Rethinking Roundhouses

Rethinking Roundhouses

Later Prehistoric Settlement in Britain and Beyond

D. W. HARDING

OXFORD
UNIVERSITY PRESS

Great Clarendon Street, Oxford, OX2 6DP,
United Kingdom

Oxford University Press is a department of the University of Oxford.
It furthers the University's objective of excellence in research, scholarship,
and education by publishing worldwide. Oxford is a registered trade mark of
Oxford University Press in the UK and in certain other countries

© D. W. Harding 2023

The moral rights of the author have been asserted

First Edition published in 2023

Impression: 1

All rights reserved. No part of this publication may be reproduced, stored in
a retrieval system, or transmitted, in any form or by any means, without the
prior permission in writing of Oxford University Press, or as expressly permitted
by law, by licence or under terms agreed with the appropriate reprographics
rights organization. Enquiries concerning reproduction outside the scope of the
above should be sent to the Rights Department, Oxford University Press, at the
address above

You must not circulate this work in any other form
and you must impose this same condition on any acquirer

Published in the United States of America by Oxford University Press
198 Madison Avenue, New York, NY 10016, United States of America

British Library Cataloguing in Publication Data
Data available

Library of Congress Control Number: 2022911704

ISBN 978-0-19-289380-2

DOI: 10.1093/oso/9780192893802.001.0001

Printed and bound in the UK by
Clays Ltd, Elcograf S.p.A.

Links to third party websites are provided by Oxford in good faith and
for information only. Oxford disclaims any responsibility for the materials
contained in any third party website referenced in this work.

To Dr Ian M. Blake

teacher, archaeologist, journalist, Outward Bound instructor, actor, and poet

Preface

In considering the proposal for this book, the Press was concerned that there was sufficient new material since *Iron Age Roundhouses in Britain and Beyond* (2009) was written to warrant a new analysis and interpretation of the topic. As evidence of the dangers of repetition, one reviewer had pointed to the similarity in chapter structure, as a result of which the writer attempted to recast the format. Working on the text, however, it became apparent that the best way to underline the extent of change in both database and interpretation was to retain essentially the same structure as in *IAR*, rendering more apparent both what was new and what was of enduring significance.

Writing this book during the Covid-19 pandemic served to underline the rapidly changing nature of data sourcing in archaeology. Initially the National Library of Scotland was closed, as were the libraries of the Society of Antiquaries of Scotland in the National Museum and of the University of Edinburgh, all of which in preparing previous books had been fundamental resources. The writer was therefore heavily dependent on online resources, particularly the increasing number of journals, British and foreign, that are becoming open access. One invaluable resource was the Archaeological Data Service (ADS), especially for 'grey literature', and continental resources such as reports from INRAP. Research has changed fundamentally from the traditional dependence upon scholarly libraries, including one's own, to access online data that may never appear in conventional published format.

In all the present writer's books since *The Iron Age of the Upper Thames Basin* (1972) and *The Iron Age in Lowland Britain* (1974) the line drawing illustrations have been his own. This not only minimizes the need for permissions to reproduce (though not, of course, acknowledgement of source), but also ensures a standardization of style that facilitates comparison and eliminates the patchwork impression that mars so many modern archaeological publications. Furthermore, there is no more reliable way of highlighting crucial anomalies in an archaeological plan than by having to focus individually on every single feature in the process of redrawing. Reconstruction drawings and elevations have been eschewed, since previous efforts have generally attracted opprobrium, doubtless because everyone is an expert when it comes to reconstructing Iron Age houses. I have, however, used photographs of life-sized reconstructions built by other agencies, since I still believe that experimental archaeology has a crucial role in demonstrating what was possible and what were practical constraints.

The period in which this book has been written may also in retrospect be seen as one in which higher education underwent a fundamental transformation, in

viii PREFACE

part induced by the coronavirus pandemic, which brought about a change from personal contact with tutors and peer group to remote learning. A second fundamental change has been the ascendancy of 'woke' attitudes, the demand for 'safe spaces' in which students can be free from exposure to ideas that might be offensive, and in which unpopular opinions are suppressed. Both are a denial of what a university should be, which is a community of students and their tutors engaged together in the intellectual evaluation of ideas, however unfashionable and unpopular, provided always that such discussion is not conducted in terms that might incite violence or infringement of law. In meeting these challenges, vice-chancellors who now see themselves as chief executives have too often shown a craven lack of leadership and judgement. Particularly disappointing has been the response of two universities with which I enjoyed a long and valued association. Edinburgh University's response to the hounding from post of a senior lecturer in Social Anthropology, whom an internal enquiry had vindicated of the charges brought against him by students, hardly does it credit, whilst its failure to defend senior staff from unsubstantiated charges of racism has been described as supine in *The Times* (Thunderer column, 2 February 2022). Equally feeble was the temporary suspension of a Durham college principal, who described students boycotting an after dinner speech by a visiting journalist as 'pathetic', hardly an immoderate term or one likely to infringe any law. Durham thereby earned itself a scathing leader in the *Times* (9 December 2021). What is disturbing is not that universities respond to complaints, but that they take no steps to take action against the bullying of staff, particularly by those who attempt to hide behind anonymity. With the burden of fees and the devaluing of qualifications by grade inflation, it seems likely that university education will decline in popularity from its later twentieth-century peak, and the subject range on offer will almost certainly decline in favour of technical, professional, and commercial training. Sadly, archaeology in universities may well fall victim to this trend.

Finally I should record my gratitude to all those who have helped me in preparing this book. I am especially obliged to Dr Stephen Dockrill, Louise Brown, and Tom Sparrow for providing images of excavations in Orkney and Shetland, to Catherine Dagg and Dr Susan Kruse for the photograph of Applecross Broch, to Joseph Fenwick and John Waddell for illustrations of the Rathcroghan survey, and to Malcolm Balmer for the Bryn Eryr reconstruction image. Rod Sylvester-Evans and Lesley Gray kindly afforded access to their high-quality A3 scanner. I am indebted to Dr Lucía Ruana and Professor Luis Berrocal-Rangel for updating me on Hispanic roundhouse research and giving me access to their research materials. Not least I thank the staff of the Oxford University Press for their professional services and unfailing courtesy in guiding this book through to publication.

Dennis Harding

Gullane, East Lothian,
Spring, 2022

Contents

List of Illustrations	xi
List of Abbreviations	xv

1. Landmarks in Roundhouse Studies — 1

Crannogs and Lake-Villages	2
Wessex between the Wars	8
Pimperne and Longbridge Deverill	12
The 1970s: Experiment and Interpretation	14
Survey and Excavation in the Tyne-Forth Region, c. 1948–1985	16
Brochs, Fieldwork and Interpretation, 1980–2000	18
Structuralism and Roundhouse Cosmology	21

2. Twenty-First-Century Archaeology: Radical Change — 25

Archaeology, Science, and Technology	26
A Change of Scale in Excavation	29
Publication of Excavations	32
Archaeological Theory	34
'House Societies'	36
Egalitarian or Hierarchical?	40
Archaeology as Entertainment	42
Archaeology and Climate Change	43

3. Analysing and Interpreting Timber Roundhouses — 45

Some Key Sites	45
Post-Ring, Double-Ring, and Central Post Construction	52
Ring-Grooves and Wall-Slots	56
'Drip-Gullies' and Drainage Trenches	64
Floors and Internal Fittings	65
Superstructure: Walls and Roofs	68
Central Four-Posters	70
Central Towers	72
Multi-Ringed Roundhouses	74
Houses with Ring-Ditches: Erosion, Storage, or Headroom?	76
'Special' Roundhouses	80

X CONTENTS

4. Analysing and Interpreting Stone-Built Roundhouses	88
Brochs, Broch Towers, and Complex Atlantic Roundhouses	88
An Architectural Perspective	89
Canonical Brochs: A Traditionalist View Reasserted?	92
The Problem of Non-Brochs with Broch Attributes	98
'Simple' Atlantic Roundhouses	100
Dun Houses	102
Radial Roundhouses	107

5. Roundhouses in Context: Settlements and Landscape	113
The Thames Valley	114
The English Midlands	122
West Yorkshire	128
The Northumberland Coastal Plain	134
Roundhouses in Hillforts	139

6. Archaeotectural Alternatives	143
The Wessex Model Reviewed	143
Oval Houses	146
Figure-of-Eight, 'Shamrocks' and Cellular Houses	147
Houses That Leave Minimal Trace	155
Rectangular Houses: Continuity or Change?	158
Aisled Houses and Aisled Halls	161
Conclusions	164

7. Regional Diversity in Britain and Beyond	165
Wales and the West	165
Ireland	175
Northern and North-Western France	187
The *Castro* Culture of the Peninsular North-West	198
Postscript	201

8. Chronology, Origins, and Aftermath	202
Neolithic Antecedents?	202
Bronze Age Circular Structures in Northern Britain	203
Middle and Late Bronze Age Structures in Southern England	212
The Roman Iron Age	215

9. Roundhouses: Space, Time, and Social Use	227
Life-Cycle of Roundhouses	227
Roundhouses and Round Houses	230
Round and Rectangular: Squaring the Circle	232
Change through Time	234
Methodology and Theoretical Afterthoughts	238
Roundhouses and Iron Age Society	242

| *Bibliography* | 249 |
| *Index* | 271 |

List of Illustrations

1.1	The pile-dwelling model of Scottish crannogs.	5
1.2	Glastonbury Lake Village Mound LXXIV house plan, substructure and section.	7
1.3	Little Woodbury reinterpreted.	11
1.4	The Pimperne roundhouse.	13
3.1	Flint Farm, Goodworth Clatford, Hampshire.	46
3.2	Groundwell Farm, Blunsdon St Andrew, Wiltshire, roundhouses.	48
3.3	Blackford, Strathallan, Bronze Age roundhouses.	49
3.4	Blackford, Strathallan, Iron Age palisaded settlement.	51
3.5	Bronze Age roundhouses with central post.	53
3.6	Iron Age roundhouses with central post.	54
3.7	Double-ring roundhouses.	55
3.8	Northamptonshire roundhouses.	57
3.9	Street House, Loftus, Yorkshire, enclosed settlement.	58
3.10	Roundhouses with polygonal ring-grooves.	60
3.11	Roundhouses with double external walls.	61
3.12	Large roundhouses with double external walls.	63
3.13	Roundhouses with central four-post settings.	67
3.14	Roundhouses with timber preservation.	69
3.15	Culduthel, Inverness, roundhouse plans 1.	73
3.16	Culduthel, Inverness, roundhouse plans 2.	75
3.17	Broxmouth, East Lothian, Roundhouse A, stage 2.	77
3.18	Roundhouses with souterrains.	81
3.19	Paddock Hill, Thwing, Yorkshire and its landscape.	83
3.20	Fison Way, Thetford, Norfolk, principal roundhouses.	85
3.21	Moss Carr, Methley, west Yorkshire, structures within enclosures A and B.	86
4.1	Beirgh, Lewis, broch and secondary structures.	91
4.2	Applecross, Wester Ross, broch, general view.	99
4.3	Bu, Orkney and Howe, Orkney, comparative plans.	101
4.4	Simple Atlantic roundhouses on Orkney.	103
4.5	Old Scatness, Shetland, post-broch buildings.	109

xii LIST OF ILLUSTRATIONS

5.1	Gravelly Guy, Oxfordshire, site plan with roundhouses.	115
5.2	Lower Thames roundhouses.	117
5.3	Horcott Quarry, Fairford, Gloucestershire, settlement plan.	120
5.4	Crick Covert Farm, Northamptonshire, Field 2 settlement, cluster development.	125
5.5	The Lodge, Kilsby, Northamptonshire, cluster settlement.	126
5.6	Dalton Parlours, west Yorkshire, Iron Age and Romano-British settlement.	129
5.7	Wattle Syke, west Yorkshire, Area 1.	131
5.8	Site M Micklefield, west Yorkshire.	133
5.9	Settlements of the Northumberland coastal plain.	136
5.10	Pegswood Moor, Morpeth, functional interpretation of settlement.	138
5.11	Welsh hillforts with roundhouses.	140
6.1	West Harling, Norfolk, Site II roundhouse.	145
6.2	Deer Park Farms, Co. Antrim, double stake-wall houses.	149
6.3	Reconstruction of the Bryn Eryr, Anglesey, houses, St Fagan's Museum, Cardiff.	152
6.4	Figure-of-eight houses and house-enclosures.	154
6.5	Later Bronze Age rectangular houses.	159
6.6	Late Iron Age–early Roman aisled houses.	162
7.1	Transition from timber to stone roundhouses in north Wales: schematic plans.	166
7.2	Defended settlements Llawhaden, Dyfed, schematic plans.	169
7.3	Cornish rounds: schematic plans.	172
7.4	Bronze Age and Iron Age roundhouses in east Devon.	174
7.5	Iron Age roundhouses in east Devon with eavesdrip-gullies.	176
7.6	Rathcroghan, Co. Roscommon, geophysical survey.	178
7.7	Corrstown, Co. Londonderry, Bronze Age settlement plan.	181
7.8	Corrstown, Co. Londonderry: Type 1 and Type 2 structures.	183
7.9	Irish Iron Age roundhouses.	185
7.10	Malleville-sur-le-Bec, Eure, site plan.	189
7.11	Malleville-sur-le-Bec, Eure, schematic plans of roundhouses.	190
7.12	Caudan, Morbihan, site plan and roundhouses.	191
7.13	Cahagnes, Calvados, site plan, with roundhouses, rectilinear buildings, and four-post structures.	192
7.14	Cahagnes, Calvados, roundhouse plans.	194
7.15	Ifs, Calvados, principal Roundhouse 4.	195
7.16	Ring-groove roundhouses in Brittany.	197

LIST OF ILLUSTRATIONS   xiii

8.1 Bronze Age houses in Northern Britain.	205
8.2 Meadowend Farm, Clackmannanshire, Bronze Age houses.	208
8.3 Scottish Bronze Age post-ring and ring-groove roundhouses.	209
8.4 Scottish Bronze Age ring-ditch houses.	211
8.5 Bronze Age roundhouses in southern England.	213
8.6 Iron Age and Romano-British roundhouses in the south Midlands.	217
8.7 Holme House, Piercebridge.	221
8.8 Stanwick, north Yorkshire, Tofts Field, 'large structures'.	222
8.9 Wattle Syke, west Yorkshire, late Roman settlement.	225

List of Abbreviations

AA4	*Archaeologia Aeliana*, Fourth Series
AA5	*Archaeologia Aeliana*, Fifth Series
ADS	Archaeology Data Service (online) York
AFEAF	Association Française pour l'Étude de l'Âge du Fer
AntJ	*Antiquaries Journal*
ArchCamb	*Archaeologia Cambrensis*
ArchJ	*Archaeological Journal*
BA	*British Archaeology*
BAR	British Archaeological Reports
CA	*Current Archaeology*
CBA	Council for British Archaeology
DAJ	*Durham Archaeological Journal*
DES	*Discovery and Excavation in Scotland*
DIRFT	Daventry International Rail Freight Terminal
GAJ	*Glasgow Archaeological Journal*
GUARD	Glasgow University Archaeological Research Division
HFC	*Proceedings of the Hampshire Field Club and Archaeological Society*
HMSO	Her Majesty's Stationery Office
IAR	Harding, D. W. 2009. *The Iron Age Roundhouse: Later Prehistoric Building in Britain and Beyond*, Oxford, Oxford University Press
INRAP	Institut national de recherches archéologiques préventives
OJA	*Oxford Journal of Archaeology*
PBA	*Proceedings of the British Academy*
PDAS	*Proceedings of the Devon Archaeological Society*
PPS	*Proceedings of the Prehistoric Society*
PRIA	*Proceedings of the Royal Irish Academy*
PSAS	*Proceedings of the Society of Antiquaries of Scotland*
RCAHMS	Royal Commission on the Ancient and Historical Monuments of Scotland
RCHME	Royal Commission on Historical Monuments (England)
SAIR	Scottish Archaeology Internet Reports
STAR	Scottish Trust for Archaeological Research
TAFAJ	*Tayside and Fife Archaeological Journal*
TBGAS	*Transactions of the Bristol and Gloucestershire Archaeological Society*
TCWAAS	*Transactions of the Cumberland and Westmorland Antiquarian and Archaeological Society*
TDGNHAS	*Transactions of the Dumfriesshire and Galloway Natural History and Antiquarian Society*
WAM	*Wiltshire Archaeological and Natural History Magazine*
WYAS	West Yorkshire Archaeological Services

1

Landmarks in Roundhouse Studies

Archaeology is not a window on the past; at best it offers a glimpse on to a stage that has been selectively ordered. Human communities direct their energies into those activities that they consider to be vital, such as providing themselves with food, shelter, and warmth. Beyond that basic provision their legacy to the archaeologist, subject to the vagaries of environmental survival, will reflect the activities they chose to engage in, or even the monuments that they chose to leave behind as their memorial. Archaeologists used to assume that what they found was 'representative', but they seldom asked 'of what?' With increasing interest in taphonomy, we are bound to ask, '*how*, and more particularly *when, in relation to the site's use*, did it get there?' in order better to inform our interpretation of its meaning.

For many years prehistorians have recognized a fundamental shift in the field record in Britain towards the Later Bronze Age, when the earlier emphasis upon ritual, ceremonial, and burial monuments gives way to settlements, field systems, and hillforts. This diversity of representation of different aspects of human activity is not immediately apparent in the continental European record. But the tradition in Britain of studying only 'selected highlights' of European prehistory has doubtless overlooked regional diversity in which the record may be as partial there as it is here. Until recently, houses were relatively sparsely represented in Britain in the Neolithic, but increasingly rectangular timber halls are being recognized from Lowland Scotland and more widely, whilst distinctive stone-built settlements are notable in the Northern Isles. Conversely, formal cemeteries are poorly represented in the Iron Age, outside well-known regional concentrations, but increasingly the diversity of funerary practice in the Iron Age beyond formal interment or cremation is being recognized.

Whilst it is certainly possible, as we shall see, to trace the tradition of building roundhouses back to the earlier Bronze Age, it is not until the later prehistoric period that roundhouses acquire iconic status. Why circular domestic architecture should dominate in Britain, in contrast to the long-standing tradition in Central and Northern Europe of building rectangular houses, is one of archaeology's unresolved questions, and it is one for which no simple solution will be offered here. We might suspect that, if an Iron Age household could be cross-examined, they would not know the answer, beyond perhaps 'because that is the way that it should be'. It may be that archaeologists, with their propensity for classification, have over-emphasized the importance of a category of 'roundhouses' based upon

Rethinking Roundhouses: Later Prehistoric Settlement in Britain and Beyond. D. W. Harding, Oxford University Press.
© D. W. Harding 2023. DOI: 10.1093/oso/9780192893802.003.0001

2 RETHINKING ROUNDHOUSES

structural morphology, which over time and space might have embodied different functional, social, and cognitive roles.

It has sometimes been fashionable among archaeologists to denigrate the collection and classification stages of field research and analysis as 'descriptive' rather than 'interpretative'. But it would be as well to remember that interpretation can only be as good as the data upon which it is based are reliable. Accordingly we may consider the stages by which roundhouses were investigated, classified, and analysed over the past one hundred and fifty years. Unsurprisingly, given circumstances of survival, the remains of stone-built roundhouses in upland Britain were recognized long before their timber-framed counterparts in Wessex and the south-east, despite the latter's traditional pre-eminence in prehistoric studies. In Atlantic Scotland brochs and related buildings were investigated from the later nineteenth century, albeit with scant regard to stratigraphy or context. In Wales and the west, at hillforts like Tre'r Ceiri and Foel Trigarn, by the beginning of the twentieth century pioneer fieldworkers recognized both stone houses and house platforms. In Wessex meantime post-built structures were seldom recognized in plan, and Iron Age communities were generally assigned to ephemeral shelters or 'pit-dwellings'.

Crannogs and Lake-Villages

In an age when antiquarian interests were primarily focused on burials and fortifications, investigation of lake-dwellings in Scotland and Ireland afforded invaluable alternative insights into prehistoric and early historic habitations. Robert Munro (1835–1920) had been a medical practitioner whose pioneering fieldwork from the late 1870s in south-west Scotland was reported in his seminal volume *Ancient Scottish Lake-Dwellings or Crannogs* (1882). Munro was not from a privileged background; late in life he admitted that he had 'struggled hard for [his] education' (1921: 33). On graduation in 1860, he had expected to proceed to the Free Church ministry, but having been totally convinced by Darwin's *Origin of Species* of 1859, this career was effectively disbarred, and two years later he re-enrolled at Edinburgh to study medicine (Clarke, 2012). Unlike some later antiquaries, Munro's interests were not parochial. He was aware of ethnographic studies of marine pile-dwellings internationally, and of the long history of lake-dwellings in Central Europe. This latter formed the focus of his Rhind Lectures of 1888, published as *The Lake Dwellings of Europe* (1890). Closer to home, he was aware of a parallel resurgence of investigation of Irish crannogs, summarized in due course by Wood-Martin in *The Lake Dwellings of Ireland* (1886).

Ethnographic studies of marine pile-dwellings popularized the image of Scottish crannogs too as built on piles over water, a model that was followed in the reconstruction at the Scottish Crannog Centre on Loch Tay (Fig. 1.1, 2). Munro, however, was well aware that excavated lake-dwellings commonly showed them to have been built on artificial mounds or reinforced natural islands in which layers of timber, brushwood, and stone had been retained within a perimeter of stakes driven into the loch bed or silts to create a platform on which the settlement was founded. He was evidently impressed by the mechanics with which these resilient structures were built, but he also addressed the question that so often strikes the impartial observer: how is it that the surviving remains, including apparent occupation levels and hearths, are found by archaeologists below water level? Has the crannog subsided, or has it been engulfed by rising water levels? In major Highland lochs today, of course, the water level is artificially controlled, but in the south-western lochs in the late nineteenth century an accumulation of factors could have been in play. Munro considered compression due to progressive accumulation of silts, as well as that resulting from the weight of the artificial island itself. In the case of sites like Buiston, of course, he was aware that draining the loch would have had a significant impact on the process of compression. But a key issue is locating an original exposed ground surface, such as a paved catwalk or *in situ* hearth, as opposed to the mass of material, including worked timbers, that simply made up the core of the mound. The unique benefits of underwater and wetland archaeology, in terms of organic and environmental preservation, are widely acknowledged. But, as Cavers (2012: 183) has warned, there remain real problems in distinguishing structural timbers of buildings from timbers driven into the loch bed to retain the sub-surface platform, and laid horizontal timbers from collapsed verticals. The benefits of preservation are rendered useless if we cannot unravel the site taphonomy.

Munro accurately identified the recurrent elements in mound construction as circles of stakes around the perimeter combining retention of the core material with the provision of a defensive stockade, together with the use of radial timbers bonding the structure in which mortice holes provided a foundation for upstanding buildings and fixtures. The exact nature of the principal building or buildings, however, eluded him. 'As to the kind of dwelling-house that no doubt once occupied this site, whether one large pagoda-like building or a series of small huts, the evidence is inconclusive, but so far as it goes it appears to me to be indicative of the former' (Munro, 1882: 205). Munro evidently believed that the builders of crannogs were competent engineers, as familiar as their modern counterparts with basic structural principles (Munro, 1882: 261). In this he was ahead of his contemporaries, whose image of prehistoric communities was one of primitive savagery, exemplified by William Donnelly's watercolour of 1899 of a boar hunt by the Clyde.

The idea that crannogs were pile-dwellings standing above water was included in that watercolour by Donnelly, who excavated the Dumbuck crannog in 1888–9

4 RETHINKING ROUNDHOUSES

(Hale and Sands, 2005: front cover). His plan of the site shows a platform of radial timbers embraced by a circle of external uprights at regular intervals, with what he described as a 'breakwater' of brushwood and stakes and a stone pavement beyond that. Setting aside the vexed issue of the forged artefacts, responsibility for which was never established, there is no reason to doubt the basic elements of construction that were recorded. In the case of Dumbuck, of course, its tidal location might justify the idea of a raised pile-dwelling even more than for crannogs sited in inland lochs that were subject to seasonal changes in water level. That model has become the accepted popular image of crannogs, and was further endorsed by Mrs Piggott's 1953 excavation at Milton Loch 1 in Kirkcudbrightshire (Fig. 1.1, 1; Piggott, 1953), where the circular platform, only a little over 10 metres across, surrounded by multiple piles sunk into the loch bed, could scarcely have accommodated more than a single building. Certainly Dumbuck, Lochan Dughaill, Argyll, and Milton Loch present convincing cases for a principal, large roundhouse (Cavers, 2012). But the evidence from Buiston was more equivocal, and has since been challenged following re-investigation of the site (Crone, 2000), though the alternative preference for a smaller round hut is scarcely more convincing. The idea that crannogs were occupied by a single substantial roundhouse was certainly endorsed by the evidence of island duns, largely stone-built and not infrequently accessed by a stone causeway. The fact that these sites were built predominantly from local stone should not render them separate from crannogs in terms of social and economic reconstruction (Harding, 2000).

As regards dating, Munro was well aware of the long chronology of lake-dwellings in Europe, but to those that he excavated in south-west Scotland he assigned a date in the early historic period. He believed that the distribution of crannogs, and more particularly their absence from those regions of south-east Scotland and the Borders that were occupied by Anglian settlers, indicated that crannogs were a manifestation of 'Celtic' settlement (Munro, 1882: 249). Furthermore, the similarity between the artefactual assemblages, notably types like composite bone combs (Munro, 1882: 278–9), and their Irish counterparts endorsed this chronology and cultural affiliation. More recent research has confirmed his assessment regarding Buiston crannog. But sampling from Loch Tay, and from a number of crannog sites in south-west Scotland, has since made it abundantly apparent that the dominant period of crannog building and occupation in Scotland was the first millennium BC.

Robert Munro was one of the specialists on the Advisory Committee for the excavations at Glastonbury, contributing a substantial opening chapter to the first volume of the excavation report (Bulleid and Gray, 1911) that set the site in its European context. Arthur Bulleid (1862–1951) had been fascinated by the Swiss lake-village finds, and abandoned his studies as a medical student to undertake the excavations at Glastonbury from 1892 to 1898, when he resumed and completed his qualifications as a doctor. He later continued and completed the

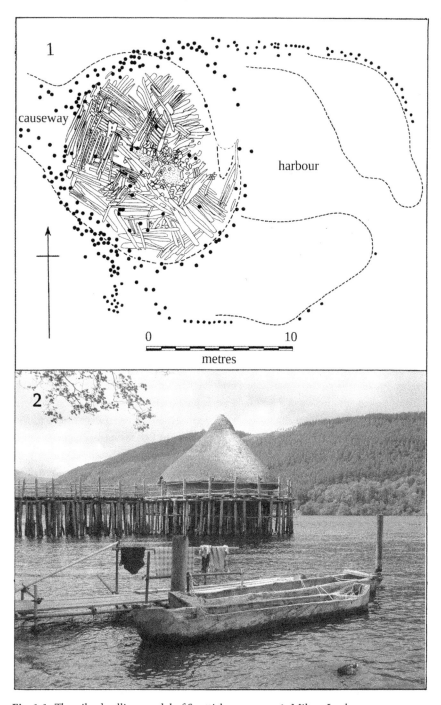

Fig. 1.1 The pile-dwelling model of Scottish crannogs. 1, Milton Loch, Kirkcudbrightshire, crannog 1. Drawing by D. W. Harding, adapted from Piggott, 1953; 2, Reconstructed crannog, Scottish Crannog Centre, Loch Tay, destroyed by fire June, 2021. Photograph by D. W. Harding.

6 RETHINKING ROUNDHOUSES

excavation with the assistance of Harold St George Gray from 1904 to 1907. Bulleid's commitment and tenacity was total; in the earlier campaign, he excavated for six months throughout the summer, employing between two and six workmen between 7 a.m. and 6 p.m., working still longer hours himself. During the winter he drew up field plans and section drawings, and processed finds for the Glastonbury Museum. He may not have excavated stratigraphically, but he drew and understood the significance of the sections through the mounds, and the accumulation of floors necessitated by the constant sinking of the settlement (Bulleid and Gray, 1911: 54). He was also a meticulous worker, spending by his own account three days lying on a plank to clean the hurdlework of Mound LVI (1911: Plate XXVII). In the later campaign, from 1904 to 1907, the excavations lasted only four to six weeks annually, but with joint directors they were able to employ eight men most seasons.

The substructure of the settlement was composed of timber and brushwood which formed the foundations for the houses. A palisade of alder and wattle-work surrounding the entire settlement retained the timber and brushwood platform and provided a protective stockade. Its very irregular outline and close proximity to the house foundations suggested that the inner lines of stakes were more crucial to the former than the latter, while their canted angles on discovery indicated the pressure they bore. The entire village enclosed 8,804 square metres (10,530 sq. yd.), and uniquely Bulleid and Gray excavated it in its totality.

The houses themselves were roughly circular, as indicated by their external walls of stakes, and between 5.50 metres and 8.50 metres in diameter (Fig. 1.2). In some cases, notably where the house had been burnt, daub fragments were found along the alignment of the stake wall. A number of houses had central hearths, and doorways were frequently distinguished by porch and threshold timbers or even paving slabs. A pivoted half 'western-saloon' door of oak need not have been typical. The floors were mostly of clay, and had commonly been resurfaced to keep pace with subsidence, but in Mound XIII an intermediate layer of radiating beams suggests that the floors needed more substantial reinforcement against rising damp. Bulleid particularly remarked the discovery of sill timbers with mortice holes that he believed were from rectangular structures, secondarily incorporated into the substructure of the settlement. The greatest length of any of these timbers was under three metres, and the height of the structures, calculated from hurdles that fitted the spacing of the mortice holes, would have been just under two metres. No rectangular buildings were apparently found *in situ*, but by their nature, sill-beam buildings do not require earth-fast foundations, so these remnants could have been from ancillary structures located around the village. Alternatively, timbers with mortice holes could have supported radial divisions in roundhouses, or external wall sill-beams in a polygonal layout that was virtually indistinguishable in elevation and roofing from a roundhouse. In effect, the

LANDMARKS IN ROUNDHOUSE STUDIES 7

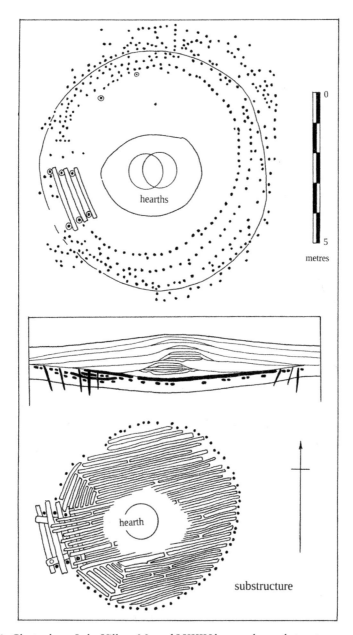

Fig. 1.2 Glastonbury Lake Village Mound LXXIV house plan, substructure, and section. Drawing by D. W. Harding, adapted from Bulleid and Gray, 1911.

sill-beam with mortice holes is simply a more sophisticated version of a ring-groove with stone packing between postholes, while the stake-wall roundhouses with porched doorways from Glastonbury are in the same class as those from Danebury or Cadbury Castle. By no means all of the mounds had definitive evidence of circular houses, and their clustering into groups suggests combinations of different component elements, as advocated by David Clarke (1972), notwithstanding the subsequent discrediting of his analysis in detail (Barrett, 1987; Coles and Minnitt, 1995).

The settlements at Meare West and Meare East were not directly comparable, other than in terms of pottery and material remains, which indicated broadly contemporary use. Otherwise, there was no evidence for a palisaded enclosure, and, though there were similar mounds with successive clay hearths, and a proliferation of artefacts, as at Glastonbury, there is limited evidence to suggest the sites' purposes. Some evidence for houses was recovered at Meare West, but the structural remains at Meare East are much more equivocal, and Coles was inclined to consider the Meare sites as intended for seasonal occupation at most, possibly for periodic gatherings and festivals. Given the abundance of metalworking materials, it is conceivable that Meare was a specialist industrial site, again perhaps occupied on a seasonal rather than permanent basis.

Wessex between the Wars

Wessex has traditionally claimed pre-eminence in prehistoric archaeology. This status stems primarily from the fact that it is the location of some of the foremost monuments in Western Europe, like Avebury and Stonehenge, and of Iron Age hillforts of monumental construction like Maiden Castle, Dorset. These sites not unnaturally attracted the attentions of pioneer antiquaries, but their investigation benefited from a wealthy class of landed gentry that sponsored the oldest county societies with an interest in antiquities. The fact that, in terms of roundhouse studies, Wessex was not a pioneer region in their investigation simply reflects their minimal survival as upstanding field monuments. Pitt-Rivers (1892: xi–xii) had lamented 'our ignorance of towns, villages, habitations', with the notable exception of lake-villages and crannogs, which he attributed to the acquisitive instinct of the sponsoring gentry, whose wish to add to their collections prompted investigation of tumuli, rather than settlements with their more mundane assemblages. In upland regions of Britain by contrast 'hut-circles' with foundations of stone survived in a landscape where later agriculture had not degraded them, while in Atlantic Scotland brochs and duns, not all as upstanding as those that had attracted antiquaries from the early eighteenth century, were nevertheless recognizable as the foundations of substantial circular buildings. Even in Wessex, however, in the unploughed sector of Hod Hill, Dorset, or intermittently along the contours of its near neighbour, Hambledon Hill, circular foundations for timber roundhouses did survive, so that the late recognition of substantial timber roundhouses is in part a reflection of the perception of prehistoric communities as primitive and rustic, epitomized in the notion that they lived in pit-dwellings, and belatedly perpetuated in the 1944 reconstruction of the Little Woodbury settlement at the Pinewood Studios (*IAR*: Fig. 4). It was also a direct consequence of the limited scale of trench excavation, which seldom opened areas of sufficient size to expose the full pattern of postholes, and certainly not without meticulous cleaning of the exposed surface in a manner that was not general at the time. Recognizing postholes or patterns of postholes had not been one of Pitt-Rivers' strong suits, and many excavations in the inter-war years fell short of his standards of fieldwork.

The interpretation of deep, beehive-shaped pits in the Wessex chalk as human habitations was exemplified by Dr R. C. C. Clay's (1924) section-drawing of a roofed pit-dwelling from Fifield Bavant Down in Wiltshire. The idea of dwelling-pits was still propagated by Wheeler (1943) in his Maiden Castle report, where he imagined a ring of mutton bones around the edge of one pit as the discarded remnants of a meal eaten by their occupants crouching around the hearth. Christopher Hawkes recalled how Gerhard Bersu, whom he had escorted to the Maiden Castle dig, had protested without avail that the occupants would have suffocated in such confined conditions. But excavators were also alert to the possibility of post-built houses on the continental model, as Reginald Smith had claimed at Park Brow, Sussex (Hawley, 1927). The options for reconstruction of Iron Age dwellings had been codified by Dorothy Liddell in her second report on excavations at Meon Hill in 1933. Her first three classes of habitation were all subterranean, 'deep underground dwellings' of the Hallstatt Iron Age A1 period, shallower pits of the same period, and beehive pits of the classic Swallowcliffe Down-Fifield Bavant Down type. Finally there were post-built houses at ground level that she dated to La Tène II (Liddell, 1935: Fig. 3). These were of indeterminate plan, since the surviving postholes were located between a dense complexity of pits, but the excavators at the time plainly did not exclude rectilinear plans on the Central European model.

Absurd though the Fifield Bavant model, and Wheeler's version of it, may now seem, the idea of a semi-subterranean building, provided it was of sufficient width relative to depth, is by no means unrealistic, and for want of evidence for regular, post-built plans, it was not impossible to imagine that some of the shallower scooped pits could have been covered by an over-arching roof as working, and perhaps living areas. Sunken buildings certainly were characteristic of later prehistoric settlement in Central Europe in the Iron Age, including *oppida* like Manching in Bavaria. In the post-Roman period the same principle is witnessed in the *Grubenhäuser* of Anglo-Saxon and Anglian settlements. The key difference, of course, is that the horizontal dimensions should exceed the vertical, allowing either greater headroom beneath a low roof or a suspended floor, below which space was potentially available for storage.

The inadequacy of the archaeological record for southern and eastern England generally, in terms of evidence for prehistoric houses, was highlighted in 1937 by Grahame Clark, who argued that houses potentially reflected better the social and economic structure of past societies than any other aspect of the archaeological record. That so little was known, especially of Neolithic and Bronze Age houses, at the time he attributed with Pitt-Rivers to the fact that archaeology had hitherto been a recreational pursuit of the leisured classes, rather than the scientific discipline that it was becoming. He cited the greater commitment to investigating houses in Jutland and Germany, and his campaign was influential in the Prehistoric Society's invitation to Gerhard Bersu to undertake the excavation at Little Woodbury in 1939, which was to become the model for the southern English Iron Age for the next generation.

The Little Woodbury excavation established beyond doubt the existence of well-planned, well-resourced, and well-engineered roundhouses as a key element of Iron Age settlements in Britain. It also established firmly the case for pits as storage silos rather than dwellings, though none of the Little Woodbury pits would have been of sufficient size to have qualified as pit-dwellings, even to advocates of that interpretation. Though Bersu chose to emphasize House 1 rather than its apparently lesser counterpart, House 2, in fact, both were double-ring houses of similar overall diameter, but of different construction (Fig. 1.3), a feature that may now be regarded as not untypical of roundhouse settlements. The one significant aspect of Bersu's plans that required reinterpretation was where plough furrows had removed the outer post-ring of House 1 on its west side, leading him to restore the replacement post-ring as if the house had expanded in overall diameter, rather than shifting its centre to one side, as in all comparable examples. In his further excavations as an internee in the Isle of Man, and in Scotland after the war, Bersu made notable contributions to the study of roundhouses at a time when research in the field had reached a point of stagnation. Perhaps because of the war, however, his initiatives did not lead to a research bonanza. Instead, Little Woodbury became an icon of the Southern British Iron Age, spawning the concepts of a 'Woodbury Culture' and a 'Woodbury Economy', that actually inhibited any appreciation of the rich diversity of settlement patterns that characterized even Southern Britain (Harding, 1974: 21).

More recently, Bersu has been presented (Sharples, 2010; Hingley, 2020) as a forerunner of the revisionist ideas of the 1990s, and he certainly was out of step with much contemporary thinking in regarding agricultural settlements as the backbone of the British Iron Age, rather than hillforts, which he did not regard as proto-urban in character, or even necessarily sites of permanent occupation. But his conclusions from the Little Woodbury excavation were hardly radical:

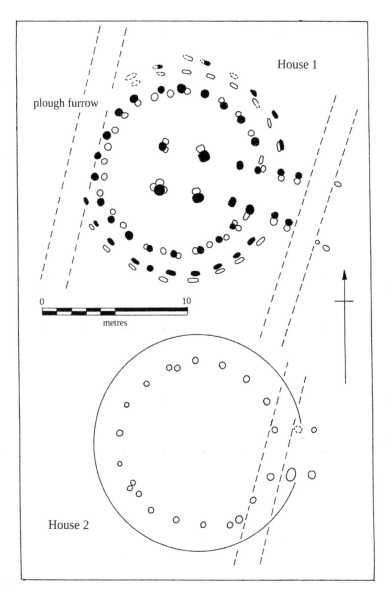

Fig. 1.3 Little Woodbury reinterpreted. Drawing by D. W. Harding, adapted from Bersu, 1940.

The main features of this civilisation (Iron Age A2-AB) with its highly developed and intensively pursued agricultural system *corroborate the ancient authors*. It was a civilisation of a self-sufficient peasant culture *with a rigidly organised social structure*. (Bersu, 1940: 107, my italics)

His endorsement of the written sources and of a hierarchical social structure would hardly rank as 'subversive' then, though it might now that egalitarianism

12 RETHINKING ROUNDHOUSES

has become the orthodoxy. He also conformed to the Hawkes system of ABC classification, then at the height of its currency. But in one regard he was certainly ahead of his peers, in regarding Iron Age society in Britain as a *civilization*, a term that at that time would hardly have been countenanced outside the Mediterranean or Near East.

Pimperne and Longbridge Deverill

In an era before large-scale area excavation, the prospects of recognizing large timber roundhouses of Little Woodbury proportions depended upon the regularity of their ground-plans being apparent from relatively small trenches. Even then there was no guarantee that the excavator would register the emerging pattern, as Bersu had observed of Bradford's interpretation of the Frilford structure (Bersu, 1940: 90, footnote 3). The Pimperne house resulted from the pioneering investigation of the site by Dr Martin Aitken, using a magnetometer, which fortuitously exposed adjacent postholes of the main weight-bearing circle.

Ironically, both Pimperne and Longbridge Deverill had been assessed as Romano-British at the time that excavation was initiated. Pimperne was a research excavation, carried out between 1960 and 1963, and was unusual in two principal respects. First, that sector of the site had never been ploughed, not even in wartime, when the enclosure was used for an anti-aircraft battery. In consequence, shallow stake-holes and construction slots survived, indicating the house's full scale, that would have been destroyed by ploughing, as they must have been when ploughing was in due course permitted in this sector of the scheduled monument. Second, the Pimperne house was planned in the field by the excavators at a scale of 1:24 (½in: 1ft) and subsequently published at 1:50 (2cm: 1m), which was unprecedented at the time. Its limitations, especially in terms of environmental analyses, stemmed largely from inadequate funding. The sum total of grants for three seasons' excavation was £235, supplemented by public donations and one excavator's army gratuity. A significant contribution in kind resulted from the fact that the excavator in question held a commission in Royal Signals, so that the entire project was based for two seasons on the Officer's Mess of 30 Royal Signals at Blandford Camp. One benefit of this was the use of a 65ft telescopic tower, mounted on a three-ton truck with outriggers, that was used to capture the unique photograph of the excavated house (Fig. 1.4).

Longbridge Deverill by contrast was funded by the Ministry of Works as a rescue excavation, the threat being a proposal for tree plantation. The final season in 1960 overlapped with the start of the Pimperne excavation, and led to the present writer's long association with Sonia and Christopher Hawkes. Like Pimperne, the site had suffered minimal damage from medieval or modern ploughing, and structures were well preserved. Only subsequently did ploughing afflict whatever

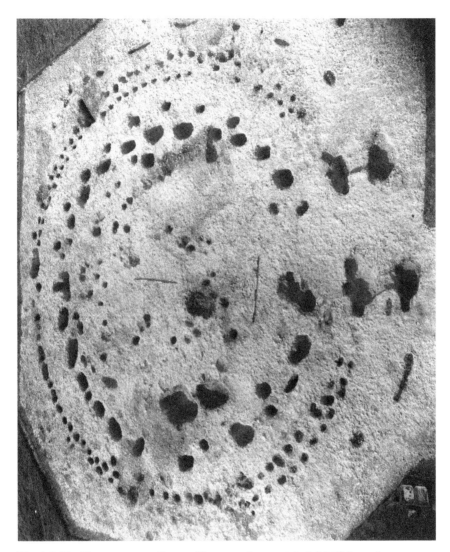

Fig. 1.4 The Pimperne roundhouse. Photograph copyright I. M. Blake and D. W. Harding.

remained. Like Pimperne too, Longbridge Deverill was totally excavated by hand, so that pottery was undisturbed in the top of posthole and pit fillings, and could be regarded as authentically *in situ*, however explained. More extensive excavation at Longbridge Deverill yielded four large roundhouses, but its particular distinction was the quantity of fine pottery from the earlier houses, notably haematite-coated furrowed bowls and large jars with deep-scored decoration, in the style first recognized in Britain at All Cannings Cross (Cunnington, 1923), with affinities to the Late Bronze Age pottery from Fort Harrouard in northern France.

The assemblage was particularly well served by Mrs Marion Cox's drawings, that accurately depict fabric and finish in a manner that recalls the equally distinctive style of Robert Gurd, who illustrated Iron Age pottery in the *Proceedings* of the Hampshire Field Club in the 1930s. An important innovation of the Longbridge Deverill post-excavation analyses was the illustration of pottery by archaeological context rather than by predetermined types, allowing study of associated material and comparison between different contexts. Regrettably, the final report gives priority to fabric analysis, a fashion that has paralysed Iron Age pottery studies for the past forty years, yielding little information of significance, and under-rating the most striking aspects of the assemblage, namely the pottery forms of bowls and jars and their highly distinctive ornamentation, which are surely the best indicators of cultural context and affiliations.

The 1970s: Experiment and Interpretation

The 1970s saw some of the most important achievements in scientific experimental archaeology, associated especially with Peter Reynolds, a classics graduate of Trinity College, Dublin, whose principal contribution to archaeology was his agricultural experiments as Director of the Butser Ancient Farm from 1972 until his untimely death in 2001. Specifically he demonstrated that pit-storage of grain was a viable practice in prehistory as a means of preserving supplies of cereals that he equally showed, from fields cultivated by hand over a period of years, could have been produced in Iron Age Wessex as a substantial surplus. He further demonstrated that, controlling weed competitors by hand at the crucial stage in the growing cycle, and thereby eliminating the need for herbicides and fertilizers, yields could be sustained year after year without crop rotation. His experimental reconstruction of Iron Age houses was initially entirely subordinate to research into agricultural practice and potential, and it was only really with the reconstruction of the Pimperne house at the Queen Elizabeth Country Park in Hampshire that he challenged some of the conventional stereotypes of prehistoric buildings.

In his building experiments Reynolds' first principle was that reconstruction had to be based on an actual excavated plan, not a hypothetical composite, since one key objective was feedback from practical experience that might illuminate unexplained features of the excavated plan. This certainly proved to be the case in the Pimperne reconstruction (*IAR*: Pls 15, 16), notably when he found himself replicating the elongated slots of the outermost circle in an attempt to bed down the somewhat irregular rafters in order to peg them firmly into the weight-bearing ring-beam. A second instance was in the replacement of upright timbers of the outer porch, which had rotted at the base through exposure to the elements. Pulling out the rotted post was simple enough, but inserting its replacement, with tenon in the lintel beam and foot bedded in the posthole, was plainly impossible without jacking up the lintel, except by replicating the lateral extension that enabled the post to be pushed sideways into its vertical position.

A second basic principle was that only materials that would have been available to the original builders should be used, and by extension, only tools that they too could have used. Whilst this might seem self-evident, it should be recalled that the central setting of four posts that held up the roof of the Little Woodbury replica in the Pinewood Studios quite unnecessarily was made of iron girders concealed in plaster to simulate timber. In practice Reynolds was not averse to using modern power tools, but only once he had convincingly demonstrated that the task could be completed with traditional equipment. This was admissible because he had no interest in calculating man-hours needed to complete the work, reckoning that the capability of skilled Iron Age craftsmen and labourers who had spent their lives doing just this kind of traditional work would have been utterly different from the capacity even of experienced modern replicators.

An important factor in Reynolds' building experiments was the monitoring of the structure and fabric of the building over time. Contrary to current archaeological opinion, he believed that substantial timber buildings with an oak framework could last for decades, if not centuries, with proper maintenance, as the survival to the present day of medieval houses and barns surely demonstrated. The Pimperne house survived the 1987 hurricane with minimal damage to its thatch, and there can be little doubt that it could have lasted half a century before requiring a major rebuild along the lines indicated by the excavated plan. Its premature dismantling, nevertheless, brought about by the lease of the site expiring, provided an opportunity to study the state of decay more closely, even though an extended life-cycle would have been preferable. Whilst some details of the reconstruction would certainly have been done differently had the exercise been repeated, Reynolds' (1993) summary of the Pimperne experiment remains a classic statement of the aims and methodology of a research agenda for a roundhouse building experiment.

The early 1970s also saw major advances in the interpretation of excavated evidence for later prehistoric roundhouses. At Moel y Gaer, Rhosesmor, Graeme Guilbert had identified the stake-wall roundhouse as a regular variant that archaeologically might only be recognizable through the deeper earth-fast paired posts of its doorway. These houses were on average 7–8 metres in diameter, and Reynolds argued that this must have been near the maximum viable size for an essentially wicker-built structure without obvious internal support, a conclusion that may require reassessment in the light of more recent research. Guilbert made further key contributions to roundhouse interpretation, being the first to recognize the double-walled roundhouse phenomenon (Guilbert, 1981), in which the outer wall, which commonly aligned with postholes of a projecting porch, was not represented by any earth-fast features, having most probably been made of turf or cob. This, of course, greatly enhanced the internal floor area of the structure, and contributed to the increasing awareness of archaeologists that they were dealing with sophisticated houses, not primitive huts. In the same vein, he identified (Guilbert, 1982) what he termed axial line symmetry, the principle of a mirror-image floor plan about a datum line through the entrance across the centre point of the circle, based initially on his work at Moel y Gaer.

By the end of the decade, similar important advances were being made in the interpretation of northern roundhouses by Peter Hill, based on his excavations in 1978–9 at Broxmouth in East Lothian. In the early 1980s Hill informally circulated a number of discussion papers which culminated in his published papers (1982, 1984) on the topic of roundhouses as cultural and chronological indicators. He was especially concerned with the 'ring-ditch' houses of south-eastern Scotland, then identified from a more limited geographical distribution and chronological range than has subsequently been recognized. He also identified what he termed the 'Votadinian' house, that is, stone-built roundhouses in the Tyne-Forth region that were common on native settlements of the Roman period, but which research was demonstrating had origins in the later pre-Roman Iron Age, as at Broxmouth. Discussion more generally challenged the long-established 'Hownam sequence' of structural progression from palisaded to univallate then multivallate enclosures, heralding a more comprehensive review of later prehistory in Northern Britain.

Survey and Excavation in the Tyne-Forth Region, c. 1948–1985

One of the most important contributions to the development of modern professional and academic archaeology, too often forgotten in an age of dependency on digital data, was the fieldwork undertaken by the three Royal Commissions for their county *Inventories*. Particularly relevant to research into later prehistoric settlements in southern Scotland were the Roxburghshire (1956) and Peeblesshire (1967) *Inventories*, the objective of which was to survey and record sites on a parish-by-parish basis, and to classify them by broad category with an evaluation of their context and dating. To clarify the latter, selective excavation was undertaken by Commission staff, notably Kenneth Steer and Richard Feachem, which, together with a programme of independent excavations, again notably by R. B. K. Stevenson of the National Museum of Antiquities and Mrs Peggy Piggott, contributed in the post-war decades to an understanding of later prehistoric settlement in the Borders that was unmatched in other parts of Britain.

Mrs Piggott's excavation at Hownam Rings in Roxburghshire in 1948 established a sequence that became a model for the Tyne-Forth region, beginning with a palisaded enclosure, and progressing through univallate and bivallate defences to culminate in a scooped settlement of the Roman period within the derelict earthworks. The more general applicability of this model of progressive complexity was later challenged, but in the Edinburgh Conference of 1981 there was still support for Jobey's case for seeing a 'trend towards enclosure' throughout the first millennium BC (Harding, 1982: 189). Also in 1947–8, Robert Stevenson had investigated two 'ditched hut-circles' at Braidwood (Stevenson, 1949), which would now be recognized as the first excavated examples of ring-ditch houses, though at the time he assumed that the ring-ditches were for drainage around and outside the central house platform. The true extent of ring-ditch houses only became apparent at High Knowes, Alnham, Northumberland (Jobey and Tait, 1966), where the ring-ditch of House 1 lay unequivocally within the defining outer ring-groove.

The initiative south of the Border was taken up by George Jobey, who was aptly described by C. E. Stevens as 'virtually a Commission in himself' (Stevens, 1966: 116). Working with his group of Extra-Mural class volunteers, Jobey surveyed and excavated sites in Northumberland for thirty years from the late 1950s, in later years extending his fieldwork into Dumfriesshire. His prompt publication of fieldwork was greatly facilitated by what might otherwise have been regarded as his greatest disadvantage, namely the minimal yield in terms of material remains, and in particular the virtual absence of pottery, which avoided the cost and effort of a time-consuming post-excavation programme. Jobey's (1962) excavations at West Brandon in County Durham were carried out in the same year as the Pimperne excavation, and like Pimperne, it was possible to expose the entire plan of the central roundhouse by hand because only a shallow topsoil covered its foundations in the sandstone bedrock. In upland Northumberland, even palisaded sites could survive as extant earthworks, so that, at High Knowes, for instance, locating the ring-ditch of a roundhouse presented no difficulty on the ground.

Though Jobey's fieldwork and published papers were largely focused on native settlements of the Iron Age and Roman period, he also later conducted pioneer fieldwork on unenclosed platform settlements, notably at Green Knowe in Peeblesshire (Jobey, 1980), a site that had earlier been investigated by Richard Feachem in the course of researching the Peeblesshire *Inventory*. Jobey showed that these platforms, recessed into the hill slope with an entrance on the forward apron, were for stake-built roundhouses up to 10 metres in diameter with a low stony bank around the perimeter, within which hearths and floors were recognized. Radiocarbon dates indicated occupation in the later second millennium, broadly contemporary with field clearance cairns in the immediate vicinity. The extent to which arable agriculture was practicable at an altitude of 275 metres (900ft) remained debatable, and at best would have been marginal.

The disadvantage, of course, arising from the paucity of material remains, in an era when radiocarbon dates were still a comparative luxury, was that dating of native settlements remained problematical. Jobey's role as a prehistorian in the University of Newcastle, and indeed the present writer's as the first prehistorian at Durham University in the 1960s, was to provide the 'native background' to the main event, which was the Roman archaeology of the frontier zone. Iron Age settlements with roundhouses plainly were occupied by the indigenous population, but how much earlier than the Roman occupation their origins might extend to was unclear. Where the houses were built of stone, even in regions where stone was readily available, it was assumed that this technical advance must have been achieved under Roman influence, and the idea that stone-built 'Votadinian' houses must date from the *pax Romana* remained firmly embedded in archaeological thinking.

Radiocarbon dating was the catalyst of the breakthrough. Though Jobey had taken charcoal samples from the palisade trenches at Huckoe in 1955–7, it was not until twelve years later that he was able to fund radiocarbon dating, based on new samples (Jobey, 1959, 1968). These confirmed that the palisaded phase of enclosure dated to the earliest Iron Age, and, alongside dates from Staple Howe in Yorkshire and Craigmarloch Wood in Renfrewshire, confirmed that palisades in the Borders too dated from that earlier horizon. Material remains from the circular stone houses and rectilinear buildings at Huckhoe still indicated reoccupation from the second century AD into the late Roman or post-Roman periods. Jobey remained active up to his retirement, participating in the 1981 Edinburgh Conference that marked the reactivation of interest in the later prehistory of south-east Scotland (Harding, 1982), which also coincided with a significant shift in fieldwork from research excavation to rescue excavation triggered by development.

Brochs, Fieldwork and Interpretation, 1980–2000

Broch studies in 1980 were still dominated by two themes, *typology* of key classes of field monuments, and *diffusionism*, a belated legacy from the inter-war and early post-war years, when any cultural innovation had to be explained as the product of folk migration or invasion. For much of the later twentieth century the foremost authority on brochs was Dr Euan MacKie, whose basic classification was set out in a series of papers from 1965. MacKie distinguished ground-galleried brochs, which were principally found in the Atlantic west, excluding Argyll, and solid-based brochs, which had just one gallery at ground-floor level to accommodate the staircase to upper floors, that were characteristic of Caithness and the Northern Isles. Much of the debate in the post-war decades had revolved around which of the two was earlier. J. R. C. Hamilton, the excavator of Jarlshof and Clickhimin, had argued for an origin in the north, where the distribution was densest. MacKie favoured the west, where he believed that broch towers had developed from an earlier form of D-shaped *semi-broch*, of which the example he had excavated at Dun Ardtreck on Skye (MacKie, 2000) afforded a model. The irony of this scheme was that the Glenelg brochs, among the finest surviving examples in Scotland, were solid-based, so explaining their presence in the west required a 'reflux movement' to bring back the northern fashion, echoing the kind of interpretative gymnastics that Sangmeister (1963) was invoking around the same time to explain the complex distribution of beakers in Western Europe.

The term semi-broch had been coined by Erskine Beveridge (1903) to describe structures that he thought were less monumental than broch towers, like Dun Mor Vaul on Tiree, later excavated by MacKie as a fully-fledged broch. MacKie had adapted the term (1991) to include two quite disparate types. One was a variant on the promontory fort, where the wall that cut off the promontory was galleried, as at Rubh' an Dunain on Skye, which has no bearing on the development of Atlantic roundhouses. The other he termed 'D-shaped semi-brochs', which were predominantly located on cliff-edges, from which an uncommitted observer might have assumed they had eroded. Since the single radiocarbon date from Dun Ardtreck was centred on the first century B C, however, it hardly provided a firm basis for claiming that the D-shaped semi-broch, even if it were an authentic regional variant, was a prototype of the fully-developed broch.

The idea that broch culture had been introduced to Atlantic Scotland from Southern Britain or beyond had been promoted by Gordon Childe and others, and was taken up by Sir Lindsay Scott (1947, 1948), J. R. C. Hamilton, and Euan MacKie in the post-war era. The diffusionist model was central to MacKie's interpretation and dating of brochs, his belief that broch culture was introduced by settlers displaced by the Belgic invasions of south-eastern England in the first century B C underlining their late dating. The fact that Southern British migrants from whatever their origins could have had no native tradition of monumental building in stone seemed not to trouble the diffusionists, any more than the fact that ceramic parallels, themselves hardly beyond debate, were drawn from disparate regions that hardly amounted to a compelling and consistent package.

A final element in the conventional interpretation of brochs related to their internal reconstruction. Particularly in relation to the Northern and Western Isles, archaeologists were conscious of the fact that natural timber resources by later prehistory would have been in short supply, and in consequence it was imagined that the internal structures of brochs would have been limited to a low range of lean-to sheds with a central open area. Internally, the space above first floor level would have been a void. Even the public display boards of sites like the Glenelg brochs thus showed the massive walls of the broch tower with something resembling a range of bicycle-sheds within, apparently with no appreciation of just how disproportionate and inconsistent with the monumental stone shell this was. By 1980 there was a growing recognition that Iron Age communities must have managed resources like timber that were essential not just for domestic building but also for enclosures and substantial fortifications, and that, where resources were limited, they must have been supplemented by renewable plantations, or by organized imports from regions that were better provided. The idea that people who, from earlier prehistory had traded widely across Britain and

Europe, and whose metalwork showed a degree of sophistication that indicated craft specialization, should not be capable of organizing and managing supplies for major building projects seems inconsistent and implausible. In consequence, the traditional interpretation of brochs experienced a process of deconstruction that dismantled typology, upset the older late chronology, and reviewed the social use of the buildings themselves.

The University of Edinburgh's Western Isles Research programme was launched in 1985, based upon its newly acquired Field Centre at Calanais Farm, adjacent to and surrounding the Calanais Standing Stones. It entailed an underwater survey of lochs in north and west Lewis carried out by Dr Nicholas Dixon and Patrick Topping, together with air survey by the present writer, and excavation of two sites on the Bhaltos peninsula of Uig at Dun Bharabhat, Cnip (Harding and Dixon, 2000), and Loch na Beirgh, Riof (Harding and Gilmour, 2000). A wider ground survey of the Western Isles had been conducted the previous summer by Ian Armit in preparation of his Edinburgh undergraduate dissertation, which he then developed in his doctoral thesis and published (Armit, 1992). Armit subsequently undertook independent excavations in North Uist, including the Iron Age site in Loch Olabhat (Armit et al., 2008), culminating in the first modern excavation of a wheelhouse at Cnip on the Bhaltos peninsula (Armit, 2006). Then in 1988 Sheffield University embarked on its Environmental and Archaeological Research Campaign in the Hebrides (SEARCH), of which the most important contribution to broch studies was the excavation at Dun Vulan, South Uist, from 1991–6 (Parker Pearson and Sharples, 1999). The Western Isles had thus been transformed from an archaeologically neglected backwater to a central focus of research, going some way towards redressing the imbalance of interest and activity between the Northern and Western Isles.

Within a few hours of work starting at Dun Bharabhat the removal of loose surface stonework had cast doubt upon the validity of conventional typology by exposing the hitherto unsuspected existence of galleries around the entire circuit of a structure that had been classified in the archaeological record as a solid-based dun. Subsequent excavation suggested on the basis of limited radiocarbon sampling that the building could have been built and occupied in the second half of the first millennium BC, rather earlier than the accepted *floruit* of brochs. Thus it illustrated a classic circular argument in archaeology, that it could not be regarded as a 'true' broch, because 'true' brochs dated to the first century BC. In fact, previously excavated brochs had produced evidence of earlier occupation. Dun Mor Vaul on Tiree (MacKie, 1974) had produced dates in the mid-first millennium BC for contexts Epsilon 2 and Eta 2, which yielded plain 'Vaul' ware of potentially early date, but this occupational evidence had been regarded by the excavator as pre-broch rather than primary broch, because, of course, brochs were later in date. Likewise, at Crosskirk in Caithness (Fairhurst, 1984) radiocarbon dates allowed the excavator cautiously to suggest an origin of the broch by 200 BC, an assessment that might now seem conservative. An even earlier date, in the fourth century BC, was subsequently obtained for the vitrified galleried dun at Langwell in Sutherland (Nisbet, 1994), but of course strict typology excluded a galleried dun from contributing to the dating of brochs. Likewise, the structure at Bu in Orkney (Hedges, 1987), dating around the mid-first millennium BC, demonstrated the potentially early beginnings of Atlantic roundhouses, but was discounted on the grounds that it lacked galleries or staircase. Excavations at Dun Vulan did not encourage an earlier dating for developed broch towers, not least because unequivocally primary contexts were not excavated and sampled (Armit, 2000), though this provoked vexed debate at the time. Throughout, the controversy was bedevilled by a rigid typology derived from a diffusionist model that dictated that broch towers could not be earlier than the first century BC. It was to address this absurdity that Armit (1991) introduced the concept of the Atlantic roundhouse, an umbrella term designed to be inclusive of regional and local variants in design, but which could still accommodate the idea of a developed broch tower as part of an integrated sequence.

The earlier origin of brochs was finally confirmed by excavations in the Northern Isles, at Old Scatness (Dockrill et al., 2015), where a structure that could not be regarded as anything other than a 'true' 'classic' broch 'tower' yielded radiocarbon dates demonstrating its construction in the second half of the first millennium BC. Archaeologists are no longer concerned with whether they originated in the north or west, since there is no reason to suppose that they originated anywhere other than where they are found. The question, 'where did they come from?' was once the first question that came to mind, both in schools and in the public domain, but which now is simply a non-question. Furthermore, we no longer have to assume that native populations can only have acquired skills in stone building from some external higher civilization, since, even discounting megalithic monuments, they had been building houses and tombs in stone since the Neolithic. The insistence on late dating, on explanations of cultural innovation that depended on external catalysts, and on no more than rudimentary structures within the sophisticated broch shell, all reflect an age when the prehistoric past was inhabited by primitive communities that were hapless victims of their environment and their own ignorance, from which we, mercifully, with the benefits of Church and Empire, had emerged. The legacy of this mindset was long enduring, but by the 1980s had finally had its day.

Structuralism and Roundhouse Cosmology

In the late 1980s and 1990s British archaeologists, observing the frequency with which roundhouse entrances were oriented towards the south-east, became fixated with the idea that the organization of internal domestic space and activities mirrored the cosmological beliefs of the Iron Age occupants, focused on diurnal and seasonal movements of the sun. The orientation of roundhouse entrances had not hitherto passed unnoticed, but had generally been supposed to relate to the maximization of daylight whilst avoiding the brunt of the prevailing south-westerly winds, a viewpoint that was now rejected as functionalist. The cosmological model was notably espoused by Oswald (1997), and developed with emphasis on structuring principles and binary oppositions by Parker Pearson (1996, 1999; Parker Pearson and Richards, 1994a, 1994b). In this approach ritual explanations became routine, and even apparently mundane groups of artefact fragments and animal bone in pits and postholes, that might otherwise have been regarded as domestic rubbish, became 'structured deposits' and accorded ritual significance (Hill, 1995). In so far as Iron Age communities may not have distinguished a clear interface between everyday and ritual, sacred and profane, it is, of course, possible that disposing of domestic rubbish embodied a ritual element, consciously or otherwise. Certainly in the case of fragmentary human remains, not infrequently found in pits, postholes, and ditches around settlements, often in liminal locations like enclosure terminals adjacent to entrances, the idea that these were deliberate deposits made more sense than the default suggestion that they were 'casual losses'. The problem is that archaeology has no mechanism for evaluating such elements or testing such hypotheses, which does not mean that they are not worth considering, subject to due qualification. The problem was that such intuitive speculation was increasingly simply asserted without qualification or supporting evidence, which is fundamentally contrary to Western intellectual process.

One argument advanced by proponents of the cosmological model was that activities such as food preparation, spinning and weaving would have taken place in that half of the house to the left of the south-east facing entrance, illuminated by the morning light, while the darker side to the right would have been reserved for sleeping and storage. This inference appeared to be endorsed by the distribution of artefacts from Longbridge Deverill Cow Down (Chadwick, 1960) and Dunston Park, Berkshire (Fitzpatrick, 1994). A similar conclusion might be drawn from the pottery distribution from the Pimperne house (Harding et al., 1993), bearing in mind that no obvious floor level was found and that the pottery sherds came almost exclusively from pits and postholes, where they ended up as a result of taphonomic processes that were not indisputably the result of everyday occupation.

A key to the new approach, derived essentially from social anthropology, was an attempt to articulate the 'structuring principles' of Iron Age society, meaning, of course, the social principles, not just their physical or architectural manifestation. The apparent north–south/left–right division was set within the context of polar opposites, light/dark, public/private, centre/periphery, and so forth that have been variously articulated in the literature since the 1990s, and which undoubtedly embody contrasts that are evident in later prehistoric roundhouses. A critical review of the cosmological model was published by Rachel Pope (2007), whose Durham doctoral thesis (2003) had analysed 570 roundhouses from Northern and Central Britain, the only substantial analyses of the data to that date or since. She expressed concern that within five years in the mid-1990s the cosmological model had progressed in archaeological publications from tentative suggestion to received fact, based upon sometimes less than accurate citation of the data and selective inclusion of sites. She further regretted the dismissal by advocates of the cosmological model of environmental issues as a retro-projection of modern functionalist values, on the grounds that basic values such as the provision of light, shelter, warmth, and food surely transcended time and were essential to the human condition. To that extent 'environmental concerns are *a part of* cosmologies' (Pope, 2007: 212). This argument is endorsed by regional and chronological shifts in the specific orientation of roundhouse entrances. Pope maintained that entrance orientation shifted from the Late Bronze through the Iron Age from south towards south-east and then east, suggesting that, with climatic deterioration, the requirement for light had to be qualified increasingly by the need to provide shelter. Conversely, in northern Scotland a predominantly south-eastern orientation, when houses in southern Scotland and northern England favoured a more easterly direction, might result from a need to maximize limited winter daylight hours in the Northern Isles (Pope, 2007: 214). The provision of a second entrance, of course, not uncommon in Central and Northern Britain, but rare in southern England, is an obvious means of resolving the issues of light and weather, but opening a second, albeit subordinate, entrance must have implications for the distribution of activities within the house.

We might observe, of course, that the idea that the rotational layout of the roundhouse reflected the movement of the sun presupposes that later prehistoric communities in Britain were aware of the principles of ancient geocentric astronomy, of which the learned class might just conceivably have been aware through long-distance diplomatic and trading contacts. It has been argued on the basis of unique Bronze Age finds like the Trundholm sun-disc and the Nebra disc that European communities in the second millennium had evolved a cosmology based upon the diurnal and annual movement of the sun, in which wheeled vehicles and ships were seen as integral, and in which the heavens may have been seen as hemispherical. How this might relate to roundhouse design, and why there should not be cosmological explanations for the layout and orientation of rectangular plans that were more common in Central and Northern Europe, remains unexplained. Sunrise to sunset, birth to death, progression through the seasons from spring to winter are all trajectories that might be projected on to a roundhouse with its focal doorway providing for entrances and exits. But these are all universal concepts that would have been integral to prehistoric societies irrespective of their local preferences in terms of domestic architecture. And might not the layout of the settlement as a whole reflect cosmological ideas more than one element within it? Whatever the answer, it is assuredly not as simplistic as archaeologists have sometimes imagined. As to the limitations of archaeological inference, as expressed in Hawkes' (1954) analysis, these issues were never 'beyond our perception', though possibly beyond our resolution, and the notion that 'today we know better' (Goldhahn, 2013: 249) is risibly self-deluding.

2

Twenty-First-Century Archaeology

Radical Change

The twenty-first century began with an information technology crisis, popularly called the Millennium Bug. Because of the way in which dates had been stored in abbreviated digital form, computer specialists had warned from the early 1990s that there could be major disruption in computer systems worldwide, causing havoc to telecommunications, public utilities, government infrastructure including defence systems, and personal records. In the event the so-called 'doomsday scenario' never materialized, which is not to say that the problem was not a real one, only that remedial action proved sufficient, and apocalyptic predictions by some sections of the press and media were fortunately not realized. What this demonstrated, however, was, first, the degree to which society at large had become dependent upon information technology, and second, the extent to which unregulated dissemination of information, or misinformation, could itself potentially generate the crisis it was predicting. Misinformation, and its dissemination, particularly through social media, has since proved to be one of the most acute issues with which governments and institutions continue to wrestle, threatening to undermine the greatest asset of the twenty-first century.

Twenty years into the new century a new crisis enveloped the world, the Covid-19 pandemic. There had, of course, been epidemics and pandemics before, when medical science was less well equipped to develop an antidote. But increased mobility and international trade has meant that preventing the spread of infectious diseases has become an impossibility. The consequent policies of lockdown and working from home have resulted in a fundamental change in lifestyles, from which it is hard to see how traditional patterns of working and socializing will ever be fully re-established. For the public at large the most serious consequence may prove to be the demise of personal contact with medical practitioners. For the academic world it will undoubtedly be the transformation of undergraduate teaching from a system based upon personal interaction with tutors and peer groups to an increasing dependence upon online programmes, with the critical loss of the most challenging and stimulating aspect of university education, impromptu face-to-face debate.

Rethinking Roundhouses: Later Prehistoric Settlement in Britain and Beyond. D. W. Harding, Oxford University Press. © D. W. Harding 2023. DOI: 10.1093/oso/9780192893802.003.0002

Archaeology, Science, and Technology

The advent of radiocarbon dating in the post-war decades heralded a new era for archaeology. It did not just afford a means of absolute dating, but in the process triggered a radical realignment of archaeological theory and practice. With the capacity for independent dating archaeologists were no longer dependent on creating type-sequences and relative chronologies into which sites and artefacts could be tentatively ordered, so that working practices were transformed, and with it in due course, approaches to interpretation. Of course, the application of radiocarbon dating was not without its problems, deriving either from the science or from archaeology. In terms of the science, the most notable issue was calibration, and for later prehistory the 'plateau' in the first millennium BC on the dendrochronological calibration graph. Archaeologically dates had to be qualified depending upon whether old timber was used, or whether the sample had been subject to the marine reservoir effect. Progressively the technique has been fine-tuned, and greater numbers of dated samples have opened up the prospect of refinement through Bayesian statistics. Now it appears that one of the final hurdles has been overcome, with the development of effective methods of dating lipids in pottery (Evershed et al., 2021), the product of actual use without risk of residual contaminants, captured in one of the most ubiquitous of all archaeological materials.

In the twenty-first century, an equally momentous series of scientific and technological changes has come about in the field of archaeogenetics. Initially popular interest focused on social studies of modern populations, with uncertainties regarding the suitability of ancient remains for DNA analysis. In the past twenty years research interest has inevitably concentrated on the major episodes of European prehistory, such as the settlement of the first farmers of the Neolithic and their integration or otherwise with indigenous Mesolithic communities. Most notable have been the results of DNA analysis of Beaker and early Copper Age burials from the Eurasiatic steppes to the Hispanic peninsula, among which the various studies of Beaker burials in Britain and Europe have led to the most radical reinterpretation in prehistoric archaeology. What is important in these developments is not simply that they provide definitive evidence that was lacking hitherto, but that they arbitrate in debates that previously provoked contested alternative opinions, based on solely archaeological data and conventional archaeological reasoning (Harding, 2020: 108–12).

A cautionary note has nevertheless been voiced regarding the equation of genetics with ethnic or cultural identity, an issue of obvious concern to a generation that is preoccupied with identity, past and present. It has been further argued that biogenetic links are not the determining factor in kinship relations (Brück, 2021), a conclusion that is hardly surprising at a time when gender is widely regarded as a matter for self-determination, irrespective of biological attributes. It is possible, of course, that these issues were determined in antiquity by society at large, rather than by the individual, and that the principle of *credo ergo est* may not have been communally acceptable.

One field of modern archaeology in which the potential for extracting information from ancient remains has been transformed in recent years is palaeopathology. This has greatly amplified our understanding of injuries and diseases, prospects of life expectancy, and the effects of diet on health. Furthermore, following in the wake of Ötzi the iceman, there have been several celebrated instances where isotope analysis has shown that individuals travelled widely in prehistory, and were often buried far from their birthplaces. The Amesbury archer and Boscombe bowmen (Fitzpatrick, 2011) are well known Beaker examples from Wessex, while more recent biochemical analyses have shown that the well-preserved young Bronze Age woman from Egtved in Jutland may have hailed from the Black Forest (Frei et al., 2015). Despite significant evidence that locally the bulk of the population remained sedentary agriculturalists, Anthony Harding concluded (2021: 34) that 'Bronze Age Europe was a place where movement was the norm, not the exception.' Since the 1960s this would not have been the prevailing view of the British Iron Age, and the dominance of roundhouses might have been cited as evidence of that insularity. It remains to be seen whether that consensus is fractured by developing science.

In terms of field archaeology, whilst recognizing the obvious need for excavation in advance of development, there has been an increasing emphasis on nonintrusive investigation as preferable to destructive excavation. The value of geophysical survey, of course, has been recognized from the 1960s, but in recent years it has been applied with conspicuous success on hillfort interiors, notably in Wessex (Payne et al., 2006) and in Dorset (Stewart and Russell, 2017). Among the more ambitious programmes was the high resolution magnetometry survey of some 170ha within the territorial oppidum of Bagendon in Gloucestershire (Moore, 2020). But perhaps the most spectacular results from remote sensing in the context of Iron Age roundhouses has been the information revealed in the Rathcroghan, Co. Roscommon, complex, including detection of circular buildings beneath the principal mound, suggesting a sequence of comparable complexity to those of other major community sites in Ireland (Waddell et al., 2009). Terrestrial survey technology has also advanced apace, with the application of laser scanning and related high-precision survey techniques, eliminating many of the errors of conventional survey and affording a degree of objectivity in the recording of stone structures that survey based upon selective points could not guarantee (Cavers et al., 2015).

Plainly the arsenal of scientific applications that the archaeologist can deploy has diversified out of all recognition in the past half century, and notably in the opening decades of the present century. But so too have the working practices of academic and professional archaeologists, a fact that could not have been made more abundantly clear than during the national and international lockdowns of the coronavirus pandemic of 2020 and 2021. A generation ago this would have brought academic research to a standstill. For field archaeology the impact was obviously disastrous, but for research that once would have been dependent upon access to libraries and archives, the availability of essential data in digital format has been transformative. In Scotland, the *Canmore* archive of sites and monuments, established by the Royal Commission on the Ancient and Historical Monuments of Scotland before its merger with Historic Scotland into a single agency, is an exemplary asset. For the rest of Britain the Archaeology Data Service facility includes access to many unpublished excavation reports in its files of 'grey literature', whilst in Ireland *excavation.ie* likewise gives access to information regarding a wide range of excavations that have yet to progress to publication. In addition, many of the major commercial fieldwork units publish online accounts of their excavations. Across Europe similar facilities are available, in some countries surprisingly more effectively than others. In effect, the whole *modus operandi* of archaeological research has been transformed, so that dependency upon the traditional specialist library like the Sackler Ashmolean or that of the Societies of Antiquaries of London or Scotland has been greatly relieved.

The IT revolution will also have its impact upon archaeology at universities, increasingly under pressure from government economies in funding. The primary advantage of residence in ancient seats of learning was the benefit of personal contact and discussion with leading scholars in the field, and with other students dedicated to the pursuit of learning. A key attraction was their specialist libraries, giving access to material that would not remotely have been available at or through most local or provincial libraries. Another was the opportunity to take part in fieldwork programmes in Britain and abroad that were both instructive and a cutting-edge contribution to research. Practical fieldwork provision is still available but with resource limitations and the changes in the organization of excavation not on the same scale as hitherto, and often designed as training exercises rather than primarily for research. Larger class sizes, the delegation of tutorial teaching to graduate assistants, and online presentations by academic staff had already eroded the key attraction of regular, small group personal contact long before Covid-19, but that crisis will doubtless have prompted many students to question the dubious value of remote learning at extortionate fees. It seems almost inevitable that a consequence will be the demise of undergraduate archaeology at many universities, or its subsuming into history or classics. In effect, we may see a reversion to the situation in Britain before the expansion of undergraduate archaeology in the 1970s. It may be hoped that a consequence of the Covid-19 crisis may be the formalization of a greater variety of remote learning archaeology qualifications. Professional postgraduate qualifications, including those requiring laboratory facilities, hopefully will continue to be provided in universities, as presumably research degrees will be. The current crisis in universities will undoubtedly hit archaeology badly, but other disciplines in the humanities will also be affected, and it is hard to see a satisfactory resolution without a nation-wide Commission of Enquiry into the objectives, administration and standards of British universities, which, as with healthcare provision, is long overdue.

A Change of Scale in Excavation

Over the past twenty years development-led excavation has not surprisingly resulted in the discovery of some individually spectacular sites, like the Pocklington chariot burials (Ware and Stephens, 2020), but it is the trans-landscape scale of major infrastructure projects that has transformed interpretation of Iron Age settlement archaeology, both in Britain and in continental Europe. In consequence, even the definition of what constitutes a site requires reappraisal, while conventional con-trasts like rural settlement as opposed to urban sites have been compromised by the diversity and complexity of new discoveries (Cowley et al., 2019). Though the great majority of later prehistoric settlements in Europe can still be regarded as rural, that label depends significantly upon our definition of urbanization. It hardly carries the same connotation if the late Hallstatt *Fürstensitze* were not the seats of aristocratic chieftains, who instead lived in country estates. Equally, for the late La Tène period, *oppida* like Manching may now appear less urban with arable fields recognized within their perimeter walls, while contemporary settle-ments in northern Gaul had ordered plans without any enclosing earthworks. The problem is that classification was devised and served a purpose in earlier stages of synthesis, but an exponential increase in the amount of new data, and the diversi-fication of that data resulting from the changing scale of exposure, now requires its radical review. The ever-accumulating database certainly reinforces previous doubts about the utility of Bronze Age, Iron Age, and Roman Iron Age divisions, and why for a century and more prehistorians have regarded AD 43 as signalling the end of the insular Iron Age. Cunliffe's *Iron Age Communities*, a masterly synthesis that went through four editions between 1974 and 2005, nevertheless encapsulated the old order of classification and interpretation, epitomized by 'developed' hillforts as central places controlled by chieftains. It was unfortunate that the miscellany of 'post-processual' models hardly afforded a sufficiently rigorous basis for any such review, as theoretical models failed to keep pace with or respond to the increasing scale and diversity of the database.

An undeniable benefit of development-led excavation, therefore, has been its impact on traditional certainties. This is evident in fields such as the rural landscape of Roman Britain (Smith et al., 2016), where the extent and complexity of roadside settlements, farmsteads, and villages has totally shifted the balance of research away from the previously disproportionate emphasis on villas. Unsurprisingly, the impact has been far greater in southern, south-eastern, and eastern England, where major infrastructure projects have exposed great swathes of settlement on an unprecedented scale, than in the north and west of Britain, where the scale of development has been more limited. The consequence of this broader perspective is that Iron Age roundhouses, for example, can be seen in the context of settlement and the surrounding landscape as a whole.

Development-led fieldwork, of course, has affected different regions of Europe to very different degrees. In northern France the impact has been disproportionately significant because previously the scale of settlement excavation had been more limited, and not conducive to detecting complete house or settlement plans. A further difference was that later prehistory in north-west Europe was better represented by cemeteries, which also yielded much more impressive inventories of artefacts, so that continental archaeology was more artefact oriented. This difference in emphasis not surprisingly made the British Iron Age appear decidedly insular, its domestic assemblages looking impoverished by comparison to cemetery assemblages from the continent. The scale of development-led fieldwork has undoubtedly helped to redress the imbalance in France between funerary and settlement evidence.

Alongside the massive increase in number and scale of development-led excavations, purely research-driven excavations have declined in number in recent decades, largely as a result of limited funds, combined with the increasing costs of post-excavation processing and specialist analyses. Long-term fieldwork projects that were linked to university training programmes, and which provided material for postgraduate research leading to dissertations are not generally now compatible with professional budgeting and publication. Whilst there have been projects funded at a very substantial level by research councils or independent foundations, these are necessarily limited in number, and have often been collaborative projects involving several institutions in Britain and abroad. Whilst some have been spectacularly successful in advancing archaeology over a broad front, others have involved research agendas that address more arcane themes. The regrettable consequence for some has been the creation of a divide between 'academic' and 'professional' archaeology, when both those terms should truly apply to all practitioners in the field, whether sponsored by universities or museums, or commercially organized.

This divide, which at one stage threatened to create a rift between academic and professional field archaeologists, was characterized by Bradley (2006) as an archaeological equivalent of C. P. Snow's 'two cultures'. What has happened in the past twenty years in fact is that there has been a significant shift in archaeological research in Britain away from universities and major museums towards the larger professional field units. This has been inevitable with universities adopting a strictly actuarial model of resource allocation, and archaeology no longer being accorded preferential status as a laboratory and fieldwork based discipline. Museums too have come under increasing pressure from local government economies. The net effect is that the only agencies in a position to undertake major archaeological fieldwork projects are the larger commercial units, not least because they have within their employed staff a range of specialist expertise that no university department of archaeology could match. One consequence has been that first-class graduates looking for a productive career in archaeology no longer regard university or museum appointments as a premium target, and have migrated into the commercial sector where the potential rewards are greater. One can hardly blame them. With universities now run by individuals who regard themselves as chief executives, with income generation supplanting academic targets as their first priority, and with the abandonment of collegiate principles that formerly bound together the academic community, we can only be thankful that a new dimension has opened up, to which the baton of research can be passed until a climate conducive to academic research in archaeology is restored to British universities.

We should nevertheless recognize the limitations of commercial archaeology. It is often mistakenly argued that all excavation is research, when development-funded investigation is undertaken to satisfy a statutory requirement of development consent, and that investigation commonly results in no finds of archaeological interest whatsoever. Research excavation is driven by research objectives, whereas development-led excavation is determined by criteria that are totally arbitrary academically. The only archaeological input may be at the planning stage, when an attempt will have been made to avoid known archaeological hotspots. The arbitrary nature of development-led excavation, however, actually has the incidental benefit that sites may be revealed in areas where archaeologists would not expect them, and therefore would not have opted to look for them, thereby redressing the imbalance of research bias. This is particularly important when it shifts the balance of site distribution, or underlines the existence of sites like unenclosed settlements or small cemeteries, the presence of which would otherwise pass undetected by ground survey or air photography. One disadvantage is that sites of any period or character may be uncovered, so that field archaeologists have to be polymaths in terms of their skills and expertise in recognizing and recovering the evidence. Now of course field archaeologists like to believe that they have developed practical techniques that are universal to good practice, irrespective of period or cultural specifics of the sites uncovered, but the reality is that most excavators only properly recognize what they are familiar with or expect to find. In the context of roundhouses, even experienced excavators familiar with the residual traces of cellular structures of Atlantic Scotland may have difficulty distinguishing them from building collapse, while in lowland situations the remains of timber foundations, like ring-grooves or beam-slots might not be so readily recognized in certain subsoils as in others, and may never have been continuous or complete features in the first place, depending upon taphonomic circumstances.

With increasingly demanding questions being asked of the database, it is alarming just how inadequate our excavated evidence is, even for outstanding classes of site like Welwyn-type burials (Harding, 2020: 59). For roundhouses, our knowledge is still extremely basic regarding ring-groove construction and 'drip gullies', and about types of construction that do not involve substantial earth-fast posts, such as stake-walling or mass-walling. How effective were drip-gullies if that was their purpose? Where was the upcast deposited, and could it have been part of mass-walled construction, or the foundations for stake-walls? Were stake-walls doubled with organic insulation between? These and similar questions are unlikely to be resolved if the site is stripped by machine down to what the excavator recognizes as archaeologically significant levels, which is generally a euphemism for natural subsoil, in which only the deepest features survive. The issue was well articulated by Poole (in Timby et al., 2007: 152) in the context of circular gullies of roundhouses of the Roman period on the Great Barford bypass: 'Where ridge and furrow has survived one might expect much better preservation below the ridge with greater truncation where the furrow had cut down. In practice any benefit of preservation below the ridge is destroyed by the use of large tracked machines to remove ploughsoil, a process which usually also removes any subsoil and palaeosol to the level of the drift or solid geology.' Oxford Archaeology, the unit responsible for this excavation, has a track record of first-class excavation and publication. But it would be naive to think that field units are equally experienced and capable elsewhere.

Publication of Excavations

In the early years of modern rescue archaeology there was a widespread crisis in publication, brought about by inadequate provision in both time and resources being made for post-excavation processing to publication and archive. In general that problem has been overcome, but the different circumstances under which modern development-led excavations are conducted have led to a different set of issues in publication. Even highly respected organizations are not immune to criticism. The first volume of publication of one major infrastructure excavation, the Heathrow Terminal 5 project, by two of the foremost and rightly respected units in Britain, was reviewed by a fellow-professional in less complimentary terms. 'Coming from a project costing millions, with all this corporate and intellectual might behind it, this should have been a big, challenging powerhouse of a book. Instead, what we have is a slim, glossy, all-colour narrative account that aspires to be "user-friendly" (its specialist work being relegated to an accompanying CD), but which can only be classed as a major disappointment' (Evans, 2007: 809).

In this instance the basic problem is that the programme adopted a pretentious theoretical framework for the site's interpretation (Andrews et al., 2000), which was unlikely ever to be realized given the extent of its truncation. The aim was to 'move beyond the *(mere)* recovery and description of archaeological remains' to 'an understanding of the history of human inhabitation' (Barrett in Lewis et al., 2006: 15, my italics). The history of inhabitation, according to Barrett, is framed by *structural conditions*, the material constraints on the landscape's inhabitants over time, and *structuring principles*, such as social conventions, control of resources, and political or supernatural forces. Critical though they might be to interpretation, these are topics that could be endlessly debated in seminars; it is hard to see how they might be applied in the course of rescue excavation, which is commonly carried out under conditions in which salvaging an adequate record of structures and associated assemblages itself presents a major challenge.

This approach was reiterated in the second volume of the site report, which subsumed much of the material presented in the first. The second volume also identified 'two main readerships', the first being those interested in the history of human inhabitation of the landscape for whom a historical narrative with detailed examples was a priority, the second being archaeologists who were 'simply content' with descriptions of structures and finds assemblages for the purposes of their own research (Lewis et al., 2010: 19). This of course perpetuates the calumny that the latter are concerned only with 'description' rather than 'interpretation', where in reality they are concerned that interpretation should have a sound basis of adequately documented data. Fortunately the great majority of professional excavators are only too conscious of this essential underpinning of interpretation.

Even assuming that an experienced excavator is capable of uncovering and recording structures and features of any period, evaluating their significance in publication is another matter altogether. With the exponential increase in the database and published record, not to mention the burgeoning corpus of grey literature, it is increasingly difficult for archaeologists, whether based in university, museum, or commercial unit, to keep abreast of even a limited specialist field. In consequence, deficiencies in the supporting bibliographies of published reports are all too apparent. In fact, the character of excavation reports has changed with the shift towards developer-led excavation, notwithstanding the ambitions of the Terminal 5 programme. As Pluciennik (2011: 37) observed,

'most excavation is now the remit of private contractors, whose circumstances demand the production of largely descriptive and predominantly empirical reports, rather than time spent on abstract or applied theory or interpretation and synthesis'. This is well exemplified by numerous substantial volumes that are copiously illustrated in colour, but with more artists' reconstructions of life in an imagined prehistoric past than technical illustrations of structures at a scale that adequately presents important detail. Roundhouse plans reproduced at the size of postage stamps suggest that the authors are unaware of the key features that they should have been looking for in excavation. The situation is compounded by the fact that careers in field archaeology are decidedly insecure and inadequately

34 RETHINKING ROUNDHOUSES

remunerated, so that the directors of excavations may have moved on before publishing their reports. In Iron Age archaeology in Scotland several of the key excavations published in recent years, or with publication pending, have been written up by individuals other than the original field director, a task which, however professional the original records, is never a satisfactory outcome.

The crucial advantage of modern development-led excavation, however, remains the landscape scale of investigation. Though excavators can hardly be expected to have personal expertise in all aspects of prehistoric and early historic material culture, the larger commercial units have a wide range of environmental expertise that enables them to bring a new and crucial understanding of landscape development over time, which is reflected in some of the more important publications of recent years. In the past, landscape archaeology was the preserve of individual archaeologists like O. G. S. Crawford and later historical geographers like Brian Roberts, and was much under-regarded. Now, with the technical and scientific capabilities of the twenty-first century, that broader overview can realize its full potential.

Archaeological Theory

The past thirty years have seen an unprecedented increase in the resources potentially available to archaeologists, both in terms of the database and in terms of the means to interrogate it. In contrast, as one authority on the history of archaeology stressed, 'while there has been an explosion in the amount of empirical information, there has been no concomitant expansion in our control over the theoretical instruments that we use to make sense of it' (Murray, 2021). Following the decades in which first processual and then post-processual theories were fashionable, at least in Anglophone countries, there has appeared to be something of a theoretical vacuum in prehistoric archaeology, leading some scholars to ask whether archaeological theory was dead (Bintliff and Pearce, 2011). One contributory factor has doubtless been the fact, detailed above, that development-led excavations, run by commercial agencies, have a different agenda, with different responsibilities in terms of outcome. Targeting an informed general public, it is hardly surprising that most publications adopt a theoretical standpoint that might be described as 'post-cultural historical common sense'. But not all archaeological publication results from excavation, and one might have expected a more robust theoretical framework to have emerged in the post-processual era.

Post-processual archaeology, of course, was never a coherent -ism, but a series of themes that reflected late twentieth- and early twenty-first century concerns, such as identity (including gender), personhood, egalitarianism and heterarchy, and so forth. What has given rise to concern, however, is not the themes themselves, but the way in which they have been asserted, the disregard for the need for evidence to sustain them, and the apparent intolerance by their exponents of contrary opinion. Bintliff (2011) went so far as to argue that theory had been assimilated into ideology. Instead of interpretations based on empirical studies or experimental evidence they are based on predetermined philosophical or political preferences, to the exclusion of alternative viewpoints. This intellectual intolerance is not just an issue in archaeology; it has infected academia generally and is manifest in the 'non-platforming' of scholars or speakers whose views do not conform to the 'woke' norm. It has likewise infected, but much more subtly, the peer review process controlling academic funding and publication.

Even if there has been no overriding -*ism* in early twenty-first century prehistory, there have been major theoretical concepts that have fuelled debate. Perhaps the most frequently discussed is identity, doubtless significant to prehistoric communities, but of enhanced importance to contemporary commentators because of the importance of gender identification to modern identity. Contemporary debate appears to focus on individual identity, where one suspects that earlier communities may have been more concerned with group identity, as is implied by the hierarchy of local and regional community names recorded in Gaul, for instance, by classical writers. Closely related to personal and group identity is a sense of *place.* It is ironic that a generation that is probably more mobile than any in history has become absorbed by the concept of place, and its inferred significance to prehistoric communities. Half a century ago, redeployment of redundant miners or heavy industry workers was genuinely inhibited by their reluctance to move more than a few miles from their traditional family homes, where they had their roots. But social and professional aspiration, and global communications, have encouraged greater mobility, so that fewer people today would feel inhibited by ties of place. It is probably true that territorial entitlement and rights of access to grazing, water sources, and arable land were prime considerations in antiquity, disputes over which were doubtless a major cause of conflict. But from isotopic analyses and DNA testing it is also abundantly clear that people could be mobile over long distances, so that we cannot presume intuitively to know how prehistoric communities regarded their spatial environment. Yet self-identification by place is as well-established in antiquity and in more recent times as identification by family or kin.

For the interpretation of archaeological evidence of buildings, most practitioners recognize the importance of reliable recording of field data as the basis for synthesis and interpretation. The process was articulated with commendable clarity by Ruano and Berrocal-Rangel (2019). The first step they termed *formal analysis*, involving constructional and stratigraphic analyses of buildings, their materials and architectural techniques, and constructional phases, together with resource implications. Second, through *functional analysis* the archaeologist tries to identify the activities that took place in the different domestic spaces. This is followed by the *typological and morphological analysis* of the structures and assemblages, the purpose of which should be simply to establish recurrence, rather than to infer predetermined outcomes. Finally *spatial analysis* addresses the relationships between different spatial areas within household layouts, the settlement, and wider landscape context. *Syntactic analysis* or *perception analysis* attempts to illuminate issues such as access to or movement within buildings, or to identify public and private space. The authors acknowledged the limitations of the model, notably that it was always dependent upon the quality and reliability of the excavated record, and the vulnerability of the interpretative process to bias from contemporary perceptions of social concepts. In effect, the *archaeotectural model* is not unlike Hawkes' (1954) ladder of inference, in attempting a sequence of interpretative stages that are increasingly difficult for the archaeological data to provide answers.

Academics, including archaeologists, should always be seeking new meaning in their data, and should be open to revising or rejecting conventional interpretations. But simply redefining established concepts does not guarantee new insights. In a survey of the British and Irish Bronze Age (Johnston, 2020) kinship is redefined, extending the term to include not only blood relationships, which is what the Anglo-Saxon root of the word implies, but relationships with animals, supernatural entities, inanimate objects, and places (Johnston, 2020: 16). No one would question that communities may have a strong association with place, to the extent that it may be part of their acknowledged identity. Equally it is possible that individuals or groups might have a particular affiliation with animals or objects. But recognizing these realities does not require the redefinition of a term that from its root defines a relationship between human beings, and which has served scholarship quite clearly in that capacity. Nor is the inclusion of animals, objects, and places compatible with the emphasis which Johnston places upon the key elements of *humanity* and *mutuality* in kinship (Johnston, 2020: 13, 15). It may be that Bronze Age communities regarded objects, structures, and places as sentient beings, but this should not bear upon our definition of kinship, rather than community or identity. It may be fashionable among social anthropologists and other allied disciplines to challenge conventional definitions, but it is not self-evident that this results in clarification or enhanced understanding. Redefinition of established terms to include meanings that they have not hitherto embraced, and for which there is no rational justification, can only lead to confusion. It certainly does not lend added value to an otherwise valid assessment of a community's symbiosis with its environment.

'House Societies'

In the 1980s and 1990s, as we have seen, it was fashionable to interpret roundhouses in terms of their possible cosmological orientation. In the early twenty-first century there has arisen a belated vogue to apply Lévi-Strauss' (1979, 1982,

1987) model of House Societies (*sociétés à maisons*) to particular regional groups within the European Iron Age, beginning with an analysis by Gonzáles-Ruibal (2006) of the Castro Culture of the north-west of the Hispanic peninsula. This triggered a new interpretation of the monumental brochs of Atlantic Scotland as a manifestation of house societies by Sharples (2020). Becker (2019) has also invoked the house society model in the context of the Irish Iron Age, where, apart from substantial structures found in what were formerly regarded as 'royal sites' on the basis of later historical associations, tangible structural evidence for a sedentary population at large is conspicuously lacking.

The first point to underline is that Lévi-Strauss was concerned with house societies and their constituent houses as corporate social units, irrespective of and even unrelated to the structural or architectural characteristics of domestic accommodation, an issue of language that archaeologists seemingly find hard to grasp. Archaeologists are invited to consider the analogy of royal houses, Oxbridge colleges (known to their members as houses), or of house communities that once commonly constituted the social allegiance of schools, particularly of independent boarding schools. As Becker explained (2019: 298), 'the existence of large or special houses in themselves is not necessarily evidence for a house society—houses do not make house societies and house societies may not have large houses.' The problem of course arises from the fact that archaeologists, unlike Lévi-Strauss and ethnographic societies, are not able to interrogate prehistoric communities personally to learn about their social structures and conventions, and are dependent instead on structural and material remains as proxies of the social conventions that produced them. Ethnographically, continuity of the corporate house is not even related to the occupation of a particular residential building, which is certainly problematical for archaeologists, who tend to think in terms of the life-cycle or 'biography' of structures, interpreting closure episodes as significant in terms of the social unit that occupied them. Archaeologists applying the model to Neolithic societies in Orkney legitimately asked, 'if the "house" is conceived as essentially an institution or abstract structuring principle, what is the status of the built house as a material and architectural construct?' (Richards and Jones, 2016: 8). If the house is the material manifestation of the social group, surely it must in some respect stand proxy for the institution?

The second point to remark is that Lévi-Strauss' discussion of house societies ranged widely over time and geographical space, raising questions regarding the utility of a model that was quite so diverse, a problem that subsequent anthropological research has compounded rather than resolved. This diversity was aptly articulated by Gillespie (2007) in her summation of a symposium of the American Anthropological Association which had addressed the relevance of the concept of house societies to archaeologists. Lévi-Strauss (1979: 47) had originally described the house as an 'ethical person, custodian of a domain composed altogether of material and immaterial property, which perpetuates itself by the transmission of its name, of its fortune and of its titles in a real or imagined line, held as legitimate on the sole condition that this continuity can express itself in the language of kinship or of alliance, and most often of both together'. The house had rights and responsibilities, and was defined by its relationship to other houses within the larger society. There could be status differences between houses, much as there could be between lineages within the structure of 'Celtic' society, as inferred from later Irish and Welsh sources. In fact, the rights and obligations of houses in relation to other houses within a house society are reminiscent of the reciprocal obligations of client and superior within 'Celtic' society. Gillespie noted that houses need not be mutually exclusive, and may even transect other social groupings such as lineages and kindred. Most importantly, the house should not be confused with a household, that is, the co-residents of a building or settlement, since membership of the house in Lévi-Strauss' terms could come from different settlements. On this basis, it is hard to see what archaeological evidence could possibly be adduced to recognize its existence.

Identification with ancestors is evidently an important aspect of house society, with the deposition of human remains or human body parts in or around the settlement, and not necessarily in formal cemeteries, being one characteristic that certainly could be recognized in later prehistoric Britain. Unfortunately it apparently need not follow that the dead should actually be related to the community in order for the latter to claim ancestral association, notably where a different social set takes over a previously occupied site after a period of abandonment, which archaeologically makes palaeopathological analysis or DNA testing in this context superfluous.

Ethnographic research underlines the fact that houses (domestic structures) are among the least definitive criteria of houses (social units), and that the structures most likely to define the social house are religious or ritual structures. In the context of later prehistoric archaeology this raises the vexed issue of conventional attributions of function to particular types of buildings, whether chambered tombs were simply tombs and whether roundhouses were just domestic residences. Among field monuments that ethnographic research has indicated could reflect house societies are trash mounds, raising the possibility that the early Iron Age monumental 'middens' of the Potterne class, identified in Wessex and beyond in recent years, could be the product of periodic communal gatherings of house societies.

One of the key roles of the house society, according to Lévi-Strauss' definition, was the custody of 'immaterial property', which ethnographers have interpreted as including origin stories, the curation and performance of traditional ceremonies, songs and dances, together with the costumes and customs that are associated with these activities, none of which are amenable to identification archaeologically, other than as they might be depicted in art, or exceptionally in the case of costumes in the survival of textiles or other materials. Material property, on the other hand, is the staple of archaeology, though entitlement to its use and custody may not be self-evident from the context in which it is found. The right to use technological knowledge to produce and to use or display special artefacts may well have been part of a house society's 'symbolic capital' (Gillespie, 2007: 36) that might be acquired or dispensed, for example, for the purpose of enhancing prestige in marriage alliances. There are plainly innumerable instances archaeologically where an exotic artefact, found well beyond its regular zone of circulation, might have been the product of such a liaison, such as the Scottish spiral bronze armlet with snake terminals from the first century AD grave from Snailwell, Cambridgeshire (Lethbridge, 1954). But the fragmentary beaded torc from the Blair Drummond, Stirlingshire, hoard (Joy, 2015), undoubtedly exotic, resembling the regional Plastic Style of the third or second century BC in south-western France, was yet apparently made of Scottish gold, suggesting that here it may have been the expertise of the craftsman that was imported through long-distance alliance. These liaisons would certainly be within the compass of the social networking of house societies, but we may well suppose that other forms of social organization could equally yield the same archaeological outcome.

One apparent means for a house to enhance its repute and material capital was by raiding and warfare, a characteristic once again in which house societies appear to mirror the traditional view of 'Celtic' society. It remains unclear, however, whether the head of a house might enhance his or her personal status and wealth by such means, or whether assets thus acquired, like the traditional material and immaterial capital of the house, were simply theirs as communal custodians. One reason for aggressive initiatives of this kind was that houses could cease to exist, either through decline in numbers or through absorption by other houses.

From this overview it will be self-evident that later prehistoric societies in Britain could easily fit with a number of aspects of Lévi-Strauss' house societies. In so far as he appears to have envisaged house societies as an intermediate phase between relatively simple kin-based societies and more complex, stratified social structures, the concept would also appear to match the relevant stage of social development. The key problem, as Gillespie recognized (2007: 39) was that Lévi-Strauss' definition (1984: 184) of the house as an institution that might exist 'on all levels of social life, from the family to the state' was so open-ended as to be practically unworkable as a model to apply to archaeological data. There is no point in adopting a concept from an allied discipline, however eminent and respected the source, unless it actually contributes to and enhances understanding. In the examples cited above from Britain, Ireland, and Europe, the definition of house societies seems in fact to focus on the structures rather than the social entities that concerned Lévi-Strauss, and therefore adds little or nothing to an understanding of the Iron Age communities in question.

Egalitarian or Hierarchical?

Discussion of social structure for the past half century or more has been driven by the premise of progression towards increasing complexity in a sequence that begins with simple, segmentary societies through kinship-based chiefdoms and culminating in proto-states that archaeologically attest to increasing craft specialization and incipient urbanization. Implicit in this model has been the assumption that early agricultural societies were essentially egalitarian, and fundamentally peaceable, whereas complex societies became increasingly hierarchical and given to aggrandizement through aggression. In recent years the rational basis for this latter assumption especially has been challenged, though the case has not always been argued on the basis of the archaeological evidence. In arguing the egalitarian nature of Iron Age communities in the peninsular north-west, Sastre and Currás (2020: 23) declared that 'interpretations have to be more attached to the archaeological evidence and not trying to impose pre-established social models on the record', a sentiment that would doubtless receive universal endorsement, whatever predetermined social models we favoured. Earle (2020: xvi) referred to a current trend in anthropological archaeology to investigate the potential and possibility of egalitarian societies existing in prehistory, a trend that had been glossed as a 'bottoms up' approach. Traditionalists, preferring to 'piece together the past' on inductive principles, might just regard that as imposing 'pre-established social models on the record'.

The contributions to the Maastricht conference, on which *Alternative Iron Ages* (Currás and Sastre, 2020a) was based, contained several contributions that argued for egalitarian societies in Iron Age Europe. The essential characteristics of segmentary societies, according to the editors, was that there was no centralization of authority or monopolization of power, nor any social differentiation based upon specialization of labour. Segmentary communities functioned symmetrically, each being independent and economically self-sufficient, whilst specialization or centres for exchange of goods and materials negated the segmentary principle. Segmentary societies were not necessarily peaceable, but warfare in decentralized and egalitarian segmentary societies was characterized as inter-communal rather than inter-personal. Hence, in the case of the Castro Culture, warfare reaffirmed identity within the complementary segmentary structure.

Currás and Sastre acknowledged the impossibility through archaeology's 'mute materiality' of establishing the nature of kinship (2020b: 135), descent, alliance, residence rules, symbolisms and so forth, but we could examine archaeologically the surviving evidence for the use of domestic and territorial space for insights into political relationships and the organization of production. What surely remains an impossibility is inferring motivation, so that Angelbeck's assertion in relation to the north-western *castros* (2020: 40) that 'households had limited integration within the *castro* overall, as families independently laboured for their own subsistence' lacks credible support. The very fact that neighbouring households were located within the *castro*'s protecting enclosure surely argues for common interest.

In several disparate regions of later prehistoric Europe a case has been made, not simply for an egalitarian social order but one based on the socio-political principle of anarchy. Armit (2019, 2020) used the term literally to mean a society 'without leaders', and pointed out that in political discourse anarchy does not have the popular implication of disorganization and chaos. Unfortunately, the standard dictionary definitions do indeed imply lack of government and lawlessness, so that the terms non-hierarchical or heterarchical might be preferred. The analysis of Late Bronze Age and Early Iron Age societies in Sardinia by González (2020) was persuasive because it drew upon a range of archaeological data, but betrayed political commitment in its reference to colonialist and capitalist influences in archaeology. The *bronzetti* were interpreted as cult images that need not reflect the reality of socio-political organization, and though the depiction of warriors in a significant proportion of examples indicated a conventional concern for the warrior ethos, there was very little evidence from *nuraghi* or villages of destruction or tangible evidence of inter-community warfare. At Broxmouth in East Lothian, by contrast, there was ample evidence of warfare in the form of bone spearheads and human trophies (Armit, 2020: 208). In the past twenty years there appears to have been a trade-off in which the 'pacified past' has been relegated in favour of the promotion of a more egalitarian prehistory.

However persuasive a case is made that Iron Age societies were fundamentally egalitarian, however, archaeologists have to recognize that in the period immediately prior to Roman conquest, regional societies emerge from prehistory as hierarchical, and in the case of Gaul or southern and south-eastern England, ruled by warrior aristocrats whose material wealth is attested archaeologically as well as by the record of ancient historians. The argument has been that social complexity and hierarchy were accelerated by contact with the Roman world, and as regards the extravagant display of wealth in burials of the Welwyn series, for example, this may as well have been triggered by a chauvinistic display of native identity in the face of external threat to indigenous culture, as by the demonstration of social hierarchy. Even so, the evidence for a deeply stratified society is irrefutable, and it is hard to believe that the social bonds of hierarchy and the mutual obligations of client relationships, personal, kin-based, or tribal, could have become so deeply embedded in a few short generations.

Even traditionalists who still subscribe to the belief that Iron Age society in Britain and Europe was stratified, however, would probably agree that the archaeological evidence suggests a greater diversity of practice regionally than was formerly acknowledged. As Earle (2020: xx) concluded: 'Were Iron Age societies of Europe egalitarian or socially stratified? The answer is most probably that they varied across the spectrum according to specific conditions of warfare, trade,

42 RETHINKING ROUNDHOUSES

agricultural intensification and the like.' Major public works, like landscape construction or building of hillforts surely would have required organizational leadership, as would have marshalling forces in conflict. But there is no reason to suppose that these roles were not endorsed by community consent, or sustained in the community's interest by what Earle termed 'group-oriented' chiefs (2020: xxi). Equally there are instances in the archaeological record where we must surely recognize that the excessively unequal distribution of wealth, in funerary or household contexts, suggests an elite status that involved personal aggrandizement and power based on autocracy rather than community interest. Consensual hierarchy might well be less conspicuous archaeologically than coercive hierarchy, but in any event presence or absence of prestige goods alone is no longer a sufficient basis for inference, without careful analysis of circumstances of deposition. In a settlement context, it is important to distinguish construction or foundation deposits or residues from closure episodes from material associated with occupation. Material found in graves may well be indicative of the status of the incumbent, but they could be prescribed by the funerary ritual as accompaniments for the dead, offerings to the gods or as part of the deposition rites, or they could be personal tributes from kin or dues from dependants or clients. All of these might be willingly contributed to a leader who was highly respected for his/her achievements on behalf of the community, and none need imply coercion or self-aggrandizement.

But whatever social system we infer, it should be compatible with the observed archaeological data, and not imported from other disciplines or presupposed on the basis of our own preferred modern political philosophy. Iron Age social reconstruction is not an appropriate canvas on which to play out controversies triggered by opposing political ideologies of the twentieth and twenty-first centuries, centred on the polarization of capitalist and Marxist economies, or upon post-colonialist or gender-liberated perspectives.

Archaeology as Entertainment

One of the key shifts in the popular perception of archaeology in the late twentieth and twenty-first centuries has been its increasing role as entertainment, promoted by television programmes like *Time Team* (Channel 4, 1994–2014), in which it ranked as the equivalent of a time-limited game challenge. Together with the acceptance by professional archaeologists of treasure hunting with metal detectors as the legitimate exercise of individual liberty, subject always to landowners' consent, rather than vandalism of the national heritage like collecting birds' eggs or poaching elephant ivory, this has contributed to the public and government perception of archaeology as a hobby for entertaining schoolchildren or tourists rather than a serious discipline for historical enquiry. On a BBC Radio 4 programme (*You and Yours*, 19 February 2021) a metal detectorist was asked if she understood why archaeologists might object to treasure hunting. She replied that she was puzzled by that, since she was only digging in topsoil, which on *Time Team* they stripped off with a mechanical digger anyway. If excavation is equated with treasure hunting, and archaeology is seen as a hobby, it is hardly surprising that the Department for Education should have considered cutting university funding for archaeology (together with media studies and performing arts), especially when leading academic archaeologists can only justify its support by virtue of its use of applied sciences or its contribution to tourism and the heritage industry (Gosden et al., 2021).

The mild ridicule with which archaeology is now regarded was well illustrated by the reception to the television programme *Stonehenge: The Lost Circle Revealed* (BBC2, 12 February 2021), based upon an *Antiquity* paper (Parker Pearson et al., 2021), which advanced the case for believing that the Stonehenge bluestones had once been part of a stone circle in Wales. 'What I loved about this winningly optimistic, dogged, rain-lashed, incredibly sodden packed lunch of a drizzling documentary was that there was nothing to go on in Pembrokeshire's bleak, miserable Proselli [*sic*] hills—but still they went on, the team lustily examining sites where the stones *once might have been*, "looking for something that would no longer exist above ground", ie "empty stokeholds" [*sic*], ie nothing. At one point they were filmed running across a field with "ground-penetrating radar", trying to work out what had happened at this point 3,500 years ago' (*The Sunday Times, Culture*, 14 February 2021).

What this ill-edited review overlooked was that the meticulous geochemistry that had identified in the Preseli Hills the quarry source of the Stonehenge bluestones (predominantly spotted dolerite) had been abandoned in the determination to identify Waun Mawn as the source circle, where the surviving four bluestones are in fact unspotted dolerite. The identification instead was based on the pentagonal footprint of a stone hole matching the shape of one of the Stonehenge bluestones, not so much science, therefore, as Cinderella. But one cannot imagine Sir David Attenborough presenting a programme on the natural world or about global warming being treated in this fashion, and archaeologists have no one to blame for the way their discipline is perceived but themselves.

Archaeology and Climate Change

Apart from political and economic crises, the biggest perceived challenge to humanity in the twenty-first century is climate change. Often bracketed together with environmental pollution, which is wholly caused by human agency and therefore potentially controllable, climate change has been endemic since the dawn of time, as archaeologists are uniquely equipped to appreciate. Since the

Industrial Revolution and more especially the advent of the atomic age, the anthropogenic contribution to climate change has doubtless been enhanced, and could be mitigated by using more sustainable practices, not just in industrial and agricultural activities, but in everyday life. Though the scale of human activity in the past hardly threatened global existence, there are clear instances of communities adapting to climate change and adopting strategies of resilience that might inform contemporary policies of mitigation. A pioneer in this approach was the Butser Ancient Farm, where Reynolds demonstrated that cereal yields could be sustained and even enhanced on a limited scale without the use of chemical herbicides and fertilizers, which were mutually necessitating. Even in the apparently esoteric field of roundhouse studies, research is now focusing upon the range of materials, construction techniques, and resourcing that were essential for sustainable building in the later prehistoric past (Romankiewicz, 2016b). When universities first became concerned with issues of climate change, it was disappointing that they consistently disregarded the potential input of archaeologists. Now some are recognizing the importance of understanding how climate change has impacted on past societies, and their responses to it, in order better to formulate strategies for sustainable development for the future. The crucial importance of an archaeological input is equally apparent in the formulation of global strategies for ocean management (Henderson, 2019), which needs a past-time perspective that respects the cultural traditions of maritime communities in order to enable sustainable coexistence.

3

Analysing and Interpreting Timber Roundhouses

The extent to which the excavator is able to recover evidence of any building must be dependent principally upon the materials of which it was constructed, the way that it was constructed, and the extent to which these impacted on the ground on which it was located. Thereafter, it depends upon the processes of attrition and degrading since the termination of its use. It follows that our interpretation will only be as good as our capacity to recognize and record reliably these factors, which in turn depends upon the techniques of excavation employed, and the excavator's skill in recognizing the structural remains.

Some Key Sites

Timber is unlikely to survive other than in exceptional circumstances, notably where the remains have been preserved in wetland conditions. Two outstanding examples that have come to light since the publication of *IAR* are Must Farm, Cambridgeshire and Black Loch of Myrton in Wigtownshire, both of which have well-preserved timber structural remains, with the additional bonus at Must Farm of a remarkable material assemblage. Occasionally, as a result of burning, charred timbers survive, as at Birnie in Morayshire, where the level of preservation could contribute significantly to our understanding of the superstructure of monumental roundhouses.

Traditionally, Wessex had been the focus of Southern British roundhouse studies, based on classic sites like Little Woodbury (Bersu, 1940), Pimperne (Harding et al., 1993), and Longbridge Deverill (Hawkes and Hawkes, 2012). An outstanding example of a large roundhouse of the early Iron Age from Flint Farm, Clatford, Hampshire, was published as *IAR* was going to press (Cunliffe and Poole, 2008). The site was initially surveyed using a high resolution caesium magnetometer, which remarkably identified not only the external gully of the principal roundhouse (CS1) but also both inner and outer ring-grooves. More remarkably, it further identified the postholes of at least two other large roundhouses, of which an arc of the main, weight-bearing post-ring of one (CS2) was uncovered in the excavated area. The site had been subject to ploughing, which evidently affected the extent of survival of features like the ring-grooves, and in accordance with

Rethinking Roundhouses: Later Prehistoric Settlement in Britain and Beyond. D. W. Harding, Oxford University Press.
© D. W. Harding 2023. DOI: 10.1093/oso/9780192893802.003.0003

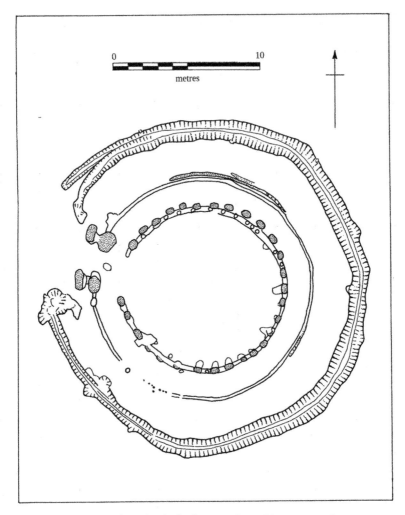

Fig. 3.1 Flint Farm, Goodworth Clatford, Hampshire, CS1. Drawing by D. W. Harding, adapted from Cunliffe and Poole, 2008.

modern practice was stripped by machine 'to the surface of natural chalk and the top of the features cut into it' (Cunliffe and Poole, 2008: 11). Given the pinpoint accuracy with which the house had been located, it is regrettable that its immediate area was not excavated by hand from topsoil in order to maximize recovery of surviving detail.

The timber roundhouse, which was located concentrically within a penannular enclosure, comprised an outer wall set in a ring-groove 15 metres in diameter and a weight-bearing circle of posts 11 metres in diameter (Fig. 3.1). It evidently had two principal construction phases. In its rebuilt phase, the inner circle comprised individual postholes slightly offset from the earlier setting of posts within a ring-groove, though the published sections hardly demonstrate this sequence as clearly as might have been hoped. Because of the offset, the assumption is that the rebuilt phase of the outer circle was represented by the very intermittent arcs of gully to the north and east of the circuit, though one might have expected the later phase to have been the better preserved. A porched entrance to the north-west possibly included elements from an earlier phase beneath the surviving later post pairs. As regards internal furnishings, a complex central structure may well have post-dated the demise of the house, but a feature on the north side of the interior occupies the same position relative to the doorway as structures at Pimperne and Longbridge Deverill, and may well have been contemporary with the occupation of the house.

Flint Farm was essentially a standard large double-ring Wessex roundhouse. A significant omission from *IAR* were the roundhouses at Groundwell Farm, Blunsdon St Andrew, Wiltshire (Gingell, 1981), which already showed a greater diversity of construction than was generally witnessed in the Wessex series (Fig. 3.2). Most distinctive is the latest of the Groundwell sequence, House 4. With a double ring-groove, the outer 19.5 metres in diameter and inner 17.5 metres in diameter, this would appear to defy the limits of conventional cone-on-cylinder construction, yet posts within its inner ring-groove plainly indicate that these were wall foundations. The excavators were surely right to infer that the double ring-groove did not represent successive building, and in hindsight it may now be seen as a classic example of an insulated double-faced outer wall. The roof was supported internally, not by a post-ring or four-post tower, but by three posts that were of more substantial construction than any others in the complex. Whether they supported a tripod or a triangular tower is not clear, but they plainly represent a variant on central tower support of a kind that will be discussed more fully below. House 2 at Groundwell Farm has just such a central tower based on four posts, whilst the eight posts of the inner ring of House 3 might just have been two successive sets of four-posters. These postholes are of distinctive ramped construction, not unlike those at Fison Way, Thetford, Norfolk (Gregory, 1991), clearly designed to facilitate replacement.

At the time that *IAR* was going to press, an excavation in Perthshire, now fully published (O'Connell and Anderson, 2020), was uncovering a series of later prehistoric roundhouse settlements dating from the Middle Bronze Age and culminating in an Iron Age palisaded homestead that challenges the conventional Wessex-derived model of roundhouses. Several of the Middle-Late Bronze Age houses from Blackford in Strathallan are not strictly circular so much as shaped like a pear-drop, with the extension being towards the entrance, though not evi-dently designed to encompass a projecting porch (Fig. 3.3). In the case of the multi-phased House 1 on site E, this shape was mirrored in the palisaded enclos-ure that, like Flint Farm, immediately contained it, and which on these grounds alone, despite the apparent absence of an entrance facing the house doorway, was

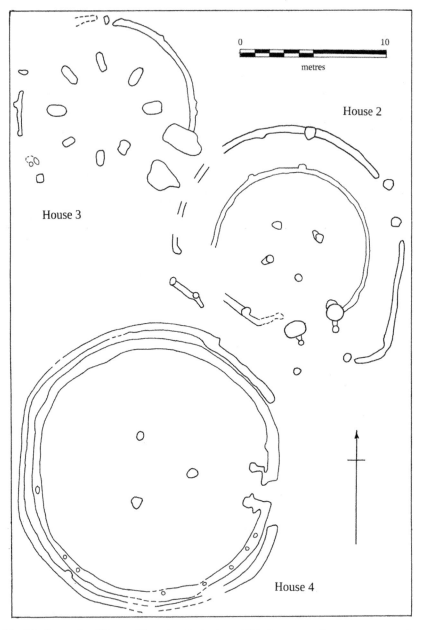

Fig. 3.2 Groundwell Farm, Blunsdon St Andrew, Wiltshire, roundhouses. Drawing by D. W. Harding, adapted from Gingell, 1981.

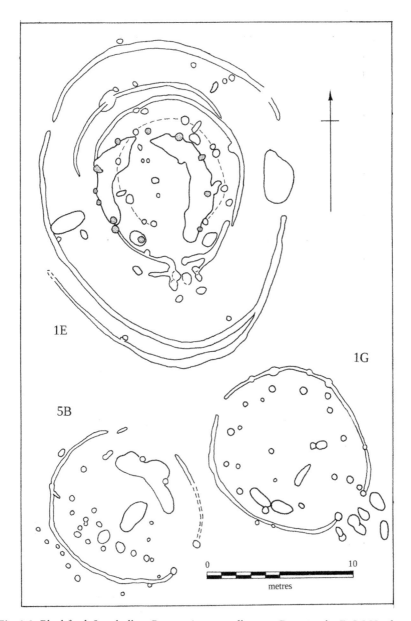

Fig. 3.3 Blackford, Strathallan, Bronze Age roundhouses. Drawing by D. W. Harding, adapted from O'Connell and Anderson, 2020.

presumably contemporary with it. The 'Reynolds principle', that the ideal house plan was a cone on a cylinder, and that any deviation represented a structural weakness, presumably applies only in a vacuum on a level plane, without regard to terrain or prevailing wind. In any event Reynolds acknowledged that the doorway was an inevitable breach of that ideal, so that local experience may perhaps have resulted in a measure of compromise.

50 RETHINKING ROUNDHOUSES

The construction of the Blackford houses in several instances deploys an outer ring-groove and an inner, roof-supporting post-ring, though the excavators argued that these were not always part of the same building phase. Several of the houses also include an arc of ring-ditch, though it is not clear in some cases whether this reflects multi-phase usage, and if so, which of the surviving other elements are integral to the ring-ditch phase. In some cases truncation has evidently reduced the ring-ditch to a series of residual pits. The roundhouses from the Iron Age palisaded enclosure on site A, however, are of quite different construction (Fig. 3.4). Both principal structures are defined by circles of small post-holes, House 1A at 12 metres in diameter and House 2A at 14 metres in diameter being the two largest structures in the Blackford complex. The problem is that neither has any evidence of further internal support, and, as the excavators were well aware, houses of the stake-wall kind from Southern Britain, which might otherwise afford comparanda, were generally considered incapable of supporting a roof over a diameter of around eight metres. However, using a temporary central king post, experimental reconstruction of a stake-walled house 13 metres in diameter was successfully achieved at Castell Henllys, Pembrokeshire (Bennett, 2010). House A1 has a pair of elongated shallow pits on its north side, and several small pits on its east, which might be the truncated remains of ring-ditches just inside the perimeter wall, but these are hardly relevant to roofing of the structure. Pit 462 contained evidence of animal bedding and faeces, which might imply the structure's use as a byre if not as a byre-house, in either case presumably requiring the shelter of a roof. Structure A1 had a further complexity in a pair of annexes flanking the south-east facing doorway, a feature without parallel in the British Iron Age, though reminiscent of some later roundhouses of the *castros* of the Hispanic north-west. Their purpose here is quite obscure, though the north-eastern annexe was filled with a pit nearly a metre deep. The suggestion that it might have been an earth closet would probably be regarded as flippant, since this is a topic that settlement archaeologists never seem to address. A pit located centrally within the doorway, if contemporary with the main structure, would certainly have complicated access, but might have supported a swinging gate to control access for smaller animals. Structure 2A had additional short lengths of truncated ring-groove on its north-west side, one on an arc with the post-ring, two others broadly concentric, which could be the truncated traces of similar annexes flanking its north-west facing doorway.

The two circular buildings within the palisaded enclosure certainly have the appearance of a related pair of roundhouses, with doorways facing the opposed entrances to the stockaded compound. Though archaeologists are rightly reluctant to base interpretations upon an absence of evidence, it is possible that internal roof support in both buildings was provided by non-earth-fast components, either posts supported on post-pads (of which one possible example was noted in Structure 1A) or more obviously by a free-standing four-post timber tower in the

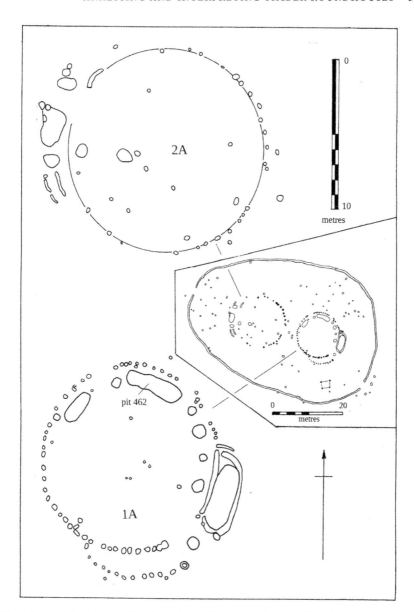

Fig. 3.4 Blackford, Strathallan, Iron Age palisaded settlement. Drawing by D. W. Harding, adapted from O'Connell and Anderson, 2020.

centre, which would have served as a constructional scaffold that became integral to the completed building. This would resolve many of the structural problems of roundhouses, especially from the Middle Iron Age in Southern Britain, where the viability of earth-fast timbers in sodden environments was plainly marginal. The roundhouse with central tower, earth-fast or free-standing, is based on different

52 RETHINKING ROUNDHOUSES

engineering principles from the post-ring roundhouse, but may be a more widespread reality than has hitherto been recognized.

Post-Ring, Double-Ring, and Central Post Construction

For many years the popular assumption, commonly perpetuated by educational reconstructions, was that prehistoric houses were circular with post-ring walls of wattle and daub, and with their thatched roofs supported by a central post on the bell-tent principle. This was a notion that *IAR* was inclined to discredit, though the evidence since has suggested that there were indeed roundhouses of this kind from the Bronze Age, with classic examples at Reading Business Park (Fig. 3.5, 1 and 2; Moore and Jennings, 1992). Examples from Easton Lane, Winchester (Fig. 3.5, 3) and Middle Farm, Dorchester (Fig. 3.5, 4) were more tentatively dated to the Middle Bronze Age. Iron Age examples include the Maiden Castle house reconstructed at Butser Hill by Peter Reynolds (1979). At Salmondsbury in Gloucestershire (Dunning, 1976) the paired Iron Age stake-wall houses both had central posts (Fig. 3.6, 3). At Mingies Ditch (Fig. 3.6, 2) the central post underlay a central hearth, suggesting, as we shall see, that the central post may have served only as a constructional rather than a permanent feature, an option that could well be more widely applicable.

By the Iron Age central post support had been generally superseded by double-ring roundhouses (Guilbert, 1981), in which roofs were supported by a main weight-bearing post-ring that would have been tied with lintels into a rigid circular framework, over which the rafters could be cantilevered with an upper ring-beam holding them into a rigid cone. The rafters would thus have extended outwards a third to a half again the span from ring-beam to apex, resting externally on an outer mass-wall or stake-wall, of which frequently no earth-fast trace survived. This inference was supported by the fact that the door posts of many Iron Age houses would otherwise have been oddly dislocated from the extant post-ring. Where the doorway is marked by a double pair of postholes, the outer wall would probably have aligned with the inner pair, the outer pair marking a projecting porch. This was the interpretation offered in the case of the post-ring roundhouse with porch from earlier excavations at Thainstone, Inverurie (Fig. 3.7, 2; Murray and Murray, 2006), where the ratio between centre-to-post-ring and post-ring-to-external wall is much closer to equal than in the case of Southern British roundhouses, perhaps reflecting the use of different roofing materials.

That ratio is plainly significant in terms of supporting the roof load. But the location of the main weight-bearing post-ring is also crucial in dividing the house in terms of social and functional use of central and peripheral space. In House 3 at Longbridge Deverill (Hawkes and Hawkes, 2012) quantities of daub in the postholes of the weight-bearing post-ring suggested that this was a substantial

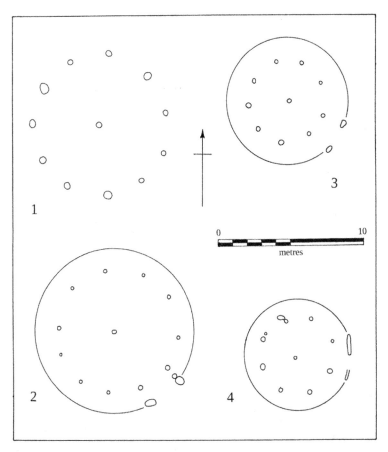

Fig. 3.5 Bronze Age roundhouses with central post. 1, Reading Business Park, Area 5, House 1; 2, Reading Business Park, Area 5, House 2; 3, Easton Lane, Winchester, CS2782; 4, Dorchester, Dorset, Bypass, Middle Farm, Structure 03252. Drawings by D. W. Harding, adapted from Moore and Jennings, 1992, Fasham et al., 1989, and Smith et al., 1997.

wall, and not just partitioned with wattle panels or textile drapes. But this need not mean that it was the external wall of the house. Support for the idea that the peripheral space was positively screened from the central area is afforded by the excavated arc of the second roundhouse (CS2) at Flint Farm. Here it was noted that the chalk within the main post-ring was more trodden than that outside it (Cunliffe and Poole, 2008: 51). At Longbridge Deverill the case for the external wall being defined by the outer post-ring of House 3 is surely clinched by the alignment of the slots on either side of the entrance porch, which must have been integral to the main structure (*IAR*: Fig. 8, 2). The outer zone could equally be accessed from the main entrance lobby, so that this area, two metres wide around the circumference of the house, and at over 60 square metres more than half as

54 RETHINKING ROUNDHOUSES

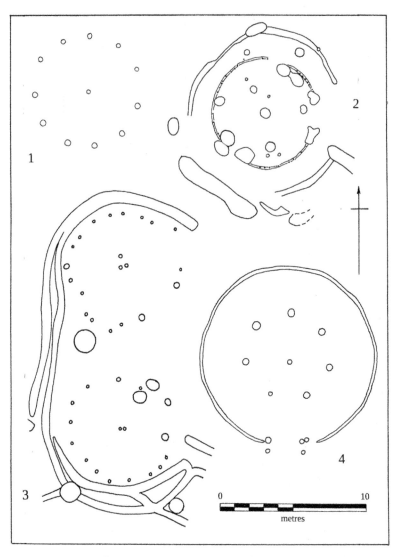

Fig. 3.6 Iron Age roundhouses with central post. 1, West Plean, Stirlingshire; 2, Mingies Ditch, Hardwick-with-Yelford, Oxfordshire, House 5; 3, Salmondsbury, Gloucestershire; 4, Burrow Farm, East Worlington, Devon. Drawings by D. W. Harding, adapted from Steer, 1956, Allen and Robinson, 1993, Dunning, 1976, and Walls and Morris, 2012.

much again as the central area, was not simply external storage space. Double-ring roundhouses, whether with external post-ring or mass-wall, evidently constituted an important variant within the timber roundhouse range, but we should allow a measure of flexibility in the division between central and peripheral space, which may have been more firmly defined in some examples than others.

ANALYSING AND INTERPRETING TIMBER ROUNDHOUSES 55

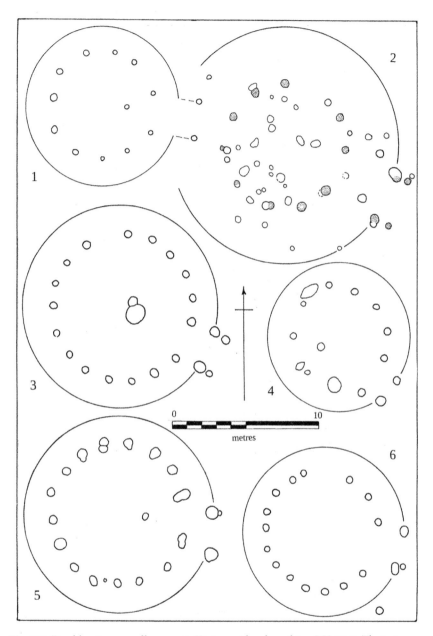

Fig. 3.7 Double-ring roundhouses. 1, Kintore, Aberdeenshire, RH 20; 2, Thainstone Business Park, Aberdeenshire; 3, Latton Lands, Wiltshire, Structure 1829; 4, Latton Lands, Wiltshire, Structure 2760; 5, Horcott Pit, Fairford, Gloucestershire, Roundhouse 6046; 6, Cotswold Community Park, Roundhouse 7721. Drawings by D. W. Harding, adapted from Cook and Dunbar, 2008, Murray and Murray, 2006, Powell et al., 2009, Lamdin-Whymark et al., 2009, and Powell et al., 2010.

It is nevertheless fundamentally different from the single-ring plan, which, with no evidence of division between central and peripheral space, most probably functioned differently in terms of social use of space.

A key factor in the ground-plans of some Iron Age timber roundhouses is the self-evident symmetry of the post-circles. Guilbert (1982) first articulated the concept of *axial line symmetry* on the basis of post-ring roundhouses from Moel y Gaer, mostly under ten metres in diameter, even allowing for the archaeologically invisible external wall, but generally provided with a projecting porch defined by two pairs of postholes. A line through the doorway and the geometric centre of the house invariably led to a key post in the weight-bearing ring. The house thus divided into two halves, each a mirror image of the other. What was unclear was whether this distinctive symmetry was a factor of engineering and construction of the house, or of its social function and usage, and Guilbert declined to offer an opinion. Regular spacing of equal sized posts in the main weight-bearing circle seems an obvious means of distributing the load evenly, and to standardize requirements of timber. The axial symmetry model can also be applied to some of the larger Wessex roundhouses. It works for House 3 at Longbridge Deverill (Hawkes and Hawkes, 2012), for House 1b at Flint Farm (Cunliffe and Poole, 2008), and for the principal house at Crickley Hill, Gloucestershire (Dixon, 2019). But for Little Woodbury and Pimperne it only applies to the replacement phase, not to the original structure without some interpretative manipulation. What is really surprising is just how many posts there were in the main weight-bearing circles of the major Wessex roundhouses – 24 at Little Woodbury Phase 1, 26 at Pimperne Phase 1, 27 at Longbridge Deverill House 3, and 29 at Flint Farm, in the latter case spaced at intervals of under a metre. Presumably the wall-plates could not much exceed a metre without impairing the strength and integrity of the ring, but the implications in terms of resource supply are substantial. At Wakerley, Northamptonshire, by contrast, the spacing in House 1 may exceed three metres, which might account for the need for replacement, since in House 2 the span is reduced to around two metres (Fig. 3.8, 1).

Ring-Grooves and Wall-Slots

Apart from post-rings of the main weight-bearing timbers, most commonly found in houses of the earlier Iron Age, the next most likely survival is the ring-groove type of wall foundation, generally though not invariably of an outer wall. Similar in appearance are the drainage-gullies that are thought to have carried away rainwater from the eaves, and hence effectively a proxy for roundhouses, the foundations of which either were not earth-fast or have not survived. Such drainage ring-gullies are not always clearly distinguished in scale of construction from wall foundation slots, though on Middle and Late pre-Roman Iron Age

ANALYSING AND INTERPRETING TIMBER ROUNDHOUSES 57

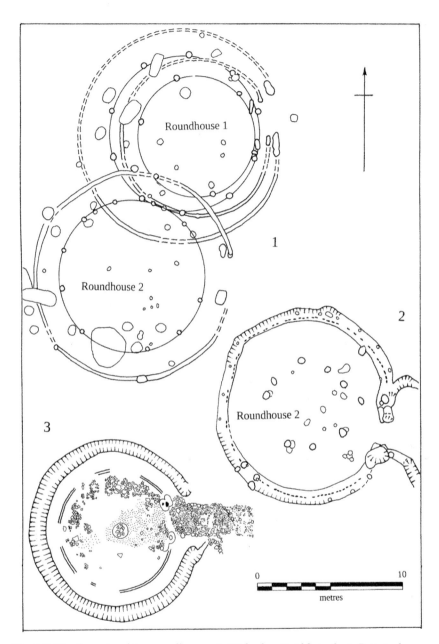

Fig. 3.8 Northamptonshire roundhouses. 1, Wakerley; 2, Aldwincle; 3, Brigstock. Drawings by D. W. Harding, adapted from Jackson, 1978, Jackson, 1977 and Jackson, 1983.

settlements they tend to be wider and deeper than house foundations. At Street House, Loftus, on the north Yorkshire coast (Fig. 3.9; Sherlock, 2019), Structure 3 in its first phase clearly had stakes set in the ring-groove, but its final phase ring-gully appears to have served as a drip-trench. In determining the size of house, it is plainly important to distinguish between the footprint of roundhouse walls and what can be no more than a proxy indicator of a roundhouse.

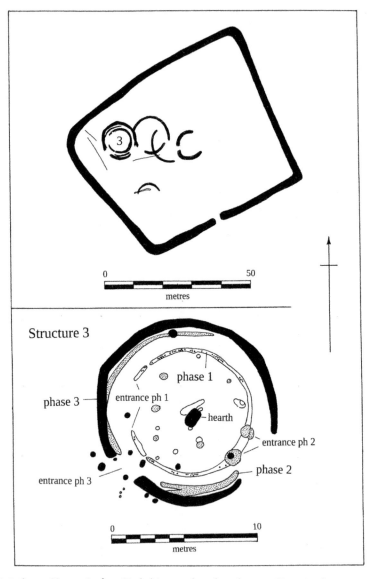

Fig. 3.9 Street House, Loftus, Yorkshire, enclosed settlement. Drawing by D. W. Harding, adapted from Sherlock, 2019.

In *IAR* the point was made that ring-groove wall construction was particularly characteristic of northern roundhouses, especially those of substantial dimensions like West Brandon, Co. Durham, House B (*IAR*: Fig.10A), or Bannockburn Fort, Stirling (Rideout, 1996), House 1 (*IAR*: Fig. 13, 3). But ring-groove construction was already well-documented in Northamptonshire in Dennis Jackson's meticulous excavations. At Wakerley (Jackson and Ambrose, 1978), successive Houses 1 and 2 attained a maximum diameter of 14 metres, equalling the size of the major Wessex roundhouses, though with fewer posts in their roof-bearing rings. At Aldwincle (Fig. 3.8, 2; Jackson, 1977) the recut ring-groove of House 2 bedded a wall of split timbers, with an outer line of intermittent posts on its outer rim. It would seem reasonable therefore to infer that the ring-groove was the foundation for an upright wall, commonly of planks or split timbers.

Where ring-grooves have a decidedly polygonal plan, however, as at Little Waltham, Essex (Fig. 3.10, 1; Drury, 1978), or Bruen Stapleford in Cheshire (Fig. 3.10, 4; Fairburn, 2003), it is possible that lengths of sill-beams could have been laid to act as the foundation for timber uprights of the outer wall. For the polygonal outline of the ring-groove house in Trench D at Birnie the excavator preferred to interpret them as foundations for prefabricated wattle panels, some stake-holes surviving within the groove, while others appeared to continue the circuit where the ring-groove itself had been eroded (Hunter, 2008: 8). Where the polygonal gully contains post or stake-holes, as at Crick Covert Farm (Fig. 3.10, 3), plainly it could not have accommodated a sill-beam. Chronologically, the polygonal plan is in evidence from the earlier Bronze Age, as from Ross Bay, Kirkcudbright (Fig. 3.10, 5; Ronan and Higgins, 2005), though whether it constituted a particular Bronze Age type is more debatable (Pope, 2015).

In a number of instances the case for an external cavity double-wall is convincing. At Melsonby, North Yorkshire (Fitts et al., 1999), it comprised a ring-groove with a concentric ring of slots and stake-holes (Fig. 3.11, 4), probably filled with straw or bracken as insulation. As noted above, in House 2 at Aldwincle, 132 split oak timbers formed the inner face of the outer wall, with an estimated 24 posts constituting the outer face, and with a cavity around 38 cm between. Both Covert Farm, Crick, House RG58 and Coton Park House RD6 display post-rings between ring-grooves and drip-gullies that could be interpreted as double-walls. This kind of wall construction appears to have been used from the earlier Bronze Age, as in the Unenclosed Platform House 5 at Lintshie Gutter in Lanarkshire (Fig. 3.11, 1; Terry, 1995), though, as the excavator pointed out, there is always the possibility that two concentric ring-grooves represented successive, rather than unitary, structures. Alternatively, where there are two, concentric ring-grooves without any surviving evidence of stakes or wall material, as at Meole Brace, Shrewsbury (Bain and Evans, 2008: Fig. 5) there will also always be the possibility that the outer ring-groove was an eavesdrip-gully. In the case of the Group 24 structure at Melton on Humberside the fact that the outer ring-groove contained postholes argues positively against this option (Fenton-Thomas, 2011: 96–7 and Fig. 67).

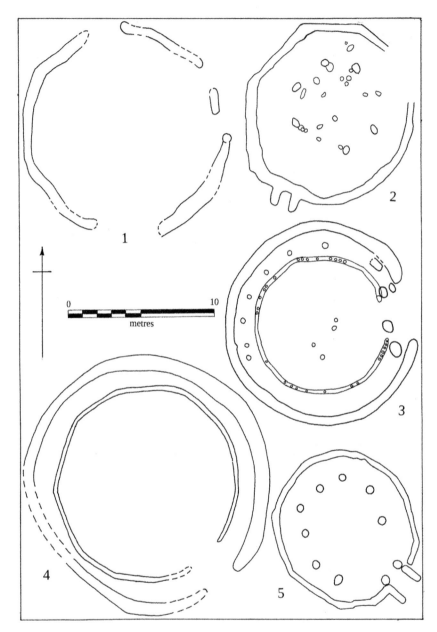

Fig. 3.10 Roundhouses with polygonal ring-grooves. 1, Little Waltham, Essex; 2, Lookout Plantation, Northumberland; 3, Crick Covert Farm, Northamptonshire, RG58; 4, Bruen Stapleford, Cheshire; 5, Ross Bay, Kirkcudbrightshire. Drawings by D. W. Harding, adapted from Drury, 1978, Menaghan, 1994, Hughes and Woodward, 2015, Fairburn, 2003, Ronan and Higgins, 2005.

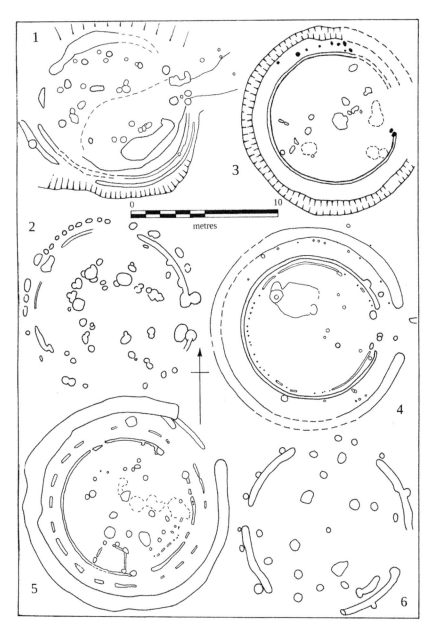

Fig. 3.11 Roundhouses with double external walls. 1, Lintshie Gutter, Lanarkshire, platform 5; 2, Wetwang Slack, Yorkshire, House 12.4; 3, South Shields, Tyne and Wear; 4, Melsonby, Yorkshire; 5, Roxby Moor, Yorkshire; 6, Dalton Parlours, Yorkshire, Roundhouse 3. Drawings by D. W. Harding, adapted from Terry, 1995, Hodgson et al., 2001, Fitts et al., 1999, Dent, 1984, Inman et al., 1985, and Wrathmell and Nicholson, 1990.

62 RETHINKING ROUNDHOUSES

Close-set double-walls pose greater problems in larger roundhouses, however, since this implies constructional geometry rather different from the Wessex model. At the Bannockburn fort roundhouse (*IAR*: Fig.13, 3) the ring-groove was packed with substantial timbers, closely spaced, of what must be an external timber wall, yet there was still evidence of an outer post-ring. The ring-groove of the Bannockburn homestead roundhouse, by contrast (Fig. 3.12, 2), appears to have supported a plank wall, which, with its outer post-ring, could have faced an insulated cavity wall. A similar interpretation could apply to the second phase roundhouse at West Brandon, where the post-ring outside the ring-groove is some 18 metres in diameter, raising questions regarding their respective functions. Were they facing for a mass wall of turf? Could they have provided peripheral storage? Were they double-walls packed with insulating materials?

A more recently excavated example is from West Stamford, Lincolnshire (Fig. 3.12, 1; Weston and Daniel, 2017), where ring-gully 2 was no less than 16 metres in diameter, with a substantial post-ring a metre beyond that. The earlier house, based on ring-gully 1, was only slightly smaller, and probably had an outer post-ring, largely obliterated by later construction. Whereas the Bannockburn homestead roundhouse and the West Brandon house had inner post-rings, however, at West Stamford an arc of posts around the northern edge of ring-gully 1 more probably is residual from an earlier building. Otherwise, internal support for the roof may have been afforded by a four- or five-post setting in the centre of the building, but individual postholes could not be linked or assigned to phase. In ring-gully 3 this central setting may have been a four-post arrangement, as noted elsewhere. The West Stamford buildings superficially might suggest a figure-of-eight, but the excavators argued on the basis of radiocarbon dates and stratigraphy that ring-gully 3 was later, and contemporary with the enclosure ditch that truncated the west side of the houses represented by ring-gullies 1 and 2.

Where the outer wall ring-groove was interrupted by the entrance, it was commonly marked by a pair of terminal posts, and sometimes by an additional pair, even where the entrance is not elaborated into a projecting porch. Distinguishing a porch from an internal vestibule may depend upon whether the outer wall was aligned with the inner or outer pair of door posts, but the intended function was probably the same, as in a modern home, to provide somewhere to leave outdoor wear or kit that one did not wish to bring into the main house. A secondary entrance is sometimes indicated by a further break in the outer wall-line, but it is often unclear whether the gap is original or the result of truncation by ploughing or machine stripping. More elaborate porches are generally indicated by more substantial postholes, so that, where the outer wall was not earth-fast, or where truncation has obliterated its line altogether, these may appear to be dislocated from the main house structure. A working rule-of-thumb is that the outer wall line in such cases would have aligned with the inner pair of the porch. The posts of extended porches almost invariably align with two posts of the inner weight-bearing circle, where these survive, but there is seldom any indication

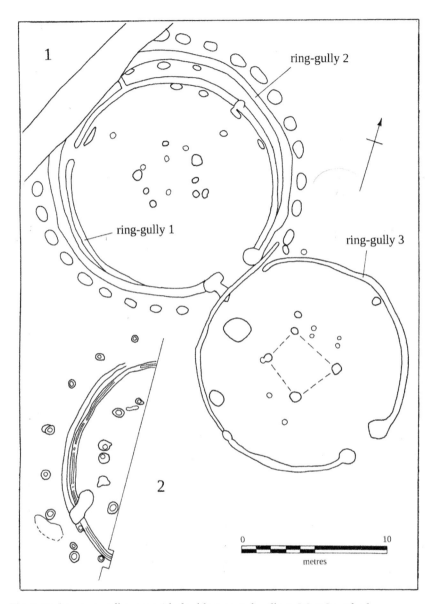

Fig. 3.12 Large roundhouses with double external walls. 1, West Stamford, Lincolnshire; 2, Lower Greenyard, Bannockburn, Stirling, Homestead 1. Drawings by D. W. Harding, adapted from Weston and Daniel, 2017 and Rideout, 1996.

whether this constituted a closed passage-way into the interior of the house, or whether there was a second set of doors suspended on the inner pair of porch posts.

A classic example of stake-wall construction within a ring-gully is House 5 at Mingies Ditch, Hardwick-with-Yelford, Oxfordshire (Fig. 3.6, 2; Allen and Robinson, 1993), where the stakes of the outer wall, spaced at around 30 cm intervals, were

64 RETHINKING ROUNDHOUSES

bedded in a ring-groove that was first recognized as a thin clay band, the fugitive remains of the bottom of the wattled panels that constituted the house walls. On the east side the ring-groove terminated in deeper postholes that evidently held the door jambs. A central posthole unusually underlay a subsequent hearth, which was nevertheless probably contemporary with the occupation of the house, so that the post may have been constructional rather than structural. At around eight metres in diameter the building accorded with Reynolds' estimated maximum for stake-wall houses. House 5 at Mingies Ditch is slightly unusual compared to the other houses in the compound, in that its surrounding ring-gully was intermittent, and showed evidence of a fence line between its segments, suggesting that its drainage function may have been incidental to defining the house site. But essentially it demonstrated that ring-gullies probably did define house sites, within which the roundhouses might have been of relatively slight construction in terms of their earth-fast foundations.

'Drip-Gullies' and Drainage Trenches

Drip-gullies have become an established concept in roundhouse literature, though often it is unclear how exactly they functioned, unless the gully's alignment is clearly designed to divert water away from the house, which most penannular gullies are not, or led to an enclosure ditch, which most do not. The effectiveness of relatively slight drip-gullies on level ground especially has been questioned, since the trench would simply fill with water from the surrounding area. At Fison Way, Thetford, some gullies are in places so shallow that they might even be the negative effect of rain water running off the eaves, rather than a positive feature designed to carry away water from the eaves. There is also the question where the upcast from the ring-gullies was deposited, internally or externally. If piled internally, it could have been integral to the house construction, if externally then it may have been intended to keep livestock away from the eaves. At South Shields (Fig. 3.11, 3; Hodgson et al., 2001) the upcast appears to have been deposited between the drip-gully and the ring-groove of the house, since around the northern circuit it afforded a foundation, of which elsewhere no trace survives, for an outer ring of earth-fast timbers. Without this fugitive remnant, the South Shields house would have been recorded as a single ring-groove house, with the ring-groove as its outer wall. Size and proportions of the South Shields plan compare closely to the double external wall with surrounding drainage gully at Melsonby (Fig. 3.11, 4), Roxby Moor (Fig. 3.11, 5), and a similar layout characterizes one phase of House R23/9 at Blagdon Park (Fig. 5.9, 2), if the concentric ring-grooves are interpreted as a double external wall. In all these examples the penannular, concentric ring-gully appears to be an integral design component. This template was evidently also applicable to roundhouses of grander proportions, as the example from Flint Farm (Fig. 3.1) has already demonstrated.

Whatever the purpose or purposes of ring-gullies around these roundhouses, the more substantial trenches that characterize Middle Iron Age settlements in the Midlands were surely intended for drainage, as at Gravelly Guy (Lambrick and Allen, 2004), where ring-trenches are often the only surviving evidence of probable house sites, in marked contrast to the post-ring houses of the earlier Iron Age. In exceptional cases, like Houses RD 5 and RD6 at Coton Park, Rugby, Warwickshire (Chapman, 2020), residual traces of wall-slot, as well as the door postholes, may permit the inference of house plans. But in substantial parts of Midland Britain, where development-led excavation has revealed extensive remains of later prehistoric settlement, it is clear that machine stripping on a large scale prior to hand cleaning of foundation deposits will have eliminated any trace of finer archaeological features such as stake-holes or wall-slots, even supposing these had survived medieval or modern ploughing. In consequence, archaeologists are increasingly reliant upon proxy indicators of structures such as stake-wall roundhouses, of which at best only the deeper door posts may be expected to survive. Where residual wall-slots or post-rings do survive, the general indication is that there was a gap of around a metre between the drainage trench and exterior house wall, a rule of thumb that appears to be compatible with the placement of the door postholes, where they are the only surviving features.

Ring-gullies for drainage are found extensively throughout Britain, even in regions where Iron Age settlement is not well represented. In north-west England, at Bruen Stapleford (Fairburn, 2003) ring-groove foundations of the outer house walls nearly 13 metres in diameter exceptionally did survive within the drainage gullies. At Poulton (Cootes et al., 2021), also in Cheshire, the ring-gullies indicate roundhouses only slightly smaller with radiocarbon dates in the second half of the first millennium BC. Similar dates were recovered for the settlement with multiple ring-gullies at Mellor, Greater Manchester (Noble and Thompson, 2005). At Duttons Farm, Lathom, Lancashire (Cowell, 2003) there was some doubt as to whether the ring-gully of roundhouse 1, with an internal diameter of ten metres and dating to the late pre-Roman Iron Age, was the wall foundation itself, or whether the external wall was supported by posts and stakes along its inner edge.

Floors and Internal Fittings

Laid floors are only seldom in evidence in lowland situations, and the probability is that, on the Wessex chalk lands, for example, the shallow natural chalk surface was exposed and rapidly became worn into a beaten floor surface. An artificial floor would only be required if the bedrock was irregular, or if the subsoil was prone to damp. In any event, ploughing and surface stripping prior to development will commonly have truncated any surviving floors, unless exceptionally, as at Brigstock, Northamptonshire, the site had escaped ploughing, in this case through its location in a country estate park (Fig. 3.8, 3; Jackson, 1983). The roundhouse was defined

66 RETHINKING ROUNDHOUSES

by a ring-groove that would not have survived ploughing, located within a drainage gully that did turn at the doorway to carry eaves water away from the access path. The approach path itself was composed of small cobbles edged with larger glacial pebbles. Within the house an area stretching from the door to the back wall had a thin surface of chalk grits, while in the northern arc of the house a layer of limestone and cobbles appears to have been the basis of a low platform, perhaps a sleeping area. An example of laid flooring from northern England, at Wolsty Hall in Cumbria (Fig. 3.13, 2), appears to have extended around the inside of the outer wall in a peripheral arc. In general, however, the layout of surviving timber floors is really only evident from wetland sites, like Black Loch of Myrton (Crone and Cavers, 2015: Crone et al., 2018).

Evidence for internal furnishings is likewise sparse, with the exception of a hearth, located generally in the centre or just off-centre, with the implication that it was a focal feature of the internal layout. Otherwise furnishings would presumably have comprised portable tables and benches, which one would not expect to survive archaeologically. The substantial paired post pits at Pimperne, Longbridge Deverill (House 3) and Dunston Park, all located on the south side of the house just inside the entrance, appear exceptional, and most probably were the foundations for a fixed piece of furniture, perhaps a dresser, or even a domestic shrine. Internal divisions within the house could have been achieved with wattle panels with minimal earth-fast securing, with movable textile or hide screens as an alternative. The probability that such divisions were used is implied not only by stone roundhouses from Northern Britain but by occasional traces like the radial slots from Roxby Moor (Fig. 3.11, 5; Inman et al., 1985). Where the subsoil was prone to damp, or was particularly irregular, it is possible that timber decking was installed to provide a level, dry living surface, in which case fittings would have been fixed to this rather than being earth-fast.

Important though the scale of recent excavation in advance of development has been, interpretation of key aspects of later prehistoric roundhouses is still dependent upon the qualitative preservation and recovery of the evidence, as demonstrated by excavations at the Black Loch of Myrton in Wigtownshire (Crone et al., 2018), where the principal timber roundhouse was constructed in the mid-first millennium BC. With an overall diameter of nearly 13 metres, it was symmetrically circular around its central stone hearth. The external wall comprised a double ring of stakes that held woven hazel wattling, potentially with insulation in the 40 cm cavity between hurdles, along the lines suggested earlier, though oddly, in view of the excellent preservation on the site, no trace of infilling remained. Near the entrance this was supplemented by oak planks, doubtless serving, as the excavators suggested, the twin purposes of reinforcing the roof support at its weakest point and presenting a prestigious frontage to visitors. The solid timber doorway was floored with logs, jointed together with countersunk battens. The main roof support was provided by a post-ring nearly nine metres in

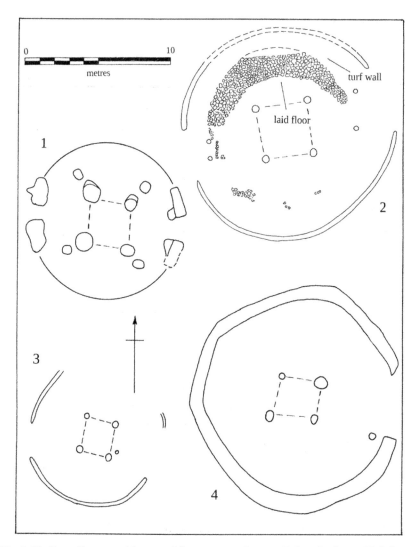

Fig. 3.13 Roundhouses with central four-post settings. 1, Dalton Parlours, Yorkshire, Roundhouse 2; 2, Wolsty Hall, Cumbria; 3, Heathrow, Middlesex, Terminal 5, Structure 9; 4, Stanwick, Northamptonshire, Building 191008. Drawings by D. W. Harding, adapted from Wrathmell and Nicholson, 1990, Blake, 1959, Lewis et al., 2010, and Crosby and Muldowney, 2011.

diameter of fourteen oak uprights, of which six had been exposed by 2018. The base of each was concave, to fit over the radial logs of the sub-floor of the house, and several displayed roughly squared holes near the base, which the excavators interpreted as tow-holes to enable the timbers to be dragged to site. These posts were linked by sill-beams that reinforced the division between central and peripheral space. Around the central hearth, though not concentric to it, was a further setting of five posts. Though shown dendrochronologically to be contemporary, they were of different construction, two having flat bases, one concave, and two with pencil-tips, suggesting that they were internal furnishings rather than part of a structural unit. Internally the floor was made up of different organic materials in different sectors of the house, while differences in the artefactual residues were also noted in different quarters. The internal stratigraphy showed a succession of floor deposits, notably of compressed layers of bracken and sedges, which from micromorphological analyses appeared to have been regularly cleaned. There was, however, no evidence of major structural rebuilding, and this, together with a suite of radiocarbon dates, argued against a protracted occupation. The nature of the house's demise is not yet entirely clear, nor whether it was partially dismantled to salvage usable building materials, but artefacts were sparse and disposable, so that a measure of deliberate salvaging is implied. The site of which this house was part, nevertheless, appears to have had a longer history as a small palisaded settlement. Recording artefact and ecofact distributions within the house has of course been standard practice for some years, though systematic salvaging of usable material at the end of the house's life will evidently limit the value of residual data, unless like Must Farm, Cambridgeshire (Knight et al., 2019), the buildings are abruptly destroyed and abandoned, leaving a genuine window on its day-to-day usage.

Superstructure: Walls and Roofs

Only very exceptionally does any trace of superstructure survive, as in the unique circumstances at Must Farm, where not only did the stumps of the timber walls survive, but also the collapsed rafters of the roof, preserving their radial disposition (Fig. 3.14, 1). The brief life-span of the Late Bronze Age settlement was stratigraphically 'encapsulated in two layers—one representing its construction, the other its demise—with material representing settlement use sandwiched between and amongst the two' (Knight et al., 2019: 655). The four largest roundhouses exceeded eight metres in diameter, and were 'founded on concentric rings of piles that were deep-set to support large roof timbers and tie-beams' (Knight et al., 2019: 653), by contrast with which the raised floors and external walkways were relatively slightly built of poles and hurdles. In the light of recent controversy over the construction of Scottish crannogs, it is worth noting that Must Farm was a pile-dwelling settlement, and the structures are described by the excavators as 'stilted' in the European *Pfahlbauten* tradition.

Preservation of timber structures was equally remarkable in the earlier deposits of the later Iron Age settlement at Deer Park Farms, Co. Antrim (Lynn and McDowell, 2011), where the roundhouses were essentially of stake-wall construction, with the wicker walls continuing uninterrupted into the roof, as was apparent

ANALYSING AND INTERPRETING TIMBER ROUNDHOUSES 69

Fig. 3.14 Roundhouses with timber preservation. 1, Must Farm, Cambridgeshire. Photograph copyright Alamy Images; 2, Deer Park Farms, Co. Antrim, Structure Theta/Eta doorway. Photograph © Crown DfC Historic Environment Division.

70 RETHINKING ROUNDHOUSES

from collapsed sections in Structure Eta that survived up to three metres in height. The doorway between Structures Theta and Eta remained *in situ* (Fig. 3.14, 2), its oak jambs a little over a metre in height with a further 50 cm bedded in the ground. Mortise and tenon joints secured the lintel, while a threshold beam braced the base of the doorway. The Deer Park Farms houses show exactly how, in normal conditions on sites that had been ploughed or stripped, only the traces of door posts would survive of stake-wall roundhouses.

For houses in which a conical thatched roof is envisaged, the presumption of a pitch of 45 degrees has been based on post-medieval vernacular building traditions. Since the enforced dismantling of the Pimperne reconstruction at the Butser Hill Demonstration area, and the deterioration of its successor, the Longbridge Deverill house at New Butser, a new reconstruction of Little Woodbury House 1 was built in 2008, which disregarded the four-poster and lowered the roof pitch to closer to 40 degrees. Bersu had come to terms with a lower pitch whilst excavating roundhouses in the Isle of Man (Bersu, 1946, 1977), but these were multiringed houses designed to carry a turf roof. All the surviving evidence for vernacular thatched buildings in Southern Britain still argues for a steeper pitch as the most effective, whilst lowering the roof-line certainly reduces the monumental impact of the building. It is worth noting, nevertheless, that Dixon (2019: 232) made a cogent case for a lower pitch for the large roundhouse at Crickley Hill.

A key feature of the major Wessex roundhouses was their substantial porched entrances. Since, as Reynolds pointed out, any breach of integrity of the cone-on-a-cylinder potentially weakened the structure, such a sizeable entrance must have been for good reason. Driving a haywain in at harvest might have been intended, but giving a grand impression and perhaps processional access might equally account for such elaboration. At Flint Farm the excavators inferred from the size of postholes that the porch was carried up to first floor level, allowing light into the loft. Experience of the Pimperne reconstruction showed that the valley between cone and porch was vulnerable to water penetration, and most reconstructions since have mitigated this by thatching roof and porch in a continuous wave. Where the entrance is not porched, but simply marked by a pair of posts in the outer wall-line, this could evidently have been achieved with minimal disruption of the cone's structural integrity, even if the house had two entrances, as an increasing number of examples outside Wessex can be shown to have had. Moderating the cone to take account of prevailing winds, as suggested earlier in respect of the Blackford houses, might have been a factor in determining the orientation of the doorway.

Central Four-Posters

The central setting of four posts within the principal house at Little Woodbury (Fig. 1.3) has for years appeared anomalous, and it plainly influenced Bersu's more fanciful elevation reconstructions. Rather than regarding it as an integral structural component of the roundhouse, some have argued that this setting was not contemporary, but a four-poster granary, fortuitously located within the area of the roundhouse, and reflecting multi-period activity. But its coincidental alignment with the roundhouse entrance and its replacement postholes matching the pattern of the post-circles still suggests that it could be integral to the house-plan. It could, of course, have been both. Having one's grain supply central to the house would seem to be quite sensible, but the possibility that a four-poster granary might have been incorporated into the structure of the house seems not to have been seriously considered by prehistorians. This is presumably because a central four-poster was not a recurrent element in excavated roundhouse plans, which need hardly be problematical, since it could have been constructed as a free-standing unit, used as a mobile scaffold during construction of the house, and finally built into its fabric as a permanent fixture. Not being earth-fast would have reduced the risk of timbers rotting, so that the absence of surviving postholes would be the norm. Even acknowledging that the Reynolds model of a cone on a cylinder would have been a viable option for the larger Wessex roundhouses, the central setting would undoubtedly have stabilized the structure by supporting radial joists to create a mezzanine or loft level. Whilst the evidence of hearths at Pimperne and Crickley Hill still suggests that the ground floor was the main level of occupation, the roof space would afford ample storage that could be accessed at harvest time through the wide double doors of the houses. The central four-post framework, of course, need not have included a grain store at all, but could alternatively have provided a framework around a central hearth, either at ground level or raised, from which spits or cauldrons could be suspended.

The alignment of the central four-post setting and the doorway is particularly conspicuous at Dalton Parlours, where several of the houses with two opposed doorways have a central four-poster, in some instances these deeper posts being the only features that survived (Fig. 3.13, 1). Similar settings also commonly occur within roundhouses defined by ring-grooves and ring-trenches.

Chronologically, four-post settings and circular buildings have a long association. The appearance of similar structures in large roundhouses on Romano-British villa sites might appear less anomalous if we accept the possibility that in the intervening period such settings would normally have been free-standing and not earth-fast. An apparent parallel at Greenbogs, Monymusk in Aberdeenshire (Noble et al., 2012), where the larger house had an outer post-ring 9.5 metres in diameter composed of thirty-four postholes with a narrow entrance on the south side, yielded radiocarbon dates demonstrating that it was Neolithic. This eastern Scottish group includes examples identified by air photography in Donside (Halliday, 2008: 86–7), and a notable example from Chapelton, Angus, where the four-post setting is proportionately larger in relation to the post-ring. There is a growing body of evidence from Southern Britain, however, to suggest that this was an established building equation from the Neolithic.

Central Towers

Roofing a timber roundhouse using the cone-on-a-cylinder model with a single span was evidently limited by the maximum practical length of the rafters, so that discoveries of roundhouses, like those at West Stamford and Bannockburn, with an overall diameter up to 18 metres, would have tested the model to its limits. At Culduthel, Inverness (Hatherley and Murray, 2021), the ring-groove buildings attain or exceed 18 metres in diameter, which would surely have been impossible to roof in a single span. In the larger buildings at Culduthel the post-pipes of the weight-bearing post-ring are up to 40 cm in diameter, from which we may reasonably infer substantial post height. Furthermore, the ratio of post-ring to overall diameter does not conform to the Wessex model, being around 1:2, compared to 3:4 in the Wessex roundhouses, implying quite different structural principles. One possible interpretation would be to adopt the reconstructed elevation proposed by Healy for the larger buildings at Fison Way, Thetford (Gregory, 1991), involving a split-level roof, supported by a central tower based upon the substantial inner post-ring. An obvious consequence of having a central tower, against which a lower level of roof rafters could be rested, with an upper cone surmounting the central tower, is that it provides an opportunity for admitting light into the interior without compromising the integrity of the roof. In effect, it provides for the equivalent of clerestory light in a rectangular building. A split-level reconstruction would allow for a full upper floor, thereby increasing the total floor area by just 25 per cent, but doubling the floor area that enjoyed full head height, as opposed to the peripheral space between the main post-ring and the outer wall. The relative roles of these contrasting spaces, and consequential issues of access, are plainly pivotal to interpreting social and economic use of space, but there is a good case for regarding buildings like Structures 4 and 10 at Culduthel (Fig. 3.15), with their penannular internal ring-ditches, as byre-houses, in which human occupation was principally on the upper floor. A split-level roof does not allow unlimited expansion of the roundhouse's diameter, however, since increased diameter means increased height, and the same practical constraints would have applied to the provision of central uprights. But the diameter of the Culduthel posts suggests that the limits may have been rather greater than archaeologists have previously supposed.

A key issue in interpreting the Culduthel plans is establishing the former position of the outer walls, where, as in the case of Structures 2 and 12 (Fig. 3.15), no evidence of these survives archaeologically. Their former existence is reasonably inferred, not just because the alternative ring-groove houses with ring-ditches demonstrably have overall diameters in that order, but because their porch posts would otherwise be oddly detached from the inner post-ring. Comparative evidence from other sites, where ploughing or mechanical stripping has removed all traces of the external wall, whether a stake-wall or a mass-wall, suggests that it

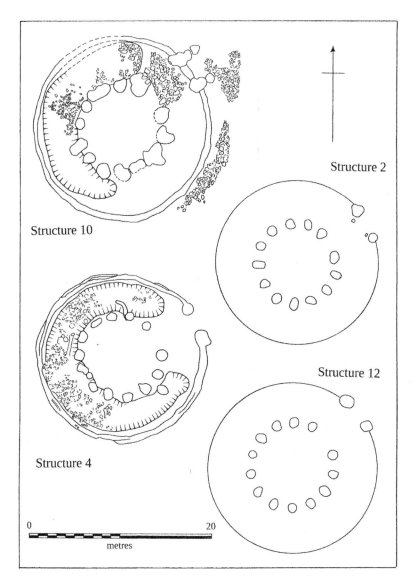

Fig. 3.15 Culduthel, Inverness, roundhouse plans 1. Drawings by D. W. Harding, adapted from Murray, 2007.

would have aligned with the door posts or the inner of a pair of porch posts, as originally proposed by the excavator of Culduthel (Murray, 2007: 30; cp House 3 at nearby Lower Slackbuie, Christie and Dalland, 2022).

A dominant factor in interpreting the Culduthel settlement plainly is the evidence for intensive industrial activity, which led in the interim report to the excavator asking 'are domestic buildings re-used for craft activity or are craft structures purpose-built?' (Murray, 2007: 70). In the final report, use of the term 'workshops' seems to imply the latter conclusion, but it remains unclear exactly what purpose would have been served by these substantial buildings in the context of metal-working. The incorporation of metalworking debris in postholes is more likely to have occurred once the posts had been withdrawn, though shelter from wind might well have been provided by the still upstanding outer mass walls of abandoned houses. The location of the Culduthel furnaces so close to the position of post-rings seems inherently unsafe and improbable had they been in contemporary use. Stratigraphic evidence is hard to come by, though in 'Workshop' 13, the anvil pit that presumably was contemporary with the adjacent furnaces, plainly cuts a posthole of the main post-ring, and thus demonstrably post-dates it (Fig. 3.16). Structure 8, which similarly has a post-ring equally detached from its door posts, was identified as a workshop, though lacking any metalworking features, on the basis of similarity to Structure 13 (Hatherley and Murray, 2021: 53). Given the stratigraphic relationship cited above, the comparison might actually suggest that both were domestic buildings with a post-ring set well within an external mass wall aligned with its door posts (Fig. 3.16), and comparable to Structures 2 and 12. The diversity of the Culduthel houses is further demonstrated by House 9 (Fig. 3.16), comprising fifteen postholes forming a circle 13 metres in diameter, with no obvious candidate for a doorway. With no external porch posts in contention, which would, if present, have required an external mass wall in excess of 18 metres in diameter, it seems more likely that House 9 was another example of a structure in which the single substantial post-ring was exceptionally itself the outer wall.

Multi-Ringed Roundhouses

In lowland Britain the standard formula for larger timber-framed houses is thus a main weight-bearing circle of posts with an outer wall that may or may not have had earth-fast foundations. Beyond that, any concentric ring, if not a drip-trench, is likely to have been constructional, as at Pimperne. Roundhouses with multiple rings as part of their structural design are not the norm in southern and eastern England, raising the obvious question, what was the purpose of an additional post-ring that would require additional resources and would have the effect of reducing internal flexibility of space? Interpretation may depend on the comparative sizes of posts in each circle. Where multiple post-circles have timbers of similar size, it might indicate a lower-pitched roof of turf, the weight of which required a greater and more regular system of support. An alternative might be that the central court was open, and that the structure was penannular with a ridged roof on the model proposed by Clarke for West Harling, which will be considered more fully later.

In the case of West Brandon in County Durham (Jobey, 1962), each of two successive phases of large timber roundhouses had no less than four constructional

ANALYSING AND INTERPRETING TIMBER ROUNDHOUSES 75

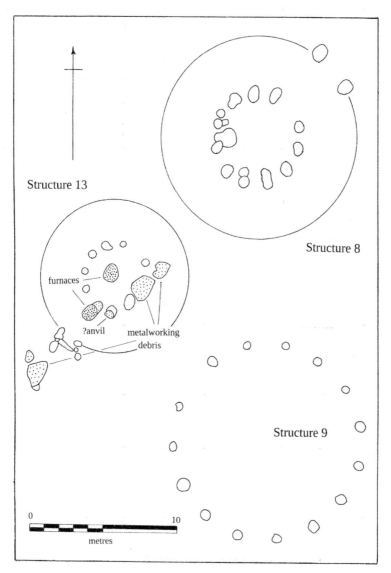

Fig. 3.16 Culduthel, Inverness, roundhouse plans 2. Drawings by D. W. Harding, adapted from Hatherley and Murray, 2021.

elements, giving an overall diameter of nearly 18 metres. Neither plan conforms in any combination to the Wessex roundhouse ratios (*IAR*: Fig. 10, A). In Phase A the depths of each posthole ring from outermost to innermost is progressively deeper, 12.5 cm, 30 cm, 33–40 cm, and 46–60 cm, respectively. The rebuilt Phase B replaced the second from outermost ring with a ring-groove of similar depth to its posthole counterpart in Phase A, suggesting that these marked the outer wall, 16 metres in diameter in both cases. Jobey (1962: 16) believed that the ring-groove had supported a solid wooden wall of split timbers. In Phase B the innermost setting comprised four posts 60–70 cm deep, and aligned with the entrance, which could have functioned in various ways, as discussed above. The roof in both phases could have been of turf, and at a much lower pitch.

A turf roof was favoured by its excavator for the house at Scotstarvit, Fife (Bersu, 1948). With an overall diameter around 18 metres, the plan is not quite as regular as West Brandon. Pope (2003) suggested that it represented a house just 13 metres in diameter, standing within and linked to a palisaded enclosure represented by the outer ring-groove, though the structure is further enclosed by an earthen bank. Other candidates for multi-ringed houses include the four-ringed structure from the Candle Stane in Aberdeenshire (Cameron, 1999), but the complexity of the entrance at this site suggests that the footprint may in fact be of two successive houses. At Dryburn Bridge House 1 is substantially larger than most of its neighbours, with an incomplete outer post-ring 14.5 metres in diameter. If, however, the outer wall aligned with the lateral projecting slots of the porch, House 1 would become triple-ringed and have a diameter of nearly 18 metres, as the original excavator claimed (Triscott, 1982: 119). An alternative would be to see the lateral slots and the postholes leading on from the southern slot as part of a projecting vestibule, comparable to that recorded in Structure A1 at Blackford.

Houses with Ring-Ditches: Erosion, Storage, or Headroom?

At the time of publication of *IAR*, ring-ditch houses were regarded as a phenomenon of the Scottish Borders, with just a few outliers north of the Forth, and representative of a relatively limited time-span within the earlier Iron Age. Their apparently recurrent association with palisaded enclosures and cord-rig agriculture had reinforced this impression (Hill, 1982). Since then both their geographical and chronological range has expanded, with examples being recorded extensively in eastern Scotland as far as the Moray Firth, and with antecedents dating to the Middle Bronze Age.

Despite, or perhaps because of the increased diversity of the database, there remain serious issues of interpretation of substantial houses with ring-ditches, most obviously dependent upon whether the ring-ditch is seen as structural or simply the product of erosion. Ironically, the prime example for analysing their structure and possible functions remains the sequential Houses A and B from Phase 1 at Broxmouth, now fully published (Armit and McKenzie, 2013), but in respect to these particular buildings broadly endorsing the original excavator's interpretation.

House A initially comprised just two concentric elements, an outer ring-groove that, had the structures not been truncated by the inner ditch of Phase 2, would have described a circle in the order of 17 metres in diameter, and an inner post-ring eight metres in diameter of which six postholes of the first phase survived of a possible thirteen. Between the two circles was a shallow ring-ditch of a kind that is generally regarded as the product of erosion through activity such as trampling by stock and regular mucking out, an explanation that would equally account for the irregular scoops recorded at High Knowes, Alnham (Jobey and Tait, 1966), and Braidwood (Stevenson, 1949). The fact that the annular hollows are regularly filled with stones or paving, at Dryburn Bridge (Dunwell, 2007) as well as Broxmouth, suggests an attempt to inhibit further erosion, and perhaps to ensure effective drainage, since retaining a surface that was dry and firm, though doubtless with softer material for bedding down, would have been paramount for over-wintering stock. By contrast, the much deeper ring-ditches at Douglasmuir, Angus (Kendrick, 1995), certainly cannot be explained as the result of erosion. In the developed stage at Broxmouth (Fig. 3.17) a further concentric ring-groove was inserted into the ring-ditch of House A, creating in plan a threefold concentric division of the interior, within which slabbed paving of the ring-ditch emphasized

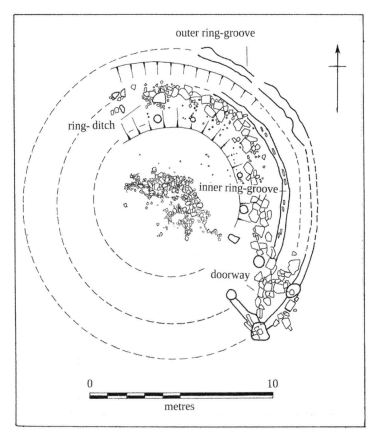

Fig. 3.17 Broxmouth, East Lothian, Roundhouse A, stage 2. Drawing by D. W. Harding, adapted from Armit and McKenzie, 2013.

78 RETHINKING ROUNDHOUSES

its separation from the outermost circuit. Stake-holes in rough alignment apparently formed radial divisions, but hardly of a sufficiently sturdy kind to have been effective as cattle stalls. House B was built over its predecessor, but with its centre offset to the south-west. It defined effectively the same area with three concentric ring-grooves, and was again subject to structural modification. It is hard to explain the purpose of dividing the interior into three concentric circuits, the limited space between which would not have made for easy manoeuvring of cattle, so that we might question whether all ring-grooves supported structural timbers as opposed to stalls or feeding troughs, fixtures that would certainly benefit from sturdy foundations. Finally, it seems that the building, possibly semi-derelict and roofless at this stage, was used for iron smelting and industrial activities, an example of how substantial roundhouses might be adapted for industrial use towards the end of their life-cycle.

Central to the reinterpretation of houses with ring-ditches is the sequence at Forest Road, Kintore, Aberdeenshire (Cook and Dunbar, 2008), where shallow ring-ditches were shown conclusively to date from the Middle Bronze Age, with a variety of constructional types being assigned to a span from the earlier second millennium BC to the later first millennium BC. It has been long accepted that post-rings, ring-grooves, and related construction techniques cannot be regarded as culturally or chronologically diagnostic (Harding, 2004: 220; 272), which would be especially true of ring-ditches if they are the consequence of usage rather than design. At Kintore, ring-ditches ranged from extended scoops to nearly full penannular hollows. Post-rings and ring-grooves were also represented, in some instances the post-rings being extremely sparse or irregular, so that their interpretation as roofed structures is not always conclusive. Whilst in general terms therefore the Kintore sequence shows the longevity of the tradition of houses with ring-ditches, it is possible that the Middle Bronze Age structures were open corrals, and that the combination of functions implicit in the byre-house concept was not widely adopted until the Late Bronze Age and Iron Age, in rather larger and better defined buildings.

The most convincing example of an early house with ring-ditch was Structure 3 on the Kintore bypass at Deer's Den (Fig. 8.4, 1; Alexander, 2000). Though truncated by the edge of the area available for excavation, it clearly had a full penannular ditch, no more than half a metre deep, with a regular post-ring based in its eastern sector on the outer edge of the ring-ditch, raising questions regarding the cause of further erosion to the outer lip, if the posts and ring-ditch were contemporary. The possibility that the ring-ditch was the product of trampling by stock is enhanced at Deer's Den by a hollow worn through the entrance passage. The excavator reasonably inferred an outer wall, possibly of turf outside the ring-ditch and aligned with the inner porch posts, thus giving an overall diameter in the order of 14 metres. An example visible on air-photographs to the west of the excavated site appeared to have an external wall-line marked by a ring-groove.

With unequivocal radiocarbon dates assigning the house to the mid-second millennium, Deer's Den affirms the antiquity of the byre-house with ring-ditch. The worn passage of the Deer's Den house raises the question why similar features have not been found in other houses with ring-ditches, if indeed cattle or other livestock were brought into the house. The answer may be that alternative, easier access was provided for stock. Where the outer wall was founded in a ring-groove, which could have supported prefabricated wattle panels, then perhaps these were removable, so that cattle could be stalled directly from outside. Where the inner post-ring was substantial, it is possible that the house was divided concentrically, and that only the inner area and upper floor were accessed through the main entrance.

What this demonstrates, of course, is the danger that archaeological classification may confuse separate and distinct structural types because of superficial similarities in plan. Many ring-ditches are shallow, notwithstanding truncation, and are most probably the result of erosion. Where post-rings are located within the ring-ditch, the two are unlikely to be contemporary if the ring-ditch is the product of erosion. Alternatively, they could have been deliberately dug and backfilled with rubble to facilitate drainage, in which case posts for stalls may have been bedded in at the same time. Deeper ring-ditches could be quite different constructions for underfloor storage, a tradition of underground storage or cellarage that includes the 'proto-souterrains' at Dalladies, Kincardineshire (Watkins, 1980a) and ends in fully-fledged souterrains. This explanation was offered for House 6 at Douglasmuir, Angus, where the ring-ditch was well over a metre deep, and steepest at its outer face, which had been revetted with wattle facing (Kendrick, 1995: 53 and Illus. 27). A similar case has been made for the C-shaped gullies that characterized several Middle Bronze Age roundhouses at Dunbeg and Glenshellach in Argyll (Ellis, online), where several were linked to channels that may have ensured ventilation for underfloor storage. The importance of access to stored produce from within the house is underlined by the discovery of a timber-lined souterrain entirely *within* the putative circuit of the associated roundhouse at Dubton Farm, Brechin (Fig. 3.18, 1; Ginnever, 2017). A post-ring comprising eleven of probable thirteen substantial uprights set in holes some 0.5 m across at intervals around 1.5 m evidently supported the roof rather than marking the outer wall, which was assumed to have been of turf or similar on the outer edge of the souterrain. This wall would thus have aligned with the posts of an east-facing doorway. The north-eastern chamber of the souterrain was lined with timber, and divided from the south-western chamber, which was slightly deeper. What was unexpected, however, was a length of ditch approaching the house from the north-west and linked to the south-west chamber of the souterrain by a short tunnel in which iron pan indicated the passage of water. A large stone in the souterrain chamber adjacent to the tunnel could have been used to plug the flow of water, which presumably serviced livestock or served other domestic functions within the house. The north-eastern chamber presumably was kept dry for storage of meat or dairy products that would benefit from the cool environment of the souterrain. No trace survived of the wooden boards that presumably covered the souterrain, and the timber lining had likewise been removed at the time the house was abandoned. This discovery, however, certainly endorses the idea that the deeper ring-ditches were constructional rather than erosional, and that more than one function was served by houses that superficially might have been conflated into a single class.

Another variant of house with ring-ditch was suggested by excavations at Thainstone Business Park East, where the twin opposed arcs of ring-ditch, doubtless correctly attributed by the excavator to erosion in use of the building, were closer to the centre of the house than its putative perimeter (Fig. 3.18, 2; McGilliard and Wilson, 2021). If the ring-ditch erosion is indicative of livestock being stalled within the house, then in this case it was radially around the centre rather than around the perimeter. The reason for this was evidently that the outer wall, probably aligned with the east-facing porched entrance, embraced the opening into the souterrain, which, unlike Dubton, then curved away externally to the south-west. Like Dubton, Thainstone East was apparently occupied in the opening centuries AD, but the example of Cyderhall, Sutherland shows that souterrains and souterrain-like structures could be associated with roundhouses from an earlier date (Pollock, 1992).

Finally, a peripheral ring-ditch could have been a means of creating more headroom, where the outer wall was relatively low. This too is a long-standing practice in prehistory and early historic times witnessed in a variety of sunken floored buildings. The danger with the ring-ditch phenomenon is that archaeological classification can confuse structures of quite different purpose, especially when so many excavated examples have been severely truncated, either by ploughing or by machine stripping. What is urgently needed is hand excavation of examples that have not suffered severe erosion in order to recover maximum evidence of construction, a prospect that should not be unattainable since ring-ditches are readily identifiable both from air photographs, and, in upland areas like the Scottish Borders, on the ground.

'Special' Roundhouses

IAR accepted as a basic premise that roundhouses, the primary purpose of which was residential and domestic, could nevertheless have had a 'ritual' dimension, in so far as Iron Age society was unlikely to have differentiated clearly between the sacred and the secular. At the same time it was argued that some sites may have served as dedicated ritual and ceremonial centres for community festivals and seasonal gatherings. Two sites, whose outstanding structural complexity might warrant their consideration as 'special' in this sense were Building 500 at Bancroft,

ANALYSING AND INTERPRETING TIMBER ROUNDHOUSES 81

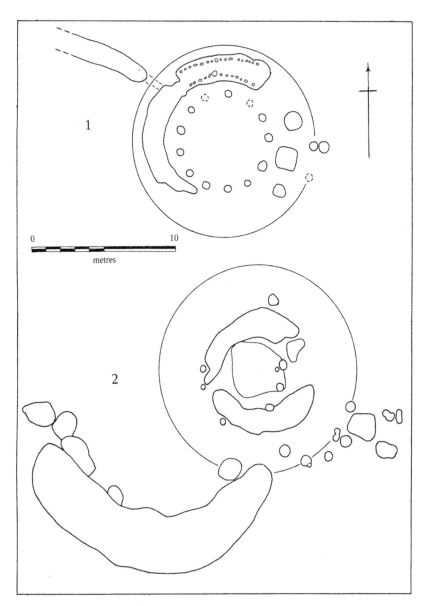

Fig. 3.18 Roundhouses with souterrains. 1, Dubton Farm East, Brechin, Angus; 2, Thainstone East, Inverurie, Aberdeenshire. Drawings by D. W. Harding, adapted from Ginnever, 2017 and McGilliard and Wilson, 2021.

Buckinghamshire (Williams and Zeepvat, 1994, Fig. 20; *IAR*: Fig. 29A), and Paddock Hill, Thwing, in Yorkshire (Manby, 2007). The Bancroft building had three post-rings, of which the middle combined posts on the west with ring-groove around the eastern half of its circuit. The inner post-ring, 11.4 metres in diameter, was the best candidate for a roof-supporting circle, while the elongated post-pipes

82 RETHINKING ROUNDHOUSES

of the middle circle suggested the use of split timbers, which might be appropriate for an outer wall. With a diameter of 16 metres, this would make it a very large house. The outermost post-ring was around a metre beyond this, and could have supported wicker panels of an outer cladding of a wide insulated double-wall, describing a circle 18.6 metres in overall diameter. Beyond this, on the eastern, uphill side was a further arc of ring-gully, which the excavators interpreted as a drip-trench. The entrance was on the east, comprising a gap in the middle ring-groove around two metres wide. There was no convincing evidence of a porch, which could have been truncated by later features. A central pit contained several fire-reddened stones, but in the absence of *in situ* burning was considered unlikely to have been a hearth.

A striking feature of Bancroft 500 is its relative isolation. Apart from one four-post structure, the only other feature assigned to the Late Bronze Age–earliest Iron Age occupation was a rectangular hollow, the floor of which had been 'met-alled' with small limestone chippings, flint and quartzite pebbles. It was distinguished only by a central pit, which was again devoid of artefacts, but appeared to have been filled with standing water. The case for regarding Bancroft building 500 as 'special' is admittedly tentative, being based upon its large size, unique plan, and apparent isolation, with features like its central pit and external hollow that are not demonstrably ritual in function, though they might not be incompatible with such an interpretation. The later presence of a Roman temple mausoleum in close proximity can hardly be invoked in terms of retrospective inference (*IAR*: 219), since the site is occupied throughout the intervening Middle Iron Age by an open settlement of more than a dozen roundhouses in a progressive linear spread, for which a domestic and agricultural interpretation would be unexceptionable. There is every reason to suppose that later prehistoric or Romano-British communities were conscious of earlier ritual foci in the landscape, but to suggest any direct link in this instance would be without foundation.

Much the same conclusion could be reached regarding Paddock Hill, Thwing, in Yorkshire (Fig. 3.19; Manby, 2007). The central timber building at Thwing was also of exceptional size, its main post-ring being 17.5 metres in diameter within an outer ring-groove no less than 26 metres in diameter. The paired post pipes of the main circle presumably indicate secondary rebuilding. But a principal issue must be whether the building could have been roofed over such a large central span. It appears to have had twin, opposed entrances facing the south-eastern and north-western entrances of the earlier Inner Monument, a circular ditch with external bank in the henge tradition, which surrounded it. They also align with the entrances of the outermost enclosing earthwork, which shares features in common with the Late Bronze Age 'ring-works' of eastern England. The case for special status of the Paddock Hill structure rests in part once again on its unusual size and layout, but also crucially on its site history and associations, and its location at a focal point in the landscape where trackways meet.

ANALYSING AND INTERPRETING TIMBER ROUNDHOUSES   83

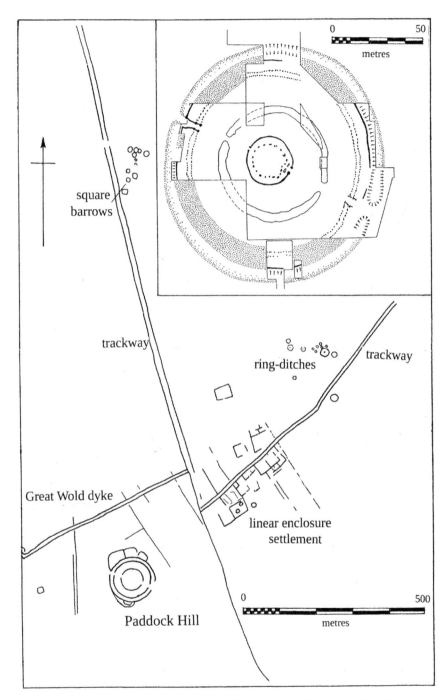

Fig. 3.19 Paddock Hill, Thwing, Yorkshire and its landscape. Drawing by D. W. Harding, adapted from Manby, 1985 and Stoertz, 1997.

A case for special status was argued for the final settlement at Fison Way, Thetford (Gregory, 1991) on the grounds that phosphate and magnetic susceptibility readings were hardly consistent with domestic occupation or animal husbandry in close proximity. The complexity of the enclosures and internal buildings certainly argued for the site's importance in the early first century AD, yet the absence of prestige goods of any kind did not suggest that it was a political or royal centre. The excavator therefore favoured a ritual interpretation, which was also taken up by Bradley (2021: 153–4), who saw Thetford as cognate to the Irish 'special' sites. An unusual aspect of Fison Way is the ordered layout of the three key roundhouses, with the focal Structure 2 apparently flanked by a matching pair on either side, facing towards the eastern entrance of the enclosure (Fig. 3.20). The role of the lesser Structures 4 and 5, and whether they were even roofed, remains unclear, though there is no positive indication that they functioned as a unit, in figure-of-eight format, with their larger partners. In the site's developed phase these buildings stood symmetrically towards one end of a widely-spaced double-ditched enclosure, which had no less than eight lines of trenching, creating a highly-schematized multiple barrier that is hard to explain in practical terms. The site also included small clusters of 'phantom' burial pits, lacking any surviving human remains or grave-goods (though some pits yielded high phosphate readings) plainly leaving interpretation unresolved. But the location of the pits, within ring-ditches, rectilinear enclosures or simply unenclosed, might be compatible with different 'house' traditions within a 'house society' of the kind proposed by Lévi-Strauss.

In Northern Britain special status was considered for the multi-ringed structure at Candle Stane, Aberdeenshire (Cameron, 1999), in view of the absence of any artefactual or environmental evidence of domestic activity, and its close proximity to the early recumbent stone circle. The overall size of the structure, at 15.5 metres in diameter, is not so exceptional for a roundhouse in north-east Scotland, but three inner, closely spaced post-rings are unusual, unless, of course, they represent successive and separate structures (Romankiewicz, 2018b). In contrast to the Candle Stane, where no other Iron Age structures were identified within the area excavated, Structure B at Seafield West (Cressey and Anderson, 2011), defined by its outer ring-gully some 24 metres in diameter, stands apart in size from the remainder of the post-ring houses, and houses with ring-ditches, which conform reasonably to recognized standards for domestic structures. Even if the ring-gully supported an independent surrounding fence, the post-ring, at 17–18 metres in diameter, could hardly realistically support a roofed building without some internal support, though these could have been obscured among the central complex of features. But the prominent location of Structure B certainly suggests that it was a focal area of the settlement.

In discussing 'special' roundhouses *IAR* naturally cited the unique sites of complex circular buildings from Ireland, notably Knockaulin and Navan, generally

ANALYSING AND INTERPRETING TIMBER ROUNDHOUSES 85

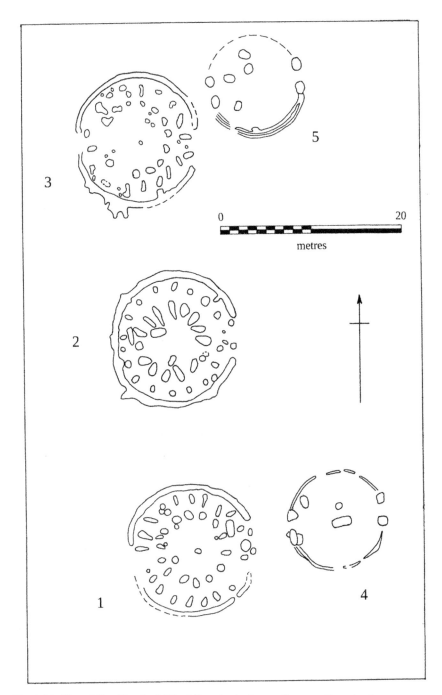

Fig. 3.20 Fison Way, Thetford, Norfolk, principal roundhouses. Drawing by D. W. Harding, adapted from Gregory, 1991.

86 RETHINKING ROUNDHOUSES

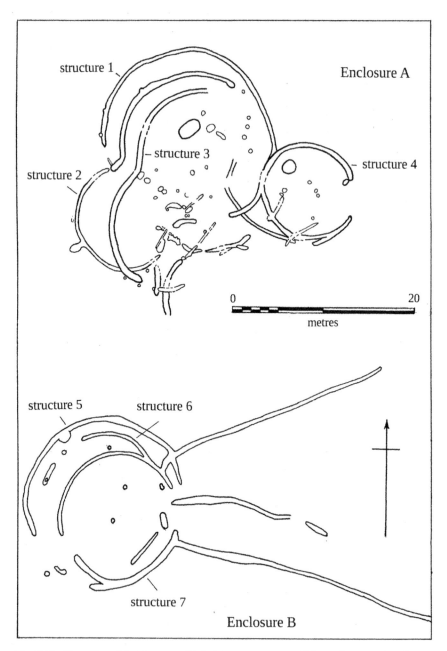

Fig. 3.21 Moss Carr, Methley, west Yorkshire, structures within enclosures A and B. Drawing by D. W. Harding, adapted from Roberts and Richardson, 2002.

accepted as having served as ceremonial centres, even if not now as 'royal' sites. One feature of those sites, including Rathcroghan, are avenues radiating outward from the circular structures, which were evidently compatible with access control or processional ways. In Britain the nearest counterparts are the 'antennae ditches' from sites like Little Woodbury or Gussage All Saints, generally regarded as serving the more mundane purpose of guiding stock into the enclosures. A more recent example from Enclosure B on Site 1 at Moss Carr, Methley in west Yorkshire leads into what might have been a large roundhouse complex (Fig. 3.21; Roberts and Richardson, 2002). Dating to the later first millennium BC, the earliest Structure 5 was demarcated by a ring-gully 18 metres in diameter, which the excavators took to be a wall foundation of an independent building. It could, however, equally have been an external fence around the near-concentric Structure 6. At 14 metres in diameter, Structure 6 was represented by more intermittent lengths of ring-gully, but appeared to have entrances on its east and south-west circuits. Stratigraphically last in the sequence was Structure 7, at 13 metres in diameter only slightly smaller than its predecessor, and likewise with doorways on its east and south-west. Radiating from the east doorway of this complex were two linear gullies that formed an avenue, widening towards the east, where only its southern arm terminated adjacent to a break in the main north–south linear dyke system. Parallel to the southern arm was a further discontinuous gully emanating from the eastern doorway, possibly associated with Structure 6, that again aligned with the break in the outer 'enclosure' ditch.

Unlike Little Woodbury and Gussage All Saints, where the 'antennae ditches' guide traffic into the enclosure paddock, the parallel between Moss Carr and the Irish sites prompts the possibility that the purpose of the site was special in some way. Yet this is hardly indicated by any notable features of the Moss Carr structures, nor by any associated artefacts or other deposits. So the possibility remains that Structure 5/6 at Moss Carr was an unroofed stock enclosure, or compound where stock could be marshalled seasonally for checking. Of course that activity may well have been crucial to a small, pastoral community, so that it might still have involved a ceremonial dimension. From an analysis of structure plans and site contexts it is clear that there is no standard formula for roundhouses of special status, so that we should resist any temptation to create a 'type' or category of 'special roundhouses'. The implications will be reviewed again in summarizing conclusions overall.

4

Analysing and Interpreting Stone-Built Roundhouses

Brochs, Broch Towers, and Complex Atlantic Roundhouses

In the years leading up to the publication of *IAR*, two issues had dominated broch studies. First was the question of dating, with advocates of early dating for the origin and development of brochs from the second half of the first millennium BC fighting a rearguard of resistance from traditionalists who wished to tie brochs to a first century BC/first century AD horizon. The second concerned the reconstruction of brochs, radicals advocating a fully-roofed building with at least one intermediate floor, as opposed to traditionalists who favoured ranges of low, lean-to buildings with an open vent to the sky. Dating had always been problematical, in that many brochs through the structural durability of their shells had seen a succession of secondary occupation, even when the broch tower had been much reduced, so that earlier investigations had often mistaken secondary occupation for primary, resulting in antiquarian attribution of brochs to Picts. This problem was still contentious into the turn of the millennium, with the publication of excavations at Dun Vulan (Parker Pearson and Sharples, 1999), though further investigations at Dun Vulan prompted by continuing erosion (Cavers, 2019) has confirmed that previously excavated deposits were entirely secondary. Perhaps the most significant sequence was that from Old Scatness, where the broch, still itself not extensively investigated, was nevertheless reliably dated to the second half of the first millennium BC. The articulated sheep bones from the broch foundations must have been relatively fresh, and had not been contaminated by the marine reservoir effect (Dockrill et al., 2015: 44–5), so presumably meet the most rigorous sample requirements. Reliable radiocarbon dates for the construction and initial occupation of brochs remain too few, not least because of problems posed by the plateau effect in the mid-first millennium BC in the calibration graph.

The internal reconstruction of brochs remains contentious in the absence of archaeologically documented *in situ* evidence for furnishings and fittings. The case for internal floors and total roofing, of course, rests in principle upon proportionality, the improbability that such a massive shell should contain minimal internal structures. At one time the present writer had hoped that the broch at Loch na Beirgh in west Lewis, where rising water levels had obliged secondary occupants progressively to raise their floor levels until they stood well above lintel

---

Rethinking Roundhouses: Later Prehistoric Settlement in Britain and Beyond. D. W. Harding, Oxford University Press.
© D. W. Harding 2023. DOI: 10.1093/oso/9780192893802.003.0004

height of the original broch entrance, would yield evidence of internal fittings preserved in the waterlogged deposits of the broch's ground floor, which still remain uninvestigated. Unfortunately, if we are right to speculate that the main living quarters were invariably on the first floor, leaving the ground floor solely for access and occasional stock, then that hope is likely to be frustrated, unless of course the whole of the first floor collapsed into the basement in circumstances that allowed its preservation. Availability or acquisition of suitable timber in tree-less environments like the Western Isles continues to pose problems for many archaeologists, though in reality this is only one particularly obvious example of the need for community resource management where substantial quantities of materials are needed. Remains of charred hurdles on the scarcement at Clachtoll, Assynt, raised the prospect that more flexible roundwood, suitably reinforced, could have played a greater part in the broch's superstructure than might have been supposed (Cavers et al., 2017). Above all, of course, there remains the question what induced this efflorescence of monumentally aggrandized building in the later first millennium BC, only for it to subside almost as suddenly into less overtly monumental houses in the early centuries AD?

There have been two important doctoral dissertations that have impacted on broch studies since the publication of *IAR*, one by a graduate architect supervised by an archaeologist (Romankiewicz, 2011), the other by an experienced professional archaeologist supervised by an architectural historian (Barber, 2016). Both focused upon the architectural and engineering aspects of brochs, with fundamental implications for traditional interpretations that were shown either to have misunderstood the technical details of the building remains or to have failed to recognize the complexity and extent of structural changes.

An Architectural Perspective

Romankiewicz's analysis of the characteristic double-walled construction of brochs clarified features and functions that are often misrepresented in archaeological discussions. First, the broch's hollow wall construction is essentially two walls, serving different but combined purposes. The inner wall, which was originally vertical, bore the main weight of the roof and upper floors of the broch. The outer wall, which was built with a batter, bore the wind load. In what conventionally was termed a solid-based broch, characteristic of the northern mainland and isles but also represented by Dun Troddan and Dun Telve in Glenelg, the double-walls are contiguous at ground level to create a solid base, above which the outer and inner walls are joined by lintels at height intervals between 1.5 and 1.8 metres, but essentially they are still two independent walls (*IAR*: Fig. 23). The technical advance of double-wall construction was thus to split the loads to achieve greater height whilst economizing on materials. The lintels do not tie the walls together in the way that stretchers do in dry-stone construction, since they only barely span the width of the gallery, except perhaps near the wall-head, where the two walls converge. In endorsement of this point we might cite the stonework capping the ground floor at Beirgh in its south-west sector, where the chunky gneiss blocks only barely spanned the intra-mural space, and even used sub-triangular stones that only projected part-way across to fill the irregular gaps (Fig. 4.1, 1). Nevertheless, doubts have been raised whether the outer wall could be free-standing without the support of the inner, and the fact that, where broch walls survive to any height, both inner and outer remain intact, suggests a degree of mutual dependency. Romankiewicz proposed a particular model whereby the double-wall was constructed with superimposed units, each comprising a corbelled outer wall and inner straight wall topped with a lintel, so that 'inner and outer walls would not have had to be free-standing over the whole building height, but only over the height of each structural unit' (2011: 109).

Romankiewicz also addressed issues of construction and reconstruction. She recognized the fact that double-walls with intra-mural staircase provided a progressive basis for building in lieu of scaffolding, with the average height between lintel levels equating to that of a mason's maximum working height. She also recognized that scarcements might similarly have served in the construction process to support internal scaffolding, which we might speculate, like central four-posters or circular settings in timber houses, could have been incorporated subsequently into the internal fittings of the building. Even if partly constructional in purpose, therefore, it seems improbable that the intra-mural galleries and cells, at least at ground and intermediate levels, would not have been used to good effect on a daily basis. The fact that, in the Beirgh sequence, radial divisions in the post-broch roundhouse occupation were not introduced until the rising floor levels necessitated by the rising water table had made inaccessible the intra-mural gallery entrances of the derelict broch (Fig. 4.1, 2), suggests that the division between central space and peripheral space was a long-standing convention.

In terms of sourcing materials for broch building, stone must surely have been quarried rather than collected from surface scatters, except in locations close to a shoreline, where a ready supply may have been available. As Romankiewicz observed, in the west especially, where galleried structures required numerous lintels, and where gneiss or granite lintels were unlikely to be available in sufficient numbers from opportunistic collection, quarrying must have been undertaken. In some circumstances, such as Dun an Ruigh Ruadh on Lochbroom, quarrying into the hill slope may also have enhanced the appearance of a lofty elevation of a broch (Romankiewicz, 2016a: 8). As anyone who has tackled dry-stone construction will know, surface collection never seems to satisfy the quantities required, not just for the major blocks but also to meet the seemingly limitless need for smaller stones to ensure level and stable courses. We are

Fig. 4.1 Beirgh, Lewis, broch and secondary structures. 1, south-west gallery triangular lintels; 2, secondary radial roundhouse with broch scarcement and gallery entrance behind. Photographs by D. W. Harding.

therefore inevitably drawn back to the question of who controlled and authorized the use of suitable supplies of materials for major construction projects.

The problems associated with timber supplies in regions that were largely treeless were notably addressed by Fojut (2005), who concluded that importation was 'not unthinkable', but required 'certain interlinked socio-political and technical assumptions' (Fojut, 2005: 199). For Shetland he argued that the island's vegetation precluded local sources, but presumably meant natural supplies rather than managed woodland. He nevertheless offered ways in which a roof framework could have been based upon, or sprung from an upper scarcement without support from ground level. Romankiewicz developed these ideas, basing her options on the broch walls themselves, converged at wall-head level to avoid the problems of water ingress into the intra-mural galleries. As to roofing materials, turf or heather thatch might seem to offer greater durability than straw or reeds, and certainly we might expect that a lower pitch than is envisaged for lowland timber roundhouses was deployed for such an exposed roof. A low conical or domed roof would be the most probable. Speculation regarding hipped roofs based on European Bronze Age house urns is misplaced, as hipped roofs on such urns generally reflect rectangular or oval plans (Sabatini, 2007).

Romankiewicz further stressed the importance of location in the siting of brochs. In terms of visual impact, the galleried dun in Loch Bharabhat, Cnip, in west Lewis (Harding and Dixon, 2000) was at the smaller end of the Atlantic roundhouse spectrum, yet, located in a small inland loch at the head of a ravine, it would have had as monumental a local impact as many larger brochs in a more expansive landscape (Romankiewicz, 2016a: 9–10). A study of broch walls and the stone of which they were built showed a 'direct correspondence between wall thickness and compression strength of specific stones', those built of sandstones being on average two metres thicker than those built of gneiss or granite (Romankiewicz, 2016a: 14–15). The fact that this capacity was not apparently exploited to create even taller towers led Romankiewicz to conclude that broch builders were not competitive, but were using local resources cost-effectively, whilst aspiring to be part of a wider inter-regional community. This, of course, need not mean that they were socially egalitarian or that resources were not controlled by local elites.

Canonical Brochs: A Traditionalist View Reasserted?

Where Romankiewicz approached brochs with the eye of a qualified architect, Barber's principal contribution lies in his focus upon the engineering factors in broch design, and in his unique talent for analysing structural anomalies. He was also able to use laser scanning techniques to survey broch sites, from which it became apparent that the basic plans of brochs at ground level were much more accurately circular than some previous surveys using conventional equipment had suggested. The most striking example of this was the laser survey conducted on behalf of the Forestry Commission of Altbreck, Sutherland (Cavers et al., 2015), which MacKie had surveyed as significantly elliptical. The difference was evidently owing to the difficulty of surveying manually on an absolute level a structure that essentially is a converging cone. Barber's conclusion not only stressed the importance of the third dimension in broch metrics but inferred that it was the circularity of the inner wall that was crucial, the external diameter being largely irrelevant. Quite how Iron Age builders had achieved this level of accuracy, since they can only at best have had basic measuring and levelling tools, remains unexplained. Modern manual survey, essentially the use of levelling instruments and tape measure, self-evidently depends upon recording specific points on a structure's ground-plan or elevation, inevitably influenced by the observer's interpretation of what he/she sees as significant. Survey and interpretation are therefore inextricably combined, prejudicing any prospect of reinterpretation by another commentator. Laser scanning by contrast records millions of points depending on programme without an individual's selection, and therefore not only is more accurate but has the potential for alternative interpretation.

Barber's fundamental premise, nevertheless, is controversial, namely that there was such a thing as a *canonical* broch, that is, one that conforms, at any rate in its initial construction, to a set of constructional or engineering rules. Given the complex design and monumental scale of several surviving brochs it is certainly not unreasonable to suppose that Iron Age architects and engineers had evolved a number of basic principles that were essential for the successful construction of broch towers, but whether this resulted from cumulative experience and handing down of traditional skills, or whether there was a specialist class of builders who understood mathematical theory and geometry as their contemporaries did in the classical world remains debatable. The concept of a 'canonical broch' is not so very different from MacKie's 'true broch', a model that was defined by much the same structural criteria, intra-mural gallery, scarcement, stacked voids and suchlike, and which MacKie had assigned to a limited first century BC–AD horizon. In defining his canonical broch, Barber added some important criteria to MacKie's check-list of architectural characteristics of broch towers, structural elements that might, even in truncated remains, betray the former presence or absence of a broch tower. First, it was crucial that the stonework of the walls should be laid formally throughout its width. Rubble infilling was incompatible with a high wall, as it induced 'hydrostatic-type pressure on the retaining walls' (Barber in Cavers et al., 2015: 159). One is reminded of Peter Reynolds' experience in experimental reconstruction of the Conderton house in the Avoncroft Museum in 1970, and the insistence of his stone masons that two wall faces with rubble infilling 'would be inherently unstable and would readily collapse if any pressure were exerted upon it' (Reynolds, 1982: 192), an injunction that plainly applies with even greater force to a broch. Accordingly, Whitegait, Caithness, could never have been a tall broch tower. Second, a complex, composite arrangement of lintels over the outer end of the broch entrance, as recognized at Clachtoll, was indicative of a high wall, designed as it was to carry maximum load (Barber in Cavers et al., 2015: 156). Barber remarked that this arrangement had been noted by Dryden at Clickhimin, but had been disregarded by archaeologists ever since. Lintels set together on their diagonals maximized their load-bearing capacity, and therefore, even in truncated field remains, could be reliably regarded as an indicator of greater weight and height. He believed that corbelling over the entrance area and some triangular lintels (though presumably not the thin facade at Old Scatness) would have served the same purpose.

The implication of this model is that any site that fails to meet the predetermined criteria can be discounted as a canonical broch, which replicates the circular arguments regarding the definition and chronology of 'true' brochs or broch towers at the time that *IAR* was published. It is highlighted by the dilemma of Dun Boredale on Raasay, which is oval on plan. Despite this MacKie had exceptionally admitted it to broch status, since it had the other diagnostic features, and plainly was a tower. Barber was disinclined to make exceptions to the rule, but acknowledged the presence of other broch tower elements and so admitted that, though eccentric, Dun Boredale was a tower. The dilemma simply demonstrates the fact that the model is a modern concept that archaeologists try to impose on Iron Age buildings. Strict application of the criteria limited Barber's analysis to some 80 brochs in all, that he apparently regarded as a totally separate phenomenon from the other several hundred, which did not meet his test of canonicity, and which therefore were dismissed as 'little more than aggrandised hut circles' (Barber, 2016: 367). He simply could not accept that broch towers might be the best preserved of a spectrum of complex Atlantic roundhouses, not all of which need have been as elaborate as his chosen few, and indeed not all of which need have served the same function.

The idea that the broch tower is a distinct and separate form of structure is central and immutable in Barber's model, and it is intrinsically linked to his short chronology.

The transition to the construction of broch towers was necessarily abrupt. The typologist's pipe-dream of an evolutionary sequence leading to the broch tower faces the same difficulty that the traditional Darwinian evolutionary biologist faces explaining the gradualist evolution of complex structures like birds' eyes or birds' wings. Gould's question, of what evolutionary use is 5% of a wing? can be applied to broch towers also, because 5% of a broch is a low circular building, and not a broch tower.   (Barber, 2016: 38)

The straightforward answer, of course, is that 5 per cent of a broch may be only a low circular building, but unlike 5 per cent of a bird's wing, it could be a perfectly serviceable low building, and 50 per cent of a broch tower, provided it adhered to the basic structural principles, could be a serviceable building intermediate between a roundhouse and a broch tower. Bonded double-walled construction may be essential for a taller tower, but there is no reason to suppose that all double-walled roundhouses were designed to attain the heights of Carloway or the Glenelg brochs, or that they required all of the 'canonical' features. Relieving voids over the main entrance may be essential, and highly desirable over interior doorways, but it is hard to believe that scarcements are structurally essential to the integrity of the shell, rather than to its interior fittings. The proportions of the galleried dun at Loch Bharabhat, Cnip, certainly do not suggest that it was designed as a tall tower, though it certainly had an upper floor. So the notion that a broch can only exist in its most developed or complex form is simply not rational, and creates unnecessary difficulties in explaining the development of the series, as well as isolating arbitrarily those that happen to have survived sufficiently to be admitted to canonicity from the greater body of remains that have not. To suggest that complex Atlantic roundhouses represent a sequence does not mean that they must have developed progressively or uniformly throughout Atlantic Scotland, though, as Gilmour has pointed out (pers. comm.), the fact that there is a common sequence from broch to roundhouse (or inner wall lining) to cellular buildings widely across the north and west does suggest a degree of common cultural development.

Equally irrational is the determination that brochs were all short-lived, and though radiocarbon dates have now obliged Barber to stretch their beginnings back to 300 BC or thereabouts, it remains much the same as the old first century BC horizon stretched a bit. To avoid conceding that any lasted more than a generation or two, he posits abandonment after initial use, sometimes precipitated by catastrophic collapse, after which, in the north-east and Northern Isles, they were reoccupied as the focus of fortified settlements, as in broch villages. Catastrophic collapse doubtless did happen, as the evidence from Clachtoll would appear to indicate, though not apparently before the broch had already undergone some structural modifications. But where collapse was comprehensive, it might have been preferable to abandon the site and to rebuild elsewhere, using the collapsed stone as a quarry, rather than double-handling stone to rebuild on the same site. This indeed might account for the apparent density of brochs in some areas. Rebuilding on the same site in any event might have been regarded as inauspicious. But there is no reason to suppose that catastrophic collapse was that frequent, and more often it would appear that brochs were occupied, continuously or intermittently, for protracted periods until they were systematically dismantled and the building materials reused for less monumental houses, roundhouses, and subsequently cellular buildings. Barber's study studiously avoids considering the

96 RETHINKING ROUNDHOUSES

secondary structures built within and around brochs, because they are not relevant to his focus on the canonical broch. Yet it is surely the sequence of occupational evidence, from later Bronze Age cellular or courtyard structures, through the period of Atlantic roundhouses, to the post-broch sequences represented particularly in the Northern Isles that provides the only context within which the monumental brochs can adequately be interpreted.

A major area of concern for Barber's study is the question of structural modifications, rebuilding, and in some cases undocumented and possibly quite radical and erroneous 'conservation' in more recent times. It is undoubtedly an important contribution of Barber's research to draw attention to the extent of structural modification that went on in brochs, even in the Iron Age. As to more recent reconstructions, it has been evident for some years that Clickhimin had been so heavily restored as to invalidate virtually any attempt at modern interpretation (Smith, 2015). Barber evidently believed that Mousa underwent substantial alteration to its basic form in late antiquity, and that many other broch towers experienced reconstruction, sometimes after catastrophic collapses. Barber has a unique eye for recognizing alterations to the structural fabric of brochs. But the present writer has always believed that it was possible for a skilled mason to rebuild sections of a stone wall virtually undetected, so that it follows that there could have been significant structural alterations that are not evident to visual inspection. At Dun Telve, for instance, Barber claimed that a series of lintels blocking access through the gallery might best be explained if the relieving void now confined to the upper wall had formerly extended down to the scarcement, an interpretation that requires the infilling to have been integrated into the irregular sloping courses with particular skill. Contrarily, where obvious breaks in building lines can be detected, there is the further possibility that these might be accounted for by separate building teams or different wagon-loads of stone, rather than by separate episodes of construction.

Barber rightly identified two inherent areas of weakness in a broch plan, the entrance, and the space over lintels where internal doorways to cells or galleries broke the integrity of the wall. MacKie had identified twenty brochs where there were corbelled cells over the entrance, presumably intended to ease the load from above, though secondary alterations could not always be discounted. Above door lintels the use of stacked voids was evidently designed to relieve the structural loading. Barber dismissed an earlier suggestion by Armit and Hope that it allowed ventilation of the intra-mural galleries, but, though the primary purpose may have been structural, it would be characteristic of the sophisticated nature of broch building to achieve a secondary benefit at the same time. A major contribution of Barber's experimental work with stone structures has been to increase awareness of the extent of probable structural alterations witnessed in surviving brochs. Though he detects evidence for collapses in many, it also became apparent that brochs could be subject to significant secondary intrusive modifications without imperilling the rest of the building.

Among acknowledged secondary developments in brochs are secondary stair-foot entrances, as witnessed at Freswick, Clickhimin, Ness, Keiss Road and Keiss Harbour, Yarrows, and Thrumster, though in some cases the broch tower itself would doubtless have been much reduced by the time the later entrance was inserted. At Old Scatness, by contrast, the excavators claimed that the stair-foot entrance could have been introduced to aid construction, allowing materials to be brought into the broch, and carefully blocked when this facility was no longer required (Dockrill et al., 2015: 48). Barber envisaged much more radical structural alterations at Mousa, where he believed (2016: 175) that the upper scarcement was a secondary addition to cope with the rising floor level, and that the entire helical staircase was a secondary insertion, which accounted for its lack of direct correspondence with gallery entrances to the interior. These changes, he argued, had been effected in or by Viking times. This radical reappraisal is necessitated by the fact that Mousa does not accord with the canonical model, either in its continuous helical staircase or in the intra-mural cavity that accommodates it extending to the wall-head. On the contrary, the single factor that argues in favour of the wall-head stair being original is the excessive wall-width to overall-width ratio of Mousa's ground-plan, which reflects the fact that its twin walls cannot converge at the top if they are to contain an intra-mural staircase to the wall head. Barber argued that the Iron Age broch had been two to four metres lower than at present, and had been 'refitted by the Vikings as a defensible citadel', including alterations designed to force the helical staircase to the wall-head (2016: 184). The stacked voids, which at Dun Troddan and Dun Telve extended to the wall-head, would likewise have done so at Mousa, but had been encased by rebuilding after the collapse of the upper part of the tower. The truth surely is that, whether or not there was a collapse in antiquity, Mousa was designed to be different from normal, residential brochs, however grand. Perhaps it was designed to serve a special function as a watch-tower (Smith, 2016), deploying broch-building technology to create a specialist structure. In fact, Barber concedes that 'it is possible that Mousa, an aberrant monument, was simply idiosyncratically built *ab initio*' (2016: 185).

A major, self-imposed, limitation of Barber's study is the omission of any consideration of the material culture of brochs, an entirely legitimate decision of choice, and hardly injudicious in a study focused on structural engineering, since the large and disparate body of material artefacts from brochs includes a majority from older excavations that lack any reliable stratigraphic context. His remark (2016: 364), nevertheless, that 'any artefact found on a broch site post-dates the monument's construction' is a source of frustration, since any experienced professional archaeologist must know that it is *its deposit* that post-dates the monument's construction, whilst the artefact itself could have been old when deposited. In practical terms, whilst an occupation deposit must of course post-date the building's construction, it may well provide evidence for contemporary occupation and use, unless it is from a context that is stratigraphically secondary.

Occupational sequences like those from Beirgh that are stratigraphically well defined may help in recognizing changes in ceramic style (Harding, 2017: 167–71), so that traditional methods of establishing chronology through cultural material should not be wholly disregarded, especially for a period when radiocarbon calibration is still problematical.

The Problem of Non-Brochs with Broch Attributes

An important implication of the Barber view of canonical brochs as buildings of tower proportions that displayed certain key architectural or engineering attributes, and the corollary that there was no intermediate stage in a progressive development of such broch towers, is that it denies a context for any building that did not aspire to such grandeur, but which did display features that might otherwise have been accommodated within a complex Atlantic roundhouse tradition. Dun Bharabhat, Cnip (Harding and Dixon, 2000), for example, had at least two ground galleries in its primary phase, one accommodating a stair to an upper floor. Its wall did not survive to a sufficient height to demonstrate the presence or absence of a scarcement, and one cannot be confident that there was any further higher level beyond first floor. The building also had a door rebate, with bar-hole, sill stone, and pivot-stone, as might be expected of a broch. But its overall footprint was modest, an oval ten by eleven metres enclosing an inner court around five metres across, and its wall construction was hardly substantial in comparison to the broch towers of the west. In fact, it had evidently suffered a catastrophic collapse, not so much through structural deficiencies themselves as resulting from inadequate foundations around the edge of the reinforced natural island on which it stood. In effect, Dun Bharabhat is a small example of a complex Atlantic roundhouse that certainly stood to two storeys in height, and would have been perfectly viable as such had it been built on dry land. But it was certainly not a broch tower in the generally accepted sense.

A similar dilemma is posed by the more recently excavated complex Atlantic roundhouse at Applecross (Peteranna, 2012). In its final Atlantic roundhouse phase it had an external diameter of 15–16 metres enclosing a circular court some 9–10 metres across (Fig. 4.2). Though there have evidently been structural alterations to this final building, it appears to have had four intra-mural spaces, and at least one entrance. The width of the walls and the width of the intra-mural galleries are far from consistent, and the quality of construction in places is poor, with undressed boulders and rubble infilling that would hardly sustain a building of

Fig. 4.2 Applecross, Wester Ross, broch, general view. Photograph courtesy Catherine Dagg with kind permission, photographed using polecam designed by John Wombell.

any height. No scarcement survived in the upstanding remains, nor in this instance any trace of a staircase.

An unusual feature of the Applecross structure was that it had been built over at least two previous structures, the arcing wall faces of which survived on its southern side. In fact, the wall of the intermediate roundhouse merged into its successor on the west side, before crossing paving at a lower level that was interpreted as potentially coinciding with an entrance to the primary building. Dating of the respective phases remains tentative, but the span represented extended from the third quarter of the first millennium BC to the mid-first millennium AD, based upon radiocarbon samples and for the later occupation upon the associated material assemblage. Applecross demonstrates well the problems of archaeological classification and structural typology. It plainly could not have supported a high tower, and would make an unconvincing contender even as a proto-broch tower. But it has intra-mural galleries, and was reasonably described by the excavators as a complex Atlantic roundhouse. The presence of intra-mural galleries in a building that evidently was not a broch tower suggests that they were not just structural features of broch building but formed part of the social or utilitarian space that the roundhouse required.

100 RETHINKING ROUNDHOUSES

The Cairns on South Ronaldsay likewise presents issues of classification. With an overall diameter of 22 metres enclosing an inner court some 11 metres across, the Cairns has a high wall-width-to-overall-width ratio, which is not uncommon for brochs in the Northern Isles. Much less common are its multiple intra-mural chambers, no less than six having been identified. Its walls had been reduced below any surviving scarcement height. It had a well-preserved entrance passage with door jambs and bar holes, but with no flanking guard chambers. Crucial evidence for construction of the walls in the north-east sector with a clay and rubble core suggested that the building could not have sustained any great height. Accordingly the excavator was disposed to regard the building as a complex Atlantic roundhouse but not a broch tower (Carruthers, 2007, 2009). Subsequent seasons of excavation showed a complex sequence of occupation from the first century BC to the end of the second century AD, when it appears that the building was deliberately reduced, with closure deposits marking the end of its occupation. The site itself nevertheless continued in use until the eighth century AD, with more than twenty secondary buildings extending over and beyond the primary Atlantic roundhouse. In effect, the Cairns shows an occupational sequence paralleled on broch sites, without its primary building ever aspiring to be a broch tower.

'Simple' Atlantic Roundhouses

In the Armit system of classification, the concept of a Complex Atlantic Roundhouse implied the existence of a 'Non-complex' or 'Simple' counterpart. Of course there were plenty of examples of stone-built roundhouses in upland zones of Britain, but to be regarded in any way as related to brochs they would need to be of substantial proportions, in overall diameter and thickness of walls. This description might well apply to Early Iron Age roundhouses such as Quanterness, Pierowall Quarry, or the Calf of Eday. At Toft's Ness, Sanday (Dockrill, 2007) the early Iron Age roundhouse was smaller in internal diameter than its Late Bronze Age precursor, though both had central hearths and radial divisions indicative of domestic usage (Fig. 4.4, 1). At the time of publication of *IAR* the best candidate for a simple (i.e. ungalleried) Atlantic roundhouse was the structure from Bu, Orkney, with an overall diameter approaching 20 metres enclosing an internal court some 10 metres in diameter. Dating to around the mid-first millennium BC, Bu was discounted as a 'true' broch by traditionalists, not only because of its early date but because it apparently lacked the key features of intra-mural cells or scarcement. However, northern brochs, unlike their western counterparts, seldom had more than one gallery at basal level (the one that accommodated the staircase to upper levels), so that limited excavation could certainly miss the crucial evidence. Furthermore, galleries in Orcadian brochs were often based well

ANALYSING AND INTERPRETING STONE-BUILT ROUNDHOUSES 101

above foundation level, so that detecting the presence of galleries depended entirely on the remains surviving to a metre or more in height. Comparison of the Bu plan and elevation with its nearest known broch neighbour at Howe (Fig. 4.3) showed that the foundations at Bu were too denuded to preserve evidence of any raised galleries, and therefore certainly not any scarcement. Likewise, any basal gallery, if located in the same quarter as Howe, would anyway not have

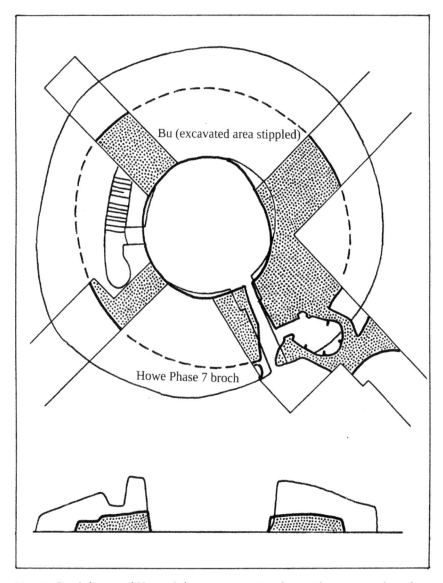

Fig. 4.3 Bu, Orkney and Howe, Orkney, comparative plans with entrances aligned. Drawing by D. W. Harding, adapted from Hedges, 1987 and Smith, 1994.

been covered by the excavated area at Bu. Any interpretation of Bu, therefore, is predetermined by factors of survival and excavation strategy.

More recently, excavations on Rousay, Orkney, just south of the Midhowe broch, have uncovered an even more impressive sequence of occupation at the Knowe of Swandro from the mid-first millennium BC continuing, whether continuously or interrupted, into the opening centuries AD (Bond and Dockrill, 2019; Dockrill et al., 2019). Structure 8 was certainly a substantial building, described by its excavators as monumental in scale, though not as yet displaying any of the defining features of broch architecture (Fig. 4.4, 2). Its overall diameter was around 20 metres, but this thickness of its walls may include refacing, and it plainly underwent several phases of occupation between its construction in the mid-first millennium BC and its latest alterations, when the entrance was redesigned, in the first–second centuries AD. The importance of Swandro, however, rests not just in its morphological relationship to brochs, but in the fact that it was the focal building within a more extensive settlement that included lesser circular and cellular buildings, in much the same way that hitherto has been associated with broch villages. The Swandro settlement was evidently of significant status, enjoying Roman imports and yielding evidence of metalworking. Structure 3, initially identified as a Pictish smithy, and employing edge-set slab construction, has since been dated to the first century AD. It yielded evidence for both iron and copper working, and two stone anvils as well as moulds and other industrial debris. Swandro doubtless will prove still more complex on further investigation, but already raises the possibility that there could be a greater diversity in contemporary architecture than simplistic evolutionary models imply.

Dun Houses

At the time of publication of *IAR*, duns were still widely regarded as a phenomenon of the west of Scotland. This was because the terminology was largely associated with the multi-volume *Inventories* of Argyll, published between 1971 and 1988 by the Royal Commission on the Ancient and Historical Monuments of Scotland, which had used the umbrella term to cover a wide range of stone enclosures smaller than its 4,000 square metre threshold for forts. Subsequently, the working distinction between *dun enclosures* and *dun houses* (Harding, 1984), the latter distinguished solely on the basis of size on the assumption that they could have been roofed, seemed to be widely accepted, even though the paucity of material associations gave no indication of the relative functions of either group. There was also still a residual preference for dating Argyll duns to the early historic period, resulting from the fact that several excavated examples had proved to have been built or reoccupied in the Later Iron Age.

ANALYSING AND INTERPRETING STONE-BUILT ROUNDHOUSES 103

Fig. 4.4 Simple Atlantic roundhouses on Orkney. 1, Toft's Ness, Sanday, Iron Age roundhouse. Photograph by Dr Stephen Dockrill, reproduced by kind permission; 2, Swandro, Rousay, Iron Age roundhouse. Photograph by Tom Sparrow, reproduced by king permission.

Clearly dating from the earlier Iron Age was the circular dun at Glashan in Argyll (Henderson and Gilmour, 2011). Enclosing an area 19 metres in diameter with a wall 4–5 metres thick, Dun Glashan must be considered on the limits of viability for roofing as a single structure, though split-roof options, as suggested for the larger timber roundhouses, might be equally applicable here. In the Armit scheme, the dun would rank as a simple Atlantic roundhouse, lacking any complex intra-mural features. Like other Argyll duns, however, it did have a medial wall face, a device that appears to have been designed to combat instability in the wall core, and as such might be regarded as a step towards consolidating the foundations to sustain a higher superstructure. It had a single rebated entrance passage on the north side, but there was no evidence within the limited area opened in the interior for postholes, stone post-pads, or conclusive evidence of a hearth. A consistent suite of radiocarbon dates indicated occupation within the second half of the first millennium BC, a conclusion which would be consistent with the limited material assemblage, which included a polished stone, hammer stone, and yellow glass bead.

More recently selective excavation of Dun Fhinn on Islay has convincingly shown that it dates from the first millennium BC (Regan, 2018; forthcoming a). Previously the roundhouse within the dun had been regarded as a probable secondary addition, for reasons that were not explained (RCAHMS, 1984: no. 211). Selective excavation established not only that the roundhouse was part of the original Early Iron Age dun layout but that the occupation of the site began by the mid-first millennium BC. The walls of the roundhouse were slighter than that of the dun enclosure, with substantial facing and a rubble core, so that the excavator inferred that the superstructure was of timber and the roof of thatch or turf. This could be broadly contemporary with occupation of the crannog exposed in the partially drained Loch nan Deala on Islay (Holley, 1996; Maričević et al., 2019), which earlier investigation had suggested as potentially Neolithic. Certainly research by the Kilmartin Museum has reinforced the probability that circular 'dun houses' are of Early Iron Age origin. What induced a shift from Later Bronze Age hut circles to more substantial dun building remains unclear, but Regan has suggested that climatic factors (Maričević et al., 2019) may have resulted in settlement instability and a need for greater protection.

The substantial stone-built roundhouse known as Comar Wood dun in Strathglass (Peteranna and Birch, 2017) was evidently constructed some time from the fourth century BC, and like several of the Atlantic roundhouses, was reused in successive episodes of reconstruction or reoccupation into the third century AD, once again underlining the longevity of site use. In this instance the dun's location, within an enclosed wall on the edge of a steep-sided knoll overlooking the strath underlined its importance strategically for defence and display. The roundhouse walls were around 22 metres in overall diameter, enclosing a court some 13 metres across, with a single entrance to the west facing the main

ANALYSING AND INTERPRETING STONE-BUILT ROUNDHOUSES   105

enclosure entrance. A secondary wall face fronted a primary facing of boulders and smaller stones that survived several courses high, but which retained a rubble core and was not of sufficient quality to sustain a monumental stone building. Surface survey had suggested the possibility of intra-mural cells, but it was not possible to confirm this through excavation. Postholes within the interior and the entrance indicated a significant timber component in the superstructure, and it is clear that the building would have had a substantial presence. The excavators drew a close parallel, both in terms of dating and in aspects of construction, with the Langwell dun from Strath Oykel, Sutherland (Nisbet, 1994), though not presumably in terms of the latter's vitrified components.

An important contribution to modern investigation of substantial, solid-walled roundhouses has been the selective excavations of the Northern Picts Project in the Tarbat peninsula between the Dornoch Firth and the Cromarty Firth. Tarlogie dun (Hatherley, 2015) was exceptionally thick-walled, resulting from successive episodes of construction over more than half a millennium. Enclosing an area some nine metres in diameter, its walls on the north side were up to eight metres thick, and around five metres thick on the south. Composite in construction, with stone facings and an earth and rubble core, it is unlikely that the building attained any great height. This conclusion would be consistent with the design of the south-east facing entrance, which was splayed in plan, from 1.8 metres wide at its inner end to 3.6 metres wide at its outer end, much wider than could be bridged for a taller superstructure. Radiocarbon dating suggested three phases of occupation, the earliest from the third quarter of the first millennium BC and the latest in the second quarter of the first millennium AD.

Cnoc Tigh (Hatherley et al., 2014), located one kilometre south-east of Portmahomack on the shores of the Dornoch Firth, also had composite walls resulting from successive episodes of construction, beginning with the earliest just over a metre wide and enclosing an area thirteen metres in diameter, and culminating in walls four metres thick. Its entrance, just a metre wide, faced west. Unusually, Cnoc Tigh did have a scarcement from its primary phase, but at a height of just 20 cm above the wall base, the excavator reasonably concluded that its purpose was more probably to carry a suspended floor than to support superstructure.

The construction of the Easter Rarichie solid-walled roundhouse (Hatherley 2014) followed a similar pattern of wall facing retaining a core of rubble and earth, within which some larger boulders may have been included in an attempt to consolidate the core. The inner wall face included substantial sandstone boulders with smaller coursed stonework between, surviving to a little over a metre in height. The walls were four metres wide enclosing an area ten metres in diameter, with an entrance facing south-east. Postholes in the interior may have supported the roof, though the limited area excavated did not reveal a coherent pattern. A regular setting of sandstone flags in the centre of the house evidently formed a hearth. Radiocarbon samples indicated occupation in the third quarter of the first millennium BC, though there was evidence of activity on the site before the construction of the stone-built roundhouse. Simultaneous excavation at Wester Rarichie examined there a roundhouse with a substantial wall, up to five metres wide, constructed of earth and turf, which yielded radiocarbon dates from the second quarter of the first millennium BC. This led the excavator to speculate whether there might have been an earlier roundhouse at Easter Rarichie that had been built of turf and earth and subsequently replaced by the surviving stone roundhouse.

The Tarbat roundhouses, though substantial, are hardly sophisticated in construction. Their walls have rubble cores and lack adequate through bonding to sustain any great height. Though the limited scale of excavation leaves the issue open, there is no confirmed evidence of intra-mural galleries or any other form of structural complexity. Their earlier Iron Age date is no basis for anticipating that they would ever have progressed to complexity in construction, and there is every reason to suppose that, like the solid-walled duns of Argyll, they are representative of self-sufficient if not elite households in the region.

Re-excavation and re-survey of the settlements at Old and New Kinord in the Howe of Cromar, first investigated by Abercromby in 1903, are of interest because these buildings, putatively roundhouses of the second century BC to second century AD, are of unusual size and of stone construction. The larger buildings, defined by massive boulders rather than coursed stone walls or wall facings, had broad foundations that micromorphological samples from the recent re-excavation (Romankiewicz et al., 2020) suggested may have supported turf walls. Later prehistoric stone structures evidently included a greater regional diversity of types and used a wider range of techniques and materials than has generally been appreciated. There is a possibility that the Old Kinord buildings were roofed with turf, but within the limited areas opened it was impossible to distinguish collapsed wall turf from potential roof turf. Investigating the interior for roof-supporting post-circles was constrained by the fact that intrusive excavation of the Scheduled Monument was restricted to Abercromby's former trenches.

One puzzling aspect of the Old Kinord structures was their overlapping layout. Paired buildings may have been simultaneously occupied, perhaps by siblings in joint land ownership, or they may have been designed as a figure-of-eight entity. The two pairs from New Kinord could be of this kind. But the Old Kinord pair (A, D) were demonstrably in sequence rather than contemporary, which, given the availability of space meant that overlap was not necessary, and indeed posed constructional problems, so that one must conclude that physical contiguity with the earlier buildings was deliberately intended to maintain continuity. An important factor at Old Kinord is the proximity of houses to souterrains, though 'souterrain' in this instance is a misnomer, since flanking banks indicate that the roof must have been at least a metre above ground level.

Finally, in the north-west, the Wedigs project (Fenton, 2015; Welti and Wildgoose, n.d.) demonstrated the capacity of field survey with selective excavation to yield important information regarding the construction and use of circular stone structures, in this instance in the Ullapool and Gairloch districts, and in south Skye. Though some radiocarbon dates indicated earlier and others later settlement, relatively few dated to the Early Iron Age, and it is not clear that all were necessarily roofed domestic buildings. Furthermore, their occupation and use may have been relatively short-lived and intermittent, as part of a pattern of local mobility within a wider landscape. As Romankiewicz has argued (Edinburgh University seminar, 31 March 2022) individual buildings may have been subject to episodic abandonment, perhaps as a result of climate change, but settlement of the landscape was continuous.

Radial Roundhouses

The anomalies of distribution and chronology of roundhouses with truncated radial piers, commonly known as wheelhouses or aisled roundhouses, were apparent at the time of publication of *IAR*, and even then suggested that the imposition of archaeological typology may have obscured subtle differences in later prehistoric and early historic buildings. In the Western Isles, where the majority of wheelhouses were adapted architecturally to their location in the machair, there was nevertheless a significant difference in size between the Cnip houses, no more than seven metres in internal diameter, and the conjoined structures at Foshigarry, where Structure C must have been around twice that diameter. Though secondary structures with radial piers were suspected at Dun Mor Vaul and Beirgh, there are no unequivocal wheelhouses in a broch and post-broch sequence in the Hebrides. On the other hand, independent dating of the Cnip wheelhouse to the first century BC or thereabouts means that its occupants were near neighbours at a time when the Beirgh broch tower was the dominant building in the landscape. In Shetland the occurrence of roundhouses with radial piers in the post-broch sequence at Jarlshof seemed to be paralleled in the later broch and post-broch occupation at Old Scatness, where modern excavation offered the prospect of refining the technological and chronological sequence.

The later broch and immediately post-broch occupation at Old Scatness was represented by Phase 5 and Phase 6 (Dockrill et al., 2015). Phase 5 was assigned to the later second and first centuries BC, contemporary with the later occupation of the broch tower itself, and otherwise represented principally by two radial roundhouses immediately to its south-west, together with several other satellite structures. There certainly were earlier buildings beneath the Iron Age village that may well have been contemporary with the earlier broch occupation, Phase 4, but these were not accessible for excavation since this would have entailed damaging the substantial remains of extant buildings that understandably were required for public display. Any pre-existing remains were evidently levelled as a foundation for the Phase 5 buildings, but at least one coherent circular setting included possible ends of aisled piers (Dockrill et al., 2015: Fig. 3.15). Structure 12 was a substantial circular house, with an internal diameter just short of ten metres, and walls that attained a metre in thickness. It had eight radial piers and two orthostatic settings that divided the interior perimeter equally into ten 'cells'. The orthostats were located hard up to the inner wall face, whereas the piers, that were otherwise straight-sided, initially had aisles between their inner ends and the wall face, thereby allowing access around the perimeter. That the passage was used was indicated by the smoothed surface of the stonework. The presence of a central hearth confirmed the division of space between a central court and peripheral cells.

Structure 14 was only marginally smaller by being elliptical in plan. It initially had six aisled piers around the southern sector of the house, and four 'long' piers around the north, where the house wall was contiguous with Structure 12. It thus likewise had ten peripheral cells, and like Structure 12 its primary entrance was to the west. A key feature of Structure 14 was its scarcement, extending across and above the surviving level of the piers (Fig. 4.5, 1), prompting comparison with the aisled roundhouse from Jarlshof. The obvious implication, as the excavators rightly observed, is that there was an upper floor or at least a mezzanine. Though there was no surviving scarcement in Structure 12, the central hearth was conspicuously moved off-centre in a subsequent episode of structural alteration, and replaced by a substantial stone that the excavators took to be a post-pad, the purpose of which was presumably to provide additional central support for the superstructure.

Both Structure 12 and Structure 14 underwent considerable structural alterations during what was evidently a protracted occupational sequence, represented internally by successive hearths, replaced floors, and accumulating occupational deposits. Significantly the aisles were blocked, perhaps in an attempt to strengthen the piers, but in due course the structure suffered a catastrophic collapse of its cells and a secondary annexe on the east side, after which it was evidently abandoned and filled with ash dumps. Perhaps most significant of the alterations to Structure 12 had been the addition to its west side of a sub-rectangular annexe, interpreted as a specialist storage and cooking area.

Phase 6 at Old Scatness, dating from the first to fourth centuries AD, is represented by a cluster of structures to the south-east of the broch and contiguous with it, of which the principal building was Structure 21, a radial roundhouse some 11.5 by 13 metres in internal diameter. The broch itself must by this time have been reduced, since the truncated remains of another radial roundhouse, Structure 16, filled its interior to create a building ten metres in diameter. Its four surviving piers were significantly tapered like those of a wheelhouse, but it had

Fig. 4.5 Old Scatness, Shetland, post-broch buildings. 1, Structure 14 radial pier and scarcement; 2, Structure 11, Phase 2, roundhouse with radial piers and central hearth. Photographs by Dr Stephen Dockrill, reproduced by kind permission.

110   RETHINKING ROUNDHOUSES

been largely destroyed in the construction of a later, Pictish-period Structure 7. Structure 21 was distinguished by its medial dividing wall, which stratigraphically appeared to be part of the primary structure. It, too, is paralleled by the aisled roundhouse at Jarlshof, where Hamilton had regarded it as secondary. Both northern and southern halves had four 'long' radial piers, creating five 'cells' in each. The entrance was to the north-west. Cells in the southern sector had drains and soak-aways, and yielded palaeoenvironmental evidence for straw and hay, suggesting its use as a byre. The northern half, by contrast more probably served for human occupation. Interpretation of the building, however, depends crucially upon the excavators' interpretation of the medial wall as supporting an upper floor, accessed possibly by an external staircase at the point of intersection between Structure 21 and the broch wall. Accordingly, in Alan Braby's reconstruction drawing (Dockrill et al., 2015: Fig. 4.32) the long radial piers support radial joists (which presumably did not need to extend the full length of the radial piers, thus in part obviating the latter's purpose) of a two-storeyed roundhouse.

Again there is evidence of structural collapse, and though remedial work was evidently undertaken, it is doubtful whether the building continued with an upper floor. Nevertheless, in its heyday it appears to have enjoyed economic prosperity, with imported Roman glassware and Roman dress ornaments signifying a relatively opulent lifestyle. From its later contexts it also yielded mould fragments for bronze handpins and penannular brooches, an activity that again affords links across the whole of Atlantic Scotland at this period.

The culmination of the Old Scatness sequence is represented by houses from the Pictish period Phase 7 settlement, dating from the fifth century AD to the Viking settlement of the ninth century (Dockrill et al., 2010). Three buildings accord closely to the structural requirements of corbelled or partially-corbelled wheelhouses, Structure 7, built within the confines of the broch interior, and Structures 6 and 11, immediately outside its walls to the south-east. These buildings are generally smaller than those of the previous phase. Discounting its two sub-rectangular annexes, the principal component of Structure 7 was an oval averaging just five metres across, and comprising six cells clustered shamrock-like around a central service area (*IAR*: Pl. 13b). Unlike earlier radial roundhouses, its piers are integral with the cell walls, curving outwards to create a curving triangular footprint. The piers have a slight flare with height, and there can be little doubt that the cells were corbelled. Within the central court, the hearth characteristically had a horseshoe-shaped surround of small orthostats. Excavation of Structure 11 was confined by the site's conservation and public presentation protocol to the final phase of what was evidently a sequence of building. The radial piers, in this instance truncated triangular in plan, were butted against the original roundhouse wall, which evidently pre-dated the building's conversion into a wheelhouse by some time. In fact, similarities between the perimeter wall's construction and the medial wall of Structure 21 were 'so distinctive in style...that the

ANALYSING AND INTERPRETING STONE-BUILT ROUNDHOUSES   111

possibility arises that they were built by the same hand' (Dockrill et al., 2010: 49), that is, in the first or second centuries A D. It need not follow, of course, that the structural sequence was uninterrupted, since AMS dates for material associated with the central hearths indicate activity between the eighth and tenth centuries A D. The cells of the wheelhouse were divided from the central service area by orthostatic kerbs, and the hearth once again had a horseshoe-shaped surround (Fig. 4.5, 2). Cell 4 (indicated by the vertical ranging pole) yielded a Class I symbol stone depicting a bear. Structure 6 was a Pictish period wheelhouse just 5.5 metres in internal diameter, set within the earlier Structure 25, reusing one section of earlier walling, on to which the triangular pier therefore abuts rather than being integral to it. The arrangement of orthostats at the inner end of the piers is here instructive, being variously set to cover the end face of the pier, or covering one half, or set sideways. Whilst the present writer at one stage believed such facing orthostats were largely ornamental, Structure 6 shows clearly that they were crucial to the weight-bearing capacity of the piers. All were set on solid slabbed foundations, and the horizontal slab that remained *in situ* over one terminal orthostat and the adjacent pier walling plainly was designed to spread the load of the corbelled cell roof. This was one of the key lessons learned from the Shetland Heritage Trust's experimental reconstruction of wheelhouse Structure 6.

The Old Scatness excavation has afforded a remarkable sequence of structural development backed up by the most reliable set of scientific dates yet available in Atlantic Scotland. As with brochs themselves it is apparent that roundhouses and cellular buildings underwent major structural repairs and alterations during their occupancy. It is equally clear that episodes of collapse were not unknown, and that any assumption that design and construction were invariably successful is unwarranted. What the Old Scatness sequence reveals, however, is that the umbrella term 'radial pier' compounds a variety of structures, from the relatively thin (or even orthostatic) piers of the earlier radial roundhouses to the integral triangular piers of the smaller Pictish period wheelhouses. A corbelled superstructure was evidently more effectively achieved in the context of the latter, whereas the larger radial roundhouses of Phases 5 and 6 probably incorporated a greater use of timber in their construction. But it is not simply in terms of their piers that the Old Scatness buildings show their diversification. The presence of a scarcement in Structure 14, paralleled in the aisled roundhouse at Jarlshof, raises the prospect that some radial roundhouses may have had mezzanine or upper floors, with obvious implications in terms of available space and the social unit that it might accommodate.

At the time that *IAR* was published it was widely recognized that radial piers might have served either or both of two functions. First, it reduced the span of timber required to roof the central court of a wheelhouse, plainly an advantage in the treeless natural landscape of the Western Isles, where the distribution was concentrated. Second, it articulated the radial division of peripheral space and the division of central space from peripheral space, which, it was argued, was fundamental to roundhouse usage. What was not adequately appreciated was that structurally piers might have supported the superstructure in different ways, not least involving the possibility in larger radial roundhouses of an upper floor level. The presence of radial piers need not invariably signal the use of corbelling, even where the inner face of the outer wall shows signs of inward coursing, since partial corbelling, that is, the combination of timber roof braced against an inward trending external wall has been suspected at Beirgh and elsewhere as a variant building technique. An undoubted indicator of corbelling, on the other hand, is an upward-flaring pier and Y-lintels, as commonly represented in aisled roundhouses in the Western Isles. Collapsed lintels that would have bridged the inner ends of the piers would equally be diagnostic of corbelling, as of course would be a mass of residual stonework, though the survival of either of the latter would obviously depend upon there having been no attempt to salvage valuable building materials. An obvious lesson from Old Scatness is that we should re-examine the evidence for aisled roundhouses and wheelhouses from the Western Isles to see whether a variety of different structures has hitherto been conflated under a single head.

5

Roundhouses in Context

Settlements and Landscape

IAR began by attempting to define a house, distinguishing between the structural remains of a building, the function of which was inferred to be residential and domestic, from a house in the sense of a household, the social unit that built and occupied the buildings in question. Archaeologically, the emphasis has generally been on the former, and classification based on size and complexity or materials of construction. A basic assumption, however, was that the house could hardly stand alone, more probably being a principal component of a group of buildings that included facilities for storage of produce, stalling of stock, and working areas, even if some of these functions were also served within the house itself. By extension, it also followed that there may be cultivated fields and stock boundaries in proximity, and trackways linking the settlement to neighbours or providing longer-distance connections through the landscape. This wider context was sometimes accessible through the survival of extant earthworks, but otherwise contextual analysis was constrained by the limits of excavation. It is this wider dimension that has been opened up to archaeologists in the past twenty years through the more extensive and even trans-landscape scale of modern development, and which may be illustrated by some selective regional reviews.

An obvious question arises where two apparently distinctive types of roundhouse, those associated with ring-ditches and those primarily identified through post-rings, for example, occur on the same site, as at Dryburn Bridge or Culduthel. Plainly they need not both have been in contemporary occupation, but, even if they represent successive episodes of occupation, we would still have to account for the difference. Houses with integral ring-ditches have been widely regarded as byre-houses, in which the ground floor with ring-ditch was for stalling cattle or livestock generally, with residential quarters on an upper floor. A simpler solution might explain the larger buildings with ring-ditch as byre-barns, with storage above and stock below. The size of building is hardly out of proportion, given that the byre-barn is generally larger than the family residence on most farms from medieval to modern times. Post-ring houses would thus be primarily residential, equally in some cases involving two floor levels. In general, however, for Iron Age roundhouses, the integration of byre-house or barn-house may seem more appropriate. In the case of Culduthel, of course, a major issue is the evidence for metalworking, and the question whether this was secondary to a

---

Rethinking Roundhouses: Later Prehistoric Settlement in Britain and Beyond. D. W. Harding, Oxford University Press.
© D. W. Harding 2023. DOI: 10.1093/oso/9780192893802.003.0005

114 RETHINKING ROUNDHOUSES

residential phase of use, or whether these substantial buildings were custom-built workshops, which has been addressed earlier.

The Thames Valley

The middle Thames Valley is characterized by settlements along the gravel terraces of the Thames and its tributaries that were not obviously enclosed by earthworks, though they could have been demarcated by hedgerows and more superficial fenced boundaries. Gravelly Guy at Stanton Harcourt (Fig. 5.1; Lambrick and Allen, 2004) was unenclosed in the sense of having no continuous enclosure ditch, but was nevertheless ordered in its spatial layout into a series of settlement units or 'blocks' of broadly comparable size and composition that the excavators interpreted as being occupied by individual, though probably related, households. Demarcation between the blocks was sometimes not easily distinguished, and might be indicated by the alignment of pits along a fence-line that had not survived archaeologically. Overall, the north-eastern and south-western limits of the Iron Age settlement were reasonably clearly defined, though the extant remains represented a palimpsest of occupation spanning some five or six hundred years, so that, of the apparent density of pits, more than 900 in total, only a limited number would have been in use at any one time. Whilst each household cluster may have had a particular role in terms of craft activities, in general they appear to have shared common functions, with no real evidence of any distinction between them in terms of social status.

The excavators of Gravelly Guy offered a provisional structural sequence, based on stratigraphic or spatial relationships where available, but otherwise using associated ceramic groups, acknowledging inherent difficulties in dating and local variability, which meant that alternative models might be advanced in detail (Lambrick and Allen, 2004: Figs 3.19 and 3.20). For our present purposes, however, it is worth noting that the double-ringed roundhouses, C and L, for instance, are assigned to the earlier Iron Age, as are the ring-groove roundhouses (E1–4, T, R, and Z), all of which are relatively slight and surely more probably wall-slots than drip-gullies. In contrast, the larger ring-gully enclosures apparently belong to the Middle Iron Age occupation. The houses within these ring-gullies are generally only positively identified from their larger door posts, suggesting that their construction was somewhat different from the earlier houses.

Whilst reports like those on Gravelly Guy and Yarnton still represent the best achievement in modern rescue archaeology, the scale of modern development-led excavation has been transformed by major infrastructure projects. Between 1999 and 2007, for example, Oxford Archaeology and Wessex Archaeology in collaboration salvaged the multi-period evidence from more than seventy hectares of land in advance of the construction of Terminal 5 at Heathrow

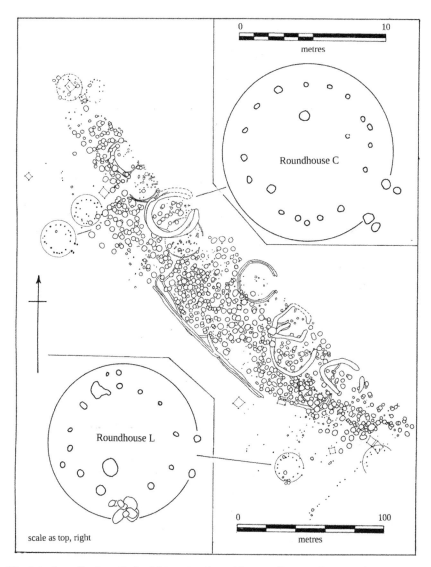

Fig. 5.1 Gravelly Guy, Oxfordshire, site plan with roundhouses. Drawing by D. W. Harding, adapted from Lambrick and Allen, 2004.

(Lewis et al., 2006, 2010). Perhaps surprisingly the area did not reveal the same density of occupation that elsewhere has complicated the process of unravelling the sequence of habitation, though severe truncation had doubtless destroyed all trace of structures with relatively shallow foundations. In fact, though the dominant landscape pattern of fields and trackways appears to have been established by the earlier Bronze Age, relatively little by way of structural evidence survived before the Middle Iron Age, around 400 BC, when the evidence takes the form principally of more than thirty penannular enclosures, several small rectilinear enclosures, several waterholes, a couple of four-poster structures, and a couple of pit clusters, one of which was interpreted as quarries for daubing clay, the other as rubbish pits. The settlement was unenclosed and structures quite widely spaced, with little evidence for grouping into social or economic units, but appeared nevertheless to respect the still extant Bronze Age trackway to the east and a field boundary to the south. Only at a relatively late stage of the Middle Iron Age was a ditched enclosure established on the south side, the earthworks of which were hardly of defensive proportions and more probably designed to contain or exclude livestock.

The penannular gullies were identified as houses or non-domestic enclosures on the simple basis of whether or not any other structural components, such as possible door posts or roof-supporting postholes were traced within the enclosure. The gullies themselves were thought to be for drainage rather than wall-trenches, so that the roundhouses that stood within them would have been smaller in diameter than the ring-gullies. This was essentially the same conclusion that Grimes had reached during his wartime rescue excavations of the site of Caesar's Camp, on the other side of the airport to the east (Grimes and Close-Brooks, 1993). If a roof with overhanging eaves was based on a low external mass wall founded on upcast from the drainage gully on its inner lip, then the diameter of the house might still have exceeded ten metres in several instances. In only one instance, Roundhouse 10 (Fig. 5.2, 1), in an area of relatively less truncation, did a credible internal post-ring survive, forming a circle nine metres in diameter, with two posts that might have framed a doorway located facing a gap in the drip-gully on its south-east side. If these constituted the weight-bearing circle of a double-ring roundhouse built on the standard ratio of 3:4, then the outer mass wall could just have been accommodated on the inner lip of the penannular gully. Within penannular gully 14 (Fig. 5.2, 2) a pair of postholes facing south-east almost certainly marked the roundhouse entrance, whilst three paired settings might have marked internal radial partitions. One other structure of interest was penannular gully 9, nine metres in diameter, within which a two metre square setting of four posts was located centrally and aligned towards a south-eastern gap in the gully (Fig. 3.13, 3). Notwithstanding its smaller overall size overall, the proportions of this structure are similar to those residential roundhouses in which an integral central setting could have been the basis of an upper floor level. One pair of penannular gullies, 19 and 26 (Fig. 6.4, 4), could have been a contemporary pair, either a dwelling with working annexe, as suggested by the excavators, or a genuine figure-of-eight building, as exemplified elsewhere.

The economy of the Heathrow Terminal 5 settlement was evidently dependent in significant measure on stock raising, with limited evidence for cereal or arable cultivation or processing. Because of adverse conditions of preservation, the faunal assemblage was generally poor (equally limiting the potential for

ROUNDHOUSES IN CONTEXT: SETTLEMENTS AND LANDSCAPE 117

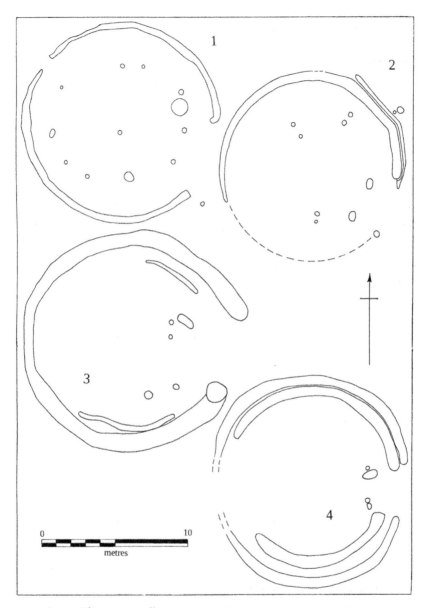

Fig. 5.2 Lower Thames roundhouses. 1, Heathrow Terminal 5, Roundhouse 10; 2, Heathrow Terminal 5, Roundhouse 14; 3, Ashford Prison, circular structure 4; 4, Ashford Prison, circular structure 3. Drawings by D. W. Harding, adapted from Lewis et al., 2010 and Carew et al., 2006.

118   RETHINKING ROUNDHOUSES

radiocarbon dating), apart from that recovered from waterholes. The evidence for cereal production was even more sparse, just a very few charred grains and a single quern fragment. Structurally the environment was unsuitable for pit storage, and the few four-post structures could have served a variety of purposes. In the late pre-Roman Iron Age and into the early Roman period there was a more fundamental reorganization of the landscape, though not necessarily as a single episode rather than cumulatively. This is most apparent in the reorientation and redesigning of the fields to the east of the Middle Iron Age settlement, but also in the creation of several new earthworks, irregular and curvilinear in layout, over the northern half of the former settlement, and bounded on the north by several linear dykes (Lewis et al., 2010: Fig. 4.3). On the floodplain to the west the older Bronze Age system was unaffected, its much degraded outline perhaps still visible in an area of summer pasture. In sum, the early Roman period saw a reversion to arable cultivation that had dominated in the Middle Bronze Age, perhaps encouraged by improvements in crop husbandry practices such as more effective drainage and manuring. Radical realignment of the landscape layout is not unknown or surprising in the lower Thames in the late Iron Age and early Roman period, and here occupation appears to have continued into the third or fourth century. The focus of settlement evidently remained within the area of the Iron Age occupation, and the several rectilinear buildings or fragmentary remains of buildings were unsophisticated architecturally, being essentially timber-framed, based on wall trenches, and presumably with timber or cob walls. There was no indication of any structures of a more pretentious design or construction.

The basic landscape pattern of field enclosures at Ashford Prison (Carew et al., 2006), three miles south of Heathrow, was likewise laid out in the Mid-Late Bronze Age, but this time seemingly with reference to an earlier ring-ditch of late Neolithic date. Again after an apparent hiatus in the later Bronze Age and earlier Iron Age, an open settlement comprising ring-gullies, some four-post structures, and a few pit groups clustered around an area where the Neolithic ring-ditch must still have been extant, since successive Iron Age buildings respected its location. As at Heathrow, the ring-gullies are regarded as defining the sites of roundhouses, which in the case of Circular Structure 3 comprised two concentric ring-gullies (Fig. 5.2, 4). There was no evidence that the inner arcs constituted wall foundations, though this possibility should not be discounted. Their apparent termination on the west side supports the possible existence of a second entrance, though there was no evidence for a second pair of door posts. The two lengths of gully within Circular Structure 4, on the other hand, presumably were traces of house walls (Fig. 5.2, 3). The darker upper filling with profuse quantities of burnt daub in Circular Structure 6, the smaller of a figure-of-eight pair (Fig. 6.4, 3), is surely indicative of a timber wall, as is 'the high proportion of burnt material, including daub' (Carew et al., 2006: 51), in the filling of Circular Structure 8.

The Iron Age farmers may have reused or modified the old Bronze Age field system in practising an economy based on animal husbandry, perhaps even on a seasonal basis. The Iron Age occupation at Ashford, however, did not extend into the Roman period, as it did in the neighbouring settlement at Hengrove Farm (Poulton et al., 2017), though both sites were subject to the imposition of a new and extensive system of fields, linear ditches, and enclosures, doubtless designed to improve drainage and enhance the potential for arable cultivation. Even this system, however, at Ashford, enclosed the Neolithic ring-ditch rather than obliterating it, suggesting continuing veneration of a traditional monument in the landscape.

At the opposite end of the Thames Valley, at Horcott Quarry near Fairford in Gloucestershire (Fig. 5.3; Hayden et al., 2017), roundhouses are abundantly represented, not by ring-gullies, but by post settings. The earlier Iron Age settlement occupied nearly 3 ha within the excavated area, and though not obviously enclosed by any perimeter works, its boundaries were very clear on its longer east and west flanks. The principal buildings were post-built roundhouses, of which there were at least a dozen, and possibly twice that number, and no less than 135 four-post structures, a greater number than has been recovered on any site in the Thames Valley. Uncertainty regarding the number of houses stems not so much from erosion issues as the density of postholes recorded, from which determining those that belonged together as an integral structure was not always straightforward. The excavators' reading of what constituted roundhouses might be contested in some cases, but the principal roundhouses and concentration of houses are reasonably clear. Post-ring diameters ranged from five to eleven metres, but seven was a representative norm. Identification was in some cases made more convincing by the larger size of postholes demarcating an entrance with porch or vestibule, from which one might also infer an outer wall line of lesser stakes that has not survived archaeologically.

The four-posters were grouped in several clusters in and around the roundhouses, not necessarily on the same group alignment. They did not appear to be related to individual houses, and were presumably therefore a common resource of the community in occupation at any given time. Broadly speaking, the houses with their south-east facing entrances were aligned on a north-east to south-west axis overlooking the former palaeochannel, with the four-posters behind them. Though there is very little evidence of structures intersecting, the assumption must be that the observed pattern represents cumulative occupation, perhaps over several centuries, rather than a single large village.

Dating of the settlement was based principally on the evidence of pottery, which included fine decorated wares akin to those represented at All Cannings Cross and Longbridge Deverill in Wiltshire, indicating occupation in the latest Bronze Age to earliest Iron Age. In the south-east corner of the excavated area there was evidence of later occupation in the Middle Iron Age, in the form of

Fig. 5.3 Horcott Quarry, Fairford, Gloucestershire, settlement plan. Drawing by D. W. Harding, adapted from Hayden et al., 2017.

ditched enclosures, a pair of pits, and possibly an arc of ring-gully, of the kind that characterized Middle Iron Age settlements elsewhere on the gravel terraces of the Thames Valley.

Debate regarding the social, political, and economic role of the Early Iron Age settlement at Horcott Quarry centres on the disproportionately large storage capacity relative to roundhouses. Assuming the conventionally accepted role of four-posters as upstanding granaries, or at least storage for arable produce, the Horcott four-posters could manifestly store far more than could conceivably be required by the resident community. Had the site been a hillfort, this would have prompted interpretation as communal storage for redistribution to a wider population. The problem with this is that the site otherwise shows no indication of being of high status in terms of either monumental enclosure or material wealth. This need not preclude exchange of surplus produce with other communities, but there is no evidence of exotic imports or of what goods might have been received in exchange.

The progression from open, dispersed occupation in the Early Iron Age to enclosed settlement in the Middle Iron Age at Horcott Quarry is matched within three miles at Horcott Pit (Lamdin-Whymark et al., 2009). Here the transitional latest Bronze Age to earliest Iron Age occupation is attested by pottery with linear, chevron, or impressed circlet ornament, some filled with white inlay, found within the postholes or pits of four or five dispersed roundhouses. With post-rings around six or seven metres in diameter, and with south-east facing entrances, these were similar to those from Horcott Quarry, with one notable difference, that their plans were much more symmetrical, conforming more closely to the principles of axial symmetry. Why this should be is a puzzle, but the purpose of strict symmetry must in part at least be to ensure maximum structural efficiency of the roof, so that we might question whether some of the more irregular plans at Horcott Quarry were from unroofed structures, or from internal fittings of houses with alternative means of roof support. Any reduction of the number of houses at Horcott Quarry, of course, would only exacerbate the imbalance between houses and granaries, unless some of the rectilinear post settings in fact were houses, as, for example in the earliest Iron Age phase at Crickley Hill, fifteen miles to the north-west. In the subsequent phase of Middle Iron Age settlement in the north-east of the Horcott Pit site, from the limited area exposed it would appear that houses were again typically demarcated by ring-gullies, with pits and some four posters assigned to the western side of the ditched enclosure.

Five miles south-west of Horcott, the earliest Iron Age occupation of Latton Lands (Powell et al., 2009) was also represented by a number of post-ring roundhouses of regular, symmetrical plan, apparently widely dispersed and unenclosed, though there may be some evidence of land division at this stage. Once again, however, ditched enclosure, field boundaries and ring-gullies demarcating roundhouses appears to have become the norm by the Middle Iron Age. During the final pre-Roman phase the layout of the central area at Latton Lands was disrupted by the construction of a rectilinear enclosure, the purpose of which is unclear, since no structures were detected within it. Its importance nevertheless is suggested by its proximity to the main entrance through the Middle Iron Age north–south linear boundary, which itself was enhanced at this time, and by the series of human burials that were subsequently inserted into its partially-silted ditch (Harding, 2016, 108–11 and Fig. 4.7). As noted elsewhere in the region, this may have been associated with an increase in pastoral activity and a reorganization of the agricultural landscape.

122 RETHINKING ROUNDHOUSES

The scale of the database of later prehistoric settlement in the Thames Valley has been totally transformed by the advent of developer-funded excavation. Salvage excavation had certainly taken place on gravel quarry sites since the 1930s, notably by E. T. Leeds and the Ashmolean Museum, but the increase in data since the 1970s (Harding, 1972) has been exponential, and has led to numerous ground-breaking publications by Oxford Archaeology, notably in its *Thames Valley Landscapes Monograph Series*. Drawing on this accumulated research, the excavators of Horcott Quarry suggested that four-posters in general were more common in the Late Bronze Age and Early Iron Age, whereas pit-storage appeared to be the norm in the Middle Iron Age. Accordingly, the overall capacity for cereal storage was no greater at Horcott Quarry than it was at Gravelly Guy or Yarnton. Plainly such an inference should not be regarded as an invariable rule, since other factors, such as geological environment, will have played an important role locally. Equally, it appeared that post-ring roundhouses were more common in the Late Bronze Age and Early Iron Age, whereas the ring-gully was especially characteristic in the region in the Middle Iron Age. The fact that structural evidence in the form of postholes of any kind, let alone groups forming a coherent plan, are seldom recovered from Middle Iron Age sites in the Thames Valley necessarily leaves a question mark over the function of ring-gullies. But, as we have seen, it need not follow that all post-ring structures, however well defined, constituted domestic dwellings.

The English Midlands

Excavation in the Midlands over a number of years has demonstrated the existence of sizeable Iron Age settlements, larger than the familiar homestead farming unit, whether enclosed or unenclosed, though the palimpsest of structures clearly indicates cumulative occupation over a protracted period of time. For these sites the term 'aggregated settlements' has been adopted, two of the key sites being those investigated in advance of commercial and civic development on the clay lands just north of Leicester at Beaumont Leys and Humberstone (Thomas, 2011). Both sites began with open settlements in the earlier Middle Iron Age, with conjoined ditched compounds appearing at Humberstone in the later pre-Roman Iron Age. Particularly characteristic of the Midlands, however, is the fact that ring-gullies or ring-trenches around house stances do not appear to have been generally adopted until the Middle Iron Age, when evidence for the house foundations themselves becomes minimal. Of the nine roundhouses from the earlier occupation at Beaumont Leys, for example, only one (Roundhouse 13) was defined solely by a deeper drainage ring-gully. The remainder appear to have had walls founded in ring-grooves or post-rings, or in the case of Roundhouse 9, a combination of the two on the same circumference. In Roundhouse 15 the short lengths of ring-groove emanated from a pair of inner porch-posts of a round-house some 11.5 metres in diameter, though regrettably the published report did not include a plan of any of these houses at a usable scale. At Manor Farm, Humberstone, ring-groove foundations survived into the first phase of enclosure in Roundhouse 1, where an outer ring-gully, 13.5 metres in diameter, and inter-preted as an eavesdrip, was almost concentric with the ring-groove within. The deep and narrow wall-slot contrasted with the outer gully, which had a wider, shallower profile that would surely have compromised any effective purpose, structural or drainage. The only other significant feature, the central hearth, nevertheless endorses a primarily domestic usage of the structure. The Humberstone roundhouses, including those from Elms Farm (Charles et al., 2000), were generally signalled by their proxy ring-trenches, with the threshold posts from the house doorways generally the only surviving traces of the houses themselves.

Covert Farm, Crick is in north-western Northamptonshire, just east of Rugby and the Warwickshire border. The extensive Iron Age settlement was exposed by the development of the Daventry International Rail Freight Terminal (DIRFT) which stripped some sixteen hectares in the vicinity of Covert Farm (Hughes and Woodward, 2015). Evidence for roundhouses and related structures almost exclu-sively consisted of ring-gullies that the excavators believed on the basis of their silty fillings not to have supported posts or walls of the houses, but to have enclosed buildings of which only occasional postholes relating to their doorways generally survived. Exceptionally an inner ring-groove most probably did repre-sent the wall of the house, notably in the case of ring-gully 58, where the presence of stake-holes and a somewhat polygonal outline might indicate the use of sill-beams or prefabricated wattle panels. Ring-gully 58 (Fig. 3.10, 3) was unusual in having a partial post-ring between the ring-gully and the structural ring-groove that could indeed have provided roof support, as the excavators believed, but which alternatively could indicate a double-wall with cavity insulation, as dis-cussed earlier. The excavators also raised doubts regarding the efficacy of ring-gullies for drainage on clay or alluvium over gravel at Covert Farm, since they would simply fill with standing water, suggesting instead that their purpose was symbolic, defining the private space of the occupants. The fact that they were evi-dently maintained and regularly recut, however, still perhaps favours a practical function.

The principal contribution of the Covert Farm excavation was recognition of the fact that the palimpsest of more than a hundred agglomerated ring-gullies and ditched enclosures, spanning the second half of the first millennium BC and into the Roman period, could be resolved into clusters, even from the earlier Iron Age, when the site distribution was more dispersed. In the earlier Middle Iron Age the clusters were not so clearly defined, but there were at least two instances in which a larger and smaller ring-gully in close proximity suggested a deliberate

124 RETHINKING ROUNDHOUSES

pairing (Fig. 5.4, Period 3.2). By the later Middle Iron Age the clusters had been reinforced by ditches linking the ring-gullies to create 'modular units' of four or five ring-gullies, with irregular compounds being created between them (Fig. 5.4, Period 4.2). The width and depth of gullies was generally greater than hitherto, and the overall number of elements had reached a peak in the sequence. The excavators commendably attempted to inform the function of various elements within the modular units by plotting the distribution of finds, an exercise that showed that the ring-gully terminals and the sector at the back of the putative house stance were favoured locations for material deposition. The problem, of course, was, first of all, that the material assemblage was limited to pottery sherds, animal bone, and charcoal and related residues, which were not particularly informative. Second, the contexts themselves are only arguably related to occupational activity within the ring-groove. Some may have been incorporated into the ring-grooves or ditches from nearby middens or working areas. And the very fact that material in the ring-gullies would inhibit any drainage purpose suggests that these might have been closure deposits, or relate to activity after the buildings themselves had been abandoned.

The second volume of the DIRFT reports (Masefield et al., 2015) presented the results of four more excavations in the development area, including a further 140 ring-gully structures. The essential unit of these 'aggregated' settlements remains the cluster of structures, predominantly defined by their enclosing ring-gullies, and either loosely grouped or actually enclosed by a generally rectilinear ditched compound. For the site at the Lodge, however, Chapman proposed an alternative interpretation (Fig. 5.5) to the prevailing view that these clusters or modules represented the houses and working areas of extended family units. The closely-spaced clusters aligned down the hill slope each displayed distinctive differences in plan, suggesting that they may have served somewhat different roles for a single community (Chapman 2015b: 114). Cluster 2, which contained the two largest ring-gullies in the series, may have been the residential core of the settlement, with ring-gully 3 surrounding the one roundhouse of which porch-posts and a short length of wall foundation groove survived, of a building that would have been at least eleven metres in diameter. Though subsequent to ring-gully 4, the latter may have been retained in use to create a pair of roundhouses, for which the excavator suggested complementary social uses rather than joint tenure of related family groups. The multiple recutting of ring-gullies implied longevity of use, and the excavator believed that the house within ring-gully 3 could have been in use for 200–250 years. Whether occupation was continuous, intermittent, or even seasonal, of course, may be another matter. In Cluster 3 ring-gullies 18 and 14 could have begun as house stances, but the later recutting of ring-gully 18 constrained the available space for a substantial structure, as did ring-gully 14. The only clue to the cluster's possible function was a quantity of cereal processing debris in the latter's terminal, suggesting the possibility that the cluster was

ROUNDHOUSES IN CONTEXT: SETTLEMENTS AND LANDSCAPE 125

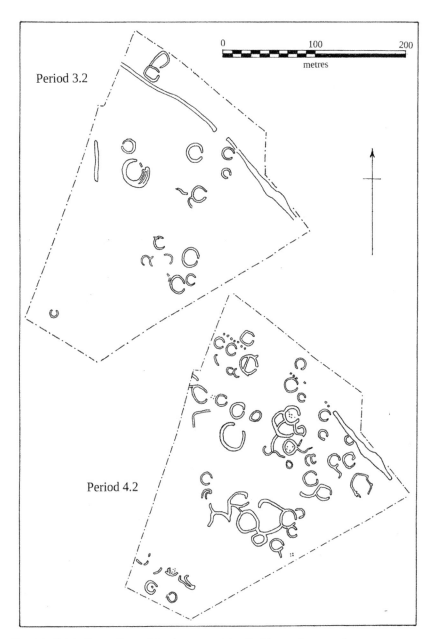

Fig. 5.4 Crick Covert Farm, Northamptonshire, Field 2 settlement, cluster development. Drawings by D. W. Harding, adapted from Hughes and Woodward, 2015.

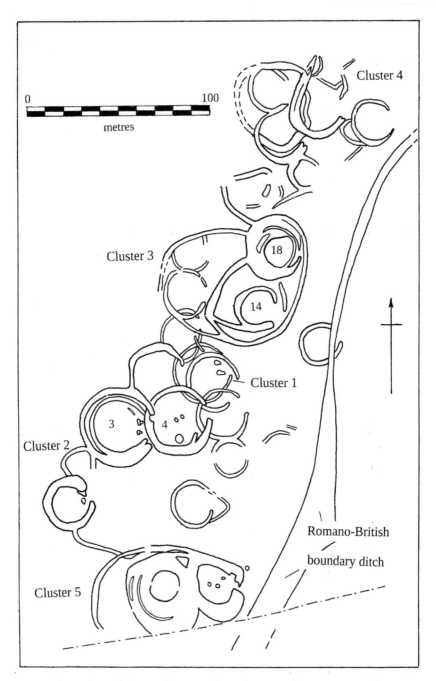

Fig. 5.5 The Lodge, Kilsby, Northamptonshire, cluster settlement. Drawing by D. W. Harding, adapted from Masefield et al., 2015.

dedicated to grain processing and storage. Cluster 4 evidently never had more than one small roundhouse, but did yield the bulk of animal bone, especially from its late phase of usage, so that it may have served for activities related to the site's primarily pastoral economy. In reviewing the functional options of aggregated settlements, it is of course possible that use of the clusters changed over time, perhaps with increasing specialization of dedicated areas.

The clusters or modules of aggregated settlements evidently include unenclosed and enclosed variants. Though there appears to be a trend towards enclosure through the Middle Iron Age, with sub-rectangular compounds like Enclosure 1 at Long Dole in the DIRFT complex (Chapman, 2015a) appearing to emphasize the notion of separate identity within a community, there is an obvious cohesion in the overall landscape layout. The gravel ridge to the south of the settlement at Nortoft Lane, Kilsby, was most probably dedicated to arable cultivation, together with the higher ground north-east of Covert Farm, Crick. The stream valley between the two doubtless afforded good pasture land, the settlements themselves providing a measure of separation between the two. To the north land-use division was reinforced by linear earthwork, with summer pastures perhaps provided by the floodplain beyond, and winter pasture on the hillside east of the Lodge (Masefield et al., 2015: Fig. 6.5). Whether the whole construct warrants the term 'village', dispersed, poly-focal, or nucleated is a matter of debate. The important contribution of the DIRFT programme is that it has shown that aggregated settlements are structured, and not just an unstructured spread.

Many of the issues highlighted by the DIRFT programme were also prominent at Coton Park, Rugby, some five miles to the north-west over the Warwickshire border (Chapman, 2020). Though the catalyst for salvage excavation was residential and commercial development, the real cause of severe truncation to the archaeological remains were the furrows of medieval cultivation (Chapman, 2020: Fig. 1.3, Fig. 1.4). The consequence is that the presence of houses is in general only attested by proxy of their enclosing ring-gullies, which, as the excavator rightly stressed, are too often casually confused with the putative houses themselves. At Coton Park the best-preserved roundhouses were the pair within the principal roundhouse Group 2, located within ring-ditch 5 and ring-ditch 6, where the east-facing door posts and some short lengths of wall slot survived. The roundhouse within ring-ditch 6 also had an outer circle of posts, of which an arc around the northern perimeter showed their spacing to be around 1.5 metres, which the excavator suggested may have supported the main house rafters, presumably over a rigid ring-beam structure. Their siting, 0.8 metres beyond the wall-slot, is comparable to the arrangement at Covert Farm, Crick, Structure RG58 (Fig. 3.10, 3), and could again indicate an insulated cavity double-wall. Finally, the Group 1 structures at Coton Park, comprising three ring-ditch compounds and a sub-rectangular enclosure, somewhat detached spatially from the

128   RETHINKING ROUNDHOUSES

rest of the settlement, were evidently dedicated to industrial or craft activities, namely copper alloy working and the working of bone, antler, and horn.

West Yorkshire

Development-led archaeology has not only intensified the database in regions that had already been well researched, it has also had an impact on areas where hitherto information regarding Iron Age settlement was much more limited. Until the turn of the millennium, the Iron Age in Yorkshire was represented overwhelmingly by the 'Arras' culture cemeteries of the Wolds, with much less known about the settlement archaeology of the region, especially of the Vale of York and west Yorkshire. A major constraint on Iron Age studies north of the Trent had always been the virtual absence of pottery until the latest pre-Roman period, limiting prospects of dating settlements before the wider application of radiocarbon dating. Nevertheless the scale of progress can be measured by comparing the state of knowledge at the time of Aidan Challis' doctoral studies (Challis and Harding, 1975) and the more recent doctoral research of Adrian Chadwick (2010). A notable achievement in settlement excavation was the excavation at Dalton Parlours (Fig. 5.6; Wrathmell and Nicholson, 1990), where a succession of Iron Age settlements continued to be occupied into the Roman period, culminating in a villa estate. Occupation dates from the second half of the first millennium BC, the earliest sub-rectangular enclosure being progressively enlarged by the addition of further irregular compounds, within which essentially were single houses or successive houses. One, House 5, was substantially larger than the others, and may have been the earliest, since the first enclosure appears to divert around it, presumably indicating that it was still in use. It comprised a ring-groove, taken in this case by the excavators to be a wall footing, 17 metres in diameter. Postholes of an inner, weight-bearing circle survived some 2.5 metres within this line around the northern sector of the house. The remainder of the houses likewise were based on ring-groove foundations, some with surviving postholes too, but all with diameters in the range 9 to 11 metres. This scale difference might suggest that Roundhouse 5 had originated as an unenclosed building, and that the shift to ditched enclosures represented a change in the social order.

At the time of publication of *IAR*, the presence at Dalton Parlours of several roundhouses with more than one entrance was regarded as exceptional, where now, as we have seen, this feature is not restricted to northern England. Equally significant perhaps are the Dalton Parlours roundhouses 1, 2 (Fig. 3.13, 1), and 3 (Fig. 3.11, 6) with central settings of four posts, less easily dismissed as coincidental four-post granaries on a site where such structures are hardly otherwise represented. Among the more significant features of the Dalton Parlours roundhouses, however, are the close concentric settings of post-rings immediately outside the ring-grooves in Houses 1, 3 (Fig. 3.11, 6), and 8, which the excavator was inclined

ROUNDHOUSES IN CONTEXT: SETTLEMENTS AND LANDSCAPE 129

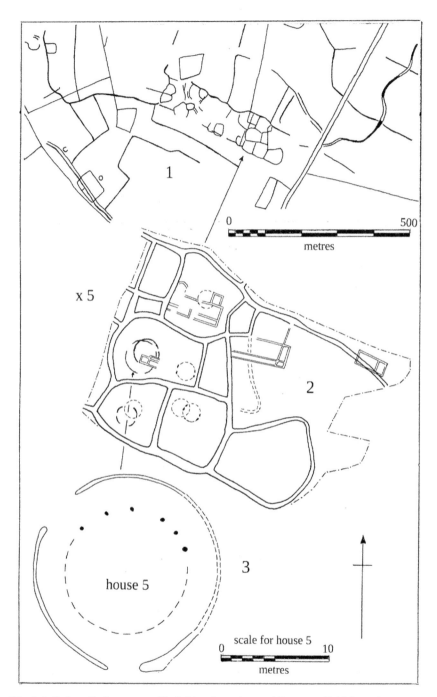

Fig. 5.6 Dalton Parlours, west Yorkshire, Iron Age and Romano-British settlement. 1, landscape reconstructed from air photography; 2, excavated settlement; 3, Roundhouse 5. Drawings by D. W. Harding, adapted from Wrathmell and Nicholson, 1990.

130 RETHINKING ROUNDHOUSES

to interpret as reinforcement for the rotting foundations of the house walls (Wrathmell and Nicholson, 1990: 279). A complete rebuild does not normally entail an increased diameter, but a similar footprint marginally offset. In retrospect, in the light of accumulating evidence from elsewhere, we might see this instead as evidence for cavity walling, the inner comprising planks, the outer hurdling, with insulating material between.

Just a mile to the north the settlement at Wattle Syke (Roberts and Richardson, 2013) shares several of the characteristics of Dalton Parlours. Exposed by the A1 upgrade scheme, with its attendant feeder route developments, the parallel linear spreads of enclosures north and south of the Wattle Dyke stream had been identified by cropmark and geophysical survey. They are described as aggregated and incremental enclosure complexes, cognate to the 'ladder settlements' of eastern Yorkshire. The northern group of 'washing line' enclosures (Fig. 5.7) continued to expand from the later pre-Roman Iron Age through into the Roman period, including the continued use of roundhouses, as late as the second or early third centuries. Unlike Dalton Parlours, however, the inhabitants of Wattle Syke never adopted Romanized masonry building practices. Most of the roundhouses at Wattle Syke occupy the ditched enclosures, generally not more than two or three per enclosure, and these not necessarily in contemporary occupation. Two roundhouses, 6 and 7, apparently occupied an area between enclosures that was open in the later pre-Roman Iron Age, though they evidently continued in use in the Roman period. Roundhouse 6 may in fact have served a special purpose in view of the presence of several burials, both animal and human, of pre-Roman Iron Age date within or cutting its footprint. Another unusual aspect of the Wattle Syke houses is the predominance of large roundhouses with diameters in the order of 13–14 metres. That their defining ring-gullies were indeed wall trenches rather than drainage gullies is demonstrated in the case of Roundhouse 3 by the presence of postholes at intervals extending away from its south-west facing doorway within the limited area of its circuit that was exposed by excavation. The ring-gully of Roundhouse 1 included post settings around its inner edge, which might indicate some structural alteration. But the apparently conflicting sections across ring-gully and postholes of course might reflect the process of dismantling the house rather than its construction, but the scalloped effect in plan certainly would be consistent with a split timber plank wall. The roundhouse may have had a doorway on the south-east, but a pair of larger posts on the north-eastern perimeter gully could indicate a secondary, opposed doorway. It is regrettable that this interesting structure was only partially within the excavated area, since a pair of substantial pits within its circuit were plausibly interpreted by the excavators as half of a four-post setting, which would broadly have been aligned on the doorways.

ROUNDHOUSES IN CONTEXT: SETTLEMENTS AND LANDSCAPE 131

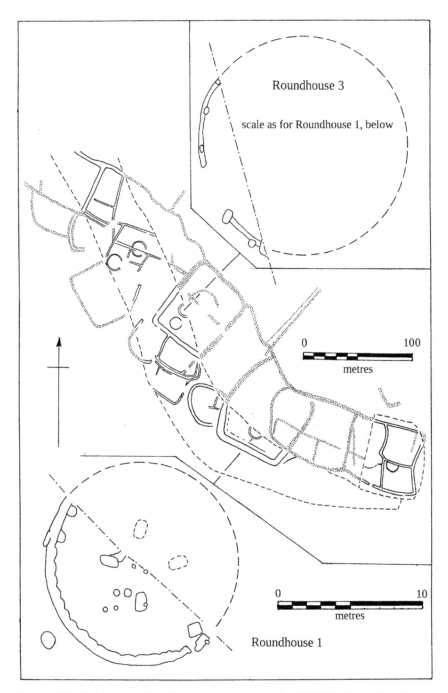

Fig. 5.7 Wattle Syke, west Yorkshire, Area 1. Drawing by D. W. Harding, adapted from Martin et al., 2013.

132 RETHINKING ROUNDHOUSES

Four-poster granaries are not in evidence at Wattle Syke, where the quantities of animal bone plainly indicate the primacy of animal husbandry in the economy. The discovery of four-posters at nearby Micklefield, also exposed by excavations on the line of the A1, and the recognition of pit clusters by air photography at Ledston, among other more recent finds, has nevertheless led to a radical review of the older conventional view of northern England as predominantly pastoral in its economy. The presence of querns at Wattle Syke, of course, may only confirm cereal processing, and not necessarily cereal cultivation, but some deposits of cereal grains, including a significant, possibly votive deposit of barley in a pit by Roundhouse 6, may indicate that cereal cultivation was an element in the local economy even before the Roman period. The layout of the Wattle Syke settlement is plainly suitable for marshalling large numbers of livestock, and though there may have been a significant shift to cereal cultivation under the Roman occupation the Wattle Syke community evidently retained its native character throughout.

The practice of arable cultivation, as we have indicated, was testified more plainly in the later pre-Roman Iron Age settlement at Site M, Micklefield (Fig. 5.8; Brown et al., 2007), in an area of extensive landscape organization, including agglomerated enclosures akin to Wattle Syke, droveways and field enclosures, and the Ledston complex less than two miles to the south-west. The settlement comprised a linear spread of pits and four-posters on a north-west to south-east alignment, bounded on the west by a substantial linear ditch from which further ditches defined arable fields or enclosures. At the north-western and south-eastern ends were single unenclosed roundhouses, though the limits of the settlement were not located within the area exposed, and could therefore have been more extensive. The south-eastern roundhouse was represented by an outer ring-gully, 16 metres in diameter, presumed to be a drainage gully, and an inner ring-groove, 11 metres in maximum diameter, within which several residual stakes indicated that this had been a wall foundation. In fact, the ring-groove was decidedly polygonal on its south-west sector, perhaps suggesting that it held prefabricated hurdle panels. The entrance was presumably on the east, where there was a gap in the outer ring-gully, though the expected matching gap in the ring-groove was obscured by secondary alterations. Several shallow pits within the house could have been from internal fixtures or partitions, but there was no coherent post-ring. Though not strictly enclosed, a short length of fencing divided the house from the main concentration of pits, whilst a noticeable gap between the pits and the north-western roundhouse suggested that a similar feature may have been truncated by machine stripping. The house itself was represented only by two surviving arcs of ring-groove that would have defined an oval structure somewhat smaller than its companion to the south-east. The whole complex had an appearance of ordered layout, without obvious multiple superimposition. The four-posters were located mostly on the north-eastern side of the distribution, with the pits densest adjacent to the linear ditch, which intersected none of them. A posthole

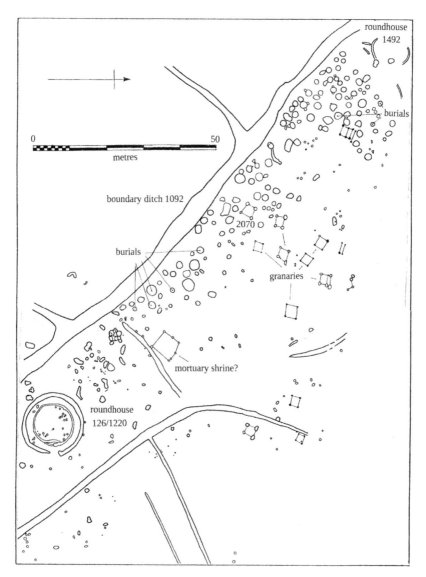

Fig. 5.8 Site M Micklefield, west Yorkshire. Drawing by D. W. Harding, adapted from Brown et al., 2007.

of one four-poster, located among the pits, contained a significant deposit of charred barley and wheat, reinforcing their interpretation as upstanding granaries, from which a date in the second half of the first millennium BC was obtained. The function of the pits, some of which were as deep as their Wessex counterparts, is less clear. Several contained human burials, three near the northern house and five closer to the southern roundhouse, suggesting small inhumation cemeteries of nuclear families.

134 RETHINKING ROUNDHOUSES

The Northumberland Coastal Plain

We have already noted that one of the incidental benefits of development-led archaeology is that the arbitrary selection of sites results in the discovery of settlement remains such as unenclosed occupation that had not registered in the archaeological record. A classic example of this was the ephemeral traces of habitation uncovered on the line of the A1 upgrading through the East Lothian coastal plain (Lelong and MacGregor, 2007), where the recorded database was previously dominated by ditched enclosures, rectilinear or curvilinear, that either survived as extant earthworks or were readily detectable through air photography. Similar conditions had determined the record of Iron Age settlement in the Northumberland coastal plain, where the fieldwork of George Jobey and air photographic survey by Norman McCord in the 1960s and 1970s had established the predominance of sub-rectangular homesteads in the regional settlement pattern of the Iron Age and Romano-British periods. Some of these settlements were characterized by outer and inner ditches, forming a square-within-a-square plan, like those excavated by Jobey at Burradon (1970) and at Hartburn (1973). At Burradon the central house most obviously belonged with the inner enclosure, overlying a succession of earlier, smaller roundhouses. Jobey considered the option that these latter might have belonged to an unenclosed phase of settlement, a possibility that he equally entertained at Hartburn. But on balance he preferred to associate the earlier occupation at Burradon with the outer ditched enclosure, rather than seeing the double-ditched homestead as an entity. Though he further recognized the Early Iron Age dating of the early pottery from Burradon, he also still believed that the later homesteads continued to flourish into the Roman period.

These conclusions were not unreasonable on the basis of the limited areas investigated in conventional research excavations. Only with the advent of large-scale site stripping has it become clear that unenclosed settlement predominated in the earlier Iron Age of the Northumberland coastal plain. Reappraisal was initiated by excavations in advance of surface mining at Blagdon Park north of Newcastle and in advance of residential and commercial development at East and West Brunton on the northern outskirts of the city (Hodgson et al., 2012). In both these settlements unenclosed occupation preceded the rectilinear ditched enclosures, with radiocarbon dates suggesting the open settlements could have flourished from the second quarter of the first millennium BC. Their layout was by no means uniform, however, the substantial Structure 1 of Blagdon Park 1 standing in apparent isolation, in contrast to the dense pattern of some two dozen roundhouses that underlay the later Phase 3 enclosures at Blagdon Park 2. Intersecting profiles of course indicate that these represent a palimpsest of successive occupation, so that no more than half a dozen, and perhaps only two or three, were necessarily in use at any one time. Few of the houses show any evidence of internal post-rings or roof support, so that their identification is based upon the surrounding ring-gully or drainage ditch, which in some cases was quite substantial. Roundhouse 23/29 in the Blagdon Park 2 unenclosed settlement (Fig. 5.9, 2), however, appears to have been founded on two, concentric ring-grooves, that would have supported a house just over ten metres in diameter, with east-facing, porched entrance. The nature of the walling was revealed by Roundhouse O at East Brunton, which had been destroyed by fire, leaving the wall slot filled with baked daub and carbonized wattles.

Whilst there is an undoubted progression towards rectilinear enclosure by the second century BC on the Northumberland coastal plain, the pattern is by no means regionally or even locally uniform. At East Brunton it was clear that there was a succession of rectilinear palisaded enclosures that preceded the later ditched enclosures, but which was overlain by an intermediate unenclosed round-house settlement. The excavators believed that the palisaded enclosures were suc-cessive, rather than unitary or double combinations, and their dating from radiocarbon sampling appeared to centre on the second quarter of the first mil-lennium BC. Plainly some of the roundhouses could have belonged to this phase of activity, though assigning all the circular structures to their respective places in the sequence was not possible. At West Brunton (Fig. 5.9, 1, A) too there was a palisade enclosure with probably contemporary roundhouse located within it. Here again demonstrating the exact sequence in the palimpsest of structural features was problematical, but from the overall layout of the site it is clear in this instance that the palisaded enclosure must have influenced the siting of the later pre-Roman Iron Age ditched enclosure.

These substantial sub-rectangular ditched enclosures were clearly not defen-sive, but may well have been designed for display as well as serving to control access, and movement of cattle. This is certainly suggested by the horn-like outworks of the ring-gully that embraced the central house in Enclosure 1 at East Brunton (Hodgson et al., 2012: Fig. 28). The roundhouse plan itself had been severely truncated by later agricultural furrows, but was apparently defined by an outer ring-groove some 16 metres in diameter. Internally, an incomplete ring of posts could have supported a central tower, whilst an arc of ditch could suggest a similar role as in byre-houses with ring-ditches. At Blagdon Park 2 the late pre-Roman Iron Age enclosure was further subdivided with a pair of paddocks flanking the trackway that led indirectly from the outer entrance to the inner enclosure (Fig. 5.9, 2, B and C), which equally would be consistent with a pastoral economy. Archaeologically, however, the faunal assemblages were very limited, on account of poor preservation in acidic soils, and it may be that more substantial enclosures reflect increasing hierarchy, in which the earthworks are an expression of individual identity, rather than a reflection of economic factors.

From air photography it is apparent that these sites were linked to a wider landscape network, but within the area uncovered by excavation relatively little

136 RETHINKING ROUNDHOUSES

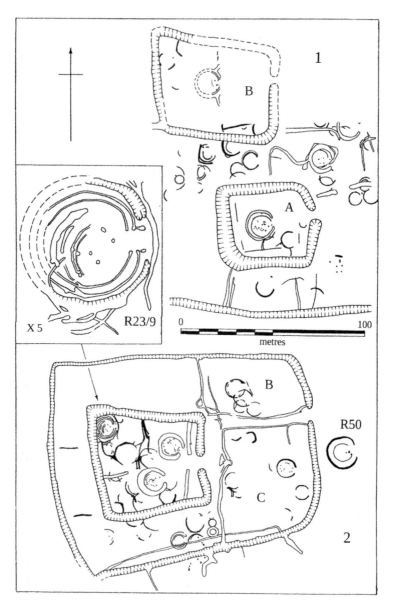

Fig. 5.9 Settlements of the Northumberland coastal plain. 1, West Brunton; 2, Blagdon Park 2. Drawing by D. W. Harding, adapted from Hodgson et al., 2012.

evidence of this could be adduced. The one significant component that was exposed at no less than four of the sites at Blagdon Park, Shotton, and Horton Grange was land division by pit-alignment. Where dated their currency appears to have been in the Late Bronze Age and Early Iron Age, so contemporary with open settlements or settlements within palisaded or slightly-built ditched enclosures. The landscape environs of the later pre-Roman Iron Age settlement was better preserved at Pegswood Moor, north of Morpeth (Proctor, 2009). The Iron Age occupation at Pegswood Moor began with a small, unenclosed settlement around the third quarter of the first millennium BC, but by 200 BC or thereabouts its principal residential focus was a sub-rectangular enclosure in which three roundhouses probably represent successive dwellings of a family unit. Structures 6 and 7 were both represented by ring-grooves that were evidently wall trenches within ring-gullies that served for drainage. Though these two could have been in contemporaneous occupation, the excavator preferred to regard all three as successive, though their diameters, between seven and eight metres, hardly ranks among the grander roundhouses. What makes Pegswood Moor special, however, is the progressive accumulation of enclosures and related features, to which the excavator was able persuasively to assign separate functions within a complex and ordered system (Fig. 5.10). Droveways and sheep races were plausibly argued, together with defined zones for storage, manufacturing, corrals for stock, and even feasting. In the latest pre-Roman phase there was a further reorganization in which the main focus of habitation shifted to a linear spread of roundhouses, again probably cumulative, on the north-western edge of the complex.

The publication of the Blagdon Park and Brunton sites especially represented a significant breakthrough in understanding of the Iron Age and Romano-British sequence of settlements in south-eastern Northumberland, and in particular the context of the substantial rectilinear ditched and double-ditched enclosures of the region. Since then continuing salvage operations in advance of surface quarrying has amplified and supplemented the database still further, including important sites at Brenkley Lane within the environs of the Blagdon estate (Wessel and Wilson, 2015) and at Morley Hill farm, Hazlerigg (Cox and Gaunt, 2018). At Brenkley Lane the principal focus of occupation was a substantial double-ditch rectilinear enclosure set within a complex of other enclosures, trackways, and boundaries that was doubtless cumulative from the late pre-Roman Iron Age. It overlay two surviving arms of a rectilinear palisaded enclosure, the orientation of which suggested a measure of continuity from the earlier Iron Age. Roundhouses were concentrated in a linear alignment not unlike that at Pegswood Moor, though their multiple ring-gullies suggested a density that was doubtless not reflected in the number of houses in occupation at any one time. The Morley Hill Enclosure 1 was unusual in having never been subject to ploughing, so that its reduced earthworks were still extant. It was a double-ditched enclosure with probable central roundhouse, its inner ditch surviving with a low internal bank

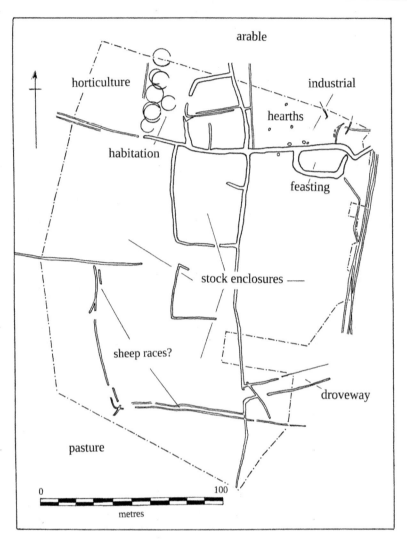

Fig. 5.10 Pegswood Moor, Morpeth, functional interpretation of settlement. Drawing by D. W. Harding, adapted from Proctor, 2009.

and larger counterscarp (Cox and Gaunt, 2018: 3). The fact that it was not built with the emphasis upon an inner bank argues against a primarily defensive purpose, and accounts for excavators on several similar sites having difficulty tracing differential silting of the ditches. Within Morley Hill Enclosure 3 multiple recutting of the gullies around the roundhouses indicates that drainage was a perennial problem, and extensions of these gullies leading into the main enclosure ditch suggest that one purpose of the more substantial enclosure ditches was to lower the ambient water level within the enclosure. The excavators nevertheless were persuaded that the ring-gullies represented wall foundations of houses rather than drip-gullies, though in some cases like Structure 17 within Enclosure 2 the ring-gully was extended from the house entrance away to the surrounding enclosure ditch, presumably to assist drainage. It therefore remains arguable how viable such foundations would have been. The fact that both the larger and smaller pair of houses in Enclosure 2 have a slightly polygonal outline perhaps endorses their interpretation as foundations for timber-panelled walls, though a low mass wall on their inner edge to support timber wall plates would have been a dryer option.

Other important sites in the vicinity will doubtless contribute to refining an understanding of these Northumberland coastal plain settlements, including the palisaded, unenclosed and enclosed sequence at Wideopen, and may yet result in revision of the time-scale of this regionally distinctive series.

Roundhouses in Hillforts

Not all hillforts contain evidence of settlement; in fact some conspicuously do not, even when subject to extensive geophysical survey (Payne et al., 2006). In others, like Hambledon Hill in Dorset or Foel Trigarn in Pembrokeshire (Fig. 5.11, 1) the density of house platforms, even allowing for the fact that they were unlikely all to be in contemporary use, nevertheless must indicate a population of some hundreds. In the Scottish Borders several hundred house platforms had been recognized at Eildon Hill by Christison (1898), and 155 were surveyed by the Royal Commission on the Ancient and Historical Monuments of Scotland (1956) at Hownam Law for the *Inventory* of Roxburghshire. These sites were described as *oppida*, and were seen as tribal centres on the eve of the Roman conquest of southern Scotland. The recognition by excavation (Rideout et al., 1992) that the Eildon house platforms almost certainly dated from the Late Bronze Age therefore came as a radical upset of the conventional interpretation of these sites, though an equally early origin for other hillfort settlements remains undemonstrated. High altitude hillforts like Hownam Law at 450 metres OD and White Meldon at 430 metres, if indeed they were enclosed at this time, were seen as potentially complementary to unenclosed platform settlements and cairnfields of the later second millennium BC, in a reversal of the older conventional view of hillfort development (Halliday, 1985: 238–40). The idea that a warmer climate in the second millennium BC may have favoured settlement at higher levels equally prompted the suggestion that the innumerable hut platforms within the outer enclosure below Tap o' Noth in Aberdeenshire might belong to this same horizon. The demonstration by the Northern Picts Project (Noble, 2020) that the outer wall and settlement at Tap o' Noth date from the early medieval period is a

140 RETHINKING ROUNDHOUSES

Fig. 5.11 Welsh hillforts with roundhouses. 1, Y Foel Trigarn, Pembrokeshire. Image AP2012 3708 Crown Copyright, reproduced with permission of the Royal Commission on the Ancient and Historical Monuments of Wales (RCAHMW) under delegated authority from The Keeper of Public Records; 2, Tre'r Ceiri, Caernarvonshire. Photograph by D. W. Harding.

salutary reminder of the need for reliable dating evidence, but still leaves open the possibility elsewhere of collective settlement of roundhouses within enclosures or on unenclosed hilltops from the later Bronze Age.

At the later end of the chronological scale, dense occupation at Hod Hill in Dorset in the later pre-Roman Iron Age is presumed to have ended abruptly with the storming of the hillfort and the punitive imposition of the Claudian Roman fort within its walls (Richmond, 1968), though there was no evidence for the destruction of the hillfort's gates or burning of its houses. In the case of Tre'r Ceiri in the Lleyn peninsula (Fig. 5.11, 2), on the other hand, the hillfort was reoccupied in the second century AD, when the gateway and defences were renovated (Hopewell, 2018) enclosing more intensive settlement, presumably with the acquiescence of the Roman military authorities. The original later pre-Roman Iron Age settlement, comprising some two dozen large roundhouses with ancillary buildings, had been abandoned for a period, and with reoccupation the roundhouses were subdivided and expanded to create more than 150 smaller units of irregular cellular plan, which surely must imply a significant reorganization of the social structure of domestic living.

In the past twenty years an important development has been the systematic geophysical survey of hillfort interiors, notably in Southern Britain. From one of the earliest of these (Payne et al., 2006) it became apparent that the density of activity within hillforts, as measured at least by geophysics, was extremely variable, and that hillforts of superficially similar layout and enclosure morphology might have quite contrasting presence or absence of interior occupation. It was also apparent that some hillforts registered a good deal of 'noise' but little in the way of coherent structural outlines. Roundhouses are invariably represented by ring-gullies, and very occasionally under optimum conditions by post settings, but without excavation of course it remains unclear whether the gullies mark the outer wall or surrounding drip-trenches. At Oldbury, Wiltshire, the roundhouses appeared to be grouped on either side of a roadway running between the east and west gateways of the hillfort, with pits scattered around. At Castle Ditches, Tisbury, Wiltshire, the palimpsest of roundhouses, pits, and small enclosures made it apparent that the surviving pattern was only a limited glimpse of a complex, multi-period sequence, but surely indicative of intensive occupation rather than temporary, seasonal, or periodic. Even so, the geophysical footprint could still be a very partial reflection of the underlying complexity of features. If ring-gullies around houses and pit storage are features that become more frequent in the Middle Iron Age in Southern Britain, where Early Iron Age settlements were characterized by post-ring houses and four-post granaries, then, depending on local conditions, Early Iron Age occupation may not be so readily detected.

Ring-gullies predominate within the interior of Pilsden Pen, Dorset, one of the hillforts surveyed as part of Bournemouth University's Durotriges Project (Stewart and Russell, 2017). Despite earlier excavation (Gelling, 1977) there remains some doubt as to whether the gullies were themselves wall foundations or drainage gullies around houses of non-earth-fast construction, not least because some of the plans of conjoined structures excavated by Gelling look more like soak-away trenches or windbreaks than actual house walls. The geophysical survey identified some double rings and potential post-rings, so that a combination of features may be involved. Pits, nevertheless, were not conspicuously present, either in excavation or in survey. In total some 50 potential houses were identified, suggesting a more intensive settlement than Gelling had suspected. What is not visible is any roadway through the settlement, though this may have been obscured by reorientation of entrances over the extended period of occupation.

Among more recent geophysical surveys of hillforts that have revealed intensive occupation with roundhouses is Clovelly Dykes in north Devon (Preece and Green, 2020; Preece, 2021). This small hillfort, made grander by no less than four additional widely spaced ramparts, occupies a prominent position at the meeting point of ridgeways with commanding views over Bideford Bay to the north and towards Dartmoor to the south. Total survey of the central compound at Clovelly Dykes, enclosing around one hectare, was undertaken using both resistivity and magnetometry. It revealed a number of ring-gullies, several in excess of 15 metres in diameter, which, without excavation, could have served as either wall foundations or drip-gullies. Ring-gullies of similar size, however, had been located among the outworks to the south, one of which on excavation had proved to be double, incorporating perhaps an inner wall with outer eavesdrip-gully. Several of the houses in the central enclosure appeared to have entrances in their north-east circuits. Just north of centre in the compound was a double rectilinear feature, which was tentatively identified as a Romano-Celtic temple, of which examples are known elsewhere within hillforts in southern England. The outline, however, appears to be slightly extended and trapezoidal, reminiscent of the Iron Age shrine at Hayling Island rather than a later Roman structure, but in either eventuality it plainly implies that Clovelly was an important regional centre in the Iron Age. The outworks were probably cumulative additions, and the excavated external roundhouse, dating to the second half of the first millennium BC, was intersected by the southern sector of one of the outer earthworks, which it evidently therefore pre-dated. The presence of roundhouses outside the central enclosure is clearly crucial to an understanding of the complex, and it must be hoped that there will be an opportunity for further survey in the outer enclosures, and indeed beyond, to establish the full nature of the site's occupation and use. For far too long the study of hillforts was constrained by the limits of their earthworks, and geophysics surely offers the ideal means, non-destructive and relatively economical, to study their role within their *immediate* locality, and the relationship between intra-mural and extra-mural communities.

6

Archaeotectural Alternatives

The term *archaeotectural* is here used, following practice initiated by a younger generation of Spanish archaeologists (Ayán Vila, 2003; Ruano, 2020), to emphasize the importance of assessing data in the context of *ancient* societies, and not on the basis of modern architectural practice, or even early modern vernacular architecture, with insufficient regard to social and cultural constraints of later prehistory. The proponents of archaeotectural approaches focus on the social use of space and the behavioural patterns of communities that used roundhouses, even though these objectives must normally be pushing the limits of inference of the archaeological database.

The Wessex Model Reviewed

Before considering alternatives to roundhouses, we should review alternative interpretations of roundhouses, since it is increasingly apparent that there is a great diversity regionally and chronologically of potential reconstructions. *IAR* accepted the then prevailing view, espoused by Peter Reynolds, that the classic model of a roundhouse was a symmetrical cone of rafters, braced with purlins, over a ring-beam of weight-bearing posts, creating, in his expression, a cone on a cylinder. He acknowledged that this was not the only possibility for roundhouse superstructure, but adopted it on the principle of Ockham's Razor, the most straightforward solution being the most likely. That principle doubtless still holds good for the great majority of Southern British Iron Age roundhouses, but it need not be an invariable or inflexible rule. Outside Southern Britain it has become increasingly apparent in recent years that the Wessex model is not the most likely, and that larger roundhouses especially may have had a radically different superstructure.

A direct corollary of the Reynolds model is the often repeated mantra that a circular plan cannot be extended beyond the practical limits of length of the rafters, which were pretty well reached in the Pimperne reconstruction. That plainly is true whilst maintaining a single unit conical roof, but if the roof is built as two separate elements, with a central tower to provide support for the rafters at the inner end, and with a vertical gap between each level of roofing, then the extension is no longer limited by the maximum feasible length of the rafters, since in principle the roof could be split into more than two sections. It instead depends on the

Rethinking Roundhouses: Later Prehistoric Settlement in Britain and Beyond. D. W. Harding, Oxford University Press.
© D. W. Harding 2023. DOI: 10.1093/oso/9780192893802.003.0006

practical maximum height of the central tower, the vertical gap required between each roof level, and, crucially, the angle of slope of the rafters. One additional factor resulting from this projected elevation is the clerestory light that can be admitted where the central 'nave' rises above the peripheral 'aisles', providing improved light for the house interior, with an upper or mezzanine floor, and providing an outlet for the otherwise inevitable ceiling smoke, without breaching the integrity of the roof.

This was the model proposed by the present writer for the massive roundhouses at Culduthel, Inverness (Harding, 2020: Fig. 13.3). Here the houses were clearly exceptional, not only in their overall diameters, up to 18 metres, but also in the massive size of their weight-bearing timbers, which were up to 40 cm in diameter and set in pits a metre deep. But the principle of the split roof with higher central tower does not demand that scale of construction, so that many Southern British roundhouses could have been built in this way. Where, however, the ratios of the post-rings conform to those identified at Pimperne and elsewhere in Wessex, we may still prefer to reconstruct the roundhouse elevation with single rafter cantilevered across the main weight-bearing circle.

Split-level roofs may not have been the only available option for roundhouses of larger diameter. The penannular (or annular) ridged roof, advanced many years ago as an interpretative reconstruction for the house plan from West Harling, Norfolk (Fig. 6.1; Clark and Fell, 1953), was particularly applicable to the plan uncovered on Site II. The principal post-ring was the outermost, comprising fourteen posts forming an oval some 15 metres across. An inner ring of nine smaller posts appeared to reverse the normal relationship in which the larger postholes might have been expected to support the taller posts. The whole structure, however, was surrounded by a penannular ditch with inner bank, on which, the excavators argued, rested the outer roof rafters. Today an outer mass wall of mixed materials might be inferred, with a drainage ditch surrounding the house. The overall diameter of the roundhouse would thus have been some 22 metres. The two hearths were hardly conclusive, one being in the north-west sector within the aisled area, the lesser hearth being in the central 'court', which of course might well have required a hearth for working activities. A gap in the earthwork on the north led to the porched entrance and into the house itself, while a second break on the south-west side could have provided access to the open central court, into which stock could have been driven for shelter. The annular ridge-roof design would thus have been a variation on the byre-house concept. The West Harling excavation also yielded a second large roundhouse with post-ring 11 metres in diameter on Site III, also within a somewhat larger ditched enclosure that cannot have been integral to its structure, the reconstruction of which remains a puzzle in the absence of any further evidence of post-rings. Hand dug by an experienced team, it seems unlikely that postholes would have been missed, but evidence may not have survived of an outer mass wall. Finally, on Site IV there was, of course, clear

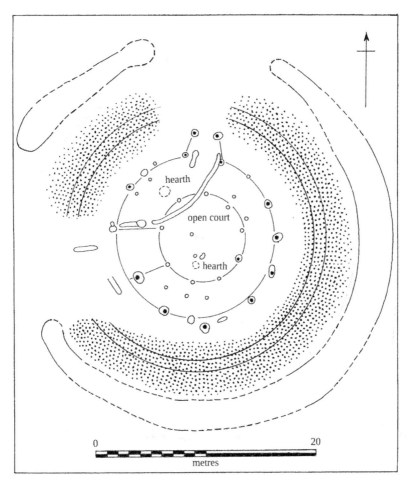

Fig. 6.1 West Harling, Norfolk, Site II roundhouse. Drawing by D. W. Harding, adapted from Clark and Fell, 1953.

evidence of rectangular structures built using a sill-beam or log-cabin (*Blockbau*) technique, as was noted in *IAR*. The penannular ridge-roof reconstruction, popularized by Rainbird Clarke (1960: Fig. 25) but otherwise today largely forgotten, represents a compromise of the two basic building plans, literally the circling of the rectangle. It is worth recalling that Bersu regarded the Little Woodbury type of large roundhouse as 'the coagulation of a farmstead composed of individual buildings round a central courtyard' (Bersu, 1940: 92), in which the central four-post tower and monumental entrance were fundamental.

Looking elsewhere for candidates for annular ridge-roof reconstructions, we might consider those plans that are at the maximum end of the range for conical roofing, and which have three post-rings or their equivalent. One possible

146   RETHINKING ROUNDHOUSES

contender is the large roundhouse from Scotstarvit, Fife (Bersu, 1948), at 19 metres overall certainly over the limit for a single, conical roof, but potentially a candidate for a split roof based on a central circular tower. Its triple ring plan, however, would equally accommodate an annular ridge-roof reconstruction, in which its somewhat asymmetrical plan would hardly be critical.

Oval Houses

Deviation from a circular plan most obviously might occur where the terrain on which the house is built is irregular. In the ethnographic example of the *pallozas* of the Ancares range of northern Spain, discussed more fully below, the thatched roofs were often far from conical or even symmetrical, yet appear to have been adequately serviceable. One variable in the equation seems to have been the porch, which, where it projected significantly from the basic cylinder, may have been integrated into the roof by extending rafters outward to create a 'pear-drop' shape.

The simplest alternative to a circular ground-plan would have been an oval plan, achieved by drawing the two halves of a circle apart by the insertion of a ridge pole to create an oblong with opposing semi-circular bay ends. This, based on a low stone wall foundation, was the staple form of the Cornish rounds of the Roman Iron Age. The architectural implications of this layout were examined by Blaylock (2004) in the context of the Tregurthy houses (Fig. 7.3, 2). In terms of area enclosed these oval houses were not so very much smaller than the large Wessex roundhouses, though usable space may have been limited by the relatively low height of the external stone walls. The wall-plates on which the rafters would have been based would surely have been levelled into the slope, but the walls may still have been not much more than a metre high. This would have meant that the door frame would have required an independent vestibule roof, bonded into the main roof, unless the wall height itself was significantly increased flanking the doorway (Blaylock, 2004: Figs. 94 and 95), as Reynolds did in the reconstruction of the Conderton, Worcestershire, house (Thomas, 2005: Pl. 45). The only question is whether the Tregurthy foundations would have been capable of sustaining a wall even of this height. A further issue is whether these oval houses had a ridge-beam, a feature which is not required to support the rafters, since each pair of the central section has its own structural integrity based on its cross-tie, whilst the hipped ends would probably have been supported by adapted tripods, likewise with half ring-beam bracing. A ridge-beam would certainly have been a constructional asset from erecting the initial rafters to thatching, and, if the evidence of Bronze Age house-urns is indicative (Sabatini, 2007), may have supported other embellishment on completion.

Figure-of-Eight, 'Shamrocks' and Cellular Houses

Figure-of-eight plans are a further variant on the roundhouse theme. At the time of publication of *IAR*, there were in Atlantic Scotland stone-built houses of the later Iron Age with a basic figure-of-eight plan, either free-standing structures, as at Buckquoy, Orkney (Ritchie, 1977) and Bostadh on Great Bernera in Lewis (Neighbour and Burgess, 1996), or within the reduced walls of derelict brochs, as at Beirgh in west Lewis (Harding and Gilmour, 2000) or at Dun Vulan, South Uist (Parker Pearson and Sharples, 1999). In fact, as was clear from the plans of these structures (*IAR*: Fig. 40), whilst the core element might have been a figure-of-eight, other cells could be aggregated to create a more complex, cellular cluster of rooms, so that the distinction between types of cellular buildings should not be over-emphasized. The core component of these figure-of-eight houses is a large, central room through which generally is the only access to a second, smaller room. These houses in Scotland are typically of Late Iron Age ('Pictish') date, with occupation at Bostadh and Buckquoy extending into the Norse period.

Ritchie (1977: 182–3) had acknowledged the limitations of the term 'figure-of-eight' in regard to the somewhat irregular plans of the Scottish, stone-built examples, but thought it useful in distinguishing those structures of broadly linear layout, like House 4 at Buckquoy, from those where the cells clustered around a central court, as in the classic 'shamrock'. This linear layout also encouraged the idea that such buildings might have had an overarching roof, rather than the cells being individually roofed, a more complex option in terms of rainwater run-off, and therefore considered less plausible. The problem is, of course, that the walls of figure-of-eight houses simply do not offer a regular base for the wall-plates of a rectangular or trapezoidal roof, even allowing for hipped ends, and any additional cells would have required separate roofing anyway. At Beirgh and Dun Vulan an overarching circular roof could have been based on the former broch walls, providing a much more substantial foundation than free-standing figure-of-eight buildings of the kind excavated at Bostadh. The reconstruction of the Bostadh house for public display opted for an overarching roof of trapezoidal plan over the figure-of-eight, and the original intention was to use turf and heather thatch (Neighbour and Crawford, 2001) in preference to straw thatch with stone weights in the blackhouse tradition.

Timber-built figure-of-eight houses, by contrast, adhere to a more regular layout of conjoined circles, whether of postholes, stake-holes, or ring-grooves. Because of their generally more ephemeral structural remains, demonstrating that these were indeed in contemporary use as integrated structures, rather than coincidentally adjacent and successive, is often problematical. At Deer Park Farms, a rath settlement of the Early Christian period in Co. Antrim (Lynn and McDowell, 2011), where houses were remarkably well preserved in the sodden conditions of the site's lower deposits, they plainly were used as an integrated unit, with the wattle-work of the adjoining walls actually woven together, with a doorway between the two. A distinctive characteristic of construction was the double-wall of stakes, which evidently was filled with organic materials for insulation, in much the same manner as has tentatively been proposed for some earlier Iron Age sites in Britain. In Structure X this filling comprised a mixture of straw, bracken heather, moss, and leaves. The only evidence for the use of stone in the construction of the houses was to buttress the material introduced to level the floors, as in the case of Structures Eta and Theta (Fig. 6.2, 1). The principal doorways, generally facing east or south-east towards the main rath gateway, were constructed of stouter materials, and in consequence had often been salvaged for subsequent reuse. The wattling of the walls effectively continued into the roof like an upturned basket, as was evident from surviving sections of inner wall up to three metres in height. Plainly, however, there would have been no point in the double-wall extending into the roof, so that, in the reconstruction at the Navan Centre, the outer wall was terminated at eaves height to provide external support for the thatch. What the Navan reconstruction of a single house did not address was the vexed issue of water run-off in the constricted point where the two cones of the figure-of-eight roofs meet.

A unique aspect of Irish Early Christian settlement archaeology is the availability of broadly contemporary legal documentary sources, notable the early eighth-century *Críth Gablach*, that refers to the separate components of figure-of-eight buildings as the 'front house' and 'back house', respectively, with the diameters of the latter given as a fraction of the diameter of the former, thus confirming the figure-of-eight format. Those sources also imply that size of house reflected the status of its occupants, though the higher ranks of free commoner might qualify for houses almost as grand as those of the lower grades of nobility (Lynn and McDowell, 2011: 605 table 34.1). At Deer Park Farms the front houses were around 6 to 7.5 metres in diameter and the back houses some 3.5 to 5.5 metres in diameter, placing them in the middle ranks of the series.

The Deer Park Farms houses are not exclusively figure-of-eight houses. Single roundhouses are also present, and to compound the problems of interpretation, single houses could become figures-of-eight in a secondary episode of construction, as in the case of Structures W2 and G (Fig. 6.2, 2). Structure Theta was built as a single house and subsequently became the back house to Structure Eta (Fig. 6.2, 1). Conversely, it is possible that a pair might be reduced, with the closure or demolition of one element and the blocking of the redundant door (Lynn and McDowell, 2011: 615), when the surviving unit reverted to a single roundhouse.

The distinction in use between single houses and figure-of-eight houses is not entirely clear, though both would appear to have been fundamentally residential. Equally, the relative function of front and back houses in figures-of-eight remains unclear, though it might be assumed that the less accessible back house was more

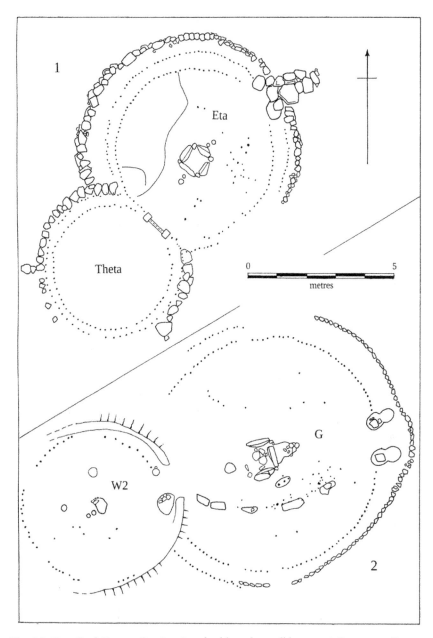

Fig. 6.2 Deer Park Farms, Co. Antrim, double stake-wall houses. 1, Structures Eta and Theta; 2, Structures W2 and G. Drawings by D. W. Harding, adapted from Waterman and Lynn, 1997.

private space. Hearths and bedding areas indicate domestic functions, and beds or daytime couches survived, notably in Structure X, where the woodwork suggested screens or canopies framing the bed. Interestingly, there was no evidence for beds in the back houses that were not arguably residual from a previous phase as single houses. Craft activities such as shoe-making and stave-making were in evidence, but not especially associated with either front houses or back houses, nor were the latter set aside for cooking or storage. It is therefore possible that the use of back houses related to some archaeologically undistinguishable social factor, such as use by a younger or older generation of the same family, or as an area used by women.

The life-span of the Deer Park Farms houses was estimated between ten and fifteen years, which would have been the maximum expectation for their wicker-basket construction. The more durable components, notably the oak jambs of the principal doorways, were evidently reused in replacement buildings. Though the structures were adequately strong and weathertight, environmental evidence shows that the houses and their occupants were infested with lice and parasitic insects, while the surrounding area was littered with rotting food waste, midden, and animal droppings. The essentially lightweight type of building contrasted with the more permanent construction of the rath enclosure itself, and may have reflected a shortage of more substantial timbers or simply a cultural tradition of transient settlement inherited from later prehistoric times.

The concept of the figure-of-eight timber houses in Ireland was evidently already known by the earlier Iron Age, with a complex sequence of interlocking ring-grooves of Phase 3ii on Site B at Navan in Co. Armagh (Waterman and Lynn, 1997; *IAR*: Fig. 45, 1). Dating to the second half of the first millennium BC, the Navan structures were regarded as domestic houses, rather than ceremonial or ritual in anticipation of the site's later usage. Each ring-groove roundhouse, some 12–13 metres in diameter had a central hearth and main external doorway to the east. To the north access was gained to what was initially supposed to have been a larger, unroofed 'yard', enclosed by a ring-groove, and in turn leading out through the east side via an avenue flanked by palisades. At around 20 metres in diameter it is arguable whether the yards were roofed or even partially roofed, so that the Navan ring-grooves may represent a distinct variation on the figure-of-eight theme. Becker (2019: 281) raised the possibility that ring-groove based walls combined with turf or sod construction, as noted elsewhere, might have enabled these 'yards', which apparently also contained hearths (Becker, 2019: 280), to be roofed. One observation that is more relevant in the light of the evidence from Deer Park Farms was that there were more ring-slots in the southern series than in the northern, indicating that renewals had not been entirely in step (Becker, 2019: 147). This might suggest that at any given stage there might have been only one element in use, so that once again it is conceivable that expansion and contraction in response to need was a factor in the figure-of-eight regime.

Unless there is positive evidence of a common doorway, it can be difficult to demonstrate that two adjacent roundhouses are part of a contemporary and integral construction, particularly where the evidence comprises a complex palimpsest of superimposed features. As at Deer Park Farms, expansion appears to have created the figure-of-eight at Bryn Eryr on Anglesey (Longley, 1998), where the initial roundhouse, built in the middle pre-Roman Iron Age, acquired a slightly smaller contiguous neighbour in a subsequent episode of occupation. More recently the paired houses from Bryn Eryr have been reconstructed as a figure-of-eight at St Fagan's National History Museum in Cardiff (Burrow, 2015). The houses at Bryn Eryr had been built with clay walls, as a thin residual spread around both the houses' perimeters confirmed. The reconstruction therefore used a traditional Welsh clom, a mixture of clay and straw, strengthened with coarse and fine stone aggregates (Fig. 6.3). The roofs were composed of spelt straw over a base of heather and gorse, again a well-documented vernacular option. An interesting statistic from the St Fagan's experimental reconstruction, given that resource management concerns invariably focus solely on timber supplies, was that it required 3.5 ha of spelt wheat to provide the thatch for the houses, a figure that plainly can be significantly increased if a greater depth of thatch is required to improve the roof's weatherproofing. Both excavated houses had principal entrances to the south-east. The reconstruction allowed internal access between the two for convenience of the public. Though archaeologically undemonstrated, since the residual footings of the house walls would have been unbroken anyway, and post-holes for jambs would only have been required if there had been a communicating door, rather than simply a screened gap, this was probably not an unreasonable inference.

One recurrent issue with the reconstruction of figure-of-eight houses was convincingly addressed by the St Fagan's reconstruction, namely, the problem of potential waterlogging between the contiguous roofs. The builders chose to introduce a ridge beam between the two roofs at mid-roof height. This, of course, caused the rainwater to run down the channels to focus at the waist of the figure-of-eight, where rain barrels were strategically placed to catch the run-off. A structural disadvantage is thus converted immediately into a social asset, answering the perennial question, 'where did they obtain their water supply?'

The fact that some of the most distinctive cellular and figure-of-eight plans derive from Late Iron Age settlements should not obscure the antiquity of this archaeotectural variant. At Links of Noltland, Westray (Moore and Wilson, 2011) a succession of Bronze Age structures comprised conjoined pairs, with entrances facing each other across a paved passageway. The smaller components contained stone-lined tanks set just inside the entrance, whilst the main roundhouses had central hearths and evidence for radial divisions projecting inwards from the wall face. Where the evidence is a palimpsest of superimposed structures, there is always the risk of coincidental alignments between adjacent buildings.

Fig. 6.3 Reconstruction of the Bryn Eryr, Anglesey, houses, St Fagan's Museum, Cardiff. Photograph by Malcolm Balmer, LRPS, reproduced by kind permission.

Nevertheless, where one is larger than the other, as at Seafield West, Inverness, Structures G and F, for example (Cressey and Anderson, 2011), a case might be made for a unitary pair, linked by a passage supported by the pairs of posts (042, 035 and 044, 037). Assuming that the main post-rings of structures F and G were not their outer walls, the two components would converge closely. The more recent discovery of Houses 2 and 3 at Portgordon, Moray (Headland, forthcoming) likewise share a double post-pair half way between the two conjoined roundhouses.

In Southern Britain a possible example of figure-of-eight construction may be noted in the sequence of structures within Enclosure A on Site 1 at Moss Carr, Methley in west Yorkshire (Fig. 3.21; Roberts and Richardson, 2002), dating to the mid-to-late pre-Roman Iron Age. All the Moss Carr structures were defined by ring-gullies, which the excavators appear to have interpreted generally as wall foundations rather than drip-trenches, despite some exceptionally large diameters, and absence of evidence for post sockets within them. Neither was there any surviving evidence of internal post settings, though a double pair of pits marks the point at which a doorway between conjoined roundhouses within Structure 2 would have been located. This clue could be crucial, if we were to regard the gullies as drainage trenches rather than actual wall-foundations, since it is clear from the example of Salmonsbury, Gloucestershire (Fig. 3.6, 3; Dunning, 1976) that the drainage gullies themselves are insufficient proof of figure-of-eight houses. Since there is no space at Salmonsbury for any outer wall beyond the post-rings, and no linking posts or gullies between the houses, it seems most appropriate to regard these as a pair, rather than a single, conjoined unit. They may still represent some form of shared land-ownership or joint tenancy by related family units, but the houses evidently functioned independently as a matching pair, rather than as an entity with social or functional subdivisions.

An early contender for a figure-of-eight conjoined pair of roundhouses was recognized by the pioneer in air photography Derrick Riley (1947), who salvaged plans of the Iron Age settlement from a gravel quarry at Standlake in Oxfordshire (Fig. 6.4, 1). Though both post-rings were about the same diameter, that of Hut 2 has the appearance of a main weight-bearing circle, around which an outer wall some ten metres in diameter would have been lost to the scraper. The smaller component, Hut 3, was represented by a post-ring with ring-groove in close combination, forming a double external wall some 7.5 metres in diameter. Riley considered both options, that they were a single structure with posts defining a corridor linking the two, and that they were separate and successive, in which option we might see the posts as one side of a south-east facing porch, matching that of its neighbour, Hut 1, though apparently rather more elaborate. Caution might favour the latter interpretation, but the coincidence of alignment of the larger and smaller elements of Huts 2 and 3 is certainly striking.

More frequently in Southern Britain the possibility of figure-of-eight construction is suggested by the house enclosure rather than the building itself, which, as

154 RETHINKING ROUNDHOUSES

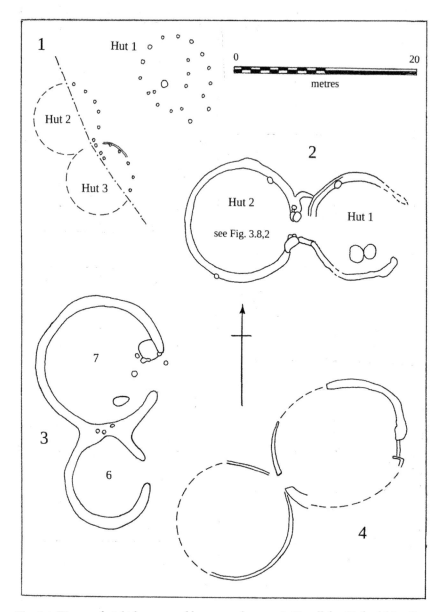

Fig. 6.4 Figure-of-eight houses and house-enclosures. 1, Standlake, Oxfordshire; 2, Aldwincle, Northamptonshire; 3, Ashford Prison, Middlesex, CS 6/7; 4, Heathrow, Middlesex, Terminal 5, Enclosure 26, Roundhouse 19. Drawings by D. W. Harding, adapted from Riley, 1947, Jackson, 1977, Carew et al., 2006, and Lewis et al., 2010.

argued above, is not an infallible indicator. In the case of Huts 1 and 2 at Aldwincle, Northamptonshire (Fig. 6.4, 2; Jackson, 1977) it is not even clear that 'Hut 1' was a house rather than an annexe or open compound. More recently, examples of figure-of-eight enclosures have been recorded at Ashford Prison (Fig. 6.4, 3; Carew et al., 2006) and at Heathrow, Terminal 5 (Fig. 6.4, 4; Lewis et al., 2010), where truncation would have eliminated any traces of the structures themselves.

Houses That Leave Minimal Trace

Posthole construction is so ubiquitous in later British prehistory that we may be inclined to overlook the obvious fact that some types of building may leave minimal trace archaeologically, while factors of taphonomy may further militate against recovery of evidence. Only where there is a glaring gap in the database are we prompted to look for evidence to fill it. So the paucity of Iron Age burials, with some limited and notable exceptions, prompts us to consider other ways in which the dead may have been disposed of in the Iron Age, but it seldom occurs to us that those other more ephemeral practices may equally have been the norm, so that chambered tombs of the Neolithic, for example, may have been the exception rather than the rule. So where there is abundant evidence of post-ring roundhouses we should not assume that was the only type of construction that was employed. In the case of Iron Age roundhouses, the one area where the archaeological record shows an unexplained blank is Kent and south-eastern England. This failure of roundhouses to register can hardly be explained through lack of excavation and research, since Kent has a long and productive tradition of archaeological discoveries in other fields, and one might have expected that major infrastructure projects like the Channel Tunnel Link would have yielded results from arbitrary exposure where planned research has drawn a blank. So we can only conclude that structures were being used that elude archaeological detection.

For Iron Age houses, there are two possible explanations for buildings that have not made a sufficient impact on the archaeological record to be detected by current technology, of which either or both might pertain. The first is that they were of such a design that did not require earth-fast foundations. The second is that they were built of materials that either have not survived or have not been recognized. The first needs qualification, however, because it is not just construction techniques such as sill-beams or log-cabin construction that will not normally register in the archaeological record. Anywhere where there has been a history of plough cultivation, posts that have penetrated into the ground less than 15–20 cm will simply not have survived, and certainly not to be detected under the conditions of most modern excavations. As a rule of thumb, posthole depth relates to girth and height of the post, so that the main weight-bearing posts of a roundhouse might survive where the lesser posts or stakes of the outer wall may not. Likewise

156 RETHINKING ROUNDHOUSES

the main paired posts of a three-aisled longhouse should survive, where those of the outer walls may not. For much of south-eastern England there appears to have been a trend towards smaller roundhouses in the later pre-Roman Iron Age, perhaps associated with a social shift towards increased functional specialization. These smaller houses did not require posts of the scale of the larger, earlier Wessex roundhouses, and accordingly the penannular drainage gully around the house stances is often the only surviving evidence for their existence. But in Kent even these proxy indicators are conspicuous by their absence. Had the community adopted a rectangular house plan, there is no assumption that it would have been a massive longhouse, and in all probability therefore its earth-fast traces would have been as vulnerable as those of smaller roundhouses. Round or rectangular, therefore, the problems of survival and recognition are similar.

There is, of course, a third possible explanation of the dilemma of missing houses, namely that they have been hiding in plain sight, that is, we consistently misinterpret the evidence, perhaps because it is so partial that it is easily mistaken for something else. How otherwise can we explain the absence of houses, for example, on the route of the A2 (Allen et al., 2012) and HS1 in Kent, when otherwise Iron Age occupation is abundantly represented by enclosure ditches and compounds, pits, and an abundance of evidence for domestic, agricultural, and even industrial activity? The one recognized Iron Age structural type that was present on these sites was the four-poster, universally interpreted since Bersu's pioneer work at Little Woodbury as upstanding granaries. Where they occur in ordered clusters, as on Site E on the A2, this may be the right interpretation, as it undoubtedly is in hillforts like Danebury. And where they occur in isolation elsewhere they might equally have been granaries for individual households, were there any evidence of adjacent houses. But the four-poster phenomenon could include similar structures of quite different purposes. They have even been interpreted as excarnation platforms. Some, as we have seen, formed the central framework within roundhouses, including examples of ring-groove construction, where the evidence for an outer wall would not survive ploughing or mechanical stripping. Lambrick (Lambrick and Robinson, 2009: 154) asked why pairs of posts interpreted as 'drying racks', once popular in the literature and endorsed by experiment at Butser Hill, had gone out of fashion. The answer, of course, is that they became the entrance posts of stake-wall roundhouses of which all other trace had been eradicated. Could some four-posters equally be the fugitive traces of a variant form of roundhouse?

It has been argued earlier that substantial roundhouses may have had central towers to support split-level roofs. But a four-post setting could equally have provided central roof support for lesser houses, braced at the top to form a rigid frame, and possibly with a further square of horizontal timbers introduced at 45 degrees to form an octagon corresponding to the upper ring-beam of the classic Reynolds reconstruction. Rafters thus supported could rest their feet on wall-plates resting on a turf or cob outer wall of the house. A four-poster would thus be the only archaeological footprint of the building, with the possible exception of the door jamb holes. Though the mass wall may have been lined externally or internally by wattling or planking, this is unlikely to have left any earth-fast trace. We have already seen a number of instances in lowland Britain in which roundhouses with earth-fast outer walls incorporated a central four-poster, and numerable instances where an outer mass-wall has been inferred for double-ring roundhouses, so that the alternative of an outer mass-wall around a four-post central roof support need occasion no surprise, particularly when it is evident that from the Middle Iron Age, earth-fast foundations appear to have been abandoned in many regions. In regions where stone was available as a construction material, and where the outer wall was based on stone footings, interior support could equally have been provided by a central four-post setting, based either on post-pits or on stone post-pads. If these had been alternative options throughout the pre-Roman Iron Age, then roundhouses on Roman villa sites with four central post-pits or stone pillar bases, like Holme House and Winterton (Stead, 1976: Fig. 26), might not have appeared to be anomalous, but based on long-standing Iron Age building traditions.

If roundhouses can be constructed with minimal earth-fast trace, as Reynolds argued many years ago on the basis of experimental reconstruction, then searching for houses in areas where there is a blank in the archaeological distribution may be fruitless. Perhaps the question that we should be asking is not why there are blanks, but why there are houses that *do* leave conspicuous traces? Presumably it is easier in the construction phase, before the several elements of a building are mutually supporting, to have posts firmly positioned in the ground. And in the longer term, earth-fast foundations will also be more solidly established, providing they are kept dry and not a potential weakness. But was it also perhaps important to their builders that the house was physically and symbolically rooted in the ground?

In terms of materials for constructing a non-earth-fast wall, the most obvious are cob or clom, turf, and perhaps peat, the use of which plainly might reflect regional differences in availability and environmental context. In many cases it is clear that wall-slots or post-rings have been eroded, but there must remain a serious possibility in subsoils prone to waterlogging that earth-fast foundations were avoided altogether by the use of mass-walls. Turf would have been an effective building material, provided it was kept dry by overhanging eaves, but its former presence might be expected to leave a low residual bank unless the site had subsequently been intensively ploughed. One of the earliest examples of a turf wall recognized as the exterior wall of a roundhouse was at Wolsty Hall in Cumbria (Fig. 3.13, 2; Blake, 1959), where the excavator assumed that it was faced by a wooden wall based in a wall-trench that might well in fact have been a drainage gully. Other mass materials include clay and straw, and cob, use of which continued in vernacular building until more recent times in lowland Britain. Recent experiments at Butser Hill (Creighton et al., 2022), based on excavations at Dunch Hill, Tidworth on Salisbury Plain, experimented with the use of stacked turves, cob (in this instance chalk mixed with straw, hair, and wool), chalk and earth, and twin hurdles with wool insulating the cavity. Archaeologically a version of cob walls was clearly in evidence at Hod Hill (Richmond, 1968), in combination with upright timbers that may have supported a ring-beam to carry the roof rafters. Here the collapsed wall spreads were between 120 and 170 cm wide, within ring-gullies some nine metres across.

Peat or turf walls would be unlikely to survive in the archaeological record once the building was abandoned and the walls exposed to weathering. In the context of the Western Isles there is the further problem that, even if their residual traces survived, the poverty and more especially the undiagnostic character of any material associations would make it unlikely that such structures would be identified correctly to date and cultural context. These factors most probably combine to account for the apparent absence of any widely recognized class of lower-order houses of earlier Iron Age date contemporary with the brochs. The ephemeral outlines of small round and oval structures defined by stony spreads or boulder alignments on Barabhas machair (MacLeod Rivett, 2018; Cowie and MacLeod Rivett forthcoming), for example, hardly conform to recognized archaeological typology, and it is unclear whether the stones represent a wall foundation or were simply piled around to protect a structure the fabric of which has left no trace.

Rectangular Houses: Continuity or Change?

At the time that *IAR* was published there were few credible candidates for rectangular houses in the British Iron Age, a situation that has hardly changed as a consequence of much more extensive development-led excavation. Among convincing plans, the aisled longhouses from Crickley Hill had been challenged by some who believed them to be coincidentally adjacent four-posters, even though several had internal hearths, and alignment along the internal roadway was consistent with the inferred position of their outer walls. One reason for contention was that the paired posts of the longhouses did not invariably form regular parallel lines, a feature that the excavator has suggested (Dixon, 2019: 225) indicated that it was the tie-beams across the pairs, rather than arcade plates along the length of the building, that supported the superstructure, in a system now known as reversed assembly. In fact, Dixon acknowledged that some of the longer settings might represent more than one structure. But the essential validity of the Crickley longhouses is attested by House 5, in which significant sections of the northern and southern outer walls survived in the form of stake-hole alignments. Whether these Early Iron Age houses represent a local influx from continental Europe, or whether they derive from an older, later Bronze Age insular tradition, as tentatively suggested by Moore (2003: 49), must remain a matter for speculation in the absence of more examples.

The two most convincing examples of post-built rectangular longhouses of the later Bronze Age are Down Farm, Woodcuts (Fig. 6.5, 1; Barrett et al., 1991), and Barleycroft Farm, Bluntisham, Cambridgeshire (Fig. 6.5, 2; Evans and Knight, 1996).

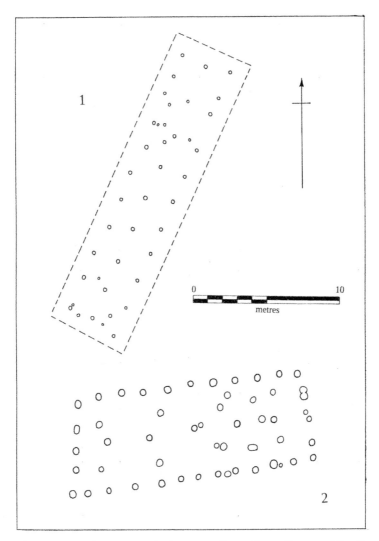

Fig. 6.5 Later Bronze Age rectangular houses. 1, Down Farm, Sixpenny Handley, Dorset, House F; 2, Barleycroft Farm, Cambridgeshire. Drawing by D. W. Harding, adapted from Barrett et al., 1991 and Evans and Knight, 1996.

160 RETHINKING ROUNDHOUSES

Both have a regular central alignment of posts, at Down Farm comprising nine posts extending just over 18 metres, at Barleycroft seven spanning 16 metres. Both have parallel outer alignments, but Barleycroft has two further rows, with fewer posts that do not form regular sets across the aisles, so that they could be from internal fixtures or subdivisions of space rather than integral to the superstructure. Whether the outer alignments coincided with the outer walls, or whether the latter lay beyond the timber framework and were of materials that have not survived is unclear in the absence of any laid or trodden floors. Subject to interpretation of these factors, however, the Down Farm and Barleycroft houses could have been equivalent in their floor areas to roundhouses with a diameter in the order of 10–12 metres.

It must be apparent from the discussion earlier of oval house plans, and, more specifically, short, aisled buildings with apsidal ends, that the distinction between circular and rectangular ground-plans can be over-emphasized. In fact, most of the rectangular buildings of the near Continent were oblong rather than rectangular in the Northern European or Central European longhouse sense, while oval and square-with-rounded-corner variants again compromised simplistic classification. Many were rather irregular in plan, and not always readily classified as single-aisled, two-aisled, or three-aisled. Furthermore, the range of size and structural complexity too suggested a great diversity of functions and social contexts.

The classic post-built rectangular longhouse itself, of course, admits of various forms. For our purposes, one of the more interesting developments is the progression in the Northern Early Bronze Age from the two-aisled house to the three-aisled house, and the reasons advanced for the change (Bech and Haack Olsen, 2012). There are intriguing hybrids like Ginnerup House 1 from northern Jutland in which one end is two-aisled and the other three-aisled, suggesting that this was not simply a technical, structural improvement, since otherwise it would surely have been implemented throughout. One reason that has been advanced for this hybrid plan is the introduction of indoor stalling for animals, creating a rectangular byre-house. It has also been suggested that the three-aisled system allows for greater ease of subdivision of space for functional purposes, and that it might make it easier to incorporate storage space in the roof.

These arguments might be equally applicable to double-ring roundhouses, which, in terms of the division of central space from peripheral space, are the circular equivalents to three-aisled longhouses.

The large roundhouse may be capable of division, such as radial division of peripheral space around communal central space, but circular building can only be otherwise divided by having several circular units in proximity, or aggregated into a cellular cluster. It has therefore often been remarked that an advantage of rectilinear building is that it is easier to divide into separate rooms for different activities or for different groups of people, women, children, dependent elderly, non-family dependents or whatever. But rectangular buildings are also amenable to the idea of communal central space with peripheral subdivisions.

Aisled Houses and Aisled Halls

In terms of social use of space, one example of continuity from the Iron Age into the Roman period has been evident for many years. With the Roman occupation came one architectural innovation that has continued to puzzle archaeologists, because it is not otherwise widely represented in the Roman world, namely the aisled house, often itself described as a single-roomed building, but, because of its aisled construction, evidently capable of subdivision. The key to continuity in the social use of space lies in the division between a central, communal area surrounded by peripheral space that could have been divided by impermanent screens or drapes, like a roundhouse but within a rectangular outline.

At the time of publication of *IAR*, the best contender for an early aisled house with potential late pre-Roman Iron Age origins was from Gorhambury, Hertfordshire (Neal et al., 1990), within the environs of the late pre-Roman Iron Age *oppidum* of Verulamium, and the situation has not been amplified much since then. Gorhambury certainly showed that rectangular houses in the late pre-Roman Iron Age could be large and not just single-roomed buildings, but the dating evidence for the earliest aisled house, Building 15 (Fig. 6.6, 1), was not indisputably pre-Roman. The excavators recognized nevertheless that the aisled plan could have had pre-Roman origins. As to domestic use, they simply stuck with the older conventional interpretation of these structures as byres or accommodation for agricultural workers. Building 15 was a simple aisled structure, 16.5 metres long by 11.5 metres wide, and comprising a double line of substantial postholes internally with an external wall trench. By the late second or early third centuries it had been rebuilt on the same site to an overall length in excess of 29 metres, but retaining the same structural layout.

More recently, the aisled house from Furfield Quarry, Kent (Fig. 6.6, 2; Mackinder, 2006; Howell, 2014), likewise in the environs of a probable late pre-Roman Iron Age *oppidum* at Loose, may have originated in the pre-Roman period, on the basis of associated pottery. Measuring 17 metres in length and 12.6 metres wide, the principal roof support was provided by a double line of six posts with smaller posts forming the outside longer walls. The south-west wall was likewise post-built, but its north-eastern counterpart appears to have been based in a wall-trench. Two dissimilar pairs of more widely spaced posts down the middle of the broad central aisle mirror a similar difference in size of the posts of the main parallel alignments, and might reflect internal divisions of space. By way of comparison, we might note that the total internal ground floor area of this house

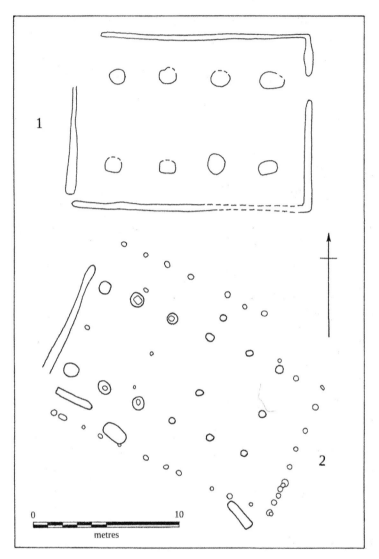

Fig. 6.6 Late Iron Age–early Roman aisled houses. 1, Gorhambury, St Albans, Hertfordshire, Building 15; 2, Furfield Quarry, Boughton Monchelsea, Kent, Building 6/1. Drawings by D. W. Harding, adapted from Neal et al., 1990 and Mackinder, 2006.

would have been 214 square metres, the equivalent of a roundhouse 16.5 metres in diameter. Rather larger was a rectangular building at Furfield Quarry that was interpreted in publication as intended for stock handling, on the questionable rationale that there were no known parallels in Kent. At least 31.4 metres in length and with its parallel posthole rows 5.5 metres apart, it could have sustained an aisled building 7.5 to 8 metres wide, somewhat longer than but comparable in width to the largest of the rectangular houses at Crickley Hill. Unlike the other aisled buildings, lesser postholes or wall-trenches of outer walls may not have survived mechanical stripping of the site. Pottery from the postholes spanned the later Iron Age and early Roman periods, and definitive dating was compromised by what might have been intrusive and what might have been residual.

In Roman Britain aisled houses are widely distributed across England and Wales, though they are more sparsely represented in the north and west (Smith et al., 2016: Fig. 3.18). They occur in the context of a variety of settlement types, farmstead, roadside settlements and villages, and in the south of England especially in association with villas. They range greatly in size, and architectural complexity, with 'developed' variants acquiring additional suites of rooms, or even becoming incorporated into later villa complexes. Whereas a previous generation regarded them as subordinate or ancillary buildings, used for agricultural or industrial activities, or housing the estate labourers, their grandeur of scale and in some cases their construction and fittings make clear that they were often the primary focus of the settlement and integral to the lifestyle of the community. Their very diversity, however, suggests that a single functional explanation would probably be inappropriate, and is in any event not the purpose of the present review.

Whatever accretions it may have acquired, the essence of the aisled hall is the division between central space and peripheral space, exactly as it had been in the larger roundhouses of later prehistory. In Wessex it is true that later Iron Age roundhouses were often smaller in size than their later Bronze Age and earlier Iron Age predecessors, perhaps indicating that already social conventions were distilling into discrete functions that required designated space, and perhaps in some parts of the south-east already transferring social practices into the context of rectangular architecture. The key may have been social convention, but practice could be maintained in the face of innovating building styles by squaring the circle, compressing the circular plan with its fundamental division of central and peripheral space into a rectangular building in which the same principle is maintained. A comparison of the Gorhambury aisled house with one phase of Little Woodbury, for example, shows that the basic format could be maintained, economizing on the number of timbers required by extending the spacing between uprights supporting a gabled or hipped roof. Both the Gorhambury and Furfield Quarry aisled buildings could have boasted a central 'nave' higher than the roofline of the flanking aisles to allow for 'clerestory' light. That, of course, is exactly the counterpart of the effect in a circular plan of having a central tower rising above the roof level of the peripheral areas of the roundhouse, as proposed earlier. So it is unnecessary to pursue the pedigree of aisled houses in terms of architectural typology from the Iron Age to the Roman period, since the concept of the communal use of space was the underlying icon, which under the Roman occupation could be reasserted at any time by the adoption of the aisled format, or more overtly by building roundhouses anew. Once established in Roman Britain, under a new regime that must have totally ruptured the older social order, it developed in various ways. Cunliffe (2013) saw the aisled building as a hall where the community could convene for public assemblies, where the local elite could hold court, decide disputes, or dispense justice. He speculated whether indeed this concept embodied in the aisled hall might not have survived into the sub-Roman period and into the Anglian and later halls of the medieval period.

Conclusions

Cunliffe surely identified the key to understanding the role of aisled buildings in Roman Britain when he described it as 'a style of building conducive to a mode of social behaviour rooted well back into the prehistoric past...the continuum was the social practice not the building form' (Cunliffe, 2008: 120, 127). This is a sentiment that could be applied more generally in the study of later prehistoric houses. Too much emphasis can be placed upon structural typology, and too little upon the social use of space that might have been the common factor in superficially different structural types. In much the same way, structural typology can suggest apparently radical differences that in reality reflect changing environmental conditions or even arbitrary circumstances of archaeological survival. Archaeological typology at best has been a mixed blessing, at worse a straitjacket that has inhibited reinterpretation of the evidence. Four-post settings in many contexts were surely upstanding granaries as Bersu suggested at Little Woodbury. But they could equally elsewhere have served a range of agricultural and domestic purposes, as shrines or excarnation platforms, or as structural components of domestic houses. And, of course, not all of the 'houses' need have been domestic houses.

7

Regional Diversity in Britain and Beyond

One reviewer of *IAR* criticized its 'traditional polarized focus of study on the extreme north and south of Britain' (Büster, 2011: 323). Whilst the book had hoped to rectify the imbalance between Wessex and Britain north of the Trent, it was plainly deficient in its treatment of Western Britain. Ireland too was deficient in excavated information regarding later prehistoric settlement, other than the plainly exceptional evidence from the so-called 'royal sites', a situation that still pertains to a degree, though it has been significantly informed through the results of excavation in advance of development in the past twenty years. The existence of roundhouses in the *castros* of the peninsular north-west had been long established, and the prospect of relating this to the later prehistoric tradition in Britain was encouraged by the discovery of Iron Age roundhouses in parts of northern and north-western France. The convention of circular rather than rectilinear plans for domestic architecture is still essentially Atlantic, though far from regionally consistent.

Wales and the West

At the time *IAR* was published a major survey of Welsh roundhouses, sponsored by the University of Wales Board of Celtic Studies, had recently been completed (Ghey et al., 2007, 2008) which summarized the state of knowledge and highlighted key issues that needed to be addressed. Though acknowledging the practical necessity of classification in reducing a great mass of data to usable order, Ghey was acutely aware of the limitations of the conventional typologies of Welsh roundhouse settlements, some of which were too broad and inclusive to be meaningful, while others included superficially similar sites that in reality might be contextually and chronologically quite different. In principle a problem with typology was that it tended to 'tidy up' diversity (Ghey et al., 2008: 20) and thereby mislead. As with sites in northern England and Lowland Scotland, especially those that were effectively aceramic, a major problem with many Welsh roundhouse settlements has been dating, placing a disproportionate dependence upon the presence of Roman pottery. Radiocarbon dating now testifies to the existence of roundhouse settlements in the later pre-Roman Iron Age, continuing in use into at least the second century AD, suggesting that the impact of the Roman occupation upon everyday life was neither immediate nor especially profound.

Rethinking Roundhouses: Later Prehistoric Settlement in Britain and Beyond. D. W. Harding, Oxford University Press.
© D. W. Harding 2023. DOI: 10.1093/oso/9780192893802.003.0007

166 RETHINKING ROUNDHOUSES

Also like Northern Britain, the shift from timber construction to the widespread use of stone has been a major concern over the years, together with the transition to rectilinear building plans. Among settlements of the Roman period in North Wales the proportion of round to rectangular house plans is about equal overall, but with roundhouses more strongly represented in hillforts and farmsteads, whereas rectangular buildings not surprisingly dominate in *vici* and roadside settlements and villages (Smith et al., 2016: 373).

The classic sequence from timber- to stone-built roundhouses was established for Wales at Moel y Gerddi and Erw-wen (Kelly, 1988), though several earlier excavations had pointed the way. Of the two sites, near neighbours on the slopes below the Moel Goedog hillfort near Harlech in the former Merionethshire, Moel y Gerddi (Fig. 7.1, 1) was the better preserved, but Erw-wen (Fig. 7.1, 2) proved to

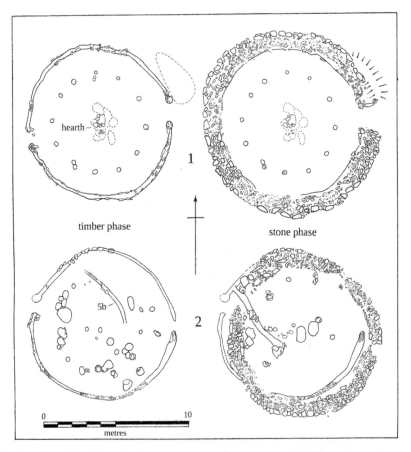

Fig. 7.1 Transition from timber to stone roundhouses in north Wales: schematic plans. 1, Moel y Gerddi, Gwynedd; 2, Erw-wen, Gwynedd. Drawings by D. W. Harding, adapted from Kelly, 1988.

have the more distinctive structural sequence. The earliest house at Erw-wen was probably represented by a truncated arc of ring-gully (5b) that, if complete, would have described a building some 9.5 metres in diameter. Its successor was of similar size, and comprised a trench with closely-spaced packing stones and edge-set slabs aligned along its outer sides. There were two diametrically opposed doorways on the west and east, both originally around a metre wide, with postholes in the trench terminals. Within the area enclosed there were numerous postholes, but none formed any convincing circle for internal roof-support. The final stone-built phase was notably eccentric in relation to its immediate predecessor. Its walls of stone, cobbles, and slabs, with larger stones on the outer faces, were around a metre wide and enclosed an area nearly nine metres in diameter. It had a single doorway on the north-west side, through which a drain extended from the interior. Part of the south-eastern arc of the timber wall-gully may have been reused, mirroring an arc of four postholes close to the stone footings on the northern circuit.

At Moel y Gerddi the timber and stone episodes of construction may have been successive, but it was essentially a case of adaptation of the same building. Otherwise similarities in size and construction are evident. The ring-gully similarly had edge-set stones along its sides, and the diametrically opposed doorways likewise had postholes in their terminals. A major distinction was the presence of a well-defined internal post-ring, which, as the excavator explained, could reflect the principle of axial line symmetry (Guilbert, 1982) whilst having an even number of posts (twelve) by virtue of the fact that there were two entrances. A central hearth was represented by shallow pits with sandstone slabs. The stone wall was undoubtedly secondary, since it blocked the western doorway. Yet it had evidently been built against the still standing timber wall, with which it was accordingly concentric, and its roof was apparently supported by the same internal post-ring, perhaps with a couple of post replacements. In terms of occupancy, the life-span of the Moel y Gerddi houses cannot have been long, and evidence of usage was not so obvious as it was at Erw-wen, where the floor had been worn to a dish profile. The material culture at both sites was aceramic and undiagnostic, but radiocarbon dating suggested occupation in the pre-Roman Iron Age, with Erw-wen perhaps having slight chronological priority over Moel y Gerddi.

Among earlier excavated sites where a similar sequence had been advanced was Castell Odo (Alcock, 1960), but the excavated evidence for timber houses there was somewhat tenuous. Fortunately, just three miles to the east, the sequence at Meillionydd (Karl et al., 2016) is based upon more positive evidence. The initial settlement on the hilltop was open, and may have extended beyond the area that was subsequently enclosed. It comprised roundhouses up to 12 metres in diameter of posthole and ring-groove construction, and probably dating from some time after 800 BC. The first phase of enclosure, represented by a palisade and ditch, was constructed around 600 BC, and maintained a tradition of timber roundhouses, mainly 9–10 metres in diameter up to a maximum of 12 metres. Phase 3 saw a major change in the site's status, with the construction of a double ring-work comprising earth and stone banks with internal quarry ditches, with roundhouses of stone construction built into the terminals of the enclosure works at the entrance. In the absence of definitive dates, this episode is assigned to *c.* 500–400 BC, and is referred to by the excavators as the site's 'monumentalizing' phase. Phase 4 sees a further radical change, with one stone-built roundhouse being built in the inner entrance passage, plainly obstructing access unless the inner bank at least was no longer a significant obstacle. In the following phase, the walls of this roundhouse were defined by outer facing stones, and in the next it was rebuilt slightly further in. By this stage it is assumed that the outer bank had fallen into disuse, while the inner bank was totally eroded, echoing the pattern at Castell Odo, where the later roundhouses were built over the denuded defences. The final Phases 7 and 8 see further roundhouses with stone-faced walls and rubble cores built into the former defences.

In sum, twelve episodes of construction have been identified at Meillionydd, spanning a period probably from the early eighth to the late third centuries BC. Only limited radiocarbon dates were available, and Meillionydd lacked either later Bronze Age pottery, as found at Castell Odo, or any later Iron Age pottery. The excavators calculated that around 550 years allowed around half a century for each building episode, a longer life-span than some archaeologists would accept for roundhouses of this kind, but certainly not beyond optimum expectation. The relatively short period in which the site boasted a double ring-work may not reflect its social status, if the enclosure works were to meet a real need for defence, as opposed to demonstrating social aggrandizement.

Among the enclosed roundhouse settlements of south-west Wales, the distinctive 'banjo' pair of Woodside and Dan-y-Coed (Williams and Mytum, 1998) remain remarkable, not least because the disproportionate elaboration of their defences and approaches in comparison to their internal areas must indicate some special status or function. The cobbled approach to Woodside (Fig. 7.2, 1) was no less than 80 metres in length, flanked by banks and ditches that at various stages were revetted with timber and stone, and which at their outer, western extremity turned north and south to present a further facade. Access was controlled by an outer gateway that may have supported a guard tower, while an inner gate was located between the ends of the main enclosure wall. The elaboration of the Woodside outworks must imply prestige and status of the occupants, though the complex network of outworks among comparable sites in south-west Wales (Murphy, 2018: Fig. 3b) was surely related to stock control and management. Internal occupation at Woodside was focused on two sets of roundhouses, backed against the north and south enclosure walls, respectively, together with a central roundhouse, the remains of which had been severely eroded by ploughing, in contrast to those in the lee of the earthworks. These were of ring-groove

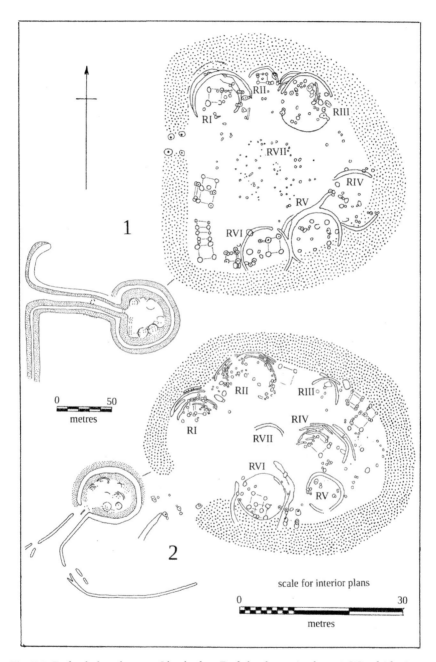

Fig. 7.2 Defended settlements Llawhaden, Dyfed, schematic plans. 1, Woodside; 2, Dan-y-Coed. Drawings by D. W. Harding, adapted from Williams and Mytum, 1998.

and post-ring construction, at maximum nine or ten metres in diameter, revealing a succession of structural phases in which the sequence was not always clear. The northern group appears, however, to have been the earlier of the two groups, with a range of four-post granaries initially occupying the south and south-west side of the interior. Subsequently a ring-groove roundhouse with internal post-ring (Roundhouse V) was built over the four-posters, to which two further continuous circular buildings were added. It is not clear whether these ever functioned as a single unit, as there is no clear entrance gap between Roundhouse V and either of its neighbours, but Roundhouses IV, V, and VI certainly look like a related suite of rooms, the functional and social role of which, within a couple of generations 70 miles to the south-east, at Whitton in the Vale of Glamorgan (Jarrett and Wrathmell, 1981), was more effectively achieved by adopting a rectilinear plan (*IAR*: Fig. 33). Dating indicates that the Woodside settlement began in the second or first century BC, and continued until the early second century AD.

Though superficially similar in plan, the construction of the Dan-y-Coed enclosure and approach works (Fig. 7.2, 2) was less substantial and less elaborate, with just a single entrance into the enclosure. A crucial difference, however, was in the construction of the roundhouses, which were stake-walled buildings, with the wattled walls bedded either in a narrow slot trench or gully, or simply in an alignment of stake-holes, as in Roundhouse VI, which at around ten metres in diameter must be on the upper limit of viability for roofing. Several of the Dan-y-Coed houses have ring-grooves that were interpreted as drainage gullies, though in several cases they must have been hard to distinguish from wall-trenches. Double-walls were ruled out because of the occurrence of capping stones, not apparently indicative of internal drains, but believed to have been placed over redundant wall-trenches (Williams and Mytum, 1998: 125), though it is not clear why these were not simply filled in. The distinction between wall-trench and drip-gully is much clearer in Houses A and B at Ffynnonwen, on the border between Ceredigion and Pembrokeshire (Murphy and Mytum, 2012, Fig. 14), where the concentricity of the two makes it much more likely that the outer gully was for drainage from the eaves, rather than simply designed to soak away groundwater from the foundations of the building.

One class of site that links south-west Wales to neighbouring regions of Cornwall and Brittany is the coastal promontory fort, some located in precipitous cliff-edge contexts that must have challenged their practicability for permanent settlement. Just such a site is the now much-eroded fort at Porth y Rhaw on the north Pembrokeshire coast (Crane and Murphy, 2010), which nevertheless has yielded evidence of sustained occupation in the first millennium BC. The earliest occupation dates from the Late Bronze Age and earliest Iron Age, in the form of ring-groove roundhouses, averaging eight to ten metres in diameter, and sharing many of the characteristics of inland sites. The latest occupation is represented by Roundhouse VIII, which had low stone foundations and a roughly laid floor of slabs. A slab-capped drain led out through a south-west facing doorway flanked by a timber porch. Pottery and a single radiocarbon date indicate a Romano-British occupation for the stone roundhouse, but the unequivocal evidence for much earlier occupation raises the possibility that other promontory forts with surviving stone roundhouses like that on St David's Head (Baring-Gould et al., 1899) might have had earlier occupation that was not detected by older investigations.

Among the Cornish promontory forts one of the most impressively defended is Trevelgue Head at Newquay (Nowakowski and Quinnell, 2011), where Croft Andrew's 1939 excavation had uncovered a single, large roundhouse with an external stone wall composed of alternate orthostats and horizontal drystone coursing (*IAR*: Fig. 20), defining an area 14 metres in diameter. That construction technique is unique in the south-west, but is commonly found in later Iron Age stone roundhouses in Atlantic Scotland and Ireland (*IAR*: Pls. 12 and 13), in both free-standing walls and those that are revetted against subsoil or accumulated rubble. In the short-lived investigations of 1939 House 1 was the only roundhouse uncovered. Subsequent survey has indicated that the area between the lynchets on which it was located includes more than a dozen potential house platforms, though none in fact the size of House 1, which remains unusual and distinctive. The publication of Croft Andrew's records now permits the reconstruction of House 1's plan, which shows two internal post-rings, though not in the classic Wessex proportions, together with an east-facing paved entrance with porch. It seems probable that the inner post-ring supported a central tower, with the second ring, seven metres in diameter, providing the principal roof-support. Nowakowski and Quinnell suggest community use, rather than a standard domestic role for this exceptional building, perhaps in connection with the site's important role in iron working. Its exceptional status appears to be underlined by the fact that, long after its primary period of use in the closing centuries of the first millennium BC, the extant ruins of the building were deliberately infilled with a mixture of midden material in the late Roman period, suggesting long survival of its known significance in local memory (Nowakowski and Quinnell, 2011: 390). Plainly House 1 had a special role within the later pre-Roman Iron Age community, but, if the putative house platforms were indeed the sites of other, smaller roundhouses, it is still possible that House 1 was the great roundhouse in a similar relationship to the others as was shown for the Phase 3 settlement at Crickley Hill (Dixon, 2019).

Characteristic of Cornwall are *rounds*, univallate ring-works enclosing an area around a hectare with a ditch no more than two metres deep and accessed through a single, simple entrance. Rounds date to the pre-Roman Iron Age, extending into the Roman period. One of the more extensively excavated examples was Threemilestone near Truro (Schwieso, 1976), where the interior was occupied by circular or oval gullies and ditches that either enclosed roundhouses, of which minimal earth-fast trace survived, or were ancillary compounds (Fig. 7.3, 1). Among these two oval ditches, 2 and 3, were larger than normal house size, being

172 RETHINKING ROUNDHOUSES

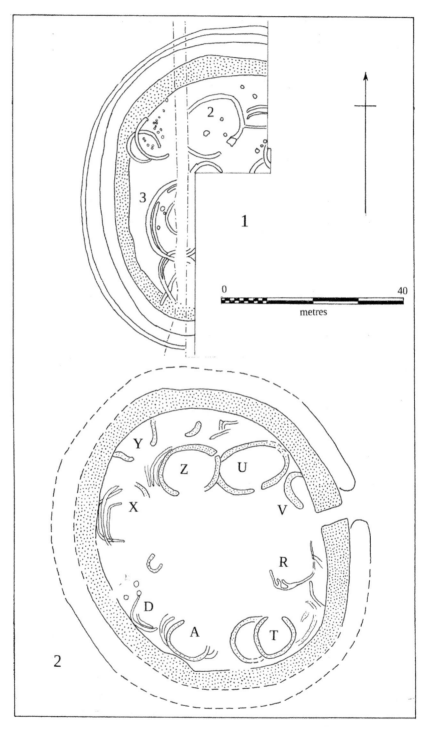

Fig. 7.3 Cornish rounds: schematic plans. 1, Threemilestone, Kenwyn, Truro; 2, Trethurgy, St Austell. Drawings by D. W. Harding, adapted from Schwieso, 1976 and Quinnell, 2004.

some 12 by 15 metres and an estimated 17 by 15, respectively, though the houses that may have stood within them would of course have been smaller. The material assemblage at Threemilestone indicated occupation entirely within the pre-Roman Iron Age. At Trethurgy Round, St Austell (Quinnell, 2004), by contrast, though the site was established around the first century BC, the round proper was not constructed until the mid-second century, with large oval houses being built in the third quarter of that century (Fig. 7.3, 2). The primary surviving evidence is the stone-faced footings of their external walls, of which there were three or four in each of the major occupational phases, together with some ancillary buildings. These were arranged peripherally around the enclosure, with every indication that the central area was left for working or communal activities.

There was evidently a long-established roundhouse tradition in the south-west from the Bronze Age, exemplified by sites on Dartmoor that are an integral part of the extensive landscape co-axial field systems (Fleming, 2008). Some later Bronze Age house platforms are cognate to the unenclosed platform settlements of Northern Britain. Nevertheless, excavation has shown the limitations of dating on the basis of site morphology, as at Gold Park on Shapley Common on the south-eastern edge of Dartmoor (Gibson, 1992). Here an unenclosed platform settlement that on surface examination certainly prompted comparison with sites in Northumberland and the Scottish Borders proved to date from the later pre-Roman Iron Age. The ring-groove with inner post-ring construction and secondary building defined by unfaced stony footings would not have been out of place in a Middle to Late Bronze Age context, but radiocarbon dates left no doubt as to its true context. Conversely, the roundhouse at Teigncombe (Gerrard, 2016), part of the Kestor complex within which Lady Fox (1954) had excavated what was regarded as a classic Iron Age settlement, proved to have been established in the Middle Bronze Age, though it was reoccupied in the Early Iron Age after a prolonged abandonment. With an internal diameter of some nine metres, its walls were constructed with a combination of massive double edge-set granite boulders and single boulders with coursing on a prepared platform some 14 metres across. By the hearth and entrance the earthen floor had been reinforced with flagstones, and a threshold stone had been set in a foundation trench across the entrance passage. Postholes and stake-holes within the building formed no regular pattern, so that the roof was probably supported by the massive walls alone.

An informative series of excavations in advance of the A30 Honiton to Exeter road improvement scheme (Fitzpatrick et al., 1999) showed that eastern Devon reflected the same patterns of roundhouse construction that were in evidence in southern England generally, with some regional variation. Middle Bronze Age houses at Patteson's Cross were of post-ring construction with south-east facing porches, and, if reconstructed as double-ring roundhouses with non-earth-fast outer walls, would have been eight or nine metres in diameter (Fig. 7.4, 1). A similar plan (Roundhouse 1) at Blackhorse (Fig. 7.4, 2), assigned by the excavators to the

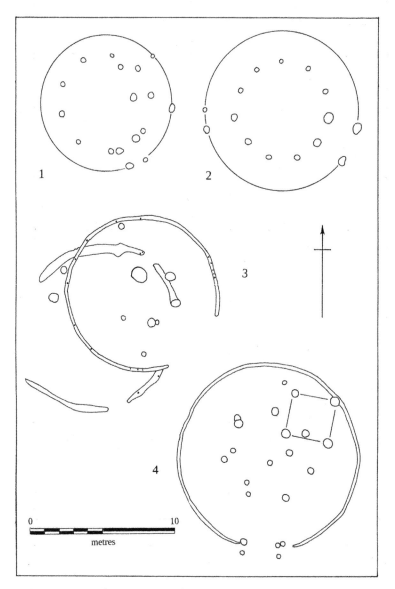

Fig. 7.4 Bronze Age and Iron Age roundhouses in east Devon. 1, Patteson's Cross, 1705; 2, Blackhorse, 1; 3, Blackhorse 136 (above, right) and 137; 4, Middle Burrow Farm, East Worlington. Drawings by D. W. Harding, adapted from Fitzpatrick et al., 1999 and Walls and Morris, 2012.

earliest Iron Age on the basis of a radiocarbon dating was nevertheless evidently in that Bronze Age tradition. The Iron Age houses employ ring-groove wall construction, but also use ring-gullies for drainage around roundhouses. Ring-groove wall foundations are evident from the Blackhorse penannular gullies 136 and 137 (Fig. 7.4, 3), of which the former, ten metres in diameter, had traces of stake-holes at intervals around its circuit. By contrast, at Langland Lane, a ring gully 13.5 metres in diameter, appears to have enclosed a roundhouse nine or ten metres in diameter, of which only the four porch posts survived (Fig. 7.5, 1). Likewise, a more substantial penannular gully 203, largely resulting from recutting, within a square, ditched compound at Blackhorse, most probably served as a eavesdrip-gully for a roundhouse some 12.5 metres in diameter, of which again only the porch posts survived (Fig. 7.5, 2). This house nevertheless is of particular interest since its radiocarbon dates and the presence of Durotrigian pottery suggest the latest pre-Roman Iron Age for its occupation. One of the better preserved larger roundhouse plans, dating to the last quarter of the first millennium BC, is from Burrow Farm, East Worlington, north of Crediton (Fig. 7.4, 4; Walls and Morris, 2012). The outer ring-groove 12.5 metres in diameter is comparable in size to the larger Wessex roundhouses. But the inner ring of seven posts, forming a circle six metres in diameter, and as the principal support for the roof effectively rendering the central post structurally redundant, departs from the geometric proportions of Wessex roundhouses, perhaps suggesting the use of different roofing materials. Perhaps the most important lesson, however, is that surviving traces of post-rings, ring-grooves, and drainage gullies are not necessarily indicators of overall house sizes, so that uncritical listing of comparative building diameters can be misleading.

A distinctive form of building in Cornwall is the courtyard settlement, typified by the classic site at Chysauster (Hencken, 1933) and conventionally dated to the Roman Iron Age. There has been long-standing debate as to whether only the peripheral cells of these cellular clusters were roofed around an open courtyard, or whether the whole complex was roofed by a single, hipped roof (Cripps, 2007: 148–53), but essentially the courtyard complex represents a shift towards the definition of separate spaces within an integrated whole, a process that is apparent in many regions of Atlantic Europe in the later Iron Age from Scotland to the Hispanic peninsula. A second issue regarding courtyard houses relates to dating. Evidence from the limited number of excavated examples supports a late dating, but it is clear from the sequence at Carn Euny (Christie, 1978) that occupation originated from the earlier Iron Age in the form of stake-wall roundhouses founded in ring-grooves and with the principal roof-support provided by an internal post-ring. The souterrain or *fogou* at Carn Euny was also evidently in use during the Early Iron Age occupation, though it continued in modified form during the later courtyard house phase. Evidence for dating *fogous*, the distribution of which is restricted to west Cornwall, has been summarized by Brindle (Smith et al., 2016: 349).

Ireland

Since the publication of *IAR*, there have been two major changes in the interpretation of Irish later prehistory that bear upon our theme. The first is that hillforts

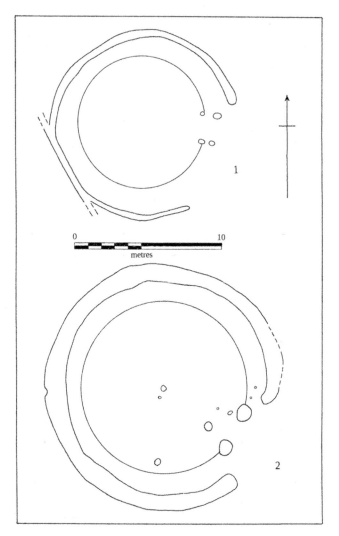

Fig. 7.5 Iron Age roundhouses in east Devon with eavesdrip-gullies. 1, Langland Lane 76; 2, Blackhorse 203. Drawings by D. W. Harding, adapted from Fitzpatrick et al. 1999.

have been shown conclusively to be a phenomenon of the later Bronze Age (most recently by O'Brien and O'Driscoll, 2017), and not of the Iron Age with Bronze Age antecedents, as in Britain. In fact, there only ever were limited points of comparison between British and Irish hillforts at the most basic level of walled enclosures, probably communal and probably multi-functional. Interestingly, however, O'Brien and O'Driscoll do not follow the fashion among some British archaeologists of denying a defensive role for hillforts. The second is that Irish 'royal sites' are no longer generally regarded in terms of their archaeology as primarily 'royal', the term 'regional' being preferred by some archaeologists to allow their interpretation as communal centres, without the contextual prejudice of later documentary sources (Becker, 2019). Perhaps the most striking achievement in the field has been the results of non-intrusive geophysical survey of the Rathcroghan complex by the ArchaeoGeophysical Imaging project of NUI Galway since the mid-1990s (Waddell et al., 2009), which revealed that the Rathcroghan Mound was surrounded by an enclosure 360 metres across (Fig. 7.6, 1), not yet definitively with reversed earthworks but otherwise comparable to Tara, Navan, and Knockaulin. Subsequent surveys (Fenwick, 2018; Fenwick et al., 2020) have revealed the complexity of the successive circular structures of the central mound, and the importance of the adjacent 'northern enclosure' and their radiating avenues (Fig. 7.6, 2). Whilst these major regional sites may no longer be regarded as 'royal', they were surely important ceremonial and ritual centres, a role which could well have carried over into the Early Christian period.

The 'deconstruction' of the 'royal' associations of the Irish sites had become inevitable once the notion had been discredited that the later Irish epics might be a 'window on the Iron Age' (Jackson, 1964). Whatever role they may have played in early historic Ireland, and archaeologically the evidence is limited, retro-projecting more than half a millennium interpretation based upon later documentary sources was always speculative. A key reason why the 'royal sites' were treated as special was, of course, because their structures were monumentally impressive in contrast to the dearth of coherent plans from settlements at large, and their special ceremonial and ritual status in the early historic period might reasonably imply long-established and socially embedded traditions (O'Driscoll et al. 2020), Their treatment as a coherent group, as Becker (2019) has argued, lent weight to the idea of continuity, whereas, despite some elements in common, like internally ditched enclosing earthworks, there was perhaps greater diversity in the series than was sometimes acknowledged. Other sites like Raffin, Co. Meath (Newman, 1995) shared some features of the 'royal sites' but did not register in the documentary record as having royal connections. Becker also challenged the idea that the 'royal sites' were primarily sites of seasonal occupation, though seasonal feasting would doubtless have been part of the communal way of life and integral to the social system.

There is still nevertheless a case for a significant shift in the later structural phases at both Navan and Knockaulin, with the 40 metre structure and the Mauve phase representing a substantial increase in the scale of building, and in the case of the Navan multi-ringed structure its covering with a massive mound to create a permanent monument in the landscape. Unique to the Navan structure furthermore is the three-aisled ambulatory that extends from its western edge to the central 'totem', which might well imply the formal, even ceremonial, control of access. Cumulatively, these factors imply a role 'beyond the household', perhaps reflecting a 'fundamental change in function' and a 'broader societal re-organisation'

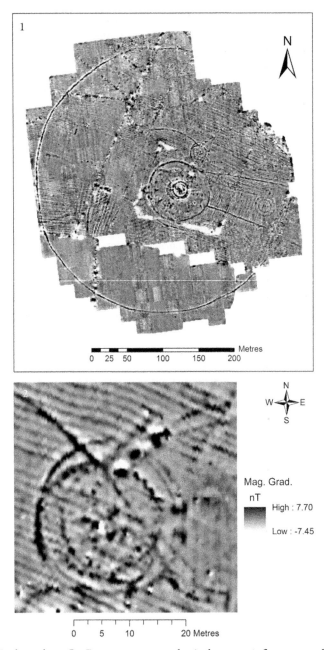

Fig. 7.6 Rathcroghan, Co. Roscommon, geophysical survey. 1, fluxgate gradiometer image of Rathcroghan Mound and encircling 360 m enclosure (© J. Waddell, J. Fenwick, and K. Barton, NUI Galway); 2, fluxgate gradiometer image of 'northern enclosure' (© J. Fenwick, NUI Galway).

(Becker, 2019: 296–7), which Becker attributed to the appearance of 'house societies' from the eighth century BC, in the wake of social and economic upheaval at the end of the Irish Bronze Age. At Navan the building of the multi-ringed structure on Site B also apparently coincided with the construction of the enclosing bank and internal ditch. Whatever their various roles may have been, it is clear that these major regional sites should not simply be regarded as hillforts of exceptional character and significance. But we should not assume from the similarity of buildings such as the figure-of-eight structures at Navan, Knockaulin, and the Rath of the Synods at Tara that these sites were necessarily contemporary. Radiocarbon dating has shown (Bayliss and Grogan, 2013) that the Navan figure-of-eight structures were in use between 255–150 *cal* BC, whereas at the Rath of the Synods they were assigned to a span AD 1–115, while the Rose Phase structures at Knockaulin are probably closer in date to the latter than the former. The enclosure of the Ráith na Rígh at Tara was probably contemporary with the bank and ditch at Navan, but the figure-of-eight structures at the Rath of the Synods were succeeded by later episodes of building extending into the opening centuries AD. Structures apparently were 'built and rebuilt – not over centuries but on a scale of generations, if not decades' (Bayliss and Grogan, 2013: 138). In general in archaeology complex palimpsests of superimposed structures are seen as evidence of longevity of occupation, and to argue that effort and resources on a substantial scale were invested in structures that were used for very short periods seems counter-intuitive. In fact, though retro-projection from much later documentary sources that are not primarily historical anyway is plainly speculative, there does seem to be a *prima facie* case at sites like Navan, Knockaulin, Tara, and Rathcroghan for continuity of activity, communal and probably ritual, over centuries if not longer. This hardly seems improbable when more than half the world today subscribes to religious beliefs and customs whose origins are older by far.

As in Britain, it is not immediately evident that all hillforts in Ireland were primarily used for residential occupation. It is equally apparent that correlating the use of individual house stances that are located physically within or around a hillfort with the construction and use of the enclosure earthworks is seldom straightforward. Nevertheless, on several of the major hillforts a combination of ground survey, LiDAR survey, and geophysical survey has indicated the presence of house stances in considerable numbers, in some instances involving a range of sizes that may well be indicative of social hierarchy within the Bronze Age communities (Cleary, 2007). At Brusselstown Ring, for example, in the Baltinglass hills of County Wicklow, 288 house sites have been identified, mostly in the range 5 m to 8 m in diameter, with some smaller structures that may have been ancillary buildings. Just fourteen structures were within a larger range of 9 m to 12 m in diameter, with just two in excess of 12 m, for the most part distributed evenly across the occupied area, though none apparently within the hillfort's inner enclosure (O'Brien and O'Driscoll, 2017: Fig. 8.33). A similar range of sizes was detected within the hillfort at Rathcoran with 10 per cent of the total here being in the larger range. One exceptionally large structure, defined by boulders forming a circle some 14 m in diameter, was located prominently on the summit in relative isolation from other buildings (O'Brien and O'Driscoll, 2017: Fig. 8.34). At Hughstown the buildings were recorded as magnetic anomalies only, and the size ranges were somewhat larger. Here again, however, a single largest structure, some 17 m in diameter, dominated the summit of the hill within its inner enclosure (O'Brien and O'Driscoll, 2017: Fig. 8.36). The potential recognition of a hierarchy in houses based upon size is remarkable, given that there is nothing comparable in the far greater number of hillforts in Britain. The assumption is that these groups represented kin-related families, with the largest, central house presumably some kind of 'big house' as a communal focus. Radiocarbon dating has now shown that the period of maximum construction and occupation of Irish hillforts was the Bishopland and Roscommon metalworking phases of the Irish Bronze Age, in absolute terms *c*. 1400–1000 BC, with a few continuing thereafter into the Dowris phase, but with virtually no new hillforts being built after 800 BC. There is some evidence for occasional reuse in the Iron Age, but in broad terms, hillforts in Ireland were a Bronze Age phenomenon, with some later survivals, where in Britain they were largely Iron Age, with some Bronze Age antecedents.

If the Baltinglass hillforts suggest a hierarchy of buildings within the settlement, a hierarchy within hillforts as a group might be implied by the associated material assemblages. In the absence of full publication it would be premature to assess the very complex sequence of activity uncovered within and outwith the hillfort at Rathgall, Co. Wicklow (Raftery, 1976). But in the present context it is worth noting that the central roundhouse, at 15 m in diameter in the 'big house' league, and attributed by the excavator to the Dowris Late Bronze Age, appears to have had a double outer wall, defined externally by a ring-groove and internally by a combination of ring-groove and post-ring. By contrast, the central circular structure partially excavated within the Late Bronze Age hillfort at Haughey's Fort, Co. Armagh, with an overall diameter in the order of 30 m, anticipates the monumental scale of the later Iron Age regional enclosures (Mallory and Baban, 2014). Like Rathgall, the claim of Haughey's Fort to be a high status site is based on the wealth of its material assemblage, including goldwork and prestigious items of bronze.

By contrast to this putative evidence for social hierarchy, the settlement at Corrstown, Co. Londonderry (Fig. 7.7; Ginn and Rathbone, 2012), showed little evidence of structural or social hierarchy. The houses, which were circular or oval in plan, ranged in size from 6.5 m across up to 12 m, in some cases the smaller buildings being interpreted as ancillary to the larger. But there was little in terms of the material assemblage, which comprised principally pottery and lithics, to suggest a social hierarchy. The dominant house type, around 85 per cent of the total of 74 houses, was defined by an outer, segmented annular ditch, commonly

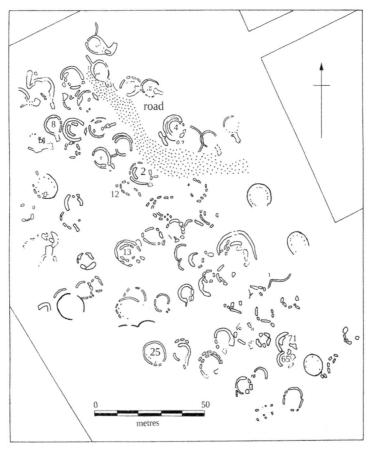

Fig. 7.7 Corrstown, Co. Londonderry, Bronze Age settlement plan. Drawing by D. W. Harding, adapted from Ginn and Rathbone, 2012.

with a broadly concentric inner ditch of similar construction (Fig. 7.8, 2). Between the two there was generally a post-ring that would certainly have provided the principal roof-support. A second post-ring, sometimes only partial, in the interior may have supported an upper ring-beam, or may simply have been secondary support for sagging rafters. To an observer of Scottish houses with ring-ditches a further element that is surely significant is the presence of postholes around the outer lip of the outer segmented ditches, as illustrated in Structure 2. This layout has evidently generated some debate in interpretation. The ditches commonly have a substantial base of cobbles, sometimes with looser stonework above, but hardly such as would warrant interpretation as a wall-foundation, which in any event would have been intermittent, given the segmented character of the ditches. Prevailing opinion therefore favours the view that the outer cobble-filled segmented ditches were initially for drainage, a view that may be supported by the presence

182 RETHINKING ROUNDHOUSES

on occasion of a length of ditch leading away from the outer house ditch. A case has been made from the excavated evidence for a mass-wall aligned between the segmented ditches, but not apparently for a mass-wall on the outer lip of the outer segmented ditch. In the case of Structure 4, for example, this would imply an overall diameter between 12 and 14 metres, but would still leave the south-facing porch projecting beyond the outer wall. Structures 8, 12, 13, and others could equally accommodate an external wall and still retain a projecting porch. The doorway was commonly on the south-east side, and was generally defined by a pair of post pits. Some had a well-defined hollow way leading from them, and in some cases surviving posts lined one side only, prompting interpretation as supporting a windbreak rather than an extended porch. Structurally, these houses most closely correlate with houses with ring-ditches from Northern Britain, though in Scotland the Bronze Age versions are seldom as complex in their footprint as these. There has been no suggestion at Corrstown that the ditches were the product of erosion rather than constructional. It is possible in some cases (Structure 4, for example) that the extant remains result from successive expansion of a smaller ditched house into a larger building. But in general the evidence for rebuilding is remarkably absent, suggesting that the settlement retained its basic layout over generations, with the implication that location was important to the occupants.

The second key structural type was characterized by an external ring-groove and internal post-ring (Fig. 7.8, 1), of a kind widely recognized across Britain and Ireland, though seldom so clearly defined as at Corrstown. Reconstruction of this type is hardly controversial, with the ring-groove supporting a plank wall or similar, and the post-ring providing the main roof-support.

The occupation at Corrstown appears from radiocarbon dating to have spanned the second half of the second millennium BC. Though the settlement may have originated in its southern half, and expanded progressively further north, there appears to be a pattern of three alignments, broadly west–east in the southern half, perhaps separated by initially open 'streets'. In the northern half of the settlement the houses appear to be aligned roughly north-west to south-east, but essentially flanking the cobbled street 70 metres long by 10 metres wide that was a distinctive element of the settlement layout. To its west the houses appear to be paired, once again suggesting that pairing was an integral part of the social structure. A question arises whether any of the paired houses, such as Structures 65 and 71, might have been occupied as figure-of-eight buildings. If the houses with segmented ring-ditches are cognate to their Northern British counterparts, and similarly interpreted as byre-houses in which the ground floor was occupied by stock, then the concept would appear to have been more fully developed at an earlier date at Corrstown, where the houses are large enough and sufficiently substantial to have supported an upper or mezzanine floor. Unfortunately, bone preservation at Corrstown was extremely poor, so that no corroboration is available from this quarter. The few ring-groove houses, on the other hand,

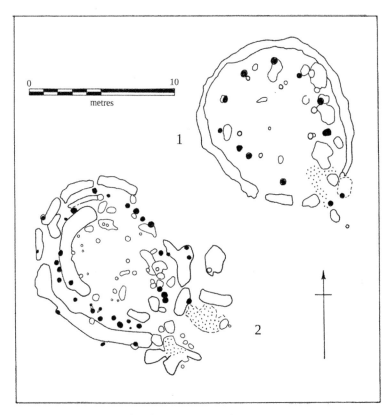

Fig. 7.8 Corrstown, Co. Londonderry: Type 1 and Type 2 structures. 1, Structure 25; 2, Structure 2. Drawing by D. W. Harding, adapted from Ginn and Rathbone, 2012.

were presumably exclusively for human occupation. The Corrstown village was apparently an open settlement, since the excavation covered a sufficient area to have exposed any enclosing earthworks, and though the planned alignments probably reflect kin groups, there is otherwise no evidence of social hierarchy.

Notwithstanding the evidence for village-sized settlements, the basic settlement unit of the Middle Bronze Age in Ireland was of just two or three houses, like those revealed by excavation in advance of the Cashel to Mitchelstown Road Improvement Scheme (McQuade and Moriarty, 2011). Post-ring and ring-groove structures were in evidence in various circular, sub-circular, or sub-rectangular plans. The roundhouse at Ballylegan (site 207) had a regular post-ring some nine metres in diameter around most of its circuit, with a clear doorway on the south-east flanked by slots that left in doubt whether the post-ring was the external wall or a roof-supporting circle with a further wattle or mass-wall that had not survived. At Phoenixtown, Co. Meath, a roundhouse ten metres in diameter was clearly defined by a ring of ten posts with sections of outer wall-slot on either side of its south-east facing entrance (Lyne, 2010). Radiocarbon dates from post-ring and door post confirmed its Middle Bronze Age construction.

By contrast with the evidence for roundhouses in the Irish Bronze Age, the number of recorded examples of Iron Age roundhouses in Ireland, outside the major regional sites, remains sparse. Despite the discovery through development-led excavation of numerous sites that have been radiocarbon dated to the Iron Age, structural remains are ephemeral, with some exceptions. One of the most impressive, and certainly the most like the major roundhouses of the British Iron Age, was the Ballycullen, Co. Dublin, house (Fig. 7.9, 1; Larsson, 2012). The outer wall of planks was bedded in a ring-groove fifteen metres in diameter, within which a circle ten metres in diameter of seventeen postholes provided the principal roof-support. A narrow gap in the south-east was certainly original, as may have been a gap in the circuit to the north-east, but a further break in the ring-groove to the west probably resulted from later disturbance. Neither possible doorway was elaborated. Several pits and a pair of L-shaped slots were possibly original internal features, though the purpose of the latter is obscure. Three further short slots extending inwards from the outer ring-groove may have supported radial divisions of internal space. Two relevant radiocarbon dates, one from the ring-groove, the other from an internal pit, indicated occupation in the second half of the first millennium BC. The material evidence, in addition to lithics, some of which may have been residual, included a pair of iron tweezers and a cylindrical blue glass bead, together unusually with undiagnostic pottery sherds, all consistent with a domestic function. The artefactual assemblage nevertheless, together with the monumental scale of the building, suggests a house of some potential status.

The roundhouse at Ballinaspig More, Co. Cork (Fig. 7.9, 2; Danaher, 2012) was evidently unenclosed and isolated. Its incomplete C-shaped plan was explained by the excavator as the result of erosion on the uphill side of the site, where the surviving postholes were shallower. The postholes of the main weight-bearing circle, some 7.5 metres in diameter, would have been substantial enough to support the roof, without the need for further internal posts, especially if there was an outer mass-wall of which no archaeological trace survived. Alternatively, an outer ring-groove might easily have been lost to truncation. Radiocarbon dating suggested activity in the second half of the first millennium BC. A similar time-scale was indicated for the intermittent ring-gully that surrounded the round-house from Knockcommane, Co. Limerick (Fig. 7.9, 3; McQuade and Molloy, 2012). The surviving structural remains in this instance comprised five substantial postholes around the northern half of the circuit, forming part of a circle 8.5 metres in diameter that was apparently completed by an arc of gully around the southern half, which might suggest a different use of internal space. Whilst the southern arc could have supported an external plank wall, the postholes of the northern circuit seem out of proportion for an external wall, and more appropriate to internal roof-support. There is ample room on the south, and just sufficient on

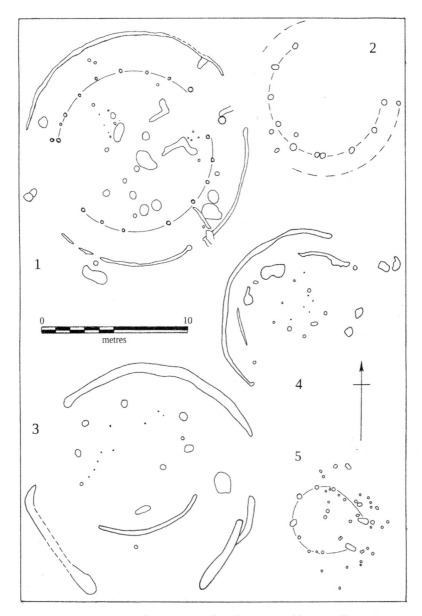

Fig. 7.9 Irish Iron Age roundhouses. 1, Ballycullen, Co. Dublin; 2, Ballinaspig More, Co. Cork; 3, Knockcommane, Co. Limerick; 4, Moneylawn Lower, Co. Wexford; 5, Coolbeg, Co. Wicklow. Drawings by D. W. Harding, adapted from Larsson, 2012, Danaher, 2012, McQuade and Molloy, 2012, McKinstry, 2011, and Frazer, 2012.

the north side for an external mass-wall, with the intermittent external gullies affording drainage around the house. The excavator suggested that a doorway might have existed on the east side of the house, and a second doorway on the west is possible. The ring-groove technique is also in evidence in the roundhouse on site 13 at Moneylawn Lower, Co. Wexford (Fig. 7.9, 4; McKinstry, 2011). Here slightly irregular concentric arcs, together with a scatter of postholes, represented the surviving footprint of a roundhouse, the outer wall of which, from its slightly polygonal plan, could have been made up of prefabricated wattle panels. Again, a radiocarbon date from this external gully indicated an Early Iron Age structure. Finally, a smaller house from Coolbeg, Co. Wicklow (Fig. 7.9, 5; Frazer, 2012), has a pear-shaped plan that extends towards its east-facing entrance, not unlike some British examples.

Development-led excavation has undoubtedly increased significantly the database of Iron Age sites in Ireland. Yet the number of settlements yielding coherent or substantial remains of roundhouses remains remarkably meagre, even by comparison with the number of Bronze Age sites now recognized. One category of site that has consistently been recognized from its distinctive plan is the ring barrow, which a generation ago was itself known only through a limited number of excavated examples (Raftery, 1981). Many of the new discoveries plainly are primarily funerary monuments, but there are others where the evidence for burial is more qualified, and whose penannular ditches in outline are hardly significantly different from those ring-ditches or ring-gullies which on British Iron Age sites are interpreted as for drainage of house stances, where the remains of the building very often have not survived truncation. In consequence the question has been asked (Ó Drisceoil and Devine, 2012: 263) whether in some instances ring-ditches might have been misinterpreted as primarily funerary, when they were in fact domestic structures analogous to those of the British Iron Age? The presence of structured deposits, even those including human remains, of course, need not signify a primarily funerary monument, since such deposits not unusually represent key moments in the life-cycles of domestic buildings.

However we view the evidence, the relative poverty of evidence for domestic settlement in the Iron Age in Ireland requires explanation. Various possible explanations have been advanced. There may have been a decline in population numbers, in which factors such as famine induced by successive failures in harvests or shortage of foodstuffs for livestock would be archaeologically undetectable. Evidence of epidemic disease, which must have afflicted communities in prehistory as much as in later documented times, would be equally elusive, except perhaps in mass burial or change in methods of disposal of the dead. It is clear that the economic structure that sustained the later Bronze Age bronze industries collapsed, though there is also evidence for iron working in Ireland from the eighth century BC (Becker, 2012). But a key factor in terms of settlement patterns is the decline of hillforts and the fact that settlements appear to be smaller and dispersed, suggesting a fundamental shift in the social structure. Some commentators have suggested that communities became more mobile, with a shift towards pastoralism, so that settlements became more transient, but it would probably be a mistake to underestimate the continuing importance of arable agriculture. Certainly the evidence of trackways through peat lands suggests that communication and mobility were important considerations. In these circumstances the rise of major regional centres like Navan, Tara, Knockaulin, and Rathcroghan might have assumed the roles formerly served by hillforts as places of assembly for communal and seasonal activities. Whilst qualifying the emphasis on pastoral farming as predominant in the Irish Iron Age, Becker suggested that one role of the major regional centres, in their earlier phases of use at any rate, may have been as gathering places 'in complex networks of agricultural production' (2019: 294–5).

Northern and North-Western France

The presence of circular building plans in later prehistory in northern France and the Netherlands was already apparent half a century ago (Harding, 1973), when examples of roundhouses dating to the Bronze Age were excavated at Dampierre-sur-le-Doubs in eastern France and at Nijnsel in Noord-Brabant. Though convincing plans at the time were few and far between, it was clear that open-area excavation on a larger scale would rapidly augment the number of known sites. By the time that *IAR* was published, the number of sites in Normandy, deploying both posthole and ring-groove construction, and with porched entrances like their Wessex counterparts, encouraged belief in 'a commonality of architectural tradition on both sides of the Channel that represents a significant modification of the conventional view of insular and Continental polarisation' (*IAR*: 88–9). In the past twenty years the number of sites uncovered as a result of development excavation has multiplied, demonstrating a considerable diversity in the size and character of roundhouse settlements. More importantly, however, it has become clear that the sequence of roundhouse settlements in northern France and their relationship with Southern British counterparts fluctuated from the later Bronze Age to the final La Tène Iron Age in a manner that undoubtedly will require reassessment as research progresses (Godard, 2013). Roundhouse settlements of the Middle and Late Bronze Age in northern France are seen as part of a cultural continuum, defined as Manche-Mer du Nord by Marcigny (Marcigny and Talon, 2009) that equally embraces the 'Deverel-Rimbury' phenomenon of southern England, reflecting cross-Channel connections, social, cultural, and commercial, rooted in a common Atlantic Bronze Age tradition. Iron Age roundhouses in northern France are not the product of this same tradition, though cross-Channel trading connections were evidently maintained into the late La Tène period.

188   RETHINKING ROUNDHOUSES

What is remarkable about the Middle-Late Bronze Age roundhouses of northern France is their similarity of size and construction. They are primarily defined by a single post-circle, commonly in the range 6 to 8 metres in diameter, also commonly with a projecting porch in the south-eastern quarter. In contrast to some of their southern English counterparts, these houses are notable for their axial symmetry, though this may be obscured by multiple episodes of rebuilding. House A at Plédéliac (Côtes d'Armor) demonstrates this (Nicolas, 2011). The same axial symmetry is displayed by a number of houses from the Late Bronze Age-early Iron Age settlement at Cahagnes (Calvados), though the majority here are more irregular in plan (Jahier, 2018). Because of their pronounced porches, generally defined by four posts, but sometimes by six, French archaeologists have followed the British interpretation of an outer mass-wall beyond the weight-bearing post-ring, giving these houses an overall diameter in excess of ten metres. A surprising number of examples nevertheless also have a central post, which presumably contributed to support of the superstructure, in construction if not essentially on completion. Where the doorway is represented solely by a single pair of posts, as in House A1 at Gravigny 'Les Coudrettes' (Eure) (Fromont et al., 2018), we must consider the probability that the post-ring, defining with the entrance an oval seven metres by eight, was the outer wall.

Among the most important later Bronze Age settlements in northern France, where the number of houses, notwithstanding successive episodes of building, might qualify them as villages or at least hamlets (*hameaux*), are Malleville-sur-le-Bec in the Eure (Mare et al., 2018), Caudin in Morbihan (Levan, 2016), and Cahagnes in Calvados (Jahier, 2018). The site of Malleville-sur-le-Bec (Fig. 7.10) is unusual in having three complementary components, apparently in contemporary use in the Late Bronze Age, namely a ring-work defined by an interrupted ditched earthwork, an open village with at least twenty roundhouses, and a cremation cemetery. From the mass of postholes within the ring-work the excavators defined three principal post-rings, not exactly concentric with the ditched enclosure, and doubtless in combination representing a succession of structural episodes. Their overall diameters, some 26, 32, and 37 metres, make a simple roofed structure unlikely, though a penannular reconstruction with open, central court would be possible. As to function, they favoured a ritual explanation rather than regarding the enclosure as a high status residence or defensive citadel (Mare et al., 2018: 94, 98). Comparisons have been drawn with the ring-works of south-eastern and eastern England, notably Mucking South Ring in Essex and Thwing in Yorkshire, for which both secular and ritual functions have been suggested. In Normandy the existence of other examples of such ring-works is suspected from air photographic survey.

The open village at Malleville-sur-le-Bec appears to have been a farming community, with limited storage capacity in pits and some four-post granaries. The houses appear to have been grouped in clusters of three or four, which could

REGIONAL DIVERSITY IN BRITAIN AND BEYOND 189

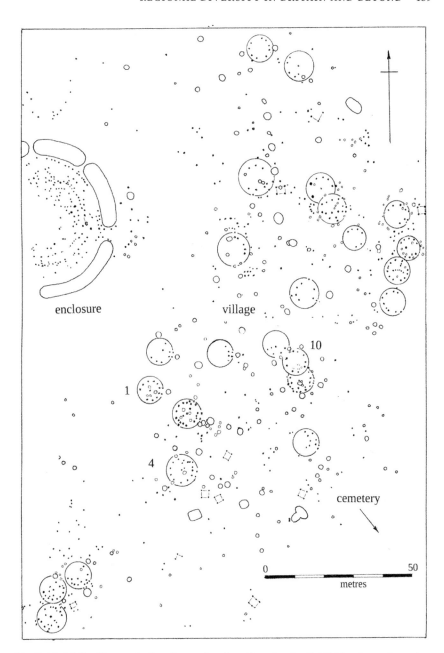

Fig. 7.10 Malleville-sur-le-Bec, Eure, site plan. Drawing by D. W. Harding, adapted from Mare et al., 2018.

represent successive generations of several family units. There is little to distinguish any one house or group of houses from the others, either architecturally or in terms of material associations. Their plans are remarkably standardized, with post-rings between six and eight metres in diameter, and those with porched doorways displaying axial symmetry and easterly orientation (Fig. 7.11). Some, but not the majority, have central posts, the role of which must remain equivocal in a building of this design. The excavators of Malleville-sur-le-Bec believed that the houses had an upper floor, so that the central post, and indeed the adherence to radial symmetry, could have been as much determined by this factor as by requirements to support the roof.

Further west, at Caudin in southern Brittany (Fig. 7.12; Levan, 2016), the houses have many features in common with Malleville-sur-le-Bec, including a greater number of houses with central postholes. The post-circles of the score of roundhouses fall within the same range of diameters, and several display the same adherence to the principles of axial symmetry. The excavator argued in

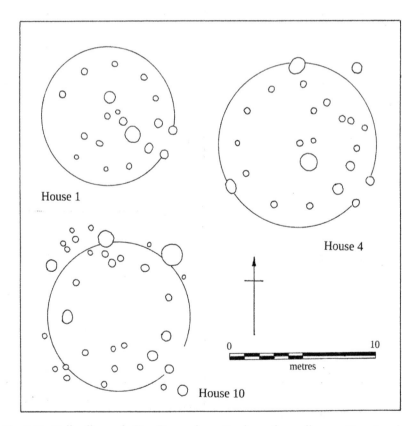

Fig. 7.11 Malleville-sur-le-Bec, Eure, schematic plans of roundhouses. Drawings by D. W. Harding, adapted from Mare et al., 2018.

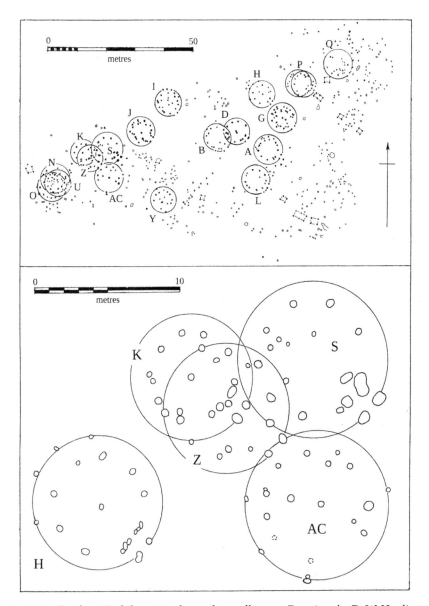

Fig. 7.12 Caudan, Morbihan, site plan and roundhouses. Drawings by D. W. Harding, adapted from Levan, 2016.

favour of a reconstruction involving an external mass-wall aligned with the outer porch posts. In several instances the Caudin roundhouses have surviving post-holes of an outer ring, coincident with the projected line of the mass-wall, so that the outer wall might have been of plastered wattle-work rather than clay cob in whole or in part. Several houses are self-evidently successive, and could have formed family clusters, though these groupings are not obviously segregated by occasional alignments of posts that presumably defined domestic or agricultural annexes.

The settlement at Cahagnes in Calvados (Fig. 7.13; Jahier, 2018) also had a total of around twenty circular or oval houses, with post-circles some seven to eight

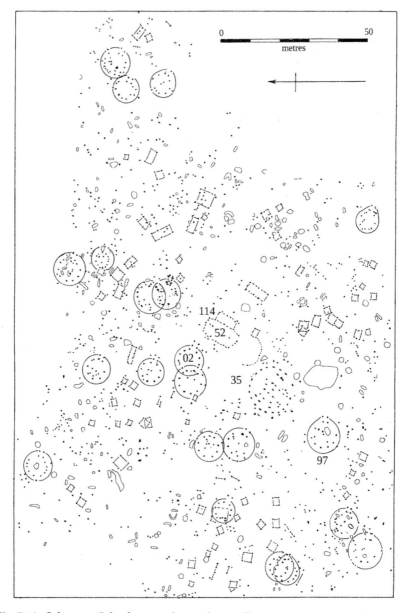

Fig. 7.13 Cahagnes, Calvados, site plan, with roundhouses, rectilinear buildings, and four-post structures. Drawing by D. W. Harding, adapted from Jahier, 2018.

metres in diameter, but by no means all so regular or symmetrical in their layout. Though several appear to conform to the principles of axial symmetry, others have much more irregular plans, though the apparent inclusion of porches seems to endorse their function as domestic dwellings. The settlement, for which again there was no evidence of enclosure within the exposed area, also included four-poster settings that could have been granaries or stores, but six- and eight-post settings as well, suggesting a range of possible functions. Centrally located was a larger circular building, 35, defined by an oval of postholes 15 metres by 16, within which and beyond which further arcs of postholes suggest a more complex layout (Fig. 7.14). One possibility is that the principal post-ring supported a ridge-roofed building with open inner court, approached by entrances flanked by paired posts on the south-east and north-west sides. In the centre a rectangular or sub-circular setting could be inferred, though the evidence was hardly definitive. The excavator considered the building's function more probably communal and ritual than domestic. The situation is compounded by the presence nearby of a larger than average rectilinear building 52 and 114, for which a communal or ceremonial function might also be applicable.

From these sites a remarkably consistent pattern emerges of later Bronze Age settlement in northern and north-western France centred on small, unenclosed villages of roundhouses in much the same fashion as those represented at Reading Business Park in southern England or at Corrstown in Ireland. The evidence for roundhouses in the Iron Age in northern France is far more equivocal. Whilst there are certainly some roundhouses dating to the La Tène period, they are by no means the norm, and are still in many regions a minority among a variety of rectilinear and apsidal plans, which appear to have become dominant towards the later pre-Roman period. Some roundhouses along the Channel and southern North Sea coasts have been attributed to cross-Channel commercial contacts, and may even represent enclaves of cross-Channel settlement, which must have been endemic in later prehistory, and not simply focused on those periods when high-status goods such as imported amphorae are prominent in the archaeological record.

The state of knowledge regarding domestic settlement in the Iron Age of Western and Central Europe was synthesized in a meeting of the Association Française pour l'Étude de l'Âge du Fer (AFEAF) in 2016 in Rennes (Villard-Le-Tiec, 2018). Plainly roundhouses were in a minority in the Iron Age, in comparison to the diversity of rectilinear plans, mostly oblong and modest in size compared to the Central and Northern European longhouses. There are also innumerable four- and six-poster structures, not all of which need have served exclusively as storage facilities, especially if four-posters were integral to roundhouses with non-earth-fast exterior walls, as is certainly suggested by the structure from La Gaubretière 'La Dugerie' in the Vendée (Guillier, 2004). But there are also occasional larger roundhouses in the Wessex tradition. Several of these roundhouses from

194 RETHINKING ROUNDHOUSES

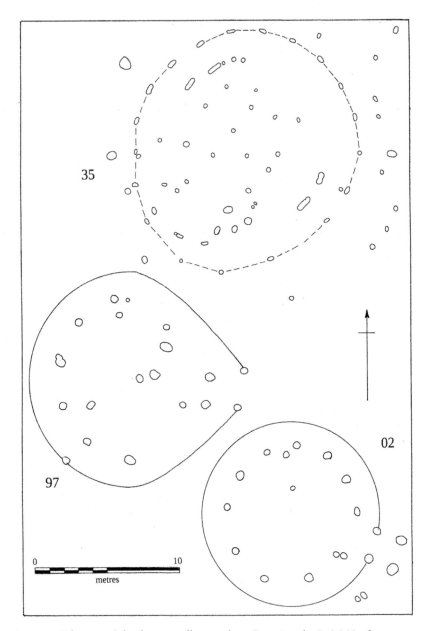

Fig. 7.14 Cahagnes, Calvados, roundhouse plans. Drawings by D. W. Harding, adapted from Jahier, 2018.

the Champagne are from palisaded enclosures (Desbrosse and Riquier, 2012). The earlier Iron Age roundhouse from Bezannes 'La Bergerie' in the Marne (Péchart, 2016; Riquier et al., 2018: 282, Fig. 9), with an overall diameter in excess of 17 metres, and apparently with entrances on the south and west sides, could have been a penannular ridge-roofed roundhouse, with stock access through the western entrance to an open central court. The principal roundhouse from the early Iron Age defended settlement at Courseulles-sur-Mer on the Normandy coast (Jahier, 2011) is also a three post-ring house, with an overall diameter of 15 metres, though in this instance the middle post-ring is the least substantial (*IAR*: Fig. 19, 3). Still the most symmetrical and substantial of the larger roundhouses is Ensemble III at Poses-sur-la-Mare in Haute-Normandie (Dechezleprêtre et al., 1997, 2000), with its main roof-supporting post-ring of 15/16 posts describing a circle 15 metres in diameter, giving an inferred overall diameter in the order of 18 metres (*IAR*: Fig. 19, 1). For a building of such proportions a porched entrance five metres wide on the east side hardly seems disproportionate. But the spacing between principal uprights of around three metres raises questions regarding the practicality of bridging them to create a rigid ring-beam to support a roof, and we may consider other possible functions of a communal or special nature for such a monumental structure.

Northern and north-western France have also yielded several roundhouse plans in which ring-groove foundations are deployed. One example of particular interest is Building 4 at Ifs (Calvados) (Fig. 7.15; Vauterin, 2011). The surviving structural framework consisted of a slightly irregular circular ring-groove, 13 metres in diameter, within which was a post-ring nine metres in diameter. Within the

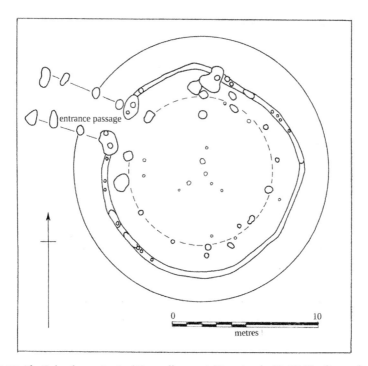

Fig. 7.15 Ifs, Calvados, principal Roundhouse 4. Drawing by D. W. Harding, adapted from Vauterin, 2011.

ring-groove traces were recovered of postholes at intervals up to a metre, with some lesser stake-holes between them. The excavators therefore concluded that the trench was the foundation for a continuous external wall of linked posts with deeper supports at regular intervals. An outstanding feature of the building, however, was its north-west facing porched entrance, the passage being no less than six metres long and supported by four pairs of posts. A more normal balance between house and porch would have been achieved had the outer wall aligned with the second or third pair of posts from the outside, creating a division between outer porch and inner vestibule. Had such a mass-wall without earth-fast foundations existed in this case, the overall diameter of the house would have been at least 16 metres, creating yet another three-ringed monumental round-house. The ring-groove in places is somewhat polygonal, suggesting that it may have supported a wall of prefabricated wattle panels, so that the post-ring could have supported a dividing wall as well as a roof-supporting post-ring, as claimed at Longbridge Deverill.

An important agricultural settlement of the early Iron Age at Inzinzac-Lochrist in the Morbihan (Le Gall, 2017) used the ring-groove technique for its half dozen circular houses and comparable foundation trenches for its rectangular houses or oblong houses with rounded ends. House 76 (Fig. 7.16, 1) is noteworthy for its double ring-groove, which the excavator interpreted as successive roundhouses, of which the larger was probably later, since its central post appears to have necessitated shifting the earlier hearth somewhat to the north-west. The position of the two doorways, facing south and north-west, nevertheless, remained unchanged, so that the footprint of the earlier house was evidently still important. The spacing between the ring-grooves is at maximum over a metre, which would be wide for wall insulation, but on the east it is certainly within the range of practicality.

One of the more striking discoveries was the roundhouse with souterrain-cellar from Bel Air, Saint-Caradec (Côtes-d'Armor) in Brittany (Fig. 7.16, 2; Barbeau and Delnef, 2020), not least because of its similarities to examples from eastern Scotland. The roundhouse itself, dating to the sixth and fifth centuries BC, was founded in a ring-groove of modest proportions at around seven metres in diameter. It demonstrated nevertheless three principal phases of construction, in the first two of which the main entrance was oriented to the east, veering to the south in its final stage, but in each case with secondary access from the west. There was no complete inner post-ring, but an arc of postholes on the south-west side looks too substantial to be simply internal partitioning. In each structural phase, however, on its south-west flank the interior led directly into a timber-revetted souterrain-cellar, with the use of which the house was evidently integral. Nearly 15 metres in length, a maximum of 2.40 metres in overall width and with an average depth around 1.85 metres, its storage capacity would surely have been considerably in excess of the needs of a single household. External access to the cellar was afforded by an entrance at its south-west end. Structurally, the parallel

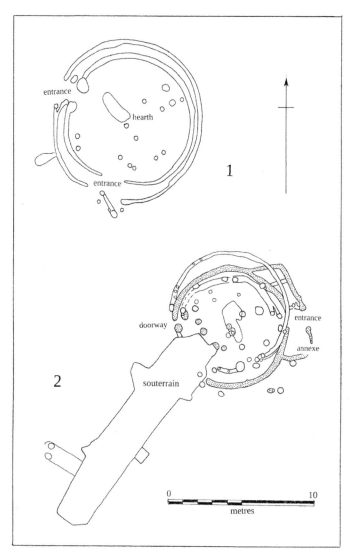

Fig. 7.16 Ring-groove roundhouses in Brittany. 1, Inzinzac-Lochrist, Morbihan, House 76; 2, Bel Air, Saint-Caradec, Côtes d'Armor, roundhouse and souterrain-cellar: Phase 2 stippled. Drawing by D. W. Harding, adapted from Le Gall, 2017 and Barbeau and Delnef, 2020.

with Thainstone East in Aberdeenshire, of somewhat later date, is nevertheless compelling. Direct access from houses into souterrains is hardly novel in Brittany, of course, but most of the known examples are in relation to rectangular or rectilinear houses (Bossard, 2020). One example, at Bénodet in Finistère (Roy, 2003), where the post-circle, if complete, would have defined a substantial roundhouse some 14 metres in diameter, included most of a small but complex souterrain.

A further facet of the Bel Air house, however, was the apparent annexe flanking its eastern entrance in its two earlier phases of use. This outer vestibule area was defined by trench foundations extending from the ring-groove and in each phase terminating in a pair of postholes marking the outer door. Once again the Scottish parallel with the annexe of Structure 1A at Blackford in Strathallan is striking, to the extent that it may be necessary to re-examine plans of houses elsewhere, particularly those that display projecting porches, to see if evidence for similar outer vestibules may have been overlooked.

The conclusion from a review of roundhouses in northern and north-western France, more than a decade after the publication of *IAR*, is therefore that Iron Age roundhouses, though important, are still very much a minority among the diversity of rectilinear plans (Milcent, 2017). Though they show some significant similarities to their British counterparts, they are effectively superseded by the La Tène fashion for rectilinear building plans (Maguer et al., 2018). The later Bronze Age, by contrast, has shown increasing similarities between roundhouse open village settlements in various parts of north-west Europe.

The *Castro* Culture of the Peninsular North-West

The issue of hierarchy or heterarchy is one that has been prominent in studies of *castro* settlements. Sastre argued that *Castro* society was complex but not hierarchical, but that emergent forms of inequality were controlled corporately. Inequalities were latent in production, especially of metallurgy, but potential social tensions, she believed, were controlled without class divisions. In agriculture inequalities of land allocation might give rise to different capacity in terms of production. In terms of settlement structures she argued on the basis of the homogeneity of buildings and material culture in the Middle Iron Age *castros* that there was minimal archaeological evidence for hierarchy. They each enclosed around a hectare and could have accommodated some 200 inhabitants. They were 'characterised by self-sufficiency' (Sastre, 2002: 215), and did not show any evidence of being in an hierarchical relationship with other more prominent *castros*. A heterarchical social structure nevertheless did not mean that neighbouring communities were not likely to have engaged in warfare, so that a defensive role for the hillfort was not discounted. *Castro* communities were effectively opposed equals, who must have engaged in exchange relationships, including the exchange of brides in marriage (Currás and Sastre, 2020b: 141). By the early centuries AD, however, there was a 'clearly defined local aristocracy operating under Roman imperial auspices' (Sastre, 2002: 233), but this she regarded as a totally new social dynamic.

The history of hillfort and roundhouse studies in the peninsular north-west, and particularly its link with Galician culture and ethnicity, has led to their typological treatment as artefacts, rather than as social constructions. In consequence, excavations into the later twentieth century failed to address social relationships of structures or to record finds in their social context (Ayán Vila, 2008: 905–6). Furthermore, until the 1990s there was a deficiency of information regarding the origins and antecedents of the roundhouses of the *Castro* culture, and especially of any timber-built houses preceding the familiar stone foundations.

The earliest *castros* are now radiocarbon dated between the tenth and ninth centuries BC, but the construction and layout of domestic space is assumed to have continued from the preceding later Bronze Age phase of unfortified settlement (Ayán Vila, 2008: 923). Some settlements appear to have had circular houses with stone foundations, but there are other sites, like the hillfort of Sacaojos, León (Misiego Tejeda et al., 1996) where timber huts not dissimilar to stake-wall construction in Britain are known. In some instances timber or made-up walls were based on a low stone foundation, with clay and straw flooring and central hearth indicating domestic usage, as at Castro Pequeno de Neixón (Alvarez Gonzáles et al., 2005), dating to the seventh and sixth centuries BC. The fact is, however, that the very small dimensions of the structures in the earliest Iron Age *castros*, at Sacaojos between three and five metres in diameter, more commonly averaging five metres, and generally not much above five, are small by British standards and suggest a rather limited domestic function. In the earlier Iron Age they are also located, sometimes in proximity to each other, but generally with open spaces around them, and we may suppose most daily activities took place outdoors. In some cases successive episodes of construction evidently maintained this pattern of occupation. In sum, Ayán Vila concluded that the Early Iron Age *castros* demonstrated a lack of demographic pressure, a lack of social hierarchy, and little socio-economic complexity (2008: 932). The central hearth was evidently an important reference point around which social activities focused.

The second phase of *castro* settlement, dating from the fifth century, saw the more general adoption of stone construction, and an increase in the density of building within the enclosure. At the Cividade de Terroso, one of the major settlements of the latest phase, on the coast midway between the Doura and Lima rivers, family units have been recognized from the fourth to second centuries, based on small, circular units, with occasionally rectilinear, oval, or D-shaped components. The circular buildings had flagged floors and central hearth that also incorporated a central support for the roof. Allowing for local variations, similar structuring principles are in evidence in the hillfort of Borneiro, at La Coruña in north-western Spain, where small clusters of circular buildings are not formally defined by boundary walls into distinct entities.

By the later second century, certain of the larger hillforts in the western coastal zone were evidently engaged in productive trade along the western seaways with the Mediterranean, together with an evident increase in population. These included the citânia de Briteiros, the citânia de Santa Luzia, and the cividade de

Terroso, which plainly fulfilled a proto-urban role as regional centres, and in which the interior layout was more organized, with some buildings that served a communal role. This development became more formalized in the Augustan period, but the concept of the courtyard cluster of domestic buildings had emerged from an older local convention. An example from the cividade de Âncora near Viano do Castelo consisted of three circular structures, one with outer vestibule, together with a rectangular building, all arranged around a paved courtyard that included a water tank. Vestibules are reckoned to have been an innovation from the Augustan period, but the concept of the courtyard complex is certainly older. The rectangular building had a hearth, benches, and a bread oven, and is therefore assumed to have been a communal hall for the resident kin group. There remains some debate regarding the size of social unit represented, whether a single nuclear family or an extended group. Similar familial enclosures or composite house groups are dominated by circular components at Terroso (Queiroga, 2003: Fig. 19). In fact, the *castros* afford a clear alternative to the monumental roundhouse model, in which we must assume that a range of social activities were accommodated within a single building, whereby different activities or individuals were assigned to separate space within a collective enclosure. In the developed *castros* these areas were more clearly segregated into 'quarters', as at the *oppidum* of Sanfins, and with Romanization the layout acquires more urban appearance. But for our present purposes, it is the concept of the familial courtyard house, based upon several component elements in which circular plans are integral, that is crucial. It is one that would not be difficult to translate into the pattern of surviving hut circles, for example, at Hod Hill in Dorset, dating likewise to the later pre-Roman Iron Age (Richmond, 1968: Fig. 2). The crucial difference, of course, is that the *castro* courtyard complexes were constructed of stone, so that their integration as a unit is more definitive. This further helps to interpret the role and use of the individual components, since the quality of construction may differ, and the walls may additionally be decorated. Hearths, raised granaries, and threshing floors may be distinguished, while the associated material assemblage may further indicate activities (Ayán Vila, 2008: 954).

A more recent line of research has focused on the *pallozas*, traditional roundhouses of the Ancares range, and related domestic and agricultural architecture of Asturias, as ethnographic models of the construction and use of roundhouses (Ruano and Berrocal-Rangel, 2019). As late as the mid-twentieth century, roundhouses up to 20 metres in diameter accommodated households of fifteen to twenty persons, in winter sharing the living space with livestock, when harsh weather conditions limited outside movement. The largest are certainly exceptional, but 15 metres is by no means unusual. What the *pallozas* demonstrate, however, is a greater variety in roofing than the Reynolds conical model implies. *Pallozas* can be built on a slope, with variable wall height and decidedly unsymmetrical conical roofs, which may be supported by several upright posts and pairs of rafters creating effectively a hipped roof on a circular ground-plan. The roof may reflect the internal division of space between human quarters and byre, and the need to ensure that smoke from the hearth does not distract the animals. These large *pallozas* can only be traced back to medieval times, but they constitute an invaluable ethnographic insight into the construction and social use of circular buildings in a region where circular house plans certainly derived from much earlier origins.

The most common structures in Asturias are rather smaller, six to nine metres in diameter if circular, between six and ten in length and five or six wide if rectangular. The ground floor was used to stable stock overnight with provision for a herdsman, and the upper floor was used as a hayloft, and they were evidently used by transhuming pastoralists in spring or autumn. A notable feature is the steep pitch of the roofs, often as much as 60 degrees, and rough walls designed to keep cattle away from the thatch. The smallest of the roundhouses are effectively beehive cells, just two to three metres in diameter and corbelled beneath sod roofs (Ruano and Berrocal Rangel, 2019: Fig. 2), which match the construction of some of the cellular structures of the later Iron Age in the Western Isles.

Postscript

In view of the predominantly North-West European distribution of circular ground-plans for domestic buildings, in Britain, Ireland, north-western France, and the north-west of the Hispanic peninsula, all areas that were inhabited by Celtic-speaking people, we should address the question whether the roundhouse might be regarded as a 'Celtic' tradition? In Spain, whilst some users of roundhouses may have been Celtic-speaking, significant groups of Celtic speakers, including the Celtiberians, had a long-established practice of rectangular building. Furthermore, there is no archaeological evidence in Central or West-Central Europe, whence Indo-European Celtic speakers originated in the older conventional view, for an older tradition of circular architecture that was progressively replaced by rectangular. Alternative claims to Celtic origins in the peninsular south-west do not alter the comparative distributions of Celtic-speaking communities and roundhouses. A persuasive critique of the archaeological and philological evidence (Sims-Williams, 2020) suggests that the most plausible origin of Celtic language was in France, whence it spread from around 1000 BC. Accordingly, there would appear to be no justification in equating roundhouses and 'Celtic' society, though it would seem reasonable to regard the later prehistoric fashion for circular domestic building as geographically and culturally common to neighbouring communities of the Atlantic seaboard.

8

Chronology, Origins, and Aftermath

At the time that *IAR* was published it was still possible to think of roundhouses as an archetype of the Iron Age in Britain, whilst acknowledging the existence of second millennium antecedents. Now, even though still best represented in the first millennium BC, with examples continuing regionally into the para-Roman Iron Age, distinctive types of roundhouse, including substantial post-ring round-houses, have been shown to characterize the Bronze Age in Northern Britain especially (Pope, 2015), leading one to suppose that they might have been equally represented in lowland England had conditions favoured their survival, or upland England and Wales had research been able to confirm their dating. Whilst recognizing that circular building plans exist from the Early Bronze Age, and possibly in the Late Neolithic too, our definition of houses should be based not so much on structural footprints as on houses as social artefacts, and how they functioned for their occupants and the community. It remains true that, from the end of the Middle Bronze Age, there appears to be a shift in emphasis in the archaeological record from funerary and ceremonial monuments to settlement remains, perhaps leading to a greater focus on the house and domestic architecture, even if the basic geometry of circular domestic building was established in Britain at least from the earlier Bronze Age. In retrospect, therefore, three questions come to the fore. When did the roundhouses as a diagnostic component of insular settlement first appear, and what was its significance? What were the circumstances of its demise? And, not unrelated perhaps to the latter issue, how far did it survive under the Roman occupation?

Neolithic Antecedents?

Faced with the obvious contrast with the widespread and long-established Continental tradition of rectangular house plans, Sharples (2010: 189) concluded that the insular preference for circular plans in domestic architecture must derive from the ritual architecture of early prehistory. The post-rings that are sometimes found beneath Bronze Age barrows had long been cited as analogous to domestic roundhouses, triggering ideas regarding the potential relationship between houses of the living and houses of the dead. But it was more particularly the monumental timber circles of the late Neolithic and Early Bronze Age, for which a ceremonial or ritual role has generally been inferred, that Sharples regarded as the 'template

---

Rethinking Roundhouses: Later Prehistoric Settlement in Britain and Beyond. D. W. Harding, Oxford University Press.
© D. W. Harding 2023. DOI: 10.1093/oso/9780192893802.003.0008

to create a domestic house that would chart and control time' (Sharples, 2010: 191). A link with ritual sites of earlier prehistory would also lend weight to the cosmological interpretation of Iron Age roundhouses. Though chronologically and spatially unrelated, the later prehistoric circular structures from the so-called 'royal sites' of Ireland presented the prospect of a relationship between substantial roundhouses and complex circular timber structures of probably ceremonial or ritual function.

Plainly there are superficial similarities in plan between Neolithic and Early Bronze Age timber circles and later roundhouses, just as there are similarities between the circular stone building techniques of Neolithic tombs and cairns and later prehistoric stone-built roundhouses. Whilst undoubtedly the earlier monuments demonstrate a degree of skill in working timber and stone, the striking element in their construction is the massive communal labour input in acquiring and erecting monolithic stones or massive timbers, rather than the constructional specialisms of domestic joinery or masonry. And it remains a fact that the surviving evidence of earlier Bronze Age domestic buildings, ephemeral and slight in contrast to the larger domestic or communal houses of later prehistory, hardly supports a direct derivation from Neolithic or Early Bronze Age ritual monuments. In terms of social significance it is surely clear that major Neolithic monuments and the later Irish sites were communal meeting places in which dispersed and possibly seasonally mobile populations had chosen to invest their resources and identities, whereas the roundhouses of the British later Bronze and Iron Ages were the devolved focus of much smaller, nuclear or extended family groups.

More important than superficial similarities of plan are the so-called structuring principles of houses, and the social conventions and beliefs that they may articulate. These have been discussed for the Orcadian later Neolithic by Richards and others (Richards and Jones, 2016), and in the context of Grooved Ware sites in Ireland (Smyth, 2011), where the distinction between domestic and ritual sites has sometimes been arguable. Defining 'house societies' archaeologically is not made easier by Lévi-Strauss' wide-ranging definition of the concept, and more especially by the fact that distinctive domestic buildings are not among his definitive criteria. But at least in the Irish Neolithic and the Orcadian Neolithic there were demonstrable 'links between houses and tombs through which concepts of lineage and continuity were channelled' (Smyth, 2011: 28) that persuaded Irish archaeologists that these may have been the product of house societies.

Bronze Age Circular Structures in Northern Britain

Among the earliest Bronze Age circular structures are ring-banks, essentially a mass-wall defining a circular building, within which evidence of posts supporting the roof may or may not survive archaeologically. In upland regions the ring-bank

204 RETHINKING ROUNDHOUSES

may still be extant, but dating has always been problematical, as material suitable for radiocarbon sampling may not survive, and material associations have often been sparse in the extreme. Generally these 'hut-circles', not always readily distinguishable from ring cairns, are of no great diameter, and architecturally do not bear obvious comparison to the complex architecture of later prehistoric roundhouses. For Scotland classic examples of earlier Bronze Age ring-bank houses are those from the site at Lairg in Sutherland (Fig. 8.1, 1; McCullagh and Tipping, 1998), where they date from around 1800 BC, continuing well into the third quarter of the second millennium. The overall diameters can be substantial: House 4 was 15 metres externally and House 3 was 17 metres by 15 metres externally. But the walls are essentially low rubble banks some 2 metres in width, though in House 4 they included coursed masonry flanking the entrance, and in House 6 a sector of the wall was faced with stone revetting on the inside. Though some internal posts were traced, there is little evidence for roof-supporting post-circles, and the probability must be that the cone of the roof rested directly on the ring-bank, thus reducing the usable internal space. The excavators were not persuaded that all of the structures were designed for domestic habitation. Though lacking a hearth, House 3 yielded a range of artefacts that would be consistent with domestic occupation. A shallow penannular depression within the house, with a similar extension to the entrance, that was attributed to erosion through use, bears similarities to later ring-ditch features thought to result from stock being stalled within the building. Almost identical features were found in House 4, and similar but more fugitive traces characterized other structures at Lairg. House 3 appears to have been converted into an open byre in a secondary phase of use, so that animal husbandry seems to have been integral to the site's economy and its domestic architecture.

Whilst at Lairg there was evidently some attempt to create faced walling, especially by the house doorway, at Bracken Rigg in Upper Teesdale (Fig. 8.1, 2; Coggins and Fairless, 1984) the use of whinstone cobbles, including some larger boulders, made it impractical to bond the stonework. The foundations therefore comprised a dump over two metres across, within which it was impossible to trace postholes, though it could doubtless have supported a wall-plate. Nevertheless, the entrance had been paved, extending into the interior, which elsewhere had been cobbled. Several hearths indicated successive episodes of occupation. An odd feature was the presence of earth-fast boulders, not simply in the walls but within the house interior, where they must have been used as furniture or work surfaces. Evidently it would have been difficult at Bracken Rigg to ground the roof rafters firmly unless perhaps with a covering of turf to stabilize the foundations. Support of the roof, however, was provided by a reasonably regular ring of six posts. The excavators considered ling as the most likely available roofing material. Some stake-holes suggested that the inner face of the perimeter wall may have been wattle lined, which may account for the slightly polygonal appearance in

CHRONOLOGY, ORIGINS, AND AFTERMATH 205

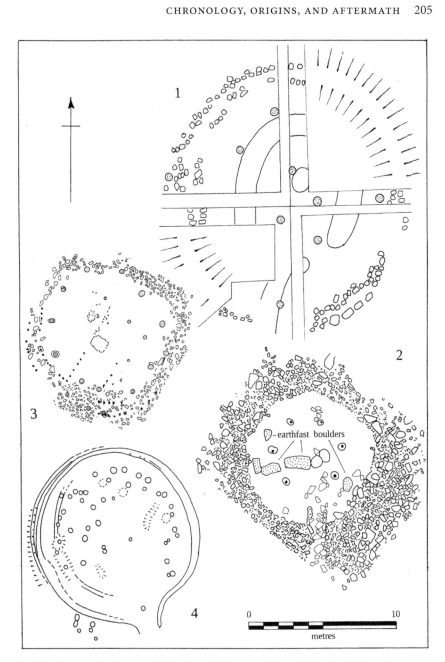

Fig. 8.1 Bronze Age houses in Northern Britain. 1, Lairg, Sutherland, House 4; 2, Bracken Rigg, Co. Durham; 3, Green Knowe, Peeblesshire, platform 4; 4, Green Knowe, Peeblesshire, platform 2. Drawings by D. W. Harding, adapted from McCullagh and Tipping, 1998, Coggins and Fairless, 1984, Feachem, 1961, and Jobey, 1980.

plan of the internal wall-face. The average internal diameter was 8.5 metres. There was a series of successive hearths just off centre, and gullies leading in from the southern doorway suggested an internal lobby. Unusually, the Bracken Rigg house stands in apparent isolation within its irregular enclosure of less than a hectare, and is the most westerly of a series of similar sites stretching along the 381 m (1,250 ft) contour overlooking the Tees.

Colin Burgess' excavation at Houseledge (Burgess, 1980; 1984: 145ff.) showed that Bronze Age ring-banks could also incorporate or overlie both post-ring and ring-groove structures, and it was unclear exactly what role the ring-bank served, except that it was made up of stones resulting from systematic field clearance. Unlike Bracken Rigg, postholes were located within the rubble ring-bank at Houseledge. Burgess, however, emphasized the distinction between these dump walls and the faced masonry of hut-circles of the Roman period, and he stressed that not all the ring-bank structures need have been domestic dwellings, citing levelled floors, doors and porches, and support for roofing (though oddly not hearths) as evidence for use as houses, as opposed to stock pens.

Ring-groove with simple internal post-ring constituted the basic house construction of the unenclosed platform settlement at Green Knowe, Peeblesshire, in this case located at around 275 metres, in a linear spread along the contour. The houses should not be regarded as a separate type on account of their platforms set into sloping topography, and though there was evidence of field clearance, the stone was not a definitive component of the houses themselves. Jobey (1980) cleared two platforms, 2 and 5, and sampled a third. The houses ranged in size from 7 to 10 metres in diameter, and were defined by ring-grooves, from some of which evidence for stake-wall construction with hurdling and daub was recovered. In the case of platform 2 (Fig. 8.1, 4) slightly eccentric ring-grooves were plainly successive, and were served by separate successive entrances facing south. By contrast, the house excavated by Feachem (1961) on platform 4 (Fig. 8.1, 3) had twin stake-circles, notably flanking the south-west doorway, that were sufficiently concentric to suppose contemporaneity. These he believed had constituted a cavity wall from which no trace of insulating material had survived. Roof-support in all cases was provided by internal post-rings. Radiocarbon dates at the time were scarce, and the few available indicated a later second millennium occupation for Green Knowe, though not all platforms need have been in use at any one time, and not all necessarily for domestic occupation.

A parallel site at Lintshie Gutter in the Upper Clyde (Terry, 1995) complemented the findings from Green Knowe. Of particular relevance are the concentric ring-grooves of House 13 and House 5 (Fig. 3.11, 1), which the excavator believed indicated cavity wall construction with turf infilling for insulation, thereby vindicating Feachem's earlier interpretation at Green Knowe. Stony rubble featured notably in the structure on platform 1, which was interpreted as a stock pen rather than a roofed dwelling. Lintshie Gutter was exceptional in the number of platforms recognized, more than thirty in all spread over 700 metres, but not all were for domestic occupation, and the chronological range spanned the first half of the second millennium BC. One date from a structural context on platform 8 indicated that the origins of the settlement could have extended back into the late third millennium.

Meadowend Farm, Kennet, south-east of Clackmannan (Fig. 8.2; Jones et al., 2018), is a remarkable Bronze Age settlement for several reasons. First, unlike Wessex or the Scottish Borders, it is not located in an area that is well documented archaeologically, and in that regard is a typical product of the era of development-led archaeology. Second, its roundhouses include the full range of structural features represented in the Iron Age, that is, post-ring, ring-groove, and ring-ditch, including double-ring examples with extended porched entrances, and its ancillary structures, secondary circular structures, and four-posters, indicate a fully-developed roundhouse settlement that cannot be regarded as a prototype or antecedent in anything less than fully-formed state. Finally it shows elements of sophistication, such as the 'extended pear-drop' plan of the Structure 1 ring-groove that is designed to integrate the projecting porch into the framework of the house, thus addressing a problem that was fundamental to the structural integrity of monumental roundhouses, including those of the Wessex Iron Age.

The earliest building on the site was Structure 5, comprising a sector of surviving ring-groove that could have described a circle or oval around eight metres across around a central post. Best-preserved at Meadowend Farm are two Middle Bronze Age houses, Structures 1 and 7 (Fig. 8.2), radiocarbon dates from which strongly suggested that they were in simultaneous occupation. Structure 1 was defined by a pear-drop ring-groove 15 metres by 13 metres, two metres within which a regular post-ring would have supported the roof. Its porched entrance was in the south-east, whilst successive hearths were located towards the front of the house, just inside the doorway. Two radial post alignments suggest an internal division of the house between front and back, which would have assigned the hearths to the front 'working' area. An unusual, and unexplained feature of Structure 1 was an arc of ring-ditch around the northern circuit *external* to the ring-groove. It seems too shallow to have been effective as a soak-away, and in the absence of independent dating evidence is only assumed to be contemporary because of its concentricity with the main building.

Structure 7 was represented by a post-ring nine metres in diameter, but with a genuine ring-ditch crescent around its northern circuit. Its hearth was centrally located, and its entrance likewise was oriented to the south-east. An external wall of turf, as suggested by the excavators, would have given the building an overall diameter still somewhat short of its neighbour's. Dating evidence suggested that Structures 1 and 7 were both built around the late sixteenth century *cal* BC (Jones et al., 2018: 69) and abandoned by the early thirteenth (Jones et al., 2018: 70), a potential span of two or three centuries. Abandonment between building phases seems improbable given the close replication of footprints, suggesting that the

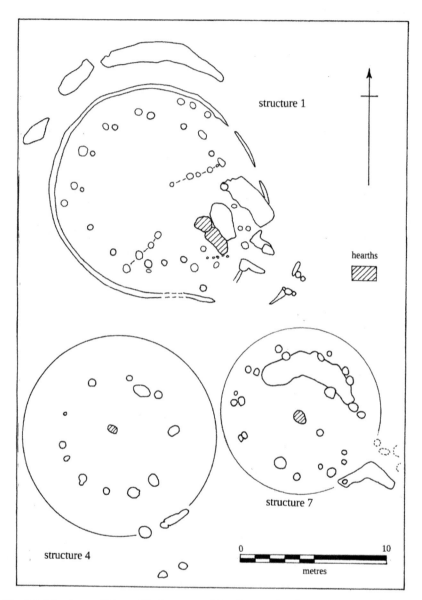

Fig. 8.2 Meadowend Farm, Clackmannanshire, Bronze Age houses. Drawing by D. W. Harding, adapted from Jones et al., 2018.

current fashion for short roundhouse life-spans is not universally supported by the evidence.

The full range of structural types is equally well represented elsewhere in Scotland in the second millennium BC. Among the earliest examples is a double-ring roundhouse some ten metres in diameter from Blairhall Burn, Amisfield, Dumfriesshire (Fig. 8.3, 2; Strachan et al., 1998), which produced a single

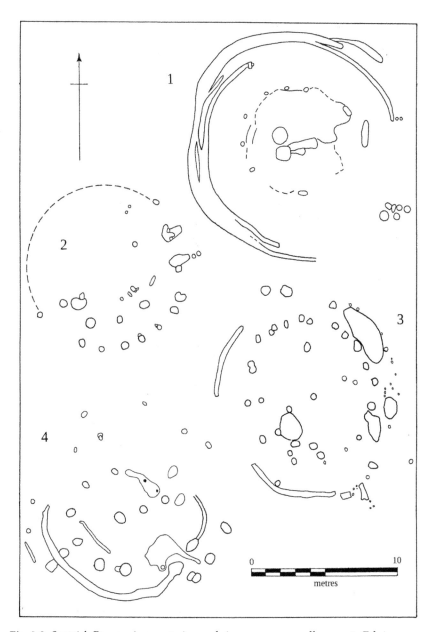

Fig. 8.3 Scottish Bronze Age post-ring and ring-groove roundhouses. 1, Ednie, Aberdeenshire; 2, Blairhall Burn, Amisfield, Dumfriesshire; 3, Lamb's Nursery, Dalkeith, Midlothian; 4, Inverkip, Inverclyde. Drawings by D. W. Harding, adapted from Strachan and Dunwell, 2003, Strachan et al., 1998, Cook, 2000, and Rennie, 2016.

radiocarbon date spanning the first half of the second millennium. Complete post-ring plans of Middle to Late Bronze Age houses were recovered from Lochinver Quarry, Elgin (Cockcroft et al. 2019). A combination of post-ring and ring-groove construction is amply demonstrated by the Middle Bronze Age at Lamb's Nursery, Dalkeith (Fig. 8.3, 3; Cook, 2000) and at Inverkip, Inverclyde (Fig. 8.3, 4; Rennie, 2016), where there was a suggestion of an external post-ring supporting either a fence around the house or grounding support for the principal rafters. At Ednie, Aberdeenshire (Fig. 8.3, 1; Strachan and Dunwell, 2003), successive ring-grooves defined an enclosing wall some 15 metres in diameter, which the excavators believed to be the outer wall of a substantial domestic house, rather than an enclosure around a lesser building. Successive entrances may be indicated by post settings on the east and south-east sides, though these could equally have defined entrances to the compound rather than doorways to the house. The central area was paved, around which a post-ring presumably held the principal roof-support, reinforcing the functional distinction between central and peripheral space. In Argyll the expectation might have been that hut-circles from the Bronze Age would have been of stone, perhaps in proximity to field systems. In fact, timber houses have also been discovered dating from the Middle Bronze Age, notably in the Oban district, where Roundhouse S1 at Dunbeg (Ellis, online) displays not only a very regular post-circle eight metres in diameter but also an unusual timber-lined gully leading from the central hearth out through the entrance, which the excavator suggested was designed for ventilation. It is interesting that this feature is linked to the arc of ditch on the north-east side of the house, which could perhaps have been the sleeping area, which underfloor ventilation would help keep dry and warm.

Field research since the publication of *IAR* has abundantly demonstrated the widespread presence of ring-ditches in Scotland in the Bronze Age, but it has also demonstrated such diversity in structures that are now grouped under the portmanteau heading of ring-ditch houses that we must surely question its utility as an archaeological classification. Most of the Bronze Age houses with ring-ditches are of relatively modest size, with the ring-ditch extending around most of the perimeter except where it has obviously been eroded. At Deer's Den (Fig. 8.4, 1; Alexander, 2000) the post-circle intrudes into the ring-ditch, and at Auchrennie (Fig. 8.4, 3; Cameron et al., 2007) it is located around the outer edge. At Oldmeldrum (Fig. 8.4, 2; White and Richardson, 2010) the post-ring is more obviously external to the ring-ditch. At Drumyocher (Fig. 8.4, 4; Johnson, 2017) the ring-ditch is a shallow dished area that occupies much of the area within the inner ring-groove, spanning some ten metres, so that it is unclear whether the external ring-groove, which, if projected, would align with the outer end of the porch, is integral to the house or formed a fence around it.

Among ring-groove structures with earlier second millennium radiocarbon dates the distinctive building from Lookout Plantation, Northumberland (Fig. 3.10, 2; Monaghan, 1994) had a markedly polygonal plan defining an area some nine

CHRONOLOGY, ORIGINS, AND AFTERMATH 211

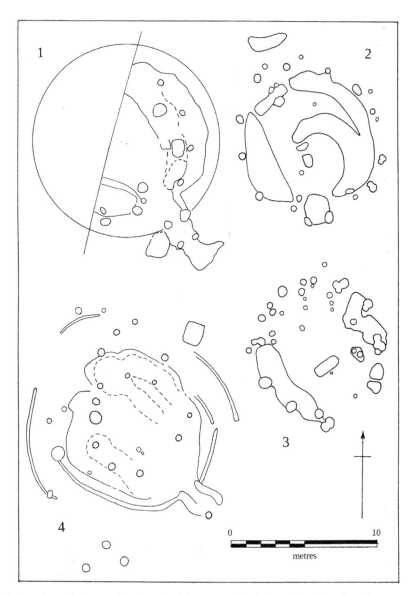

Fig. 8.4 Scottish Bronze Age ring-ditch houses. 1, Deer's Den, Aberdeenshire, Structure 3; 2, Oldmeldrum, Aberdeenshire, House 2; 3, Auchrennie, Angus, Structure A; 4, Drumyocher, Aberdeenshire, Structure 4. Drawings by D. W. Harding, adapted from Alexander, 2000, White and Richardson, 2010, Cameron et al., 2007, and Johnson, 2017.

metres across. Its inner setting of seven postholes was centred slightly towards the rear of the house, assuming that its entrance was defined by the outer projecting 'horns' of the ring-groove on its south-west side. Pope (2015: 173–4 and note 11) compared this entrance to that of the unenclosed house from Melville Nurseries, Dalkeith (Raisen and Rees, 1995), which also had a continuous annular

212 RETHINKING ROUNDHOUSES

ring-groove that showed marginal polygonality in its oval outline, and speculated that its single Early Iron Age date might just be unrepresentative. One clear difference was the intermittent but regular *external* post-ring at Melville Nurseries, which once again raises the possibility of a double cavity wall, though in this case the ring-groove is the more substantial component. The Ross Bay, Kirkcudbright, house was dated to the mid-second millennium (Fig. 3.10, 5; Ronan and Higgins, 2005). It too was slightly off-circular in its polygonal ring-groove and internal post-ring, and its porched entrance comprised a more regular pair of flanking gullies with posts at their inner ends.

Middle and Late Bronze Age Structures in Southern England

There has never been any doubt that circular ground-plans for domestic buildings in southern England extended back into the Bronze Age, with examples like Plumpton Plain on the South Downs known from the 1930s (Holleyman and Curwen, 1935) and Itford Hill from the early 1950s (Burstow and Holleyman, 1957). Whilst these sites underlined the insular tradition of circular building, their smaller dimensions and simpler layout in contrast with the major Wessex roundhouses of the earlier Iron Age suggested a significant difference in terms of social and economic usage. The reinterpretation of the Shearplace Hill, Sydling St Nicholas, Dorset, plans (Avery and Close-Brooks, 1969) showed that some of the roundhouses of the Middle Bronze Age could have been larger than originally supposed on the basis of their post-rings, and demonstrated that the porched entrance was already a focal feature in the second millennium, a landmark of reinterpretation that has been widely acknowledged by subsequent researchers. But interestingly that reinterpretation was based upon the alignment of the exterior wall of the houses with the *outer* pair of porch posts, whereas most interpretations since of houses in which the outer wall has not survived have been based on the principle that it aligned with the *inner* pair of porch posts. Guilbert (1981) qualified the Avery/Close-Brooks interpretation by suggesting that the outer ditch was in fact a drip-gully, thereby reducing the maximum diameter of the Shearplace house marginally. But more importantly, the ring-groove, still accepted as an outer wall line, could then align with the porch slots just inside the outer pair of porch posts (Fig. 8.5, 1).

The Shearplace post-ring describes a reasonable circle, though the postholes are hardly of consistent size; some also appear to have been replaced. Some Middle Bronze Age houses have much less regular post-circles, and show no sign of replacement. Their lack of symmetry or consistency of size suggests that the timbers themselves were not of a consistent standard, and therefore perhaps not the product of managed woodland plantations. But in many cases we may question whether they were structural in function at all, as opposed to providing

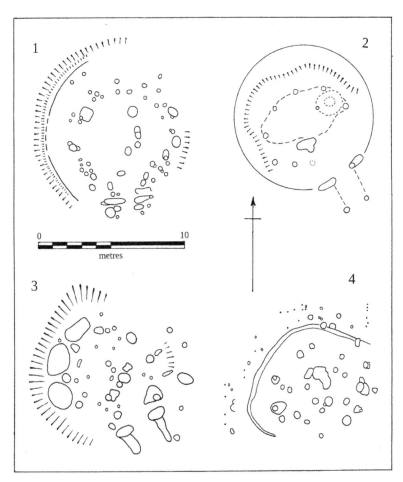

Fig. 8.5 Bronze Age roundhouses in southern England. 1, Shearplace Hill, Sydling St Nicholas, Dorset, House A; 2, Itford Hill, Sussex, enclosure III, House B; 3, Black Patch, Sussex, platform 4, House 3; 4, Black Patch, Sussex, platform 3, House A. Drawings by D. W. Harding, adapted from Rahtz and ApSimon, 1962, Burstow and Holleyman, 1957, Drewett, 1982, and Tapper, 2011.

a scaffold in the construction process, and thereafter, if retained, supporting furniture or fittings, or internal partitions within the house. If the roof was essentially a cone with its rafters bedded into the ground, made rigid by a ring-beam below the apex, or indeed an upturned basket with its poles similarly bedded, then technically it would require no internal support, until perhaps the roof began to sag under the weight of thatch. Accordingly, of course, if the post-ring was not structural, then the absence of secondary replacement has no bearing on the issue of the building's life-span.

At Black Patch, Sussex, Drewett (1982) had been particularly concerned with identifying the outer wall of the houses, and in his Hut 4 on platform 4 he located five postholes on the upper lip of the terrace which he believed were where rafters had been bedded. In order to maintain level eaves, the roof at the front of the house would thus have required supporting on a low mass-wall, which he suggested could have been composed of flint nodules, as proposed by Musson (1970) for a comparable structure at Amberley Mount. Drewett's reconstruction, for a house with an interior diameter around eight metres, included internal roof-supporting timbers, but with a ring-beam nearer the apex the cone would essentially have been self-supporting. Of the platform 4 houses at Black Patch, Hut 3 (Fig. 8.5, 3) has a convincing inner post-ring of six or eight postholes of broadly similar proportions, which accord with the principles of axial symmetry through the porched entrance. By contrast the selection of a post-ring from the postholes in Hut 1, though appearing plausible, seems a trifle contrived from the total number of postholes available. One conclusion might be that there were different building types represented at Black Patch, perhaps serving different purposes, though it is hard to correlate the distribution of finds with possible functions. Functions anyway could have changed during the life-span of a building, and without cumulative floor levels and distinctive stratigraphic horizons such changes could be hard to detect archaeologically. Subsequent excavations at Black Patch (Tapper, 2011) produced further evidence in Hut A (Fig. 8.5, 4) for rafters having been grounded on the upper edge of the terrace, beyond which a line of stake-holes, too far from the terrace edge to have been structural, may nevertheless have supported a hurdle fence designed to prevent livestock from straying on to the roof. Again there was evidence for a low wall of flint around the doorway in the south-east sector. Based on the Black Patch evidence, we may infer that the Itford Hill houses likewise had an outer wall based on the higher slope at the back, and possibly on a built wall at the front, flanking the doorway (Fig. 8.5, 2).

Raising the eaves off a low foundation by building an external stake- or mass-wall plainly increases the usable internal floor area, and transforms the capacity of the house. This evidently was a transition that could have occurred at various times in different regions, depending presumably not just upon engineering capability but upon the social needs that the house was required to serve. Otherwise it is hard to point to any convincing structural progression in terms of component elements, central post, post-ring, and so forth, not least because it is not always possible to be confident which role these served, structural, constructional, maintenance and repair, or related to internal fittings. But it is increasingly clear that large roundhouses of complex construction were already current in the Middle Bronze Age, and that there is no unilinear progression towards aggrandizement or complexity.

The Roman Iron Age

Older studies of the Southern British Iron Age ended with the Roman Conquest, a convention that was consistent with the prevailing historical model. Any consideration of social or cognitive dimensions would acknowledge that traditional relationships and beliefs must have persisted in the native communities despite political and economic change, though doubtless in varying degrees regionally, dependent upon the degree of contact local groups had with the Roman authorities, and the extent to which there was resistance or mutual collaboration. Archaeologically the extent to which local groups adopted Roman fashions may be measured in terms of material structures and artefacts. The social impact of the destruction of the traditional order by the imposition of a new political authority is much harder to measure, but that too might just be reflected in the continuing occurrence or recurrence of a predominant element of Iron Age settlement that was the roundhouse.

Information regarding the rural settlement of Roman Britain has been immeasurably transformed by the scale of development-led archaeology, which has resulted in an exponentially-increased database and a greater appreciation of the diversity of settlement compared to the days when discussion of 'the countryside' as opposed to 'towns' focused largely on villa typology. The database for *The Rural Settlement of Roman Britain* (Smith et al., 2016) included some 2,659 circular or curvilinear buildings from settlements in England and Wales, or 43 per cent of the total number of structures identified. Not surprisingly it showed that the decline in the use of roundhouses in the south and east preceded that in the north and west, where significant numbers persisted into the third and fourth centuries.

In the river valleys of the south Midlands material evidence of settlement continuity is not always matched by the structural evidence. At Yarnton (Hey et al., 2011) settlement continued from the earlier Iron Age through to the Roman period, yet after the Middle Iron Age, all structural trace of the domestic occupation that must have been contained within the rectilinear ditched enclosures, and which is attested by material artefacts and domestic debris, is absent. Again excavators have frequently invoked the idea that non-earth-fast footings of turf or cob may have been used, and the fact that these putative roundhouses, even by the Middle Iron Age, were generally only attested by the proxy of their penannular drainage gullies, evidently points to increasing problems with waterlogging, resulting from a higher water table, towards the end of the first millennium B C. This was evidently not triggered by climatic change, but by hydrology and alluviation (Robinson, 1992), and affected the Thames Valley, the Nene, and the Ouse at different times and in somewhat different ways. On sites where there appears to be continuity of settlement, presumably individual house drainage gullies were replaced by a more radical network of deeper enclosure ditches that no longer

216 RETHINKING ROUNDHOUSES

mirror individual houses, or site functions were reorganized and dwellings moved to drier ground. There is some evidence for such a level of site reorganization in the first centuries BC/AD, before the more radical reorganization that affected many settlements in southern and midland England in the early second century, which was presumably induced by political and administrative considerations.

One region of Southern Britain where the roundhouse tradition appears to have remained strong during the Roman period is the south Midlands, notably the Nene Valley in Northamptonshire, where roundhouses are found on farming settlements and within villa estates. The straightforward assumption that this was a case of continuity of local convention unabated by the disruption of landscape organization, however, is belied by the fact that many of the later Iron Age settlements had already been abandoned, so that direct site continuity is not the norm. One exception is the extensive settlement at Stanwick, Northamptonshire (Crosby and Muldowney, 2011). In the Roman period Stanwick was not strictly a roadside settlement, since it was set back from the Roman road from Irchester to Titchmarch, and its layout was determined by an Iron Age linear boundary ditch that, though silted up by the early Roman period, still constrained the pattern of settlement until major reorganization accompanied the construction of a winged corridor villa in the mid-fourth century AD. As in other parts of the Midlands, roundhouses were represented in the Middle and Late pre-Roman Iron Age by their external drainage gullies, though in one instance in particular, a two-phased house in the cluster closest to the boundary ditch on its north side (Roundhouse 192051) retained a partial wall-slot with stake-holes in its first phase, with several more substantial internal postholes that could have supported an inner post-ring of a house some ten metres in diameter (Fig. 8.6, 1). In its second phase the ring-groove was more complete, confirming a somewhat polygonal outline, whilst the inner setting of postholes could have included a substantial four-post framework. The roundhouse is located somewhat eccentrically within the drainage gullies, with the southern wall of Phase 1 unusually close to the drainage gully, and the entrance of Phase 2 decidedly offset from the gap in the gully to its east. Though some drainage gullies may have persisted, the later first century AD (Phase 7) saw the introduction of the 'earliest stone or stone-footed buildings surviving on the site' (Crosby and Muldowney, 2011: 33).

The shift to stone foundations at Stanwick is informative, because it affects round and rectangular plans equally. The crucial factor is that these are not stone walls to the eaves, but stone foundations, generally in a foundation trench, but perhaps at most three or four courses high, which is presumably why, even allowing for stone-robbing, there is not more debris. They are intended simply to raise a timber superstructure (or possibly cob) above the damp that would rot earth-fast timbers, performing the same function that might previously have been achieved by a low turf wall or one made of other archaeologically fugitive materials.

CHRONOLOGY, ORIGINS, AND AFTERMATH 217

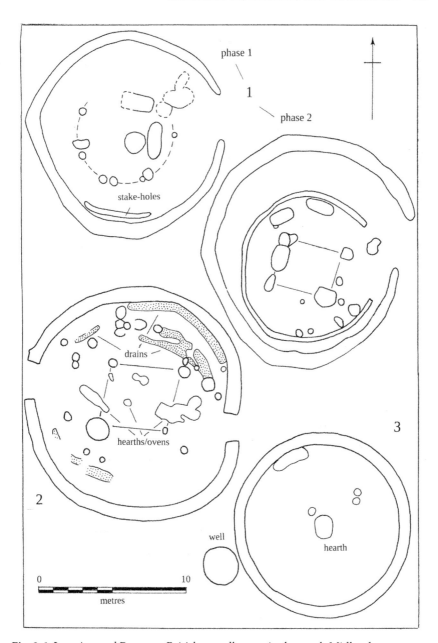

Fig. 8.6 Iron Age and Romano-British roundhouses in the south Midlands. 1, Stanwick Northamptonshire, Building 192051; 2, Redlands Farm, Stanwick, Northamptonshire, Roundhouse 369; 3, Higham Ferrers, Northamptonshire, Building 10920. Drawings by D. W. Harding, adapted from Crosby and Muldowney, 2011, Keevill and Booth, 1997, and Lawrence and Smith, 2009.

218   RETHINKING ROUNDHOUSES

The existence of turf foundation walls inside ring-trenches has been previously surmised. But if we acknowledge that the purpose was to raise footings (and perhaps floors too) above damp ground, then of course rectangular structures constructed in a similar fashion in the later pre-Roman Iron Age in southern and south-eastern England could have been much more widespread than the archaeological record suggests, in the absence of clearly rectangular drainage gullies to stand proxy for them. So the apparent shift to stone-founded rectangular houses is not a change in architectural fashion, simply a change of materials that makes them archaeologically visible.

Three miles south-west of Stanwick lies the site of Higham Ferrers (Lawrence and Smith, 2009). Here the nearest pre-Roman Iron Age occupation, a few hundred metres to the north-east, had come to an end at least a century before the early second century AD settlement came into existence. There is, therefore, no evidence of direct site continuity, though this may mean no more than that there was a local shift of focus within a continuously inhabited landscape, a conclusion that would be consistent with the discovery, just a mile to the south-east, of a sequence of shifting occupation from the Middle Iron Age to the second century AD (Mudd, 2004). Higham Ferrers is an authentic roadside settlement, though ironically for an apparently archetypical Romano-British settlement type, in its earliest phase it was dominated by circular structures that appear to have functioned as domestic houses (Fig. 8.6, 3). Each had stone wall-footings, and two had adjacent wells, underlining the importance for both occupants and livestock of a convenient water supply, a consideration too often overlooked in discussions of Iron Age houses. By the later second century, however, the settlement was mostly composed of rectangular buildings, though the one surviving roundhouse appears to occupy a central location within a compound created by its rectangular counterparts, a position it continued to enjoy until the fourth century. This building appears to have served a domestic function, in the third century acquiring radial divisions in one half of its interior. It is perhaps arguable whether the internal layout and functioning of roundhouses in the Roman period should inform our interpretation of their role in later prehistory, but it is also a salutary reminder that, but for the use of durable footings, such simple divisions would not survive if they depended upon textile or hide drapes or wattled hurdles.

The fact that roundhouses continued in use in the Nene Valley into the later fourth century, of course, need not mean that they still served the same residential function as in the Iron Age. In fact, one was identified as a horse-mill and another contained corn-drying or malting ovens, showing that they were also used for specialist agricultural or other purposes. The smaller of the two circular structures with stone foundations at Redlands Farm, two kilometres south-west of the Stanwick complex, was tentatively identified as a threshing barn (Keevill and Booth, 1997: 25), not least because its wide main entrance, stone floor, and limestone trackway leading to it would have allowed wheeled farm vehicles to unload directly into the building. The larger roundhouse (Fig. 8.6, 2), on the other hand, with an internal diameter of 13.7 metres and an overall diameter of 15.5 metres, was more probably a byre-house, a function that would certainly have been facilitated by its two opposed entrances. Roof-support or an upper floor level may have been provided by a central four-post framework, initially based in postholes and subsequently on post-pads. These two buildings were evidently constructed in the third century, after the foundation of the villa, their relationship to which is unclear. Viewed in terms of their comparative sizes, however, it certainly cannot be assumed that the roundhouse was in any sense regarded by the inhabitants of the settlement as inferior or subordinate to the villa buildings.

One of the most challenging instances of roundhouses on the site of a Roman villa, however, remains the example from Holme House, Piercebridge, where artefacts associated with structural elements of the building, as opposed to the upper, late filling of its major post-pits, proclaimed its occupation as second century, in significant part coincident with the adjacent villa buildings. In *IAR* two possible interpretations were advanced. One was that this might be an instance of dual proprietorship, the equivalent, using contrasting rectilinear and circular architectural traditions, of the concept of paired occupation of 'unit villas' (Smith, 1978), in which the roundhouse still occupied the prime central position in the enclosure, with the villa accommodated to one side, and in its original form, at any rate, offering no greater internal floor space. Alternatively it was suggested (*IAR*: 165, 290) that the two contrasting buildings reflected a desire to adopt the comforts and privileges of novel Roman living standards, whilst not giving overt offence to traditional values in dealings with the local community, an idea encapsulated in a modern colonialist context by Mattingly's (2007: 375) 'Mandela model'. This interpretation still seems to be essentially valid. Even though the glassware from the roundhouse was mostly of utilitarian blue/green vessels in contrast to the apparently more highly regarded colourless table wares found in the villa, and the fact that pork and chicken were consumed in the villa, but not in the roundhouse, just oysters being common to both, these distinctions could still be consistent with the use of the buildings to emphasize or to downplay Roman fashions. Cool and Mason (2008: 297) could find 'no simple clear-cut division between the two buildings'. The reason for the building of a small villa and the adoption of Roman manners at such an early date, estimated as early in the second century AD, was evidently problematic, since there was hardly time for the son of a native elite family to have been recruited into the army, acquired Roman habits, served his time and returned to build a villa in the style to which he had become accustomed. However, recognition that the native *oppidum* at nearby Stanwick (North Yorkshire) was not the centre of anti-Roman resistance, as imagined by Wheeler (1954), but instead was the capital of a pro-Roman faction that was engaged in commercial exchange with the Roman world, perhaps even as a client kingdom under Cartimandua (Haselgrove, 2016), now allows the

220 RETHINKING ROUNDHOUSES

possibility of precocious adoption of Roman fashions at Piercebridge, that may have been brought to a premature end by the establishment of a military presence at Piercebridge at the end of the second century (Cool and Mason, 2008 302ff.).

Reconstructing the origins and development of the roundhouse settlement at Holme House, however, remains problematical, not least because the option of radiocarbon dating was not available at the time of excavation, and none of the 'native' pottery or other artefacts from the site can be dated earlier than the Roman period. The format of the site, with roundhouse located centrally within a sub-rectangular compound plainly accords with a known pre-Roman Iron Age pattern. Equally, the complexity of the postholes and post-pits within the stone-founded roundhouse implies a sequence of building with multiple recutting of key settings that would normally indicate a protracted period of use. The interim report (Harding, 1984, text reproduced with additional illustration in Cool and Mason, 2008) tentatively envisaged four stages of development for the house, of which the first was least well documented on grounds of truncation by later episodes, while the last was most confidently identified by its substantial setting of four central post-pits.[1] These four stages have here been reduced to two (Fig. 8.7), an earlier ring of six postholes, each subject to recutting, of which one underlay the chord wall, and a later setting of four massive post-pits that was associated with the circular stone wall and chord wall. The earlier post-ring presumably supported a substantial roundhouse of a type now recognized at Stanwick, of which the outer walls must have been of turf or cob, and the entrance to which would have been destroyed by the later, surviving circular stone wall. The later setting of four pits had substantial stone post-pads in their bases, presumably to counter settlement from the weight of the timber framework, which must imply a substantial central tower supporting the roof and upper floor. The timbers themselves were doubtless salvaged on abandonment, at the same time as the limestone footings of the walls. The partially filled pits were left to silt up over time, so that their upper filling included some late Roman scraps from the later ephemeral reuse of the south-eastern quarter of the site. The chord wall on the west side of the roundhouse, presumably supporting a raised dais, now has a local parallel in the smaller and later roundhouse at Ingleby Barwick (Willis and Carne, 2013). Initially thought to have been from an earlier, rectangular building that had been intersected by the roundhouse, its external continuation was expressly investigated beyond the area initially exposed, with negative results. The chord must therefore be integral to the roundhouse. No hearths were located within the house, but in a byre-house with upper floor these would in all probability have been on that upper level.

---

[1] Unfortunately the plan of the roundhouse reproduced in Cool and Mason, 2008, is not the one used in the interim report (Harding, 1984), the internal features having their on-site context labels, rather than the numbers assigned to them in the explanatory text. Likewise the possible structural sequence shown in Cool and Mason, 2008: Fig. 7.7 is not the sequence alluded to in the text, and should be disregarded.

CHRONOLOGY, ORIGINS, AND AFTERMATH 221

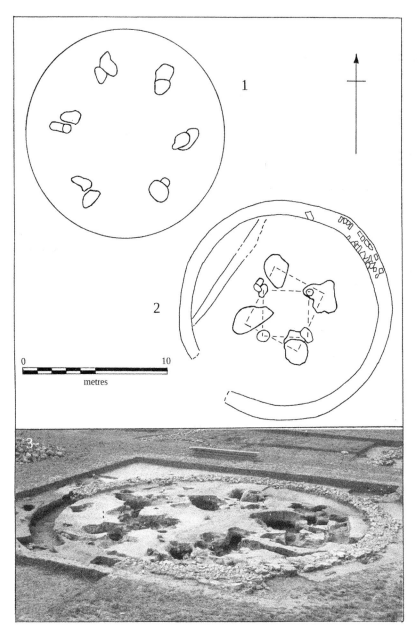

Fig. 8.7 Holme House, Piercebridge. 1, post-ring structure; 2, stone-founded roundhouse with four-post tower; 3, view of excavated roundhouses from north-east. Drawings by D. W. Harding; photograph © D. W. Harding.

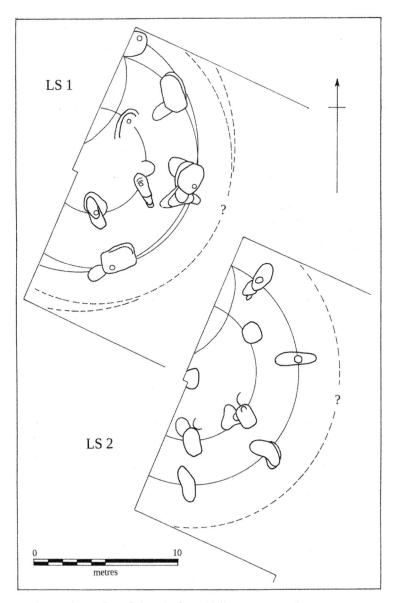

Fig. 8.8 Stanwick, north Yorkshire, Tofts Field, 'large structures'. 1, LS1; 2, LS2. Drawings by D. W. Harding, adapted from Haselgrove, 2016.

The substantial post-pits of the Holme House roundhouse are now no longer exceptional, since the excavation of the 'large structures' in the Tofts Field at Stanwick, north Yorkshire, just to the south (Fig. 8.8). These structures raise fundamental issues of reconstruction, notably in the wide spacing between the major post-pits, and the inherent implausibility that the outer ring of post-pits

CHRONOLOGY, ORIGINS, AND AFTERMATH   223

constituted the outer wall of a roofed building. If the inner ring of post-pits supported a central tower, against which rafters could have rested, then there could have been an outer mass-wall, even though this would have been over 20 metres in diameter. But it is clear that there was a novel form of construction being deployed in the region in the late pre-Roman Iron Age, the purpose of which is by no means demonstrably domestic.

The coexistence of a substantial roundhouse with more obviously Romanized buildings is not easy to parallel. In *IAR* the structural sequence at Whitton, Glamorgan (Jarrett and Wrathmell, 1981) was regarded as a classic example of the progression from native Iron Age roundhouses to the adoption of rectilinear building plans, in which the latter replaced the former, with no real evidence for chronological overlap. At the same time it was recognized that the later, rectangular buildings were all sited around the inner edges of the sub-square enclosure, apparently leaving vacant the prime central location where the major Roundhouses D1 and D2 had dominated the earlier phases of occupation (*IAR*: Fig. 33). The excavators, of course, had suggested the former existence of a third, if not fourth large roundhouse, on the basis of two surviving pairs of postholes that matched the door posts of the extant houses. The ring-groove of one of the latter had been truncated in part, and of the other much reduced, so that these shallow features were plainly vulnerable to erosion. But in any event it is clear that at Whitton, as at Holme House, it is the principal roundhouse that essentially determined the pattern of occupation in the homestead.

Roundhouses on high-status rural sites evidently could fulfil a variety of roles, social, political, or even religious, but the more usual expectation in northern England would be for a progressive shift from roundhouse settlements to those in which rectilinear building plans predominate. Evaluating progressive 'Romanization' in this regard has in the past depended upon the focus of research, which has tended to emphasize military sites, towns, and roads, the infrastructure of colonial administration. An understanding of how far this really made an impact upon traditional rural settlement has been greatly amplified in the past twenty years by the scale of investigation in advance of development.

One such site is Heslington East in the south-east of the city of York (Antoni et al., 2009; Roskams and Neal, 2020). It occupies the southern edge of a glacial moraine across the Vale of York, and is spread from east to west over a distance of a kilometre or more. The Iron Age occupation focused on the spring line, and the system of fields, settlement enclosures, and droveways is laid out with regard to several wells that evidently served the needs of stock and the human community. In the later pre-Roman Iron Age two principal sub-rectangular enclosures in the western area of the site both contained one larger roundhouse that had been rebuilt on more than one occasion. These were represented by ring-gullies, none of which in the western complex actually contained evidence of posts (Antoni et al., 2009: 114), and which most probably were for drainage and therefore outside the

224 RETHINKING ROUNDHOUSES

alignment of the outer house wall. In one instance large porch posts were aligned between the terminals of the ring-gully, but the porch could have projected beyond the line of the outer wall itself. Other smaller circular buildings may have served ancillary functions related either to the mixed agricultural economy of the settlement or to its secondary industrial activities, which included not only iron smelting and smithing but apparently copper and possibly silver working, as well as the manufacture and repair of jet. Roundhouses were not confined to the enclosures, however, with one group of three houses possibly part of an external related cluster.

Some 700 metres to the east was an isolated square enclosure containing two roundhouses with diameters in the order of seven metres. Located side by side, they were more probably successive than a contemporary pair, since their entrances were diametrically opposite, one oriented to the south-east, the other to the north-west. The dating of these houses was not certain, but they could have been built as late as the first century AD. Further east again was the latest group of roundhouses, with ring-gullies around nine metres in diameter, within which there were evidently several postholes (Roskams and Neal, 2020: 72). The ring-gully of the latest rebuild contained south Gaulish Samian of Flavian date, so that the occupants, who were availing themselves of Roman imports, nevertheless chose to retain their traditional Iron Age building style. This illustrates what Roskams and Neal (2020: 126) describe as a 'prestige overlay', making the important distinction between the acquisition of new ceramic styles for the presentation of food and the more fundamental adoption of new ways of preparing food, which took another couple of generations. In effect, the initial impact of the Roman conquest and military advance north was not nearly as disruptive as has sometimes been presented. Clearly the creation of a network of roads and forts did have an impact on their immediate environs and supply zones, but for much of the landscape control of land and production appears to have been largely unaffected. The period around AD 200, on the other hand, appears to have been a watershed (Roskams and Neal, 2020: 128). At Heslington East the focus of settlement shifted to the central area between the former Iron Age settlements, which were abandoned. New roads were built across the site, together with a new network of enclosures that probably signalled a new system of land tenure in which the imperial power exercised greater control. At the same time there evidently was a shift in agricultural output, with a greater emphasis upon cattle raising and the cultivation of bread wheat. The introduction of corn dryers would have improved crop processing and improved plough technology would have facilitated cultivation of heavier soils. Similar radical changes are evident elsewhere in Yorkshire, with the decline, for example, of 'ladder settlements' in the Wolds. It was also at around this time that the sequence of roundhouse settlements at Dalton Parlours was finally succeeded by the construction of the villa complex.

At Wattle Syke (Fig. 8.9; Martin et al., 2013), less than a mile north of Dalton Parlours, and conceivably in the Roman period under the same administrative

CHRONOLOGY, ORIGINS, AND AFTERMATH 225

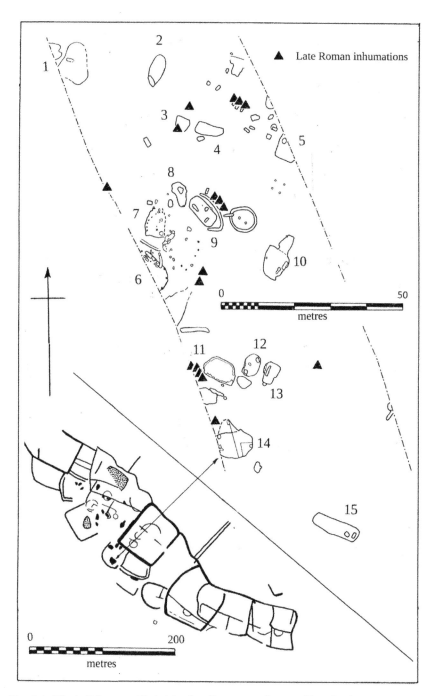

Fig. 8.9 Wattle Syke, west Yorkshire, late Roman settlement. Drawing by D. W. Harding, adapted from Martin et al., 2013.

jurisdiction, there is, perhaps surprisingly, no evidence of the adoption of rectilinear architecture, either in timber or in stone. How long the roundhouse tradition, which had characterized the settlement since around the fourth century BC, lasted is debatable, because of the lack of sealed contexts on a site where settlement appears to have been continuous from the second half of the first millennium BC through to the fifth century AD. In the early Roman period the enclosure system in the northern complex was amplified, but dwelling structures are notable for their absence, and it is conceivable that there was some reorganization of domestic and agricultural sectors. In the late Roman period, however, the site undergoes a transformation, with the appearance of sub-rectangular or sub-oval structures with sunken foundations, of a type which has occasionally been noted elsewhere, but not previously in northern England in quite this concentration. Individual structures can range from 6 to 10 metres in length and 4 to 5 metres in width. The sides of the hollows in some cases were stone-revetted, most clearly in Structure 5, whereas in Structure 6 the edges of the sunken foundations were reinforced with a series of timber posts. In the case of Structure 7 there may have been a combination of the two. These, or a low wall on the lip of the hollows formed from upcast from the pit could have supported roof rafters. Otherwise, there was no evidence for roofing, comparable to the posts that supported a gable roof over post-Roman *Grubenhaüser*, for example, and the ground plans are so irregular and the sunken foundations relatively shallow so that some of these features might have been no more than unroofed working areas. Buildings 10 and 11 have attached and detached annexes, respectively, that raise issues regarding roofing comparable to those posed by figure-of-eight buildings. As to function, ovens, quern fragments, and carbonized grain indicate that some of these structures were associated with processing of cereals, while hammerscale from Building 13 suggested industrial activity. Whether any served as domestic dwellings, therefore, remains contentious, but certainly in eastern Scotland there are domestic structures of the Late Iron Age that have similar sunken foundations. In the case of the Wattle Syke sunken structures, however, it is hard to imagine that a symmetrical, wind- and weatherproof superstructure was other than rectilinear, or perhaps a hipped oval, rather than a roundhouse in the conventional sense. The interpretation of the ring of postholes between Structures 6, 7, and 9 as a roundhouse (Structure 10) may, as the excavators acknowledged, be a coincidental contrivance.

At Wattle Syke, the roundhouse tradition has effectively come to an end. Beyond the Roman frontier it continued, notably in the post-broch radial roundhouses of the Atlantic north and west. Thereafter it devolved into a range of cellular variants, including figures-of-eight and 'shamrocks', which, though incorporating circular units, in terms of use of space represent a developed social order.

9

Roundhouses

Space, Time, and Social Use

Those who are ignorant of history are destined to re-invent the wheel badly
Anonymous schoolmaster, 1950s

In 2018, the excavators of Roundhouse 2 at the Black Loch of Myrton were able to state unequivocally on the basis of multiple dendrochronological samples taken from structural oak timbers, on some of which even the bark survived, that the house was built in the spring and summer of 435 BC, but that preparations for construction, in terms of felling timber, had begun a year to eighteen months previously (Crone et al., 2018: 152). This astonishingly precise assessment is not simply the achievement of modern scientific analyses: it requires also the application of field techniques informed by a cumulative understanding of prehistoric buildings that would simply not have been possible a couple of generations, much less a century ago. In fact, we might qualify one of the excavators' conclusions, namely that preparations for construction by felling trees had begun somewhat earlier, since this implies that this was undertaken by the builders themselves. An alternative view might suppose that the Iron Age equivalent of a quantity surveyor sought supplies from whoever controlled the managed woodlands, and that it was the latter who had already cut the trees and who would therefore have had stocks of seasoned oak. This is not just a cavilling distinction, since it implies a level of social infrastructure and technical proficiency in traditional crafts such as house-building, with the implication of mathematical and geometric knowledge, with which Iron Age communities are seldom credited. The same skills and social infrastructure must surely also have pertained throughout Atlantic Scotland, where the existence of brochs defies any notion that their builders were technologically or culturally unsophisticated.

Life-Cycle of Roundhouses

The archaeologist is fundamentally and essentially constrained by the arbitrary survival of material evidence of past societies, and the skill with which it is recovered and recorded, both of which determine the reliability of its interpretation. Interpretation must begin with the presumption that much if not most of the definitive data from lowland roundhouses built of timber, clay, and thatch will

Rethinking Roundhouses: Later Prehistoric Settlement in Britain and Beyond. D. W. Harding, Oxford University Press.
© D. W. Harding 2023. DOI: 10.1093/oso/9780192893802.003.0009

have perished without leaving trace. Plough damage is almost inevitable but not inevitably total, and even on shallow chalk downland sites some residual features may survive. So where large roundhouses can be pinpointed through geophysical survey it is surely wanton to strip the topsoil mechanically when pressures of development do not demand it. What does survive may be misleadingly partial, and excavators may not even agree on what it is they have uncovered. The dilemma is abundantly shown by what excavators regard as the extent of the house, some quoting the diameter of the post-ring, as if it defined the outer wall, others citing a ring-gully, even when there is no evidence that it supported a structural wall rather than surrounding it, others hypothesizing a mass-wall of which no trace survives at all.

Perhaps the most important outcome of the Butser Hill reconstruction of the Pimperne roundhouse, crucially based upon an actual excavated plan, was the realization that the plan was not just a two-dimensional drawing of a structure, but a palimpsest reflecting the various stages of activity in the life-cycle of the house. In *IAR* in consequence emphasis was placed upon the distinction between *structural features*, 'those that are essential to sustain a house as a viable engineering entity' that answer the question 'will it stand up?' and *constructional features*, those 'that are necessary as part of the building process' that answer the question 'how did they get it up in the first place?' (*IAR*: 213–14). Recognizing the mounting evidence for special closure episodes on some roundhouses, *IAR* further concluded that one might try to isolate *inaugural features* and *abandonment features* in the archaeological record (*IAR*: 216).

More than a decade on, with the exponential increase in the number of excavated roundhouses, though regrettably hardly any with the degree of structural detail recovered from the Pimperne house, excavators are well aware of the potential for constructional as well as structural features. One of the abiding anomalies about roundhouse plans is why some should be so symmetrical while others are highly irregular. Where the main post-circle is irregular, we might question whether these ever constituted the primary support for the building, or whether that was achieved by some other means, with the extant postholes evidence of secondary support inserted ad hoc as the need arose, thereby reflecting the basic structure, but more erratically. Alternatively, some have suggested that most surviving postholes in timber-built roundhouses were for constructional timbers that would have been removed or truncated on completion. Others have even suggested that key features of Atlantic roundhouses, such as scarcements and intra-mural staircases were primarily intended as aids to construction rather than being integral to the roundhouse design. Only in the early twenty-first century could academics seriously suggest that such a monumental class of building was designed primarily for the benefit of the builders.

Archaeological plans, as recovered by excavation, evidently are a composite of successive episodes of activity. Those episodes might now be defined as

- structural design
- construction
- inauguration
- occupation (including furnishing and fittings)
- maintenance and repair
- closure and dismantling

On complex sites, of course, this cycle could be repeated on the same or adjacent locations.

The distinction between structural and constructional in the Pimperne reconstruction was best exemplified by the outermost shallow slots, which Reynolds unwittingly replicated when trying to bed the somewhat irregular rafters over the weight-bearing ring-beam, which he achieved by scuffing out identical lateral slots with the base of the rafters. The fact that the Pimperne slots were regularly spaced around the circuit, as the principal rafters would have been, supported this interpretation, in preference to the idea that they may have been ad hoc secondary external supports. In other instances, however, constructional and structural functions may not be so distinct, or arbitrary. A central tower, for example, could well have served as a useful scaffold in the course of construction, but might thereafter have afforded built-in support for an upper floor level, a central tower to support a split roof, a focal store for grain, a framework around a central hearth, or all of these. The same principle plainly could apply to brochs, in which intra-mural galleries, staircases, and scarcements could clearly aid construction, and yet be integral to the subsequent use of the broch.

Inauguration and closure deposits are not infrequently inferred, but are not always demonstrably associated with the construction or destruction event. At Cnip in west Lewis the deposit of cattle bones and the head and beak of a great auk behind the wall of wheelhouse 2 (Armit, 2006: 32, 220) could hardly be more conclusive. More typical are the pits containing human and animal burials around Structure 27 at Melton on Humberside (Fenton-Thomas, 2011: 89–93, 369–71), which stratigraphically post-date the demise of the building, though there is no means of judging by what period of time. Physical proximity, however, suggests that the deposits respected the former presence of the roundhouse, and were a final act of the closure ritual. In a number of instances, including Longbridge Deverill and Birnie, houses appear to have been destroyed by fire in intentional closure episodes, rather than by accident or aggressive attack. The circumstances are obscure, and there is no evidence that a funerary pyre, for example, was involved, but it is possible that firing was seen as an act of physical or spiritual cleansing, if the occupant had died of disease, or if the house was associated with misfortune.

Evidence of occupation at one time would have been equated simply with the material remains found within and around a building, without close scrutiny of the taphonomic circumstances of deposit. By the time of publication of *IAR* archaeologists were challenging such assumptions in regard to Wessex roundhouses (Webley, 2007), which for the most part retained no surviving trace of floors, and only occasionally hearths, resulting from a long history of plough agriculture. In Atlantic Scotland there is a greater chance of identifying a stratigraphic sequence of occupation and abandonment, not least because construction in stone, even if reused, generally involves rebuilding over the levelled debris of earlier occupation. But even here some of the more striking deposits have been interpreted or reinterpreted as foundation or closure deposits rather than everyday occupational detritus (Waddington, 2014). At the Howe, for example, the majority of significant deposits were associated with structural change, at transitional moments in the life-cycle of the settlement. Red deer bones were one important component of these special deposits, but human burials and body parts are also often represented, though their context is not always adequately recorded in older reports (Armit and Ginn, 2007: 134, Table). It is fairly evident that, when houses were abandoned, they were generally stripped of any contents worth salvaging, so that the excavated inventory is a poor reflection of everyday reality. Only in the event of catastrophic destruction, as at Must Farm, do we see just how total the stripping of associated artefacts must have been.

In several instances we have noted evidence for internal radial divisions in roundhouse plans, where posts may have supported partitions. Where more substantial structures were required, such as cattle stalls in byre-houses, the radial disposition of postholes might well be mistaken for structural settings. The size of the post in this instance might not reflect its height so much as the buffeting from stock that it was expected to withstand.

Evidence of maintenance and repair, short of complete rebuild, is hard to detect, though the elongation of postholes, as notably at Fison Way, Thetford, may be a tell-tale sign of uprights being replaced without removing the roof or dismantling the lintels of the ring-beam. The most obvious and regular repair to timber buildings in lowland Britain would have been the replacement of the thatched roof, which, provided the basic structure was sound, would leave no earth-fast impression. Major posts of the main weight-bearing circle could be replaced at this stage too using the same hole from which a rotting post was extracted, so that, once again, evidence of repair would be archaeologically undetectable.

Roundhouses and Round Houses

One obvious conclusion from a review of roundhouses is that there are roundhouses and round houses. Whilst they may share similar structural and engineering characteristics, some are of a scale or complexity of construction that must have made a social and symbolic statement beyond basic utility. Roundhouses like Pimperne and the Longbridge Deverill examples were monumental compared to many later prehistoric houses, and considerably more sophisticated in construction. Of course it is possible to trace an insular tradition of building domestic structures to a circular plan back into the second millennium, but that does not make all the same in function, or in social, economic, or ritual significance. The most obvious aspect of the 'great houses' is their symmetry of plan, and the fact that their scale of construction, like the number of posts of their weight-bearing circle, is more than sufficient to support a building that might have been required only for a generation, and which could certainly have lasted for several generations. The symmetry of construction, though doubtless maximizing load-bearing efficiency, may well reflect a belief in a greater cosmic order. The principle of axial symmetry is based on the idea that the posthole plan on each side of the axial line through the entrance is a mirror image of the other. It thus matches the concept of fold-over symmetry exemplified in insular La Tène art, as for instance in mirror ornament, which must likewise embody some symbolic significance. Equally, the fact that the substantial timber roundhouses of the Late Bronze Age and Early Iron Age have post-circles and door posts that are earth-fast may not simply reflect building considerations of stability, but perhaps also met a symbolic need to embed the foundations, especially of liminal locations like doorways, firmly in the ground as a physical assertion of the right to place. Ring-gullies around houses that archaeologists interpret as for drainage from the eaves could equally be a tangible assertion of entitlement and definition of site. The second observable fact is that some of the roof-supporting circles, like those at Culduthel, are more than adequate to bear the load of the roof, which certainly did not require timbers 40 cm in girth, the use of which must represent a positively profligate consumption of resources. Like Victorian engineers, these builders were making a statement in the scale and grandeur of their building. These are houses in which there has been an investment of resources and effort over and above the basic requirements of utility. The fact that they share a common circular plan with a great variety of other structures that might be interpreted as dwelling houses throughout Britain and parts of North-Western Europe is certainly significant, but does not require them to be explained in the same way.

Jon Henderson (2007: 101) recognized that domestic structures also embodied ritual and ideological significance, so that circularity reflected more than simple functionality. In our analyses of roundhouses, therefore, we should not simply categorize ground-plans, but also look for evidence of domestic roundhouses acquiring special significance for their households and kin groups. It is hard to know what archaeologically might reflect that special quality. It might have been the use of a central king post, perhaps as part of a foundation ritual, even when one was structurally not strictly necessary. It might have been reflected in axial roundhouse geometry, the structural efficiency of which may not have been its sole recommendation. And, perhaps most probably, it was reflected in the particular use of radial division of space and the implicit contrast between the role of central space and peripheral space. It may also have been reflected in the south-eastern orientation of the main doorway of the house, which need not be in contradiction to the practical expedient of maximizing early morning sunlight and minimizing exposure to prevailing winds. Indeed, the one may have been a direct consequence of the other, and indistinguishable in the minds of Iron Age householders.

After the Early Iron Age in Southern Britain monumental timber roundhouses give way to buildings of medium size range, commonly found in clusters, and presumably indicative of a modified social order. In Northern Britain the substantial roundhouse apparently survived longer, notably in the stone-built Atlantic roundhouse series, but also locally in north-eastern Scotland in some exceptionally substantial timber roundhouses. But the alternative 'cluster' model is not invariably a later development, and in Atlantic Europe generally it is in evidence in various forms at various times. In larger 'cluster' settlements in midland England the roundhouses often are of a medium size range of 8–10 metres in overall diameter, which was presumably sufficient for an extended family unit with access to adjacent storage and other facilities. It may indicate a shift away from communality of activities under one roof to segregation and specialization of activities or social groups. So we may make a further distinction between houses that are functionally multi-purpose, however subdivided internally, from those that are functionally discrete and segregated, even if they are contiguous in a cluster that separates them from neighbours.

Round and Rectangular: Squaring the Circle

Henderson (2007: 100–101) saw circular house plans as 'a common way of enclosing space around a central hearth', and as such 'the most logical development from the campfire arrangement or tent'. Certainly some of the ephemeral traces of Mesolithic shelters suggest that they were erected on flexible poles, presumably either with woven cane and straw roofs or covered with hides. For smaller shelters a central pole was hardly necessary, and would have conflicted with the presence of a central hearth. But where one was used, the outline of the building is effectively predetermined to be circular. But simple shelters could equally have been oblong in plan, based on a ridge-pole supported by a pair of uprights, thereby spanning the hearth, and even providing support for suspending items over it. The archaeological evidence of earlier prehistoric shelters and huts suggests that both options were employed, often leaving archaeological footprints that were roughly circular, oval, oblong, rectilinear with rounded corners, or simply irregular in outline. The archaeologist's tendency to select examples that conform to typology disguises the fact that on many sites the distinction between curvilinear and rectilinear is by no means clear-cut. In earlier prehistory much of the daily activities must have taken place in the open air, with the aid of wind-breaks and temporary covers, so that the overnight shelter was not so clearly the focus of domestic life. So at what point does a shelter become a house, and at what point do roundhouses and rectangular houses conform to a degree of architectural formality that signifies a significant distinction in their role? A key moment must have been when many everyday activities within the domestic context were routinely performed within the house, at which point conventions would have become established as to which activities took place where, and in turn the construction of the house may have been adapted to chime with established conventions.

It would be unrealistic to attempt to identify any universal law that determined whether round or rectangular, curvilinear or rectilinear house plans were adopted in any given geographical, chronological, or cultural context. But there are perhaps two factors in particular that commend rectangular plans. The first is where space is at a premium, within the confines of an enclosed community, for instance, where rectilinear plans tend to make more economic and efficient use of space. As a consequence, such plans predominate in urban contexts in the Middle East and the Mediterranean in prehistory. Enclosed towns, as opposed to larger communities assembled together, are a relatively late introduction into North-Western Europe, and in Northern and Western Britain and Ireland they do not appear before the early medieval period. Of course, this rule of thumb does not invariably apply. In the Hispanic *castros* roundhouses still dominate the interior occupation, though radical reorganization into quarters with an increase in rectilinearity under Roman influence characterizes major sites like Sanfins from the Augustan period. In Britain some hillforts are densely occupied by roundhouses, which has tempted some to think of them as *oppida*, though there may be little else to suggest that the character of settlement was urban or proto-urban.

The second contributory factor relates to the division of functions and activities within the house, which may be more readily achieved in a rectangular layout than in a circular one, simply by division into separate rooms or by the addition of rooms. As early as the Neolithic in Central and North-Western Europe longhouses of the *Linearbandkeramik* series were divided into functional rooms across the narrow width of the building, sometimes with corridors emphasizing the division. We have already noted the Early Bronze Age hybrid house from Ginnerup in northern Jutland which combined two-aisled with three-aisled construction to achieve different functional units under one roof. In much later times even in dispersed settlements a byre-house is readily created by having living and sleeping quarters in one end and livestock and storage in the other. Achieving a similar separation of functions and activities in a circular building is more difficult, other than by separating upper and lower floors levels, and appears to have been achieved in plan by agglomerating several smaller roundhouses and ancillary buildings around a courtyard, again as notably at the Cividade de Terroso or the Citânia de Sanfins (Queiroga, 2003: Fig. 19). In the context of the

Southern British Iron Age, the tendency to create clusters of circular buildings from the Middle Iron Age might correspond to a progressive separation of activities into dedicated space. Exceptions can always be found, which is why it would be delusional to imagine that there is any universal law, pragmatic or cosmic, that governed preference and practice in prehistory. But these two factors seem to have been significant in the Old World in later prehistory.

Throughout this study it has been stressed that architectural typology alone, unqualified by consideration of social use, could prove misleading, and this principle could be equally true of rectangular houses as for roundhouses. In *IAR*, in discussing the stalled 'wags' of north-eastern Scotland, which at the time of excavation at Forse and Yarrows in Caithness had been regarded exclusively as byres, the suggestion was advanced that they might alternatively be seen as 'a translation into a rectilinear plan of the arrangement of the classic wheel-house, of peripheral compartments around a central space' (*IAR*: 194). That squaring of the circle only becomes possible if there was a concept of rectangular house that was not just a linear sequence of rooms but a central hall, around which the outer aisles formed peripheral spaces. In Britain that concept is essentially and uniquely the basis of the so-called aisled hall or aisled villa of the Roman period, which we have seen, could have had its origins, architecturally as well as conceptually, in the pre-Roman Iron Age. In fact, the elements common to rectangular aisled buildings and circular aisled buildings become most apparent when both are reconstructed with the central 'nave' higher than the flanking 'aisles', with the provision of clerestory light. Viewed thus in terms of social use of space, the geometric form of the footprint becomes little more than a technicality.

Change through Time

It is clear that there are significant changes in the way in which roundhouses are built, or at least in what survives as a proxy record of their building, not just regionally but over time. There could be a variety of reasons for this, some local, some more widespread, with no expectation that they will be synchronous, but the most likely changes could probably be accommodated under one of three heads:

- pressures resulting from changing environmental conditions;
- problems with sourcing building materials;
- pressures from changing social, cultural or political conditions.

Changes in environmental conditions do not result only from climate changes on a global or continental scale. In the river valleys of central England the change from ground-plans based on post-rings in the earlier Iron Age to those indicated by ring-gullies in the Middle and Later pre-Roman Iron Age has been attributed to a need for drainage on settlement sites, resulting in a shift to non-earth-fast wall construction to avoid bedding major structural timbers in damp foundations. Hydrological factors and alluviation have been shown to have had a particular impact in the Upper Thames Valley, with similar possible effects, though not coterminous, in the Nene and Ouse catchment areas. The earliest indications of a rising water table by the later Bronze Age was from Yarnton (Hey et al., 2011), resulting in seasonal flooding in the earlier Iron Age. By the Middle Iron Age this process had resulted in significant alluviation, a process that became more extensive in the Roman period. Some areas of the floodplain nevertheless remained relatively dry, as appears to have been the case at Reading Business Park in the Late Bronze Age. Robinson and Lambrick (2009: esp. Fig. 2.6) argued that, for the Upper Thames Valley, the rise in water table was triggered by extensive woodland clearance to create grazing land, a process that would have reduced water loss through transpiration and increased surface water run-off. During the Iron Age arable extensification on the Cotswold slopes, which in the Roman period saw the creation of a number of villa estates, would have increased erosion and initiated the process of alluviation. The catalyst for these changes most obviously would be population growth, demanding greatly increased productivity during the Iron Age together with a shift in the balance between pastoral and arable agriculture. The process has been well documented in the Thames Valley, with its long history of salvage archaeology in advance of development. How far similar processes affected other regions is less clear, but the impact of population growth, unchecked by disease, famine, or warfare, could have resulted in fundamental changes in economic and settlement patterns.

It is now generally accepted that timber for building larger roundhouses of the Little Woodbury-Pimperne class would have required the availability of managed woodlands. The quantities of suitable-quality timber, on the scale that Reynolds (1993) inferred, would simply not have been available from opportunistic collection. Whether some of the smaller round huts and houses with less substantial and regular ground-plans could have been accomplished on the basis of opportunistic collection of timbers, perhaps gathered over a protracted period of time in anticipation of the next building project, remains debatable. What is clear, however, is that the idea of woodland management must have originated rather earlier than the widespread introduction of domestic roundhouses, since major communal building projects, defensive, ceremonial, or funerary, would have demanded management of resources from the Neolithic onwards. From the later Bronze Age hillforts regularly had enclosing ramparts that were timber-framed, and entrances that were reinforced or elaborated with timber-lined passages and gateway towers. The rampart circuits of southern English hillforts would have required timber beams in the thousands derived from tens of hectares of managed woodland, and though they might essentially have been one-off constructions, hillfort entrances at least suggest that rebuilding and repair would have imposed a significant ongoing demand for timber. In fact, the later trend towards dump ramparts might have been a consequence of depleted supplies as much as a tactical change away from box-construction, in southern England broadly coinciding with the decline of monumental timber roundhouses. Roundhouses evidently did have a limited life-span, though perhaps not as short as some have estimated. The cases in which it appears that the posts were withdrawn and presumably reused contrasts with those examples in which the house was burnt or otherwise dismantled in a 'closure episode' that perhaps corresponded to a death or generational reorganization. At any rate, the shorter the life-span of houses, the greater must have been the demand upon diminishing supplies of timber, which certainly could have been a factor in the decline of the largest roundhouses.

Availability of timber has always been an issue in the interpretation of Atlantic roundhouses, particularly in view of their concentrations in the Northern and Western Isles, where the lack of natural woodland in the Iron Age has always been regarded as a major stumbling block. The failure of archaeologists to give credence to the idea that communities were capable either of maintaining managed woodlands in suitably sheltered locations or of importing timber from the mainland, is indicative of just how embedded in modern scholarship has been the concept of the primitive rusticity of Iron Age society, despite the manifest sophistication of surviving field monuments or prestigious material artefacts. The ready discussion of the role of driftwood, doubtless used but surely never a realistic source for monumental building, reinforces this misguided notion of Iron Age communities as passive victims of their parlous predicament. The Northern and Western Isles were inhabited by maritime communities whose livelihood had long depended on seafaring. Neighbouring communities in Brittany in the Iron Age were recorded by Caesar (*dBG*, 3, 13) as having ocean-going vessels that outperformed his own ships in all but speed, and were so sturdily built of oak that they resisted not only storms but attack with the ram and grappling hooks. There is no sound reason to believe that Atlantic Scotland was any less well provided. If a regular supply route had been established between Shetland and the eastern mainland, however, it is conceivable that this may have been disrupted in the early centuries AD by Roman exploration up the North Sea coast, contributing to the demise of Atlantic roundhouses in the north.

A similar attitude has always inhibited interpretation of monumental stone buildings. The evidence for Iron Age quarrying is not surprisingly deficient, but it is simply not realistic to imagine that stone for building brochs was gathered from surface scatters, except in close proximity to shoreline or outcropping supplies. Furthermore the quantities needed would have required a suitable source that presumably belonged to someone, whose authority would have been required to use it. Assuming that the occupants of brochs were the local elite, of course, this supply may have been within its own jurisdiction, since in general the stone used is local. At Carloway in Lewis, for example, there is a good source of the preferred tabular gneiss just a few hundred metres to the east of the site, the coincidence of which may well have helped determine the broch's location.

Our third criterion, changing social, cultural, or political circumstances, was most likely triggered by contact with external agencies, travellers, traders, or settlers, though the response may locally be either innovation or resistance. The most obvious example of fundamental social, cultural, and political change, of course, was the Roman conquest, to which the native response in terms of domestic buildings has been shown to have been regionally variable (Smith et al., 2016). The survival of a native tradition of roundhouses on the northern and western fringes of the Roman province is hardly surprising, but the continuing use of roundhouses, and not simply as secondary or ancillary buildings, on sites of Romanized villas shows a degree of ambivalence in the adoption of Roman lifestyles. Classical civilizations fairly evidently did regard rectangular architecture for domestic buildings as superior to circular, just as they regarded stone, brick, and tile as superior to timber and thatch. These, together with cultivation and agriculture were the hallmarks of civilization in contrast to pastoralists who lived in circular huts made of perishable materials. So when Strabo (IV, IV, 3) recorded the Gauls living in large domed houses made of planks, wickerwork, and thatch he was not so much conveying an ethnographically observed fact as glossing his view of their relatively primitive culture compared to that of Greece and Rome. The idea that some estates in Roman Britain may have maintained buildings in both traditions, therefore, rectangular to conduct official business of the Romanized province and circular for transactions and social commitments with the local community, is a clear measure of insular independence. The resurgence of circular buildings on villa sites in the late Roman period suggests that the roundhouse had acquired symbolic status. For most of the rural population, however, it is evident that rectangular buildings became predominant by the early second century, though, as with the acquisition of a novel eating and drinking service, the adoption of architectural fashion need not imply total conversion to new social conventions.

It has been generally accepted that the Iron Age in Britain was a period of population expansion, notably in southern and eastern England and the south Midlands, culminating around the second century AD. Since the 1970s it has been assumed that this did not involve any significant immigration, though cross-channel mobility should not be discounted in either direction, and increasing application of DNA testing may well show surprising examples of enclaves of settlement that have not made a notable impact on the archaeological record. Recent DNA research has indicated large-scale migration into Southern Britain during the Middle to Late Bronze Age (Patterson et al., 2021), that is, at around

238 RETHINKING ROUNDHOUSES

the same time that large roundhouses appear in the archaeological record. There is no basis for assuming a direct connection, of course, still less an explanation. Population increase, however generated and at whatever period, inevitably places an additional burden on food production. This requires either improved farming techniques or agricultural extensification, bringing new land into cultivation or pasture, or a combination of both. It may also result in a shift in balance between pastoralism and arable farming. A case could be made archaeologically for all of these in lowland Britain in the Middle and Late pre-Roman Iron Age. How an increase in population might have affected the character and role of roundhouses within domestic and agricultural settlements is more difficult to assess, but if a greater number of individuals were surviving into adulthood, it may have required a reorganization and redistribution of domestic space. There is archaeological evidence for groups of smaller roundhouses in the later pre-Roman Iron Age in Wessex and the Thames Valley, suggesting a shift towards structural units with more specialized functions, but this was certainly not universal. Not only were large timber roundhouses being built and occupied in the opening centuries AD in north-east Scotland, but preliminary results from an enclosed settlement at Cressing in Essex (Greef and Moan, online) suggest the presence of large roundhouses in the Boudiccan period, and likewise from the later pre-Roman Iron Age at the extensive open settlement of Winterborne Kingston in Dorset (Russell and Cheetham, 2016).

Population expansion cannot be assumed to have been uniform throughout Britain, and even locally there may have been quite different trends. A cogent case for a decline in population in Essex, for example, was based upon a significant drop in the number of roundhouse settlements known from the Late pre-Roman Iron Age (Sealey, 2016), which certainly could not be attributed to widespread adoption of non-earth-fast rectangular buildings, since roundhouses remained in evidence well into the Roman period. The period of apparent decline, from late second to the end of the first century BC, coincided with the period in which Caesar records the enmity between the Trinovantes and their neighbours, so that we should not discount political unrest and hostilities, with all attendant disruptions, as a factor in the equation.

Methodology and Theoretical Afterthoughts

Archaeological interpretation has been bedevilled by two basic and related concepts that were fundamental in its pioneer stages, namely typology and developmental sequence. At best these can be a means of 'piecing together the past' in the Childean sense, but this quasi-narrative approach may not reflect the actuality of past societies. Our attempts to induce order into the chaos of an increasingly diverse database is what scholarship is all about, but past societies were not invariably or even by inclination ordered in the sense that our attempts to rationalize and categorize the data assume. The reality may have been much more diverse. Classification based on technical traits of artefacts is one thing; Late Bronze Age swords, for example, are so idiosyncratic technically that it is hard to believe that those with similar arcane traits were not related in date, origin, and workshop tradition. But with structures there is always the risk that classification based upon superficial morphological similarities, especially when inferred from partial surviving evidence, will mistakenly conflate quite different structures. An obvious example might be structures of apparent figure-of-eight plan, that could have been two similar houses located side by side or two circular components of a unitary building. Assuming that proximity is deliberate, not coincidental or consecutive, we should distinguish between sibling pairs and unitary entities, the latter only really recognizable archaeologically where there is a clear structural link like a doorway between the two. This means that structures that only survive through their surrounding drip-gullies can hardly be identified positively as figure-of-eight buildings, though the structures that formerly stood within them may well have been linked by a mutual passageway. If the Deer Park Farms model is indicative, then those potential figures-of-eight in which one element is larger than the other are more probably unitary constructs than those in which equal size might indicate occupancy by a sibling pair. The absence of a separate doorway from the lesser element might confirm their unitary function, but in many cases erosion of the traces of the outer wall will have rendered this inconclusive. A more complex example of potential confusion is within the portmanteau category of 'ring-ditch houses'. Some of the shallower ring-ditches are evidently the product of erosion, probably the result of stalling livestock in byre-houses. But in other instances the ditches were surely deliberately dug, perhaps for below-floor storage, in anticipation of souterrains. In the case of eroding ring-ditches, the stratigraphic relationship between postholes on the lip of the ring-ditch and the ring-ditch itself can be hard to determine, since the erosion could have continued to extend around the post after it was erected.

Even where identification is clear, assigning to class may impede interpretation by emphasizing distinctions rather than similarities. The site on the margins of the Black Loch of Myrton may be rightly classified as a wetland settlement rather than a crannog, but, as the excavators have argued (Crone: lecture to Royal Archaeological Institute, 9 March 2022), it is a palisaded settlement in a wetland environment, and as such should be considered in the context of palisaded settlements generally. A parallel case could be advanced regarding crannogs that, because of the obvious technical issues of underwater excavation, are too often treated as a class apart from their terrestrial neighbours, to the detriment of understanding of both. Typological classification may have its uses in the initial stages of reducing a massive dataset to some semblance of order, but that order will be an illusion unless the criteria for distinguishing classes are meaningful in

240 RETHINKING ROUNDHOUSES

terms of their interpretation rather than coincidental in terms of superficial morphology.

The implication from typological classification, therefore, that sites or structures that shared the same morphological characteristics shared the same function or significance, in retrospect seems like one of the prime fallacies of prehistoric archaeology. More specifically, it now seems simplistic to assume that sites and structures had only one function, that houses were just domestic dwellings, or that burials were simply a means of disposing of or commemorating the dead. At least by the Iron Age, burial practices regularly included deliberate deposits in and around settlements, the implication of which must surely be that the dead were seen as still having a role within or around the settlements of the living. It therefore seems likely that the world of the living and the other world of the dead and the supernatural were not regarded as distinct and separate, which would accord with later myth and epic tales from the Celtic-speaking regions. These tales assuredly do not open a 'window on the Iron Age', but they may help explain how Iron Age communities viewed their world. In terms of our appreciation of reality, the world may not have been remotely like that, only in the imagination of fireside tales, which may have been as real in the minds of Iron Age communities as was their actual more humdrum existence.

Christopher Hawkes in lectures observed in the context of the cognitive capacity of Iron Age societies that 'we should not make the mistake of thinking that these people were rational'. As students we regarded this as a rather patronizing attitude, supposing that prehistoric people were less sophisticated than ourselves. But this was assuredly not what he meant to imply. His point was rather that their thinking was intuitive rather than rational in a post-Enlightenment sense, and in contrast to classical rationality, the probability was that later prehistoric societies did not see a strict division between the 'real' world and the 'other world', the world of the imagination, of spirits and of the dead. This would certainly account, for example, for the archaeological recognition, not just of burials within the area of settlements, but of fragments of human bone, not carelessly discarded about the settlement, but meaningfully deposited in and around the focal points of everyday life. It seems probable that spirits of ancestors inhabited the houses of the living, and that the house, or at least the 'big house', was not just a place for living and sleeping, but a symbolic and spiritual focus of the household or the community. It also seems highly probable that later prehistoric peoples identified with places and inanimate objects, not as part of their kin identification, but as part of their cultural community.

Definitions of archaeology conventionally focus on the study of the past through material remains, but the crucial element is the study of structural and material remains in their taphonomic context, that is, in the physical context of their deposition and their recovery. Having spent much of one's career telling students that archaeology is not synonymous with excavation, it is hard to admit that it is in effect the excavated *context* that distinguishes archaeology from the study of antiquities as artefacts. By this definition, studying a Greek vase or late La Tène mirror in a grave would be archaeology, but studying various styles of vase painting or mirror ornament require the critical apparatus of the art historian rather than that of the archaeologist. The crucial factor that distinguishes archaeology from the study of antiquities is therefore *context*, and the inferences that can be drawn from association or relationships. In this regard the key is stratigraphic relationship, which in many excavations seems no longer to be deemed critical, or is a casualty to recovery under the pressures of development, but without which the value of salvage is largely nullified. The same rationale of course is the principal justification for deploring uncontrolled use of metal detectors.

Critics of this definition of archaeology may object that it is too limiting, that archaeology as a discipline must include the capacity to reconstruct past ways of life, which of course is the purpose of studying the material remains of past societies. It is a regrettable feature of contemporary archaeology that any evaluation that is firmly based upon archaeological evidence is derided as 'descriptive', whilst to qualify as 'interpretative' it appears that ideas must be wholly intuitive and divorced from conventional requirements of rational argument. But rational interpretation means facing the reality of limits of inference of archaeological evidence, and recognizing when we cross the boundary between inference and hypothesis. That, of course, is where analogy or comparative evidence drawn from other disciplines comes into play, which is entirely reasonable, allowing for the fact that other disciplines have their own theoretical models and critical apparatus, with their own limitations. A principal divide in terms of theory among English-speaking archaeologists is between those trained in history, language and literature, or classics, for whom written documents are a key resource in the process of reconstructing past cultures in context, and those for whom archaeology is essentially the past tense of social anthropology, who understandably invoke ethnographic models to infer past social patterns. But disciplinary inclination is also determined in substantial measure by the diversity of archaeology itself, since it is unlikely that a specialist in Roman military archaeology would adopt the same theoretical models as a specialist in Early Man. In contrasting the approaches of those trained in the Humanities and those trained in the Social Sciences I am not oblivious to the fact that an increasingly vital cohort of archaeologists have their primary training in the Physical and Biological Sciences. Whilst these specialists unquestionably are major, even definitive contributors to contemporary archaeology, my suspicion is that experts in terrestrial remote-sensing would still regard themselves as geophysicists and those who study plant and animal remains would still identify as palaeo-botanists or palaeo-zoologists in terms of their disciplinary orientation.

It is this reality that accounts for the apparent 'death of archaeological theory' (Bintliff and Pearce, 2011). The cultural-historical model that dominated earlier twentieth-century prehistory in Britain was simply an inheritance from the humanities-based stable of most practitioners at that time. Its demise dates not from the sustained criticism of diffusionism of the 1960s and early 1970s but from the publication of Clark's *Prehistoric Europe: The Economic Basis* in 1952, which introduced the English-speaking Old World to a totally different socio-economic perspective. In North America, of course, archaeology had a different pedigree, with close links to anthropology from a much earlier stage. Processualism was a new theoretical model, seeking general laws or processes by testing hypotheses against archaeological data for 'goodness of fit'. Post-processualism, as its name implies, is not a theoretical model at all, but a relative term only, applicable to a rag-bag of approaches to archaeological data. It has no unitary coherence or leading exponents, for the simple reason that its diversity reflects the multiplicity of contributions from various disciplinary sources, what has been called the *à la carte* approach to archaeological theory (Pearce, 2011: 85). We may be content with this reality, since it reflects the simple truth that archaeology is not an independent discipline that can stand alone, but a method-ology that is fundamentally embedded in a range of adjacent disciplines.

Roundhouses and Iron Age Society

In attempting to articulate the differences between civilization and savagery (Harding, 2020: 254) a basic list of criteria naturally focuses primarily upon social and economic considerations; only the presence or absence of literacy might be regarded as a direct measure of cognitive achievement. Yet it is clear that prehis-toric societies must have had numeracy and mensuration skills, to be able to con-duct basic transactions of trade, or in the present context to marshal resources in the required quantities for building their houses. Beyond pragmatic numeracy required for basic transactions, the question whether later prehistoric communi-ties had the capacity to resolve abstract mathematical problems without some form of notation, and reliant solely upon memory and oral transmission, is more contentious.

Smaller round huts and houses could doubtless be built locally with traditional community craft skills, perhaps including even skills like corbelling in stone, but monumental roundhouses in timber or stone must have presented problems of a different magnitude. Builders must have had the requisite knowledge of geometry, the means to measure, and to create levels, as well as having the tools to cut tim-ber, to shape stone and to fashion joints. Traditional stone and woodworking skills can be assumed, but the grander timber roundhouses and certainly monu-mental brochs represent a level of achievement that implies an understanding of mathematics, geometry, and physics that is of a further order from the gener-ational acquisition and transmission of traditional crafts. A basic understanding of the laws of physics might be acquired over time through practical experience, doubtless including structural failures and catastrophes. The notion of a specialist caste of itinerant professional dun builders has gone out of fashion, but the idea that such knowledge was available among the learned elite within local communities need hardly occasion surprise, since later prehistoric communities in the Mediterranean and Middle East, who were no more developed physically than the inhabitants of North-Western Europe, evidently had such cognitive capacity. Standard systems of mensuration have often been inferred from the Neolithic onwards, whilst basic levelling can be achieved with plumb bob and wooden frame by anyone familiar with the concept of equilateral triangles. Achieving accuracy with such basic equipment must have taken great patience and repeated efforts. But to apply such knowledge to complex constructions without any apparent system of notation must have raised special problems.

Later prehistoric Britain is pre-eminently represented by settlements in which the roundhouse is the recurrent characteristic. This is more widely represented than any other structural and material manifestations of everyday life and death, not excluding pottery, which is by no means universal. Not all settlements include substantial roundhouses, the constructional complexity of which can indicate a level of investment of effort and resources that exceeds basic necessity. But in some regions substantial roundhouses are in evidence by the Middle Bronze Age, and in some areas survive as late as the para-Roman Iron Age. In Southern Britain the zenith of substantial timber roundhouses still appears to have been the Late Bronze Age and Early Iron Age. In timber roundhouses the dominant features include a principal weight-bearing post-ring that conforms to a symmetrical axial pattern and entrance orientation that defined the internal layout, and may well have been based upon symbolic conventions. Doorways may be elaborated with porch or vestibule in a manner that suggests that access was regulated by social conventions. Hearths located in the centre or off-centre of the interior suggest a division of space between communal central space and peripheral personal or specialized space. The radial division of peripheral space is only formalized in stone in the radial roundhouses of the Western and Northern Isles, and occasionally in brochs, but it is sometimes suggested by traces of timber partitions in lowland timber roundhouses.

Storage was doubtless a key function of these larger roundhouses, notwithstanding the existence of special external storage facilities such as pit-groups and four-post granaries. Whether or not farming settlements in southern England were capable of a surplus, as Reynolds believed, and as Strabo certainly implied (*Geography*, 4.5.2), which would account for large-scale storage on a scale seen in some major hillforts, domestic supplies would surely be kept most securely within the house, where they would have been readily accessible. The width of entrances to the Wessex roundhouses argues for access at harvest time to wagons for storing produce, hay, or straw in the loft or mezzanine floor of the house. Roof space might also have been used for curing meat or fish in the smoke from the fire, which experiment showed hung not far above head height in the Butser reconstructions. Straw and hay might also have been stored around the perimeter of the interior, incidentally providing a measure of insulation and retaining warmth in the house. Underfloor storage appears to have been used in some northern roundhouses, leading eventually to the incorporation of souterrain storage within, or adjacent to and accessible from the house. Storage in the house is therefore well-attested in the archaeological record, so that the concept of a barn-house would not be incompatible with the scale and design of some larger timber-built roundhouses.

Most of the Wessex roundhouses seem to have been based upon ground floor occupation, as indicated by their hearths, with storage above in the roof space. Their basic proportions, that is the ratio of diameter of post-ring to outer wall, suggests a common standard construction based on the principle of a cone on a cylinder, with an inferred roof of straw or reed thatch with a pitch in the order of 45 degrees. Further north by contrast different ratios apply with the probability that different roofing materials were used, such as heather thatch or turf, probably at a lower pitch. In some larger roundhouses, especially in those in Northern Britain where shallow ditches have been eroded within the interior, livestock may have been kept on the ground floor, with human quarters at first floor level. Byre-houses in which stock were introduced overnight or over winter could have taken different architectural forms in different regions, most obviously in the Atlantic north-west, if we accept that the basement level of brochs was given over to livestock.

Either of these variants, barn-house or byre-house, could have benefited from the introduction of a four-post structure centrally within the interior, either based on earth-fast posts or free-standing but built into the fabric. It could have supported a free-standing grain store that formed the focus of the building physically and metaphorically, or it may have supported an upper floor of the byre-house on which the household lived and slept. In either model it may also have supported a central tower, enabling the roof to be split between the outer roof and an upper roof, with clerestory light between. The central tower, of course, need not have been based on a four-post framework, and could equally have taken the form of a post-ring. Apart from alleviating the problem of excessive rafter lengths, this arrangement would have provided light into the interior, and allowed smoke to escape, essential if the upper floor level was to be occupied. The introduction of a central tower to support a split-level roof would have departed completely from the radial ratios of Wessex timber roundhouses, though not necessarily from the principles of axial symmetry or the division between central and peripheral space.

These substantial roundhouses, whether in timber or in stone, may have acquired a special status in some communities that we might equate with the anthropological concept of the 'big house', fulfilling a community role that transcended the basic role as the focus of the household. Plainly not all roundhouses need have achieved this status, even among those of comparable architectural footprint, so that interpretation is a matter of inference from the associated assemblages, if these survive and are adequately recorded. In Southern Britain it is unlikely that any of the roundhouses identified from the proxy remains of drainage gullies from the Middle Iron Age onwards will have sufficient surviving evidence of the house itself or its layout to warrant such an inference, and it may be in any event that the social organization of settlements had changed with the apparent fragmentation or specialization implicit in the cluster-group arrangement. But certainly the larger post-built roundhouses could well have acquired a special communal status, and possibly even a dedicated ritual role, though archaeologically this will always be hard to demonstrate. Even in predominantly domestic roundhouses, nevertheless, it seems likely that relics of ancestors could have been curated, though they may well have been removed when the house was abandoned. Fossil sea-urchins from Pimperne, with their conical shape and radiating pattern evocative of a roundhouse in construction, seem plausibly explained as magical charms (*IAR*: 222), but need signify nothing more.

The social unit that occupied these large roundhouses seems most likely to have been a nuclear family, together with dependants making up the household. Those dependants would have included fostered or adopted children, and the family may have been enlarged if polygyny was still practised in Iron Age Britain. In the West Brandon kind of homestead only one large house is represented, at Little Woodbury there was a secondary roundhouse, and at High Knowes, Alnham, both were twinned, perhaps a sibling pair. In settlements like Dryburn Bridge, on the other hand, even allowing for the houses not being all in contemporary occupation, there would certainly have been several at any one time, possibly including both barn-houses and byre-houses as part of the residential pattern. In larger settlements, like those of the Upper Thames or south Midlands, where there is some evidence for clustering of less substantial units into groups, presumably each group might represent a nuclear family within a larger community of related kin. But within these clusters, functions that had been combined in the larger houses presumably had been devolved into separate adjacent buildings within the compound. Even within the Late Bronze Age villages of southern England, Ireland, and northern France clusters of buildings may have formed related groups, or sequentially-related structures, sometimes including distinctive architectural footprints. House clusters, therefore, must always have been an alternative settlement form to Bersu's single homestead (*Einzelhof*), with no presumption in principle that either alternative represented an earlier or later stage of social development.

Archaeology may reveal nothing in the structural or material assemblage to support the notion that society was hierarchical, but that need not mean that it was not so in principle, or could not become so in practice if occasion required. It seems perfectly plausible to believe that social hierarchy in normal everyday circumstances would have had consensual support, allowing the exercise of more rigorous authority in times of severe hardship or conflict, and then in the community interest rather than for personal or individual advantage. Acknowledging the limitations of later documentary sources, they might at least suggest the possibility of a system of mutual obligation, whereby a social elite was not inevitably exploitative and self-serving.

Among social anthropologists it has been widely observed that there is a close relationship between social hierarchy and agricultural intensification (Sheehan et al., 2018), though rather than demonstrating a simple causal relationship, studies of many Austronesian island communities suggested that the two co-evolved. In the British Iron Age there is abundant evidence in the increase in number and extent of settlements for agricultural extensification, and it would therefore hardly be surprising if there had been at the same time a developing social hierarchy. The problem is how we might expect to recognize this archaeologically. It is widely acknowledged that Iron Age settlements in Britain are not generally noted for the wealth of their surviving material assemblages, not at least in terms of personal material wealth, and it has often been remarked that Iron Age settlements are not generally distinguished by marked disparity in size or elaboration of houses that might be attributed to a social hierarchy. One notable exception is the Period 3 occupation at Crickley Hill, where the central large roundhouse and the lesser houses around it, reasonably deemed to be residential because of the presence of hearths, are of a totally different order, so much so that we might infer that the central 'big house' was a communal building, rather than simply the residence of an elite ruling family. Otherwise differences are less obvious. House 5 at Dalton Parlours is larger than others on the site, but also appears to have been the earliest. At Dryburn Bridge House 1 is potentially rather larger than its neighbours, and might well be seen as a special building fulfilling the role of a communal 'big house'. Among the Borders defended villages, both High Knowes B and Braidwood have central roundhouses that are somewhat larger than their neighbours, so that some disparity of size is in fact not uncommon. The problem is that the concept of house size as an indicator of social hierarchy carries echoes from contemporary Western capitalist societies that are anachronistic in the context of Iron Age communities. The idea that material remains might signify social rank carries similar qualifications, and in any event it is clear from discoveries like Must Farm that later prehistoric communities did not normally leave their material possessions lying around for the benefit of archaeologists when a house was vacated. Formal closure events might well have involved the systematic removal of anything that might be recycled.

Nevertheless, the absence of any material evidence for social hierarchy has encouraged numerous scholars to infer egalitarianism or heterarchy as the social norm, in contrast to social distinctions based on personal wealth, grandeur of living space, or extravagant display of possessions, all inequalities that they are familiar with in their own lives, and which they assume that social hierarchy in prehistory would equally have manifested. The reality more probably is that status was not displayed in this way in the Iron Age, and that wealth was measured in terms of land holding or stock holding, in so far as property was owned by an individual. More especially, as Karl has convincingly argued (2011), status and regard in the community was probably based upon the number of dependants an individual had, those for whom they provided surety, or for whom they had promoted partnerships or resolved conflicts. These are qualities that are unlikely to be reflected in the presence of intrinsically valuable goods about the house, though they might result in a settlement being elaborated with additional enclosure works or through some other display of an individual's control of labour and resources. In fact, the Irish sources suggest that status among those of noble rank was measured in number of their clients or dependants, whereas among non-noble freemen status may well have been reflected in material possessions. On this basis, a comparative evaluation based on twenty-first-century standards would almost certainly misjudge the archaeological evidence totally.

Notwithstanding variations in plan, construction materials, and techniques, the recurrent characteristics of ordered layout, orientation, and division of internal space may lead us to conclude that substantial roundhouses in later prehistoric Britain must have reflected fundamental aspects of social order and convention. Whilst circular ground-plans constituted the dominant building tradition in Britain for more than two millennia, it was not exclusively British, but was significantly represented in northern France and Brittany as well as in the north-west of the Hispanic peninsula. As such we may be justified in thinking of later Bronze Age and Iron Age society in large parts of Atlantic Europe as a 'roundhouse society', not in the social anthropologist's sense of defining a particular social structure, but in reference to an archaeological artefact that articulated it. That it became a symbol of identity is intriguingly demonstrated in its survival and reappearance in elite settlements of the Roman period, alongside but assuredly not inferior to other more fashionable building types. Though not exclusive to Britain, the roundhouse became an icon of community identity in timber and stone that endured for some two millennia in a manner unparalleled in Britain before or since.

Bibliography

Alcock, L., 1960. 'Castell Odo: an embanked settlement on Mynydd Ystum, near Aberdaron, Caernarvonshire', *ArchCamb*, 109: 78–135.

Alexander, D., 2000. 'Excavation of Neolithic pits, later prehistoric structures and a Roman temporary camp along the line of the A96 Kintore and Blackburn bypass, Aberdeenshire', *PSAS*, 130: 11–76.

Allen, T., Donnelly, M., Hardy, A., Hayden, C., and Powell, K., 2012. *A Road through the Past: Archaeological Discoveries on the A2 Pepperhill to Cobham Road-Scheme in Kent*, Oxford, Oxford Archaeology Monograph No. 16.

Allen, T. and Robinson, R., 1993. *The Prehistoric Landscape and Iron Age Enclosed Settlement at Mingies Ditch, Hardwick-with-Yelford, Oxon*, Oxford, Oxford Archaeological Unit.

Alvarez Gonzáles, Y., López Gonzáles, L., and López Marcos, M., 2005. 'Recuperación e posta en valor do conxunto arqueolóxico de Os Castros de Neixón', in X. M. Ayán Vila, ed., *Os Castros de Neixón (Boiro, A Coruña): a recuperación dende a Arqueoloxía dun espazo social e patrimonial*, Serie Keltia, Noia, Toxosoutos: 93–123.

Andrews, G., Barrett, J., and Lewis, J., 2000. 'Interpretation not record: the practice of archaeology', *Antiquity*, 74: 525–30.

Angelbeck, B., 2020. 'Interpreting the dialectic of sociopolitical tensions in the archaeological past: implications of an anarchist perspective for Iron Age Societies', in B. Currás and I. Sastre, eds., *Alternative Iron Ages: Social Theory from Archaeological Analysis*, Abingdon, Routledge: 29–49.

Antoni, B., Johnson, M., and McComish, J., 2009. *The University of York, Heslington East, York: Assessment Report*, York, York Archaeological Report No. 2009/48.

Armit, I., 1991. 'The Atlantic Scottish Iron Age: five levels of chronology', *PSAS*, 121: 181–214.

Armit, I., 1992. *The Later Prehistory of the Western Isles of Scotland*, Oxford, BAR British Series 221.

Armit, I., 2000. 'Review of Parker Pearson, M. and Sharples, N., 1999, *Between Land and Sea: Excavations at Dun Vulan, South Uist*', *Antiquity*, 74: 244–5.

Armit, I., 2006. *Anatomy of an Iron Age Roundhouse: The Cnip Wheelhouse Excavations, Lewis*, Edinburgh, Society of Antiquaries of Scotland.

Armit, I., 2019. 'Enclosure, autonomy and anarchy in Iron Age Scotland', in T. Romankiewicz, M. Fernández-Gotz, G. Lock, and O. Büchsenschütz, eds., *Enclosing Space, Opening New Ground. Iron Age Studies from Scotland to Mainland Europe*, Oxford, Oxbow Books: 101–10.

Armit, I., 2020. 'Hierarchy to anarchy and back again: social transformation from the Late Bronze Age to the Roman Iron Age in Lowland Scotland', in B. Currás and I. Sastre, eds., *Alternative Iron Ages: Social Theory from Archaeological Analysis*, Abingdon, Routledge: 195–217.

Armit, I., Campbell, E., and Dunwell, A., 2008. 'Excavation of an Iron Age, early historic and medieval settlement and metalworking site at Eilean Olabhat, North Uist', *PSAS*, 138: 27–104.

250 BIBLIOGRAPHY

Armit, I. and Ginn, V., 2007. 'Beyond the grave: human remains from domestic contexts in Iron Age Atlantic Scotland', *PPS*, 73: 113–34.

Armit, I. and McKenzie, J., 2013. *An Inherited Place: Broxmouth Hillfort and the South-East Scottish Iron Age*, Edinburgh, Society of Antiquaries of Scotland.

Avery, D. M. E. and Close-Brooks, J., 1969. 'Shearplace Hill, Sydling St Nicholas, Dorset, House A: a suggested re-interpretation', *PPS*, 35: 345–51.

Ayán Vila, X. M., 2003. *Archaeotecture: Archaeology of Architecture*, Oxford, BAR International Series 1175, Archaeopress.

Ayán Vila, X. M., 2008. 'A round Iron Age: the circular house in the hillforts of the north-western Iberian peninsula', *e-Keltoi: Journal of Interdisciplinarian Celtic Studies*, Vol. 6, *The Celts in the Iberian Peninsula*, Article 19.

Ayán Vila, X. M., 2018. 'Las casas del fin del mundo: el espacio doméstico de la edad de hierro en el noroeste', in A. Rodríguez Díaz, I. Pavón Soldevila, and D. Duque Espino, eds., *Más allá de las casas, familias, linajes y comunidades en la protohistoria peninsular*, Cácres, Universidad de Extremadura: 265–94.

Bain, K. and Evans, C., 2008. 'A late Iron Age and early Romano-British enclosure at Meole Brace, Shrewsbury', *Shropshire History and Archaeology*, 86: 121–51.

Barbeau, S. and Delnef, H., 2020. 'Une habitation et sa cave du premier âge du Fer en centre Bretagne', *Revue Archéologique de l'Ouest*, 36: 99–119.

Barber, J., 2016. *Approaching the mind of the builder. Analysis of the physical, structural and social constraints on the construction of the broch towers of Iron Age Scotland*, PhD thesis, University of Edinburgh.

Baring-Gould, S., Burnard, R., and Enys, J., 1899. 'Exploration of a stone camp on St David's Head', *ArchCamb*, 5th ser. 16: 105–31.

Barrett, J., 1987. 'The Glastonbury Lake Village: models and source criticism', *ArchJ*, 144: 409–23.

Barrett, J., Bradley, R., and Green, M., 1991. *Landscape, Monuments and Society. The Prehistory of Cranborne Chase*, Cambridge, Cambridge University Press.

Barrett, J., Freeman, P., and Woodward, A., 2000. *Cadbury Castle, Somerset: The Later Prehistoric and Early Historic Archaeology*, London, English Heritage Archaeological Report 20.

Bayliss, A. and Grogan, E., 2013. 'Chronologies for Tara and comparable royal sites of the Irish Iron Age', in M. O'Sullivan, C. Scarre, and M. Doyle, eds., *Tara from the Past to the Future*, Dublin, Wordwell: 105–44.

Bech, J.-H. and Haack Olsen, A.-L., 2012. 'Early Bronze Age houses from Thy, northwest Denmark', *Studien zur nordeuropäischen Bronzezeit*, 1: 9–12.

Becker, K., 2012. 'The introduction of iron working to Ireland', in A. Kern and J. Koch, eds., *Technologieentwicklung und- transfer in der Hallstattzeit und Latènezeit. Beiträge zur internationalen Tagung der AG Eisenzeit und des Naturhistorischen Museums Wien, Hallstatt 2009*, Langenweissenbach, Beier and Beran, Beiträge zur Ur- und Frühgeschichte Mitteleuropas, 65: 173–80.

Becker, K., 2019. 'Iron Age settlement and society: reframing Royal Sites', *PPS*, 85: 273–306.

Bennett, P., 2010. 'Reconstruction and interpretation of an Iron Age fort', *ArchJ*, 167, Supplement 1: 23–7.

Bersu, G., 1940. 'Excavations at Little Woodbury, Wiltshire. Part 1: the settlement as revealed by excavation', *PPS*, 6: 30–111.

Bersu, G., 1946. 'Celtic homesteads in the Isle of Man', *Journal of the Manx Museum*, 72–3: 177–82.

Bersu, G., 1948. '"Fort" at Scotstarvit Covert, Fife', *PSAS*, 82: 241–63.

Bersu, G., 1977. *Three Iron Age Round Houses in the Isle of Man*, Douglas, Manx Museum and National Trust.

Beveridge, E., 1903. *Coll and Tiree*, Edinburgh, William Brown.

Bintliff, J., 2011. 'The death of archaeological theory?' in J. Bintliff and M. Pearce, eds., *The Death of Archaeological Theory?*, Oxford and Oakville, Oxbow Books: 7–22.

Bintliff, J. and Pearce, M., eds., 2011. *The Death of Archaeological Theory?*, Oxford and Oakville, Oxbow Books.

Blake, B., 1959. 'Excavations of native (Iron Age) sites in Cumberland, 1956–58', *TCWAAS*, 59: 1–14.

Blaylock, S., 2004. 'Possible architectural solutions for large oval buildings', in H. Quinnell, *Trethurgy. Excavations at Tregurthy Round, St Austell: Community and Status in Roman and Post-Roman Cornwall*, Truro and London, Cornwall County Council and English Heritage: 190–201.

Bond, J. and Dockrill, S., 2019. *Knowe of Swandro Data Structure Report 2018 Field Season*, Bradford, School of Archaeological and Forensic Sciences.

Bossard, S., 2020. *Les souterraines gaulois en Bretagne et Normandie occidentale: architectures de stockages enterrées*, Rennes, Presses universitaires de Rennes.

Bradford, J. and Goodchild, R., 1939. 'Excavations at Frilford, Berks, 1937–8', *Oxoniensia*, 4: 1–70.

Bradley, R., 2006. 'Bridging the two cultures – commercial archaeology and the study of prehistoric Britain', *AntJ*, 86: 1–13.

Bradley, R., 2013. 'Houses of commons, houses of lords: domestic dwellings and monumental architecture in prehistoric Europe', *PPS*, 79: 1–17.

Bradley, R., 2021. *Temporary Palaces: The Great House in European Prehistory*, Oxford, Oxbow Books.

Bradley, R., Haselgrove, C., vander Linden, M., and Webley, L., 2016. *The Later Prehistory of North-West Europe: The Evidence of Development-Led Fieldwork*, Oxford, Oxford University Press.

Brossler, A., Early, R., and Allen, C., 2004. *Green Park (Reading Business Park) Phase 2 Excavations 1995 – Neolithic and Bronze Age Sites*, Thames Valley Landscapes Monograph 19, Oxford, Oxford Archaeology.

Brown, F., Howard-Davies, C., Brennand, M., Boyle, A., Evans, T., O'Connor, S., Spence, A., Heawood, R., and Lupton, A., 2007. *The Archaeology of the A1 (M) Darrington to Dishforth DBFO Road Scheme*, Lancaster, Oxford Archaeology North.

Brück, J., 2019. *Personifying Prehistory: Relational Ontologies in Bronze Age Britain and Ireland*, Oxford, Oxford University Press.

Brück, J., 2021. 'Ancient DNA, kinship and relational identities in Bronze Age Britain', *Antiquity*, 95: 228–37.

Bulleid, A. and Gray, St G., 1911. *The Glastonbury Lake Village, Volume 1*, Glastonbury, Glastonbury Antiquarian Society.

Burgess, C. B., 1980. 'Excavations at Houseledge, Black Law, Northumberland, 1979, and their implications for earlier Bronze Age settlement in the Cheviots', *Northern Archaeology*, 1: 5–12.

Burgess, C. B., 1984. 'The prehistoric settlement of Northumberland: a speculative survey', in R. Miket and C. Burgess, eds., *Between and Beyond the Walls: Essays on the Prehistory and History of North Britain in Honour of George Jobey*, Edinburgh, John Donald: 126–75.

Burrow, S., 2015. 'From Celtic village to Iron Age farmstead: lessons learnt from twenty years of building, maintaining and presenting Iron Age roundhouses at St Fagan's National History Museum', https://exarc.net/ark:/88735/10219.

Burrow, S., 2020. 'Pre-Iron Age domestic buildings in Wales', *ArchCamb*, 169: 71–103.

Burstow, G. and Holleyman, G., 1957. 'Late Bronze Age settlement on Itford Hill, Sussex', *PPS*, 23: 167–212.

252 BIBLIOGRAPHY

Büster, L., 2011. 'Review of Harding, D., *The Iron Age Round-House: Later Prehistoric Building in Britain and Beyond*, Oxford, Oxford University Press, 2009', *European Journal of Archaeology*, 14: 323–4.

Cameron, K., 1999. 'Excavation of an Iron Age timber structure beside the Candle Stane recumbent stone circle, Aberdeenshire', *PSAS*, 129: 359–72.

Cameron, K., Rees, A., Dunwell, A., and Anderson, S., 2007. 'Prehistoric pits, Bronze Age roundhouses, an Iron Age promontory enclosure, early historic cist burials and medieval enclosures along the route of the A92 Dundee to Arbroath', *TAFAJ*, 13: 39–73.

Carew, T., Bishop, B., Meddens, F., and Ridgeway, V., 2006. *Unlocking the Landscape: Archaeological Excavations at Ashford Prison, Middlesex*, London, Pre-Construct Archaeology Limited.

Carruthers, M., 2007. 'The Cairns, Windwick Bay', *DES*, 8: 145–6.

Carruthers, M., 2009. 'The Cairns, Windwick Bay', *DES*, 10: 137–8.

Cavers, G., 2012. 'Crannogs as buildings: the evolution of interpretation', in M. Midgley and J. Sandars, eds., *Lake Dwellings after Munro*, Leiden, Sidestone Press: 169–88.

Cavers, G., 2019. 'Dun Vulan, Bornais', *DES*, 20: 212–13.

Cavers, G., Barber, J., Johnstone, N., and Sleight, G., 2017. 'Clachtoll broch, Clachtoll: conservation and excavation', *DES*, 18: 101–2.

Cavers, G., Barber, J., and Ritchie, M., 2015. 'The survey and analysis of brochs', *PSAS*, 145: 153–76.

Chadwick, A., 2010. *Fields for discourse. Landscape and materialities of being in South and West Yorkshire and Nottinghamshire during the Iron Age and Romano-British periods. A study of people and place*. PhD thesis, University of Wales, Newport.

Chadwick, S., 1960. 'Longbridge Deverill Cow Down', in S. S. Frere, ed., *Problems of the Iron Age in Southern Britain*, London, Institute of Archaeology, University of London, Occasional Paper 11: 18–20.

Challis, A. and Harding, D., 1975. *Later Prehistory from the Trent to the Tyne*, Oxford, BAR British Series 20.

Chapman, A., 2015a. 'Iron Age settlement at the Long Dole', in R. Masefield, A. Chapman, A. Mudd, J. Hart, P. Ellis, and R. King, *Origins, Development and Abandonment of an Iron Age Village: Further Archaeological Investigations for the Daventry International Rail Freight Terminal, Crick and Kilsby, Northamptonshire*, DIRFT Volume II, Oxford, Archaeopress: 13–60.

Chapman, A., 2015b. 'Iron Age, Roman and Anglo-Saxon settlement at the Lodge', in R. Masefield, A. Chapman, A. Mudd, J. Hart, P. Ellis, and R. King, *Origins, Development and Abandonment of an Iron Age Village: Further Archaeological Investigations for the Daventry International Rail Freight Terminal, Crick and Kilsby, Northamptonshire*, DIRFT Volume II, Oxford, Archaeopress: 114–66.

Chapman, A., 2020. *Coton Park, Rugby, Warwickshire: A Middle Iron Age Settlement with Copper Alloy Casting*, Oxford, Archaeopress.

Charles, B., Parkinson, A., and Foreman, S., 2000. 'A Bronze Age ditch and Iron Age settlement at Elms Farm, Humberstone, Leicester', *Transactions of the Leicestershire Archaeological and Historical Society*, 74: 113–220.

Christie, P., 1978. 'The excavation of a souterrain and settlement at Carn Euny, Sancreed, Cornwall', *PPS*, 44: 309–434.

Christie, C. and Dalland, M., 2022. *The excavation of a prehistoric settlement at Lower Slackbuie, Inverness*, Edinburgh, Society of Antiquaries of Scotland, SAIR 100.

Christison, D., 1898. *Early Fortifications in Scotland: Motes, Camps and Forts*, Edinburgh and London, Blackwood.

Clark, J. G. D., 1937. 'Prehistoric houses', *PPS*, 3: 468–9.

Clark, J. G. D. and Fell, C., 1953. 'The Early Iron Age site at Micklemoor Hill, West Harling, Norfolk, and its pottery', *PPS*, 19: 1–40.

Clarke, D. L., 1972. 'A provisional model of an Iron Age society and its settlement system', in D. L. Clarke, ed., *Models in Archaeology*, London, Methuen: 801–69.

Clarke, D. V., 2012. 'A man changed by Darwin', in M. Midgley and J. Sandars, eds., *Lake Dwellings after Munro*, Leiden, Sidestone Press: 37–54.

Clarke, R. R., 1960. *East Anglia*, London, Thames and Hudson.

Clay, R. C. C., 1924. 'An Early Iron Age site on Fyfield Bavant Down', *WAM*, 42: 457–96.

Cleary, K., 2007. *Irish Bronze Age settlements: spatial organisation and the deposition of material culture*, PhD thesis, University College Cork.

Cockcroft, D., Hunter, P., Potter, M. and Waddington, C., 2019. *Archaeological Excavations at Lochinver Quarry, Elgin, 2013–2019*, Archaeological Research Services online report 2019/176.

Coggins, D. and Fairless, K., 1984. 'The Bronze Age settlement site at Bracken Rigg, Upper Teesdale, Co. Durham', *DAJ*, 1: 5–21.

Coles, J. and Minnitt, S., 1995. *Industrious and Fairly Civilized: The Glastonbury Lake Village*, Taunton, Somerset County Museums Service and Somerset Levels Project.

Cook, M., 2000. 'Excavation of Neolithic and Bronze Age settlement features at Lamb's Nursery, Dalkeith, Midlothian', *PSAS*, 130: 93–113.

Cook, M., 2006. 'Excavations of a Bronze Age roundhouse and associated palisaded enclosure at Aird's Quarry, Castle Kennedy, Dumfries and Galloway', *TDGNHAS*, 80: 9–28.

Cook, M., 2016. *Prehistoric Settlement Patterns in the North-East of Scotland: Excavations at Grantown Road, Forres, 2002–2013*, Edinburgh, Society of Antiquaries of Scotland, 61.

Cook, M. and Dunbar, L., 2008. *Rituals, Roundhouses and Romans: Excavations at Kintore, Aberdeenshire 2000–2006*, Edinburgh, STAR.

Cool, H. and Mason, D., 2008. *Roman Piercebridge: Excavations by D. W. Harding and Peter Scott 1969–1981*, Durham, The Architectural Society of Durham and Northumberland.

Cootes, C., Axworthy, J., Jordan, D., Thomas, M., and Carlin, R., 2021. 'Poulton, Cheshire: the excavation of a lowland Iron Age settlement', *Journal of the Chester Archaeological Society*, NS 91: 103–78.

Cowell, R., 2003. *Prehistoric and Romano-British Excavations at Duttons Farm, Lathom, Lancashire, Third Interim Report, 1999–2002*, Liverpool, National Museum.

Cowie, T. and MacLeod Rivett, M., forthcoming. 'The long Iron Age on the Barabhas machair, Isle of Lewis'.

Cowley, D., Fernández-Gotz, M., Romankkiewicz, T., and Wendling, H., 2019. *Rural Settlement: Relating Buildings, Landscape and People in the European Iron Age*, Leiden, Sidestone Press.

Cox, S. and Gaunt, J., 2018. *Enclosed Iron Age Settlements on Land East of Morley Hill Farm, Hazlerigg, Newcastle upon Tyne*, Edinburgh, Headland Archaeology, ADS.

Crane, P. and Murphy, K., 2010. 'The excavation of a coastal promontory fort at Porth y Rhaw, Solva, Pembrokeshire', *ArchCamb*, 159: 53–98.

Creighton, T., Osgood, R., and Pope, R., 2022. 'An experiment in earthen walls: Operation Nightingale, Butser Ancient Farm and the Dunch Hill roundhouse', *CA*, 383: 28–35.

Cressey, M. and Anderson, S., 2011. *A Later Prehistoric Settlement and Metalworking Site at Seafield West, Inverness, Highland*, Edinburgh, Society of Antiquaries of Scotland, SAIR 47.

Cressey, M., Finlayson, B., and Hamilton, J., 1998. 'Seafield West, near Inverness', *DES*, 1998: 52–4.

254 BIBLIOGRAPHY

Cripps, L., 2007. 'Re-situating the later Iron Age in Cornwall: new perspectives from the settlement record', in C. Haselgrove and T. Moore, eds., *The Later Iron Age in Britain and Beyond*, Oxford, Oxbow Books: 140–55.

Crone, A., 2000. *The History of a Lowland Scottish Crannog: Excavations at Buiston, Ayrshire, 1989–90*, Edinburgh, STAR Monograph 4.

Crone, A. and Cavers, G., 2015. 'The Black Loch of Myrton: an Iron Age loch village in south-west Scotland', *Antiquity* Project Gallery, August.

Crone, A., Cavers, G., Allison, E., Davies, K., Hamilton, D., Henderson, A., Mackay, H. McLaren, D., Robertson, J., Roy, L., and Whitehouse, N., 2018. 'Nasty, brutish and short? The life cycle of an Iron Age roundhouse at Black Loch of Myrton, SW Scotland', *Journal of Wetland Archaeology*, 18, no. 2: 138–62.

Crosby, V. and Muldowney, L., 2011. *Stanwick Quarry, Northamptonshire. Raunds Area Project: Phasing the Iron Age and Roman Settlement at Stanwick*, London, English Heritage Research Report 54.

Cunliffe, B., 1984. *Danebury: An Iron Age Hillfort in Hampshire, Vol. 1, the Excavations 1969–78: The Site*, London, CBA Research Report 52a.

Cunliffe, B., 2005. *Iron Age Communities in Britain*, 4th edition, Abingdon, Routledge.

Cunliffe, B., 2008. *The Danebury Environs Roman Programme: A Wessex Landscape during the Roman Era, Volume 1: Overview*, Oxford, English Heritage and Oxford School of Archaeology.

Cunliffe, B., 2013. ' "For men of rank...basilicas": aisled halls reconsidered', in H. Eckardt and S. Rippon, eds., *Living and Working in the Roman World: Essays in Honour of Michael Fulford on his 65th Birthday*, Portsmouth, *Journal of Roman Archaeology* Supplementary Series 95: 95–110.

Cunliffe, B. and Poole, C., 1991. *Danebury: An Iron Age Hillfort in Hampshire, Vol. 4, the Excavations, 1979–88: The Site*, London, CBA Research Report 73a.

Cunliffe, B. and Poole, C., 2008. *Flint Farm, Goodworth Clatford, Hants, 2004, The Danebury Environs Roman Programme Volume 2, Part 6*, Oxford, Oxford School of Archaeology.

Cunnington, M., 1923. *The Early Iron Age Inhabited Site at All Cannings Cross Farm, Wiltshire*, Devizes, George Simpson.

Currás, B. and Sastre, I., eds., 2020a. *Alternative Iron Ages: Social Theory from Archaeological Analysis*, Abingdon, Routledge.

Currás, B. and Sastre, I., 2020b. 'Segmentary societies: a theoretical approach from European Iron Age archaeology', in B. Currás and I. Sastre, eds., *Alternative Iron Ages: Social Theory from Archaeological Analysis*, Abingdon, Routledge: 127–48.

Danaher, E., 2012. 'A possible Iron Age homestead at Ballinaspig More, Co. Cork', in C. Corlett and M. Potterton, eds., *Life and Death in Iron Age Ireland in the Light of Recent Archaeological Excavations*, Dublin, Wordwell: 79–92.

Darwin, C., 1859. *On the Origin of Species by Means of Natural Selection*, London, John Murray.

Dechezleprêtre, T., Billard, C., Blancquaert, G., Fournier, P., and Langlois, J.-I., 1997. 'Les constructions à plan circulaire de Haute-Normandie', *Revue Archéologique de l'Ouest*, 14: 49–56.

Dechezleprêtre, T., Cousyn, P., Léon, G., Paez-Rezende, L., and Rougier, R., 2000. 'Architecture des bâtiments de l'âge du Fer en Haute-Normandie', in S. Marion and G. Blancquaert, eds., *Les installations agricoles de l'âge du Fer en France septentrionale*, Paris, Éditions Rue d'Ulm/Presses de l'École normale supérieure: 321–38.

Dent, J., 1984. *Wetwang Slack: an Iron Age cemetery on the Yorkshire Wolds*, MPhil thesis, University of Sheffield.

Desbrosse, V. and Riquier, V., 2012. 'Les établissements ruraux palissadés halstattiens en Champagne', in M. Schönfelder and S. Sievers, eds., *L'âge du Fer entre la Champagne et la* vallé du Rhin, Actes du XXXIVe colloque de l'AFEAF, Aschaffenburg 2010, Mainz, RGZM: 3–28.

Dixon, P., 2019. *Crickley Hill Volume 2: The Hillfort Settlements*, Crickley Hill Archaeological Trust.

Dockrill, S., 2007. *Investigations in Sanday, Orkney, Vol. 2: Tofts Ness, Sanday. An Island Landscape through Three Thousand Years of Prehistory*, Kirkwall/Edinburgh, The Orcadian/Historic Scotland.

Dockrill, S., Bond, J., and Gaffney, C., 2019. 'The 2019 excavations and geophysical survey', *Orkney Archaeology Review 2019*: 87–105.

Dockrill, S., Bond, J., Turner, V., Brown, L., Bashford, D., Cussans, J., and Nicholson, R., 2010. *Excavations at Old Scatness, Shetland Volume 1: The Pictish Village and Viking Settlement*, Lerwick, Shetland Heritage Publications.

Dockrill, S., Bond, J., Turner, V., Brown, L., Bashford, D., Cussans, J., and Nicholson, R., 2015. *Excavations at Old Scatness, Shetland, Volume 2: The Broch and Middle Iron Age Village*, Lerwick, Shetland Heritage Publications.

Drewett, P., 1982. 'Late Bronze Age downland economy and excavations at Black Patch, East Sussex', *PPS*, 48: 321–400.

Drury, P., 1978. *Excavations at Little Waltham, 1970–71*, Chelmsford, CBA Research Report No. 26, Chelmsford Excavation Committee Report 1.

Dunning, G., 1976. 'Salmonsbury, Bourton-on-the-Water, Gloucestershire', in D. W. Harding, ed., *Hillforts, Later Prehistoric Earthworks in Britain and Ireland*, London, Academic Press: 76–118, 373–401, and 488–94.

Dunwell, A., 2007. *Cist Burials and an Iron Age Settlement at Dryburn Bridge, Innerwick, East Lothian*, Edinburgh, Society of Antiquaries of Scotland, SAIR, 24.

Earle, T., 2020. 'Preface', in B. Currás and I. Sastre, eds., *Alternative Iron Ages: Social Theory from Archaeological Analysis*, Abingdon, Routledge: xv–xxi.

Ellis, C. online, n.d. *Case Study 4: Dunbeg and Glenshellach*, Scottish Archaeological Research Framework, https://scarf.scot.

Evans, C., 2007. 'Review of Lewis, J. et al., *Landscape Evolution in the Middle Thames Valley: Heathrow Terminal 5 Excavations, Volume 1, Perry Oaks*', Oxford and Salisbury, Oxford Archaeology and Wessex Archaeology.

Evans, C., forthcoming. 'Seeing differently: rereading Little Woodbury', *Bericht der Römisch-Germanische Kommission*.

Evans, C. and Knight, M., 1996. 'An Ouse-side longhouse. Barleycroft Farm, Cambridgeshire', *PAST, Prehistoric Society Newsletter*, 23.

Evershed, R., Casanova, E., Knowles, T., and Dunne, J., 2021. 'Radiocarbon dating of pottery has arrived', *BA*, March/April: 30–34.

Fairburn, N., 2003. 'Brook House farm, Bruen Stapleford: excavation of a first millennium BC settlement', *Journal of the Chester Archaeological Society*, 77: 9–57.

Fairhurst, H., 1984. *Excavations at Crosskirk Broch, Caithness*, Edinburgh, Society of Antiquaries of Scotland.

Fasham, P., Farwell, D., and Whinney, R., 1989. *The Archaeological Site at Easton Lane, Winchester*, Trust for Wessex Archaeology/Hampshire Field Club.

Feachem, R. W., 1961. 'Unenclosed platform settlements', *PSAS*, 94: 79–85.

Fenton, J., 2015. *Prehistoric Roundhouses of Wester Ross and Parts of Skye*, Gairloch, privately published.

Fenton-Thomas, C., 2011. *Where Sky and Yorkshire and Water Meet: The Story of the Melton Landscape from Prehistory to the Present*, York, On-Site Archaeology Monograph No. 2.

Fenwick, J., 2018. 'The late prehistoric "royal site" of Rathcroghan, Co. Roscommon: an enduring paradigm of enclosed sacred space', *Emania*, 24: 35–51.

Fenwick, J., Daly, E., and Rooney, S., 2020. 'Rathcroghan revisited: a renewed archaeological and geophysical exploration of selected areas of the focal ritual complex', *Emania*, 25: 81–98.

Ferreira da Silva, A., 1995. 'Portuguese castros: the evolution of the habitat and the proto-urbanization process', *PBA*, 86: 263–89.

Fitts, R., Haselgrove, C., Lowther, P., and Willis, S., 1999. 'Melsonby revisited: survey and excavation 1992-1995 at the site of the discovery of the Stanwick, North Yorkshire Hoard of 1843', *DAJ*, 14–15: 1–52.

Fitzpatrick, A., 1994. 'Outside in: the structure of an Early Iron Age house at Dunston Park, Thatcham, Berkshire', in A. Fitzpatrick and E. Morris, eds., *The Iron Age in Wessex, Recent Work*, Salisbury, Trust for Wessex Archaeology: 68–73.

Fitzpatrick, A., 2011. *The Amesbury Archer and the Boscombe Bowmen, Bell Beaker Burials at Boscombe Down, Amesbury, Wiltshire*, Salisbury, Wessex Archaeology.

Fitzpatrick, A., Butterworth, C., and Grove, J., 1999. *Prehistoric and Roman Sites in East Devon: The A30 Honiton to Exeter Improvement DBFO Scheme, 1996–9, Vol. 1: Prehistoric Sites*, Salisbury, Wessex Archaeology.

Fleming, A., 2008. *The Dartmoor Reaves: Investigating Prehistoric Land Divisions*, 2nd edition, Oxford, Windgather Press.

Fojut, N., 2005. 'Brochs and timber supply – a necessity born of invention?' in V. Turner, R. Nicholson, S. Dockrill, and J. Bond, eds., *Tall Stories? 2 Millennia of Brochs*, Lerwick, Shetland Amenity Trust: 190–201.

Fox, A., 1954. 'Celtic fields and farms on Dartmoor, in the light of recent excavations at Kestor', *PPS*, 20: 87–102.

Frazer, W., 2012. 'Mud hut redux: roundhouse vernacular at Coolbeg, Co. Wicklow, and Iron Age social organisation', in C. Corlett and M. Potterton, eds., *Life and Death in Iron Age Ireland in the Light of Recent Archaeological Excavations*, Dublin, Wordwell: 121–39.

Frei, K. M., Mannering, U., Kristiansen, K., Allentoft, M., Wilson, A., Skals, I., Tridico, S., Norsch, M., Willerslev, E. Clarke, L., and Frei, R., 2015. 'Tracing the dynamic life story of a Bronze Age female', *Scientific Reports*, 5, 10431. https://doi.org/10.1038/srep10431.

Fromont, N., Noël, J.-Y., Dietsch-Sellami, M.-F., and Juhel, L., 2018. 'Une occupation du Bronze final à Gravigny, "Les Coudrettes" (Eure)', in S. Boulud-Gazo and M. Mélin, eds., *Contributions à l'archéologie de l'âge du Bronze dans les espaces atlantiques et Manche-Mer du Nord, Vol. 1, Actes de la Table Ronde de Rouen (2005)*, Le Poiré-sur-Vie, Association pour la Promotion des Recherches sur l'Âge du Bronze: 59–76.

Gelling, P., 1977. 'Excavations at Pilsden Pen, Dorset, 1964–71', *PPS*, 43: 263–86.

Gerrard, S., 2016. 'Archaeology and bracken: the Teigncombe prehistoric roundhouse excavation', *PDAS*, 74: 1–63.

Ghey, E., Edwards, N., and Johnston, R., 2008. 'Categorizing roundhouse settlements in Wales: a critical perspective', *Studia Celtica*, XLII: 1–25.

Ghey, E., Edwards, N., Johnston, R., and Pope, R., 2007. *Characterising the Welsh Roundhouse: Chronology, Inhabitation and Landscape*, York, Internet Archaeology 23.

Gibson, A., 1992. 'The excavation of an Iron Age settlement at Gold Park, Dartmoor', *PDAS*, 50: 19–46.

Gillespie, S., 2007. 'When is a house?' in R. Beck, ed., *The Durable House: House Society Models in Archaeology*, Occasional Paper 35, Carbondale, Southern Illinois University: 25–50.

Gingell, C., 1981. 'Excavation of an Iron Age enclosure at Groundwell Farm, Blunsdon St Andrew, 1976–7', *WAM*, 76: 33–76.

Ginn, V. and Rathbone, S., 2012. *Corrstown: A Coastal Community. Excavations of a Bronze Age Village in Northern Ireland*, Oxford and Oakville, Oxbow Books.

Ginnever, M., 2017. 'An Iron Age settlement and souterrain at Dubton Farm East, Brechin, Angus', *TAFAJ*, 23: 1–12.

Godard, C., 2013. 'L'implantation des habitations circulaires en Bretagne et en Normandie à l'âge du Fer: un échange d'hommes et de savoirs', *Revue archéologique de l'Ouest*, 30: 165–86.

Goldhahn, J., 2013. 'Rethinking Bronze Age cosmology: a North European perspective', in H. Fokkens and A. Harding, eds., *The Oxford Handbook of the European Bronze Age*, Oxford, Oxford University Press: 248–65.

González, R., 2020. 'Anarchy in the Bronze Age? Social organization and complexity in Sardinia', in B. Currás and I. Sastre, eds., *Alternative Iron Ages: Social Theory from Archaeological Analysis*, Abingdon, Routledge: 74–94.

Gonzáles-Ruibal, A., 2006. 'House societies vs kinship-based societies: an archaeological case from Iron Age Europe', *Journal of Anthropological Archaeology*, 25: 144–73.

Gosden, C., Drury, P., Gerrard, C., Pretty, K., and Milner, N., 2021. 'Rise of science degrees and decline of arts', *The Times, Letters*, 6 February.

Greef, A. and Moan, P., online, n.d. 'Tye Green, Cressing, Essex: an Iron Age village with evidence of Boudiccan reprisals?', *In Touch*, Issue 54: 12–13, Oxford Archaeology.

Gregory, T., 1991. *Excavations at Thetford, 1980–82, Fison Way*, 2 vols., East Anglian Archaeology Report No. 53, Dereham, Norfolk Museums Service.

Grimes, W. F. and Close-Brooks, J., 1993. 'The excavation of Caesar's Camp, Heathrow, Harmondsworth, Middlesex, 1944', *PPS*, 59: 303–60.

Guilbert, G., 1981. 'Double-ring roundhouses, probable and possible, in prehistoric Britain', *PPS*, 47: 299–311.

Guilbert, G., 1982. 'Post-ring symmetry in roundhouses at Moel y Gaer and some other sites in prehistoric Britain', in P. Drury, ed., *Structural Reconstruction: Approaches to the Interpretation of Excavated Remains of Buildings*, Oxford, BAR British Series 110: 67–86.

Guillier, G., 2004. 'Un petit habitat ouvert de l'âge du Fer à "La Dugerie", commune de Gaubretiere (Vendée)', *Revue Archéologique de l'Ouest*, 21: 55–61.

Hale, A. and Sands, R., 2005. *Controversy on the Clyde. Archaeologists, Fakes and Forgeries: The Excavation of Dumbuck Crannog*, Edinburgh, RCAHMS.

Halliday, S., 1985. 'Unenclosed upland settlement in the east and south-east of Scotland', in D. Spratt and C. Burgess, eds., *Upland Settlement in Britain: The Second Millennium BC and After*, Oxford, BAR British Series 143: 231–51.

Halliday, S., 2008. 'The later prehistoric landscape', in S. Halliday and J. Stevenson, eds., *In the Shadow of Bennachie: A Field Archaeology of Donside, Aberdeenshire*, Edinburgh, RCAHMS/Society of Antiquaries of Scotland: 79–111.

Hamilton, J. R. C., 1956. *Excavations at Jarlshof, Shetland*, Edinburgh, HMSO.

Hamilton, J. R. C., 1968. *Excavations at Clickhimin, Shetland*, Edinburgh, HMSO.

Harding, A., 2021. *Bronze Age Lives*, Berlin, de Gruyter.

Harding, D. W., 1972. *The Iron Age in the Upper Thames Basin*, Oxford, Clarendon Press.

Harding, D. W., 1973. 'Round and rectangular, Iron Age houses, British and foreign', in C. F. C. Hawkes and S. C. Hawkes, eds., *Greeks, Celts and Romans: Studies in Venture and Resistance*, London, J. M. Dent: 43–62.

Harding, D. W., 1974. *The Iron Age in Lowland Britain*, London, Routledge & Kegan Paul.

Harding, D. W., ed., 1976. *Hillforts: Later Prehistoric Earthworks in Britain and Ireland*, London, Academic Press.

Harding, D. W., ed., 1982. *Later Prehistoric Settlement in South-East Scotland*, Edinburgh, Department of Archaeology, University of Edinburgh, Occasional Paper No. 8.

Harding, D. W., 1984. *Holme House, Piercebridge: Excavations 1969–70. A Summary Report*. Edinburgh, University of Edinburgh Department of Archaeology, Project Paper No. 2.

Harding, D. W., 1987. *Excavations in Oxfordshire, 1964–66*, Edinburgh, University of Edinburgh Department of Archaeology, Occasional Paper No. 15.

Harding, D. W., 2000. 'Crannogs and island duns', *OJA*, 19: 301–17.

258 BIBLIOGRAPHY

Harding, D. W., 2004. *The Iron Age in Northern Britain: Celts and Romans, Natives and Invaders*, London, Routledge.

Harding, D. W., 2016. Death and Burial in Iron Age Britain, Oxford, Oxford University Press.

Harding, D. W., 2017. *The Iron Age in Northern Britain: Britons and Romans, Natives and Settlers*, 2nd edition, Abingdon, Routledge.

Harding, D. W., 2020. *Rewriting History: Changing Perceptions of the Archaeological Past*, Oxford, Oxford University Press.

Harding, D., Blake, I., and Reynolds, P., 1993. *An Iron Age Settlement in Dorset, Excavation and Reconstruction*, Edinburgh, Edinburgh University Department of Archaeology, Monograph 1.

Harding, D. W. and Dixon, T. N., 2000. *Dun Bharabhat, Cnip: An Iron Age Settlement in West Lewis, Vol. 1. Structures and Material Culture*, Edinburgh, Department of Archaeology, University of Edinburgh.

Harding, D. W. and Gilmour, S. M. D., 2000. *The Iron Age Settlement at Beirgh, Riof, Isle of Lewis: Excavations 1985-95, Vol. 1. The Structures and Stratigraphy*, Edinburgh, Department of Archaeology, University of Edinburgh.

Haselgrove, C., 2016. *Cartimandua's Capital: A Late Iron Age Royal Site at Stanwick, North Yorkshire*, London, CBA Research Report 175.

Hatherley, C., 2014. *Archaeological Excavations at Easter and Wester Rarichie, Ross and Cromarty: Archaeological Assessment Report*, Aberdeen, University of Aberdeen Department of Archaeology.

Hatherley, C., 2015. *Archaeological Excavations at Tarlogie Farm Dun, Ross and Cromarty: Archaeological Assessment Report*, Aberdeen, University of Aberdeen, Department of Archaeology.

Hatherley, C. and Murray, R., 2021. *Culduthel: An Iron Age Craft Centre in North-East Scotland*, Edinburgh, Society of Antiquaries of Scotland.

Hatherley, C., Sveinbjarnarson, O., and Noble, G., 2014. 'Tarbat, Cnoc Tigh', *DES* 15: 125–6.

Hawkes, C. F. C., 1954. 'Archaeological theory and method: some suggestions from the Old World', *American Anthropologist*, 56: 155–68.

Hawkes, C. F. C., Myres, J. L., and Stevens, C. G., 1930. *St Catharine's Hill, Winchester, HFC* 11, Winchester, Hampshire Field Club.

Hawkes, S. C., 1994. 'Longbridge Deverill Cow Down, Wiltshire, House 3: a major round house of the Early Iron Age', *OJA*, 13: 49–69.

Hawkes, S. C. and Hawkes, C. F. C., 2012. *Longbridge Deverill Cow Down: An Early Iron Age Settlement in West Wiltshire*, Oxford, Oxford University School of Archaeology Monograph 76.

Hawley, W., 1927. 'Further excavations on Park Brow', *Archaeologia*, 76: 30–40.

Hayden, C., Early, R., Biddulph, E., Booth, P., Dodd, A., Smith, A., Laws, G., and Welsh, K., 2017. *Horcott Quarry, Fairford and Arkell's Land, Kempsford*, Oxford, Oxford Archaeology, Thames Valley Landscapes Monograph 40.

Headland, forthcoming. *An Iron Age Settlement near Portgordon, Moray*, Edinburgh, Society of Antiquaries of Scotland, SAIR series.

Hearne, C. and Adams, N., 1999. 'Excavation of an extensive Late Bronze Age settlement at Shorncote Quarry, near Cirencester, 1995-6', *TBGAS*, 117: 35–73.

Hedges, J., 1987. *Bu, Gurness and the Brochs of Orkney*, 3 vols., Oxford, BAR British Series.

Hencken, H. O'N., 1933. 'An excavation by H. M. Office of Works at Chysauster, Cornwall, 1931', *Archaeologia*, 83: 237–84.

Henderson, J., 2007. *The Atlantic Iron Age: Settlement and Identity in the First Millennium BC*, London and New York, Routledge.

Henderson, J., 2019. 'Oceans without history? Marine cultural heritage and the sustainable development agenda', *Sustainability*, 11, no. 18: 5080.

Henderson, J. and Gilmour, S., 2011. 'A 1st millennium BC Atlantic roundhouse in Argyll: survey and excavation at Loch Glashan', *PSAS*, 141: 75–102.

Hey, G., Booth, P., and Timby, J., 2011. *Yarnton. Iron Age and Romano-British Settlement and Landscape*, Oxford, Oxford Archaeology, Thames Valley Landscapes Monograph 35.

Hill, J., 1995. *Ritual and Rubbish in the Iron Age of Wessex*, Oxford, BAR British Series 242.

Hill, P., 1982. 'Settlement and chronology', in D. W. Harding, ed., *Later Prehistoric Settlement in South-East Scotland*, Edinburgh, Department of Archaeology, University of Edinburgh Occasional Paper No. 8: 4–43.

Hill, P., 1984. 'A sense of proportion: a contribution to the study of double-ring roundhouses', *Scottish Archaeological Review*, 3: 80–6.

Hingley, R., 2020. 'Egalitarianism in the southern British Iron Age: an "archaeology" of knowledge', in B. Currás and I. Sastre, eds., *Alternative Iron Ages: Social Theory from Archaeological Analysis*, Abingdon, Routledge: 127–48.

Hodgson, N., McKelvey, J., and Muncaster, W., 2012. *The Iron Age on the Northumberland Coastal Plain: Excavations in Advance of Development 2002–2010*, Newcastle upon Tyne, Tyne and Wear Museums Archaeological Monograph 3.

Hodgson, N., Stobbs, G., and van der Veen, M., 2001. 'An Iron Age settlement and remains of earlier prehistoric date beneath South Shields Roman fort', *ArchJ*, 158: 62–160.

Holley, M., 1996. 'Loch nan Deala', *DES*, 1996: 21.

Holleyman, G. and Curwen, E., 1935. 'Late Bronze Age lynchet settlements on Plumpton Plain, Sussex', *PPS*, 1: 16–38.

Hood, A., 2010. 'Later Iron Age and early Roman settlement at Willand Road, Cullumpton', *PDAS*, 68: 61–84.

Hopewell, D., 2018. *The Tre'r Ceiri Conservation Project: Re-examination of an Iconic Hillfort*, Bangor, Gwynedd Archaeological Trust Report 1417.

Howell, I., 2014. 'Continuity and change in the Late Iron Age-Roman transition within the environs of Quarry Wood *oppidum*: excavations at Furfield Quarry, Boughton Monchelsea', *Archaeologia Cantiana*, 134: 37–66.

Hughes, G. and Woodward, A., 2015. *The Iron Age and Romano-British Settlement at Crick Covert Farm, Northamptonshire, Excavations 1997–1998*, DIRFT Volume I, Oxford, Archaeopress.

Hunter, F., 2000–2010. *Excavations at Birnie, Moray. Interim Reports*, Edinburgh, National Museums of Scotland.

Inman, R., Brown, D., Goddard, R., and Spratt, D., 1985. 'Roxby Iron Age settlement and the Iron Age in north-east Yorkshire', *PPS*, 51: 181–213.

Jackson, D., 1977. 'Further excavations at Aldwinkle, Northamptonshire', *Northamptonshire Archaeology*, 12: 9–54.

Jackson, D., 1978. 'Excavations at Wakerley', *Britannia*, 9: 115–242.

Jackson, D., 1983. 'The excavation of an Iron Age site at Brigstock, Northamptonshire, 1979–81', *Northamptonshire Archaeology*, 18: 7–32.

Jackson, D. and Ambrose, T., 1978. 'Excavations at Wakerley, Northants, 1972–75', *Britannia*, IX: 115–242.

Jackson, D., Harding, D., and Myres, J. N. L., 1969. 'The Iron Age and Anglo-Saxon site at Upton, Northants', *AntJ*, 49: 202–21.

Jackson, K., 1964. *The Oldest Irish Tradition: A Window on the Iron Age*, Cambridge, Cambridge University Press.

Jahier, I., 2011. *L'enceinte des premier et second âges du Fer de La Fosse Touzé (Courseulles-sur-Mer, Calvados)*, Paris, Éditions de la Maison des sciences de l'homme.

Jahier, I., 2018. 'Un habitat groupé du Bronze final: Premier âge fu Fer à Cahagnes (Calvados)', in S. Boulud-Gazo and M. Mélin, eds., *Contributions à l'archéologie de l'âge du Bronze dans les espaces atlantiques et Manche-Mer du Nord, Vol. 1, Actes de la Table Ronde de Rouen (2005)*, Le Poiré-sur-Vie, Association pour la Promotion des Recherches sur l'Âge du Bronze: 267–320.

Jarrett, M. and Wrathmell, S., 1981. *Whitton: An Iron Age and Roman Farmstead in South Glamorgan*, Cardiff, University of Wales Press.

Jobey, G., 1959. 'Excavations at a native settlement at Huckhoe, Northumberland', *AA4*, 37: 217–78.

Jobey, G., 1962. 'An Iron Age homestead at West Brandon, Durham', *AA4*, 40: 1–34.

Jobey, G., 1968. 'A radiocarbon date for the palisaded settlement at Huckhoe', *AA4*, 46: 293–5.

Jobey, G., 1970. 'An Iron Age settlement at Burradon, Northumber; land', *AA4*, 48: 51–95.

Jobey, G., 1974. 'Excavations at Boonies, Westerkirk, and the nature of Romano-British settlement in eastern Dumfriesshire', *PSAS*, 105: 119–40.

Jobey, G., 1980. 'Green Knowe unenclosed platform settlement and Harehope cairn', *PSAS*, 110: 72–113.

Jobey, G. and Tait, J., 1966. 'Excavations on palisaded settlements and cairnfields at Alnham, Northumberland', *AA4*, 44: 5–48.

Johnson, M., 2017. *Excavation of Prehistoric Roundhouses and Post-Medieval Kilns at Drumyocher and Hospital Shields, Aberdeenshire*, Edinburgh, Society of Antiquaries of Scotland, SAIR 70.

Johnston, R., 2020. *Bronze Age Worlds: A Social Prehistory of Britain and Ireland*, Abingdon, Routledge.

Jones, E., Sheridan, A., and Franklin, J., 2018. *Neolithic and Bronze Age Occupation at Meadowend Farm, Clackmannanshire: Pots, Pits and Roundhouses*, Edinburgh, Society of Antiquaries of Scotland, SAIR 77.

Joy, J., 2015. 'Connection and separation: narratives of Iron Age art in Britain and its relationship with the Continent', in H. Anderson-Whymark, D. Garrow, and F. Sturt, eds., *Continental Connections: Exploring Cross-Channel Relationships from the Mesolithic to the Iron Age*, Oxford, Oxbow Books: 145–65.

Karl, R., 2011. 'Becoming Welsh: modelling first millennium BC societies in Wales and the Celtic context', in T. Moore and X.-L. Armada, eds., *Atlantic Europe in the First Millennium BC: Crossing the Divide, Oxford*, Oxford University Press: 336–57.

Karl, R., Möller, K., and Waddington, K., 2016. *Characterising the Double Ringwork Enclosures of Gwyneddd: Meillionydd Excavations June and July 2015: Interim Report*, Bangor, Bangor Studies in Archaeology Report No. 14, School of History, Welsh History and Archaeology.

Keevill, G. and Booth, P., 1997. 'Settlement sequence and structure: Romano-British stone-built roundhouses at Redlands Farm, Stanwick (Northants), and Alchester (Oxon)', in R. Friendship-Taylor and D. Friendship-Taylor, eds., *From Roundhouse to Villa*, Northampton, Upper Nene Archaeological Society: 19–45.

Kelly, R., 1988. 'Two late prehistoric circular enclosures near Harlech, Gwynedd', *PPS*, 54: 101–52.

Kendrick, J., 1995. 'Excavation of a Neolithic enclosure and Iron Age settlement at Douglasmuir, Angus', *PSAS*, 125: 29–68.

Knight, M., Ballantyne, R., Zeki, I., and Gibson, D., 2019. 'The Must Farm pile-dwelling settlement', *Antiquity*, 93, no. 369: 645–63.

Lambrick, G. and Allen, T., 2004. *Gravelly Guy, Stanton Harcourt: The Development of a Prehistoric and Romano-British Community*, Thames Valley Landscapes Monograph No. 21, Oxford, Oxford University School of Archaeology.

Lambrick, G. and Robinson, M., 2009. *The Thames through Time: The Archaeology of the Gravel Terraces of the Upper and Middle Thames*, Thames Valley Landscapes Monograph No. 29, Oxford, Oxford University School of Archaeology.

Lamdin-Whymark, H., Brady, K., and Smith, A., 2009. 'Excavation of a Neolithic to Roman Landscape at Horcott Pit near Fairford, Gloucestershire, in 2002 and 2003', *TBGAS*, 127: 45–129.

Larsson, E., 2012. 'An early Iron Age farmstead at Ballycullen, Co. Dublin', in C. Corlett and M. Potterton, eds., *Life and Death in Iron Age Ireland in the Light of Recent Archaeological Excavations*, Dublin, Wordwell: 141–55.

Lawrence, S. and Smith, A., 2009. *Between Villa and Town: Excavations of a Roman Roadside Settlement and Shrine at Higham Ferrers, Northamptonshire*, Oxford, Oxford Archaeology Monograph No. 7.

Le Gall, J., 2017. *Morbihan, Inzinzac-Lochrist, Kermat III. Un grand domaine agricole des Vie-IVe siècles avant notre ère*, Rapport final d'opération fouille archéologique, Cesson-Sévigné, INRAP Grand-Ouest.

Lelong, O. and MacGregor, G., 2007. *The Lands of Ancient Lothian: Interpreting the Archaeology of the A1*, Edinburgh, Society of Antiquaries of Scotland.

Lethbridge, T., 1954. 'Burial of an Iron Age warrior at Snailwell', *Proceedings of the Cambridge Antiquarian Society*, 47: 25–37.

Levan, M., 2016. *Caudan, Morbihan, ZAC de Lenn Sec'h (lot 1). Une succession d'édifices circulaires: un hameauy du Bronze final*, Cesson-Sévigné, INRAP Grand Ouest.

Lévi-Strauss, C., 1979. 'Nobles sauvages', in *Culture, Science et développement: contributions à une histoire de l'homme. Mélages en l'honneur de Charles Morazé*, Toulouse, Privat: 41–55.

Lévi-Strauss, C., 1982. *The Way of Masks*, London, Jonathan Cape.

Lévi-Strauss, C., 1987. *Anthropology and Myth: Lectures 1951–1982*. Oxford, Blackwell.

Lewis, J., Brown, F., Batt, A., Cooke, N., Barrett, J., Every, R., Mepham, L., Brown, K., Cramp, K., Lawson, A., Roe, F., Allen, S., Petts, D., McKinley, J., Carruthers, W., Challinor, D., Wiltshire, P., Robinson, M., Lewis, H., and Bates, M., 2006. *Landscape Evolution in the Middle Thames Valley: Heathrow Terminal 5 Excavations Volume 1, Perry Oaks*, Oxford and Salisbury, Framework Archaeology.

Lewis, J., Leivers, M., Brown, L., Smith, A., Cramp, K., Mepham, L., and Phillpotts, C. 2010. *Landscape Evolution in the Middle Thames Valley: Heathrow Terminal 5 Excavations Volume 2*, Oxford and Salisbury, Framework Archaeology.

Liddell, D., 1935. 'Report on excavations at Meon Hill, second season, 1933', *HFC*, XIII, Part 1: 7–54.

Longley, D., 1998. 'Bryn Eryr: an enclosed settlement of the Iron Age on Anglesey', *PPS*, 64: 225–73.

Lyne, E., 2010. *M3 Clonee—north of Kells Motorway Scheme Report*, Irish Archaeological Consultancy.

Lynn, C. and McDowell, J., 2011. *Deer Park Farms: The Excavation of a Raised Rath in the Glenarm Valley*, Norwich, Stationery Office/Belfast, Northern Ireland Environment Agency.

McCullagh, R. and Tipping, R., 1998. *The Lairg Project 1988–1996: An Archaeological Landscape in Northern Scotland*, Edinburgh, STAR Monograph 3.

McGilliard, S. and Wilson, D., 2021. *Bronze Age and Iron Age Archaeology at Thainstone Business Park, Inverurie, Aberdeenshire: An Investigation of Structures and Funerary Practices*, Edinburgh, Society of Antiquaries of Scotland, SAIR 95.

MacKie, E. W., 1965. 'The origin and development of the broch and wheelhouse cultures of the Scottish Iron Age', *PPS*, 31: 93–146.

262 BIBLIOGRAPHY

MacKie, E. W., 1974. *Dun Mor Vaul, an Iron Age Broch on Tiree*, Glasgow, Glasgow University Press.

MacKie, E. W., 1991. 'The Iron Age semi-brochs of Atlantic Scotland: a case study in the problems of deductive reasoning', *ArchJ*, 148: 149–81.

MacKie, E. W., 2000. 'Excavations at Dun Ardtreck, Skye, in 1964 and 1965', *PSAS*, 130: 301–412.

Mackinder, T., 2006. *East Field, Furfield Quarry, Boughton Monchelsea, Maidstone, Kent: An Archaeological Post-Excavation Assessment*, London, Museum of London Archaeological Services.

McKinstry, L., 2011. *Site 13 Moneylawn Lower Townland, Co. Wexford*, Castlecomer, Valerie J. Keeley Ltd.

MacLeod Rivett, M., 2018. *Barabhas Machair: Surveys of an Eroding Sandscape*, Edinburgh, Society of Antiquaries of Scotland, SAIR 76.

McQuade, M. and Moriarty, C., 2011. *Hearth and Home: Bronze Age Structures in South Tipperary*, National Roads Authority, Transport Infrastructure Ireland.

McQuade, M. and Molloy, B., 2012. 'Recent Iron Age discoveries in south County Tipperary and County Limerick', in C. Corlett and M. Potterton, eds., *Life and death in Iron Age Ireland in the Light of Recent Archaeological Excavations*, Dublin, Wordwell: 175–87.

Maguer, P., Achard-Corompt, N., Gaudefroy, S., and Robert, G., 2018. 'Maisons et dépendances à l'âge du Fer dans le Nord et l'Ouest de la France: de La Tène moyenne à La Tène finale', in A. Villard-le-Tiec, ed., *Architectures de l'âge du Fer en Europe occidentale et centrale*, Actes du 40e colloque international de l'AFEAF, Rennes 2016, Rennes, Presses universitaires de Rennes: 303–47.

Mallory, J. and Baban, G., 2014. 'Excavations in Haughey's Fort East', *Emania*, 22: 13–32.

Manby, T., 1985. 'The Thwing project', *Prehistory Research Bulletin*, Yorkshire Archaeological Society, 22: 2–6.

Manby, T. G., 2007. 'Continuity and monumental traditions into the Late Bronze Age? Henges to ring-forts, and shrines', in C. Burgess, P. Topping, and F. Lynch, eds., *Beyond Stonehenge: Essays on the Bronze Age in Honour of Colin Burgess*, Oxford, Oxbow Books: 403–24.

Marcigny, C. and Talon, M., 2009. 'Sur les rives de la Manche. Qu'en est-il du passage de l'âge du Bronze à l'âge du Fer à partir des découvertes récentes?' in A. Daubigney, P.-Y. Milcent, M. Talon, and J. Vital, eds., *De l'âge du Bronze à l'âge du Fer en France et en Europe occidentale (x–viii siècle avant J.-C.). La moyenne vallée du Rhône aux âges du Fer*, Actes du XXXe colloque de l'AFEAF: 385–403.

Mare, E., Ghesquiere, E., Goff, I., Marcigny, C., Nicolas, T., and Zech-Matterne, V., 2018. 'Malleville-sur-le-Bec, un village à l'Âge du Bronze final (Eure)', in S. Boulud-Gazo and M. Mélin, eds., *Contributions à l'archéologie de l'âge du Bronze dans les espaces atlantiques et Manche-Mer du Nord, Vol., Actes de la Table Ronde de Rouen (2005)*, Le Poiré-sur-Vie, Association pour la Promotion des Recherches sur l'Âge du Bronze: 77–266.

Maričevič, D., Batchelor, R., and MacLeod, A., 2019. 'Loch nan Deala crannog, Islay', *DES*, 20: 42.

Martin, L., Richardson, J., and Roberts, I., 2013. *Iron Age and Roman Settlements at Wattle Syke*, Leeds, Archaeological Services WYAS.

Masefield, R., Chapman, A., Mudd, A., Hart, J., Ellis, P., and King, R., 2015. *Origins, Development and Abandonment of an Iron Age Village: Further Archaeological Investigations for the Daventry International Rail Freight Terminal, Crick and Kilsby, Northamptonshire*, DIRFT Volume II, Oxford, Archaeopress.

BIBLIOGRAPHY 263

Mattingly, D., 2007. *An Imperial Possession: Britain in the Roman Empire, 54 BC–AD 409*, London, Penguin Books.

Menaghan, J., 1994. 'An unenclosed Bronze Age house site at Lookout Plantation', *AA5*, 22: 29–41.

Milcent, P.-Y., 2017. 'The Atlantic Early Iron Age in Gaul', in A. Lehoerff and M. Talon, eds., *Movement, Exchange and Identity in Europe in the 2nd and 1st Millennia BC: Beyond Frontiers*, Oxford, Oxbow Books: 79–98.

Misiego Tejeda, J. C., Sanz Garcia, F. J., Marcos Contreras, G. J., and Martin Carbajo, M. A., 1996. 'Excavaciones arqueológicas en el castro de Sacaojos (Santiago de la Valduerna, León)', *Numantia, Arqueología en Castlla y León*, 7, 43–66.

Monaghan, J., 1994. 'An unenclosed Bronze Age house site at Lookout Plantation, Northumbrland', *AA5*, 22: 29–41.

Moore, H. and Wilson, G., 2011. *Shifting Sands. Links of Noltland, Westray: Interim Report on Neolithic and Bronze Age Excavations, 2007–09*, Edinburgh, Historic Scotland.

Moore, J. and Jennings, D., 1992. *Reading Business Park: A Bronze Age Landscape*, Thames Valley Landscapes: The Kennet Valley, Vol. 1, Oxford, Oxford Archaeological Unit.

Moore, T., 2003. 'Rectangular houses in the British Iron Age? "Squaring the circle"', in J. Humphrey, ed., *Re-searching the Iron Age*, Leicester, Leicester University Monographs 11: 47–58.

Moore, T., 2020. *A Biography of Power: Research and Excavation at the Iron Age Oppidum of Bagendon, Gloucestershire (1979–2017)*, Oxford, Archaeopress.

Mudd, A., 2004. 'Iron Age and Roman enclosures near Higham Ferrers: the archaeology of the A6 Rushden to Higham Ferrers bypass', *Northamptonshire Archaeology*, 32: 57–94.

Munro, R., 1882. *Ancient Scottish Lake-Dwellings or Crannogs*, Edinburgh, David Douglas.

Munro, R., 1890. *The Lake Dwellings of Europe*, London, Cassell and Co.

Munro, R., 1921. *Robert Munro, M.A., M. D., LLD: Autobiographical Sketch*, Glasgow, MacLehose, Jackson and Co.

Murphy, K., 2018. 'The Atlantic coast', *Internet Archaeology*, 48.

Murphy, K. and Mytum, H., 2012. 'Iron Age enclosed settlements in west Wales', *PPS*, 78: 263–313.

Murray, H. and Murray, J., 2006. *Thainstone Business Park, Inverurie, Aberdeenshire*, Edinburgh, Society of Antiquaries of Scotland, SAIR 21.

Murray, R., 2007. *Culduthel Mains Farm, Inverness, Phase 5: Excavation of a Late Prehistoric Settlement: Assessment Report*. Edinburgh, Headland Archaeology, online.

Murray, T., 2021. 'Review of Harding, D. W., *Rewriting History*, Oxford, Oxford University Press', *Antiquity*, 95: 267–9.

Musson, C., 1970. 'House-plans and prehistory', *CA*, 10: 267–75.

Mytum, H. and Meek, J., 2020. 'Experimental archaeology and roundhouse excavation signatures: the investigation of two reconstructed Iron Age buildings at Castell Henllys, Wales', *Archaeological and Anthropological Sciences*, 12: 78.

Neal, D., Wardle, A., and Hunn, J., 1990. *Excavation of the Iron Age, Roman and Medieval Settlement at Gorhambury, St Albans*, English Heritage Archaeological Report No. 14, London, Historic Buildings and Monuments Commission.

Neighbour, T. and Burgess, C., 1996. 'Traigh Bostadh (Uig Parish)', *DES*, 1996: 113–14.

Neighbour, T. and Crawford, J., 2001. 'Bernera: reconstructing a figure-of-eight house at Bosta', *CA*, 175: 294–300.

Newman, C., 1995. 'Raffin Fort, Co. Meath: Neolithic and Bronze Age activity', in E. Grogan and C. Mount, eds., *Annus Archaeologiae. Archaeological Research 1992*, Dublin, Organisation of Irish Archaeologists, 55–66.

264 BIBLIOGRAPHY

Nicolas, E., 2011. *Plédéliac, Côtes d'Armor. Nord du bourg: deux bâtiments de l'âge du Bronze*, Cesson Sévigné, INRAP Grand Ouest.

Nisbet, H., 1994. 'Excavations of a vitrified dun at Langwell, Strath Oikel, Sutherland', *GAJ*, 19: 51–74.

Noble, G., 2020. 'The problem of the Picts', *CA*, 364: 28–35.

Noble, G., Greig, M., and Millican, K., 2012. 'Excavations at a multiperiod site at Greenbogs, Aberdeenshire, Scotland, and the four-post timber architecture tradition of late Neolithic Britain and Ireland', *PPS*, 78: 135–72.

Noble, P. and Thompson, A., 2005. 'The Mellor excavations 1998 to 2004', in M. Nevell and N. Redhead, eds., *Mellor: Living on the Edge. A Regional Study of an Iron Age and Romano-British Upland Settlement*, Manchester, University of Manchester Field Archaeology Centre: 17–34.

Nowakowski, J. and Quinnell, H., 2011. *Trevelgue Head, Cornwall: The Importance of C. K. Croft Andrew's 1939 Excavations for Prehistoric and Roman Cornwall*, Truro and London, Cornwall Council/English Heritage.

O'Brien, W., 2017. 'The development of the hillfort in prehistoric Ireland', *PRIA*, 117C: 1–59.

O'Brien, W. and O'Driscoll, J., 2017. *Hillforts, Warfare and Society in Bronze Age Ireland*, Oxford, Archaeopress.

O'Connell, C. and Anderson, S., 2020. *Excavations in a Prehistoric Landscape at Blackford, Perth and Kinross, 2007–8*, Edinburgh, Society of Antiquaries of Scotland, SAIR 93.

Ó Drisceoil, C. and Devine, E., 2012. 'Invisible people or invisible archaeology? Carrickmines Great, Co. Dublin, and the problem of Irish Iron Age settlement', in C. Corlett and M. Potterton, eds., *Life and Death in Iron Age Ireland in the Light of Recent Archaeological Excavations*, Dublin, Wordwell: 249–65.

O'Driscoll, J., Gleeson, P., and Noble, G., 2020. 'Re-imagining Navan Fort: new light on the evolution of a major ceremonial centre in Northern Europe', *OJA*, 39, no. 3: 247–73.

Oswald, A., 1997. 'A doorway on the past: practical and mystical concerns in the orientation of roundhouse doorways', in A. Gwilt and C. Haselgrove, eds., *Reconstructing Iron Age Societies*, Oxford, Oxbow Books: 87–95.

Parker Pearson, M., 1996. 'Food, fertility and front doors in the first millennium BC', in T. Champion and J. Collis, eds., *The Iron Age in Britain and Ireland: Recent Trends*, Sheffield, John Collis Publications: 117–32.

Parker Pearson, M., 1999. 'Food, sex and death: cosmologies in the British Iron Age with particular reference to East Yorkshire', *Cambridge Archaeological Journal*, 9, no. 1: 43–69.

Parker Pearson, M., Pollard, J., Richards, C., Welham, K., Kinnard, T., Shaw, D., Simmons, E., Stanford, A., Bevins, R., Ixer, R., Ruggles, C., Rylatt, J., and Edinborough, K., 2021. 'The original Stonehenge? A dismantled stone circle in the Preseli hills of west Wales', *Antiquity*, 95, no. 379: 85–103.

Parker Pearson, M. and Richards, C., 1994a. 'Ordering the world: perceptions of architecture, space and time', in M. Parker Pearson and C. Richards, eds., *Architecture and Order: Approaches to Social Space*, London, Routledge: 1–37.

Parker Pearson, M. and Richards, C., 1994b. 'Architecture and order: spatial representation and archaeology', M. Parker Pearson and C. Richards, eds., *Architecture and Order: Approaches to Social Space*, London, Routledge: 38–72.

Parker Pearson, M. and Sharples, N., 1999. *Between Land and Sea: Excavations at Dun Vulan, South Uist*, Sheffield, Sheffield Academic Press.

Patterson, N., Isakov, M., and Booth, T., 2021. 'Large-scale migration into Britain during the Middle to Late Bronze Age', *Nature*, 601: 588–94.

Payne, A., Corney, M., and Cunliffe, B., 2006. *The Wessex Hillfort Project: Extensive Survey of Hillfort Interiors in Southern England*, London, English Heritage.

Pearce, M., 2011. 'Have rumours of the "Death of Theory" been exaggerated?', in J. Bintliff and M. Pearce, eds., *The Death of Archaeological Theory*, Oxford and Oakville, Oxbow Books: 80–9.

Péchart, S., 2016. *Bezannes (Marne) ZAC Site 1, rapport de fouille archéologiques*, Reims, Reims métropole.

Peteranna, M., 2012. *Applecross Broch Community Archaeology Project. Data Structure Report on the 2006–2010 Excavations*, online.

Peteranna, M. and Birch, S., 2017. *Excavation and Survey at Comar Wood Dun, Cannich, Strathglass, Inverness-shire, Archaeological Reports Online*, 23, Glasgow, GUARD Archaeology.

Piggott, C. M., 1948. 'Excavations at Hownam Rings, Roxburghshire, 1948', *PSAS*, 83: 45–67.

Piggott, C. M., 1953. 'Milton Loch crannog 1: a native house of the second century AD in Kirkcudbrightshire', *PSAS*, 87: 134–52.

Pitt-Rivers, A. H. L. F., 1892. *Excavations in Bokerly and Wansdyke, Dorset and Wilts, Excavations in Cranborne Chase Vol. 3*, London, printed privately.

Pluciennik, M., 2011. 'Theory, fashion, culture', in J. Bintliff and M. Pearce, eds., *The Death of Archaeological Theory?* Oxford and Oakville, Oxbow Books: 31–47.

Pollock, R., 1992. 'The excavation of a souterrain and roundhouse at Cyderhall, Sutherland', *PSAS*, 122: 149–60.

Pope, R., 2003. *Prehistoric dwelling: circular structures in North and Central Britain*, PhD thesis, Durham University.

Pope, R., 2007. 'Ritual and the roundhouse: a critique of recent ideas on the use of domestic space in later British prehistory', in C. Haselgrove and R. Pope, eds., *The Earlier Iron Age in Britain and the Near Continent*, Oxford, Oxbow Books: 204–28.

Pope, R., 2015. 'Bronze Age architectural traditions: dates and landscapes', in F. Hunter and I. Ralston, eds., *Scotland in Later Prehistoric Europe*, Oxford, Oxbow Books: 159–84.

Poulton, R., Hayman, G., and Marples, N., 2017. *Foragers and Farmers – 10,000 Years of History at Hengrove Farm, Staines. Excavations between 1997 and 2012*, Woking, Spoilheap Monograph 12.

Powell, K., Laws, G., and Brown, L., 2009. 'A Late Neolithic/Early Bronze Age enclosure and Iron Age and Romano-British settlement at Latton Lands, Wiltshire', *WAM*, 102: 22–113.

Powell, K., Smith, A., and Laws, G., 2010. *Evolution of a Farming Community in the Upper Thames Valley. Excavation of a Prehistoric, Roman and Post-Roman Landscape at Cotswold Community, Gloucestershire and Wiltshire, Vol. 1: Site Narrative and Overview*, Oxford, Oxford Archaeology.

Preece, C., 2021. 'The neglected hillfort: Clovelly Dykes', *BA*, Jan.–Feb.: 16–18.

Preece, C. and Green, T., 2020. *Clovelly Dykes: Survey, Research and Excavation 2017–19*, Westward Ho! North Devon Archaeological Society.

Proctor, J., 2009. *Pegswood Moor, Morpeth, a Later Iron Age and Romano-British Farmstead Settlement*, London, Pre-Construct Archaeology Monograph No. 11.

Queiroga, F. M. V. R., 2003. *War and Castros: New Approaches to the Northwestern Portuguese Iron Age*, Oxford, BAR International Series 1198.

Quinnell, H., 2004. *Trethurgy. Excavations at Trethurgy Round, St Austell: Community and Status in Roman and Post-Roman Cornwall*, Truro and London, Cornwall County Council and English Heritage.

Raftery, B., 1976. 'Rathgall and Irish hillfort problems', in D. W. Harding, ed., *Hillforts: Later Prehistoric Earthworks in Britain and Ireland*, London, Academic Press: 339–57, 478–82, and 532–9.

Raftery, B., 1981. 'Iron Age burials in Ireland', in D. Ó Corráin, ed., *Irish Antiquity: Essays and Studies Presented to Professor M. J. O'Kelly*, Cork, Tower Books: 173–204.

Rahtz, P. and ApSimon, A., 1962. 'Excavations at Sydling St Nicholas, Dorset, England', *PPS*, 28: 289–328.

Raisen, P. and Rees, T., 1995. 'Excavations of three cropmark sites at Melville Nurseries, Dalkeith', *GAJ*, 19: 31–50.

Ramírez Ramírez, M. L., 1996. 'La casa circular durante la primera Edad del Hierro en la Valle del Duero', *Numantia, Arqueología en Castlla y León*, 7: 67–94.

RCAHMS, 1956. *An Inventory of the Ancient Monuments of Roxburghshire*, Edinburgh, HMSO.

RCAHMS, 1967. *Peeblesshire. An Inventory of the Ancient Monuments*, Edinburgh, HMSO.

RCAHMS, 1984. *Argyll, an Inventory of the monuments, Volume 5. Islay, Jura, Colonsay and Oronsay*, Edinburgh, HMSO.

Regan, R., 2018. 'Dun Fhinn, Ardtalla, Islay, excavation', *DES*, 19: 35–6.

Regan, R., forthcoming, 'Dun Fhinn, Islay. Excavation, woodland exploitation and building an Iron Age chronology for Argyll', Society of Antiquaries of Scotland.

Regan, R. and Campbell, E., 2022. *Two Iron Age Duns in Western Scotland; Excavations at Barnluasgan and Balure, North Knapdale, Argyll*, Edinburgh, Society of Antiquaries of Scotland, SAIR 99.

Rennie, C., 2013. 'A room with a view: excavations at Ravelrig Quarry', *PSAS*, 143: 137–56.

Rennie, C., 2016. 'Excavation of a Bronze Age ring-groove house at Inverkip, Inverclyde', *Scottish Archaeological Journal*, 38: 51–69.

Reynolds, P. J., 1979. *Iron-Age Farm: The Butser Experiment*, London, British Museum.

Reynolds, P. J., 1982. 'Substructure to superstructure', in P. J. Drury, ed., *Structural Reconstruction: Approaches to the Interpretation of the Excavated Remains of Buildings*, Oxford, BAR British Series 110: 173–98.

Reynolds, P. J., 1993. 'Experimental reconstruction', in D. W. Harding, I. M. Blake, and P. J. Reynolds, *An Iron Age settlement in Dorset*, Edinburgh, Department of Archaeology, University of Edinburgh: 93–113.

Richards, C. and Jones, R., 2016. 'Images of Neolithic Orkney', in C. Richards and R. Jones, eds., *The Development of Neolithic House Societies in Orkney*, Oxford, Oxbow Books: 1–15.

Richmond, I., 1968. *Hod Hill Volume Two: Excavations Carried Out between 1951 and 1958*, London, British Museum.

Rideout, J., 1996. 'Excavation of a promontory fort and palisaded homestead at Lower Greenyards, Bannockburn, Stirling, 1982–5', *PSAS*, 126: 199–269.

Rideout, J., Owen, O., and Halpin, E., 1992. *Hillforts of Southern Scotland*, Edinburgh, Historic Scotland/AOC Limited.

Riley, D., 1947. 'A Late Bronze Age and Iron Age site on Standlake Downs', *Oxoniensia*, 11–12: 27–43.

Riquier, V., Maitay, C., Leroy-Langelin, E., and Maguer, P., 2018. 'Maisons et dépendances à l'âge du Fer dans le Nord et l'Ouest de la France: du premier âge du Fer au début de La Tène', in A. Villard-le-Tiec, ed., *Architectures de l'âge du Fer en Europe occidentale et centrale*, Actes du 40e colloque international de l'AFEAF, Rennes 2016, Rennes, Presses universitaires de Rennes: 273–301.

Ritchie, A., 1977. 'Excavation of Pictish and Viking farmsteads at Buckquoy, Orkney', *PSAS*, 108: 174–227.

Roberts, I. and Richardson, J., 2002. *Iron Age and Romano-British Settlement Enclosures at Moss Carr, Methley, West Yorkshire*, Leeds, Archaeological Services WYAS.

Roberts, I. and Richardson, J., 2013. *Iron Age and Roman Settlements at Wattle Syke*, Leeds, West Yorkshire Archaeological Services.

Robinson, M., 1992. 'Environment, archaeology and alluvium on the river gravels of the South Midlands', in S. Needham and M. Macklin, eds., *Alluvial Archaeology in Britain*, Oxford, Oxbow Monographs 27: 197–208.

Robinson, M. and Lambrick, G., 2009. 'The palaeohydrology of the Thames and its floodplain', in G. Lambrick and M. Robinson, *The Thames through Time: The Archaeology of the Gravel Terraces of the Upper and Middle Thames*, Thames Valley Landscapes Monograph No. 29, Oxford, Oxford University School of Archaeology: 29–33.

Romankiewicz, T., 2011. *The Complex Roundhouses of the Scottish Iron Age*, 2 vols., Oxford, BAR British Series 550.

Romankiewicz, T., 2016a. 'Land, stone, trees, identity, ambition: the building blocks of brochs', *ArchJ*, 173: 1–29.

Romankiewicz, T., 2016b. 'Building (ancient) lives: new perspectives on the past for a sustainable future', *The European Archaeologist*, 48: 25–30.

Romankiewitcz, T., 2018a. 'Rounding up roundhouses. What can the remains of the Birnie roundhouses tells us after excavations?' in C. Herbert and J. Trythall, eds., *Forgotten, Hidden, Lost: Unearthing Moray's Archaeology. Proceedings of the Elgin Museum Archaeology Conference 2017*, Elgin, Moray Society: 74–9.

Romankiewicz, T., 2018b. 'Room for ideas: tracing non-domestic roundhouses', *AntJ*, 98: 17–42.

Romankiewicz, T., Bradley, R., and Clarke, A., 2020. 'Old Kinord, Aberdeenshire: survey and excavation of an Iron Age settlement on Deeside', *PSAS*, 149: 221–48.

Ronan, D. and Higgins, J., 2005. 'Bronze Age settlement at Ross Bay, Kirkcudbright', *TDGNHAS*, 79: 47–69.

Roskams, S. and Neal, C., 2020. *Landscape and Settlement in the Vale of York: Archaeological Investigations at Heslington East 2003–13*, London, Society of Antiquaries Research Report 82.

Roy, E., 2003. *Découverte d'une entité agricole de l'âge du Fer "route de Kernéost" à Bénodet dans le Finistère, rapport de fouille*, Cesson-Sévigné, INRAP Grand-Ouest.

Ruano, L., 2020. 'Atlantic dwellings in the first millennium BC: a transnational approach to the social organization of space', *Emania*, 25: 137–51.

Ruano, L. and Berrocal-Rangel, L., 2019. 'Rural domestic patterns in northwestern Iberia', in D. Cowley, M. Fernández-Gotz, T. Romankiewicz, and H. Wendling, eds., *Rural Settlement: Relating Buildings, Landscape and People in the European Iron Age*, Leiden, Sidestone Press: 281–7.

Russell, M. and Cheetham, P., 2016. 'Finding Duropolis: a new kind of Iron Age settlement', *CA*, 313: 12–18.

Rydberg, J., Martinez Cortizas, A., and Skelton, A., 2019. 'It's in your glass: a history of sea level and storminess from the Laphroaig bog, Islay (south west Scotland)', *Boreas*, 49: 152–67.

Sabatini, S., 2007. *House urns: a European Late Bronze Age trans-cultural phenomenon*, Gothenburg Archaeological Theses No. 47, Department of Archaeology and Ancient History.

Sangmeister, E., 1963. 'La civilisation du vase campaniforme', in P.-R. Giot, ed., *Les civilisations antlantiques du Néolithique à l'Âge du Fer*, Actes du premier colloque Atlantique, Brest, 1961, Rennes: 25–56.

Sastre, I., 2002. 'Forms of social inequality in the Castro Culture of north-west Iberia', *European Journal of Archaeology*, 5, no. 5: 213–48.

268 BIBLIOGRAPHY

Sastre, I. and Currás, B., 2020. 'Reconsidering egalitarianism for archaeological interpretation', in B. Currás and I. Sastre, eds., *Alternative Iron Ages: Social Theory from Archaeological Analysis*, Abingdon, Routledge: 9–28.

Schwieso, J., 1976. 'Excavations at Threemilestone Round, Kenwyn, Truro', *Cornish Archaeology*, 15: 51–67.

Scott, Sir Lindsay, 1947. 'The problem of the brochs', *PPS*, 13: 1–37.

Scott, Sir Lindsay, 1948. 'Gallo-British colonies: the aisled roundhouse culture in the north', *PPS*, 14: 46–125.

Sealey, P., 2016. 'Where have all the people gone? A puzzle from Middle and Late Iron Age Essex', *ArchJ*, 173: 30–55.

Sharples, N., 2010. *Social Relations in Later Prehistory: Wessex in the First Millennium BC*, Oxford, Oxford University Press.

Sharples, N., 2020. 'Monumentalising the domestic: house societies in Atlantic Scotland', in B. Currás and I. Sastre, eds., *Alternative Iron Ages: Social Theory from Archaeological Analysis*, Abingdon, Routledge: 284–305.

Sheehan, O., Watts, J., Gray, R., and Atkinson, Q., 2018. 'Coevolution of landesque capital intensive agriculture and sociopolitical hierarchy', *Proceedings of the National Academy of Sciences (USA)*, 115: 3628–33.

Sherlock, S., 2019. *A Neolithic to Late Roman Landscape on the North-East Yorkshire Coast: Excavations at Street House, Loftus, 2004–17*, Hartlepool, Tees Archaeology Monograph 7.

Sims-Williams, P., 2020. 'An alternative to "Celtic from the East" and "Celtic from the West"', *Cambridge Archaeological Journal*, 30, no. 3: 511–29.

Smith, A., Allen, M., Brindle, T., and Fulford, M., 2016. *The Rural Settlement of Roman Britain*, London, Society for the Promotion of Roman Studies, Britannia Monograph 29.

Smith, B., 2015. 'How not to reconstruct the Iron Age in Shetland: modern interpretations of Clickhimin broch', Tenth Hermann Pálsson Lecture, *Northern Studies*, 47: 1–31.

Smith, B., 2016. 'Did the broch of Mousa have a roof? and why not!' *New Shetlander*, 276: 417.

Smith, B. B., 1994. *Howe: Four Millennia of Orkney Prehistory*, Edinburgh, Society of Antiquaries of Scotland Monograph 9.

Smith, G., 2018. 'Hillforts and hut groups in north-west Wales', *Internet Archaeology*, 48.

Smith, J. T., 1978. 'Villas as a key to social structure', in M. Todd, ed., *Studies in the Romano-British Villa*, Leicester, Leicester University Press: 149–86.

Smith, R., Healy, F., Allen, M., Morris, E., Barnes, I., and Woodward, P., 1997. *Excavations along the Route of the Dorchester By-pass, Dorset, 1986–8*, Salisbury, Wessex Archaeology.

Smyth, J., 2011. 'The house and group identity in the Irish Neolithic', *PRIA*, 111C: 1–31.

Stead, I., 1976. *Excavations at Winterton Roman Villa and Other Roman Sites in North Lincolnshire*, Department of the Environment Archaeological Reports No. 9, London, HMSO.

Steer, K., 1956. 'The Early Iron Age homestead at West Plean', *PSAS*, 89: 227–51.

Stevens, C. E., 1966. 'The social and economic aspects of rural settlement', in C. Thomas, ed., *Rural Settlement in Roman Britain*, London, CBA Research Report No. 7: 108–28.

Stevenson, R. B. K., 1949. 'Braidwood fort, Midlothian; the exploration of two huts', *PSAS*, 83: 1–11.

Stewart, D. and Russell, M., 2017. *Hillforts and the Durotriges*, Oxford, Archaeopress.

Stoertz, C., 1997. *Ancient Landscapes of the Yorkshire Wolds: Aerial Photographic Transcription and Analysis*, Swindon, RCHME.

Stone, J. F. S., 1941. 'The Deverel-Rimbury settlement on Thorny Down, Winterbourne Gunner, South Wiltshire', *PPS*, 7: 114–33.

Strachan, R. and Dunwell, A., 2003. 'Excavation of Neolithic and Bronze Age sites near Peterhead, Aberdeenshire, 1998', *PSAS*, 133: 137–72.

Strachan, R., Ralston, I., and Finlayson, B., 1998. 'Neolithic and later prehistoric structures, and early medieval metal-working at Blairhall Burn, Amisfield, Dumfriesshire', *PSAS*, 128: 55–94.

Tapper, R., 2011. *Middle and Late Bronze Age settlement on the South Downs: the case study of Black Patch*, DPhil thesis, University of Sussex.

Terry, J., 1995. 'Excavation at Lintshie Gutter unenclosed platform settlement, Crawford, Lanarkshire', *PSAS*, 125: 369–427.

Thomas, J., 2011. *Two Iron Age 'Aggregated' Settlements in the Environs of Leicester: Excavations at Beaumont Leys and Humberstone*, Leicester, Leicester Archaeology Monograph 19.

Thomas, N., 2005. *Conderton Camp, Worcestershire: A Small Middle Iron Age Hillfort on Bredon Hill*, London, CBA Research Report 143.

Timby, J., Brown, R., Hardy, A., Leech, S., Poole, C., and Webley, L., 2007. *Settlement on the Bedfordshire Claylands: Archaeology along the A421 Great Barford Bypass*, Oxford and Bedford, Oxford Archaeological Unit and Bedfordshire County Council.

Triscott, J., 1982. 'Excavations at Dryburn Bridge, East Lothian, 1978–79', in D. W. Harding, ed., *Later Prehistoric Settlement in South-East Scotland*, Edinburgh, University of Edinburgh, Department of Archaeology Occasional Paper No. 8: 117–24.

Vauterin, C.-C., 2011. *Ifs ZAC Object'Ifs Sud: Habitats et lieux funéraires protohistoriques et vestiges antiques, Vol. 1, Cercles de l'âge du Bronze, habitats et mobiliers protohistoriques*, Cesson-Sévigné, INRAP Grand-Ouest.

Villard-le-Tiec, A., ed., 2018. *Architectures de l'âge du Fer en Europe occidentale et centrale*, Actes du 40e colloque international de l'AFEAF, Rennes 2016, Rennes, Presses Universitaires de Rennes.

Waddell, J., Fenwick, J., and Barton, K., 2009. *Rathcroghan: Archaeological and Geophysical Survey in a Ritual Landscape*, Dublin, Wordwell.

Waddington, K., 2014. 'The biography of a settlement: an analysis of Middle Iron Age deposits and houses at Howe, Orkney', *ArchJ*, 171: 61–96.

Walls, S. and Morris, B., 2012. 'Excavation of an Iron Age roundhouse at Middle Burrow Farm, East Worlington', *PDAS*, 70: 107–32.

Ware, P. and Stephens, M., 2020. 'Pocklington: more than chariots', *BA*, July/August: 24–31.

Waterman, D. and Lynn, C., 1997. *Excavations at Navan Fort 1961–71*, Belfast, Northern Ireland Archaeological Monographs 3, Stationery Office.

Watkins, T., 1980a. 'Excavation of an Iron Age open settlement at Dalladies, Kincardineshire', *PSAS*, 110: 122–64.

Watkins, T., 1980b. 'Excavation of a settlement and souterrain at Newmill near Bankfoot, Perthshire', *PSAS*, 110: 165–208.

Webley, L., 2007. 'Using and abandoning roundhouses: a reinterpretation of the evidence from Late Bronze Age-Early Iron Age southern England', *OJA*, 26: 127–44.

Welti, A. and Wildgoose, M., n.d. *Wedigs Project 2012–2014 Final Report. A Study of West Coast Circular Structures*, online report.

Wessel, J. and Wilson, D., 2015. *Brenkley Lane Surface Mine: Archaeological Excavation*, Edinburgh, Headland Archaeology, ADS.

Weston, P. and Daniel, P., 2017. *Stamford West, Lincolnshire: Archaeological Excavation*. Sheffield, Wessex Archaeology, online.

Wheeler, R. E. M., 1943. *Maiden Castle, Dorset*, Society of Antiquaries of London Research Report No. XII, London and Oxford, Oxford University Press.

270   BIBLIOGRAPHY

Wheeler, R. E. M., 1954. *The Stanwick Fortifications, North Riding of Yorkshire*, Oxford, Society of Antiquaries of London Research Report No. XVII, London and Oxford, Oxford University Press.

White, R. and Richardson, P., 2010. *The Excavation of Bronze Age Roundhouses at Oldmeldrum, Aberdeenshire*, Edinburgh, Society of Antiquaries of Scotland, SAIR 43.

Williams, G. and Mytum, H., 1998. *Llawhaden, Dyfed: Excavations on a Group of Small Defended Enclosures, 1980–4*, Oxford, BAR British Series 275.

Williams, R. J. and Zeepvat, R. J., 1994. *Bancroft: A Late Bronze Age/Iron Age Settlement, Roman Villa and Temple-Mausoleum*, 2 vols, Aylesbury: Buckinghamshire Archaeological Society.

Willis, S. and Carne, P., 2013. *A Roman Villa at the Edge of Empire: Excavations at Ingleby Barwick, Stockton-on-Tees, 2003–04*. York, CBA Research Report 170.

Wood-Martin, W., 1886. *The Lake Dwellings of Ireland*, Dublin, Hodges, Figgis and Co, London, Longmans Green and Co.

Wrathmell, S. and Nicholson, A., 1990. *Dalton Parlours Iron Age Settlement and Roman Villa*, Wakefield, West Yorkshire Archaeological Service.

Index

For the benefit of digital users, indexed terms that span two pages (e.g., 52–53) may, on occasion, appear on only one of those pages.

Abercromby, Lord 106
'aggregated' settlement 122–7
   see also 'ladder' settlement, 'washing line' settlement
aisled hall 161–4, 234
Aitken, Martin 12
Aldwincle, Northamptonshire 49, 59, 153–5
All Cannings Cross, Wiltshire 12–14, 119–20
alluviation 215–16, 234–5
Altbreck, Sutherland 92–3
Amberly Mount, Sussex 214
Amesbury archer 27
anarchy 41
Âncora, cividade de, Viano do Castelo 199–200
Angelbeck, B. 40–1
'antennae ditches' 84–7
Applecross, Wester Ross 98–9
Armit, Ian 20–1, 41, 96–7, 100–2, 104
Arras culture 128
Ashford Prison, Middlesex 117–19, 153–5
Auchrennie, Aberdeenshire 210–11
Avery, Michael 212
axial line symmetry 15–16, 56, 121, 167, 188–93, 214, 230–2, 243–4
Ayán Vila, X. M. 199

Bagendon, Gloucestershire 27
Ballinaspig More, Co. Cork 184–6
Ballycullen, Co. Dublin 184–5
Ballylegan, Tipperary 183–4
Bancroft, Buckinghamshire 80–2
Bannockburn, Stirling, fort 59, 62, 72
   homestead 62–3, 72
Barabhas machair, Lewis 151–3
Barber, John 92–8
Barleycroft Farm, Bluntisham, Cambridgeshire 159–60
Barrett, J. 32–3
Beakers 18–19, 26–7
Beaumont Leys, Leicestershire 122–3
Becker, K. 36–7, 150, 177–9, 186–7
Beirgh, Riof (Berie, Reef), Isle of Lewis 20, 88–91, 98, 107, 111–12, 147
Bel Air, Saint-Caradec, (Côtes-d'Armor) 196–8

Bénode, (Finistère) 196–8
Berrocal–Rangel, L. 35–6
Bersu, Gerhard 9–12, 70–1, 144–5, 164, 245
Beveridge, Erskine 19
Bezannes 'La Bergerie', (Marne) 193–5
Bintliff, J. 34–5
Birnie, Morayshire 45, 59, 229
Blackford, Perthshire 45–52, 70, 76
Blackhorse, Devon 173–6
Black Loch of Myrton, Wigtownshire 45, 65–8, 227, 239–40
Black Patch, Sussex 213–14
Blagdon Park, Northumberland 64, 134–9
Blair Drummond, Stirlingshire 38–9
Blairhall Burn, Amisfield, Dumfriesshire 208–10
Blaylock, S. 146
Borneiro, La Coruña 199
Boscombe, Wiltshire, bowmen 27
Bostadh, Great Bernera, Isle of Lewis 147
Braby, Alan 108–10
Bracken Rigg, Upper Teesdale 204–6
Bradford, J. S. P. 12
Bradley, Richard 30–1, 84
Braidwood, Midlothian 16–17, 76–8, 246
Brenkley Lane, Northumberland 137–9
Brigstock, Northamptonshire 49, 65–6
Brindle, T. 175
Briteiros, citânia de, Braga 199–200
Broxmouth, East Lothian 16, 41, 76–8
Bruen Stapleford, Cheshire 59–60, 65
Brusseltown Ring, Co. Wicklow 177–9
Bryn Eryr, Anglesey 151–2
Bu, Orkney 20–1, 100–2
Buckquoy, Orkney 147
Buiston, Ayrshire 2–4
Bulleid, Arthur 4–8
Burgess, Colin 206
burials 1, 155, 186, 240
   animal 130
   fragmentary 21–2
   human 121, 130, 132–3, 229–30
   'phantom' 84
   Welwyn-type 32, 41
   see also cemeteries

272 INDEX

Burradon, Northumberland 134
Butser Ancient Farm, Hampshire 14, 43–4, 52, 70, 156–8, 228, 243–4

Cadbury Castle, Somerset 6–8
Caesar, Gaius Julius 236, 238
Cahagnes (Calvados) 188, 192–4
Cairns, South Ronaldsay, Orkney 100
Calanais Farm Field Centre, Isle of Lewis 20
Calf of Eday, Orkney 90, 100–2
Candle Stane, Aberdeenshire 76, 84
Carloway, Isle of Lewis 95, 236–7
Carn Euny, Cornwall 175
Cartimandua 219–20
Castell Henllys, Pembrokeshire 50
Castell Odo, Caernarvonshire 167–8
Castle Ditches, Tisbury, Wiltshire 141
Castro Culture 36–7, 40–1, 50, 165, 198–200, 233
Caudin (Morbihan) 188, 190–2
Cavers, G. 2–3
cemeteries 1, 30, 38, 128, 188
    see also burials
Chadwick, Adrian 128
Challis, Aidan 128
Chapelton, Angus 71
Chapman, A. 124–7
Childe, V. Gordon 19, 238–9
Christison, D. 139–41
Chysauster, Cornwall 175
Clachtoll, Assynt 88–9, 93–6
Clark, Sir Grahame 10, 74, 241–2
Clarke, David 6–8
Claerke, Rainbird 144–5
Clay, R. C. C. 9
Clickhimin, Shetland 18–19, 93–4, 96–7
Close-Brooks, Joanna 212
Clovelly Dykes, Devon 142
Cnip, Isle of Lewis 20, 107, 229
Cnoc Tigh, Easter Ross 105
Coles, John 8
Comar Wood, Inverness-shire 104–5
Conderton, Worcestershire 93–4, 146
Cool, Hilary 219–20
Coolbeg, Co. Wicklow 184–6
Corrstown, Co. Londonderry 180–3, 193
Coton Park, Rugby, Warwickshire 59, 65, 127–8
Cotswold Community Park 55
Courseulles-sur-Mer (Calvados) 193–5
courtyard settlements 175
Cox, Marion 12–14
Craigmarloch Wood, Renfrewshire 18
crannogs 2–4, 8–9
Crawford, O. G. S. 34
Cressing, Essex 237–8

Crickley Hill, Gloucestershire 56, 70–1, 121, 158–9, 171, 246
Crick, Covert Farm, Northamptonshire 59–60, 123–5, 127–8
Críth Gablach, 148
Croft Andrew, C. K. 171
Crosskirk, Caithness 20–1
Culduthel, Inverness 72–5, 113–14, 144, 230–1
Cunliffe, Sir Barry 29, 163–4
Currás, B. X. 40–1
Cyderhall, Sutherland 80

Dalladies, Kincardineshire 79–80
Dalton Parlours, Yorkshire 61, 67, 71, 128–30, 224–6, 246
Dampierre-sur-le-Doubs (Doubs) 187
Danebury, Hampshire 6–8
Dan-y-Coed, Dyfed 168–70
Darwin, C. 2, 94
Deer Park Farms, Co. Antrim 68–70, 147–50, 238–9
Deer's Den, Aberdeenshire 78–9, 210–11
dendrochronology 26, 66–8, 227
Deverel-Rimbury culture 187
diffusionism 18–21, 241–2
DIRFT 123–7
    Lodge 124–7
    Long Dole 127
    Nortoft Lane, Kilsby 127
    see also Crick, Covert Farm
Dixon, Nicholas 20
Dixon, Philip 70, 158–9
DNA analysis 26, 35, 38, 237–8
Donnelly, William 3
Douglasmuir, Angus 76–80
Drewett, P. 214
Drumyocher, Aberdeenshire 210–11
Dryburn Bridge, East Lothian 76–8, 113–14, 245–6
Dryden, Sir Henry 93–4
'drying-racks' 156
Dubton Farm, Brechin, Angus 79–81
Dumbuck, R. Clyde 3–4
Dun an Ruigh Ruadh, Lochbroom 90–2
Dun Ardtreck, Skye 18–19
Dun Bharabhat, Cnip, Isle of Lewis 20–1, 92, 95, 98
Dun Boredale, Raasay 94
Dunch Hill, Tidworth, Wiltshire 157–8
Dunbeg, Argyll 79–80, 208–10
Dun Fhinn, Islay 104
Dun Glashan, Argyll 104
Dun Mor, Vaul, Tiree 19–21, 107
Dunstan Park, Berkshire 22, 66

Dun Telve, Glenelg, Inverness-shire 89–90, 96–7
Dun Troddan, Glenelg, Inverness-shire
    89–90, 97
Dun Vulan, South Uist 20–1, 88, 147
Duttons Farm, Lathom, Lancashire 65

Earle, T. 40–2
East Brunton, Northumberland 134–5
Easter Rarichie, Easter Ross 105–6
Easton Lane, Winchester, Hampshire 52–3
East Worlington, Devon, Middle Burrow
    Farm 54, 173–5
Ednie, Aberdeenshire 208–10
egalitarianism 40–2, 92, 246–7
Egtved, Jutland 27
Eildon Hill, Roxburghshire 139–41
    see also hierarchy
Erw-wen, Merionethshire 166–7
experimental archaeology 14–15, 50, 93–4,
    96–7, 110–11, 151–2, 157
    see also Butser Hill

Fairford, Gloucestershire, Horcott Pit 50, 121
    Horcott Quarry 119–22
Feachem, Richard 16–17, 206
Ffynnonwen, Ceredigion 170
field systems 1, 173
field clearance cairns 17, 206
Fifield Bavant Down, Wiltshire 9–10
Fison Way, Thetford, Norfolk 47, 64, 72, 84–5, 230
Flint Farm, Goodworth Clatford,
    Hampshire 45–7, 52–6, 64, 70
Foel Trigarn, Pembrokeshire 2, 139–41
fogous 175
Fojut, Noel 92
Forse, Caithness 234
Fort Harrouard, (Eure et Loir) 12–14
Foshigarry, North Uist 107
four-posters, granaries 116–22, 128–30, 132–3,
    141, 156, 164, 188–90, 192–5, 243–4
    towers 11, 47, 50–2, 62–3, 67, 70–1, 90,
    128–31, 144–5, 156–7, 164, 193–5, 218–19,
    222–3, 229, 244
Fox, Lady Aileen 173
Freswick, Caithness 97
Frilford, Oxfordshire (Berkshire) 12
Furfield Quarry, Kent 161–4

Gelling, Peter 141–2
gender 26–7, 34–5, 42
geophysical survey 27, 130, 141–2, 175–7,
    179–80, 227–8
    see also magnetometry
Ghey, E. 165–6

Gillespie, S. 37–9
Gilmour, Simon 95
Ginnerup, Jutland 160, 233–4
Glastonbury, Somerset 4–8
Glenshellach, Argyll 79–80
Glenelg, Inverness-shire 18–20
    see also Dun Telve and Dun Troddan
Gold Park, Dartmoor, Devon 173
Gonzáles, R. A. 41
Gonzáles-Ruibal, A. 36–7
Gorhambury, Hertfordshire 161–4
Gravelly Guy, Stanton Harcourt, Oxfordshire 65,
    114–16, 122
Gravigny "Les Coudrettes" (Eure) 188
Gray, Harold St George 4–6
Great Barford, Bedfordshire 32
Greenbogs, Monymusk, Aberdeenshire 71
Green Knowe, Peeblesshire 17, 205–7
Grimes, W. F. 116
Groundwell Farm, Blunsdon St Andrew,
    Wiltshire 47–8
Grubenhäuser 9–10, 224–6
Guilbert, Graham 15–16, 56, 212
Gurd, Robert 12–14
Gussage All Saints, Dorset 84–7

Hambledon Hill, Dorset 8–9, 139–41
Hamilton, J. R. C. 18–19, 108–10
Harding, Anthony 27
Hartburn, Northumberland 134
Haughey's Fort, Co. Armagh 180
Hawkes, Christopher 9, 11–14, 23–4, 35–6, 240
    Sonia 12–14
Hayling Island, Hampshire 142
Hazlerigg, Northumberland, Morley Hill
    Farm 137–9
Healy, F. 72
Heathrow, Middlesex , Caesar's Camp 116
    Terminal 5 32–3, 67, 114–18, 153–5
Henderson, Jon 231–3
Hengrove Farm, Middlesex 119
Heslington East, York 223–4
hierarchy 11–12, 35–6, 41–2, 179–82,
    198–9, 245–7
Higham Ferrers, Northamptonshire 217–18
High Knowes, Alnham, Roxburghshire 16–17,
    76–8, 245–6
Hill, Peter 16
hillforts 1, 10, 139–42, 175–7, 179–80, 186,
    235–6, 243–4
    see also Castro Culture
Hod Hill, Dorset 8–9, 141, 157–8, 199–200
Holme House, Piercebridge 156–7, 219–23
Hope, John 96–7

274 INDEX

Horcott, *see* Fairford
Horton Grange, Northumberland 135–7
Houseledge, Northumberland 206
'house societies' 36–9, 84, 177–9
house urns 92, 146
Howe, Orkney 100–2, 229–30
Hownam Law, Roxburghshire 139–41
Hownam Rings, Roxburghshire 16
   'Hownam Model' or 'sequence' 16–17
Huckoe, Northumberland 18
Hughstown, Co. Kildare 179–80
Humberstone, Leicestershire 122–3

Ifs (Calvados) 195–6
Ingleby Barwick, Teesside 220
Inverkip, Inverclyde 208–10
Inzinzac-Lochrist, (Morbihan) 196–7
isotope analysis 27, 35
Itford Hill, Sussex 209, 212–14

Jackson, Dennis 59
Jarlshof, Shetland 18–19, 107–11
Jobey, George 16–18, 74–6, 134, 206
Johnston, R. 36

Karl, R. 237
Keiss Harbour, Caithness 97
Keiss Road, Caithness 97
kinship 36–8, 40–1
Kintore, Aberdeenshire, Forest Road 55, 78
Knockaulin, Co. Kildare 84–7, 175–9, 186–7
Knockcommane, Co. Limerick 184–6
Knowe of Swandro, Rousay, Orkney 102–3

'ladder settlements' 130, 224
   see also 'aggregated settlements' and
     'washing-line settlements'
La Gaubretière 'La Dugerie', (Vendée) 193–5
Lairg, Sutherland 203–6
lake-villages 4–9
Lambrick, George 156, 234–5
Lamb's Nursery, Dalkeith, Midlothian 208–10
Langland Lane, Devon 173–6
Langwell, Sutherland 20–1, 104–5
Latton Lands, Wiltshire 55, 121
Ledston, Yorkshire 132–3
Leeds, E. T. 122
Lévi-Strauss, C. 15–16, 38–9, 203
Liddell, Dorothy 9
Links of Noltland, Westray, Orkney 151–3
Lintshie Gutter, Lanarkshire 59, 61, 206–7
Little Waltham, Essex 59–60
Little Woodbury, Wiltshire 8–12, 14–15, 45–6,
   56, 70, 84–7, 144–5, 163–4, 235–6, 245
Lochan Dughaill, Argyll 3–4

Lochinver Quarry, Elgin, Moray 208–10
Loch nan Deala, Islay 104
Loch Olabhat, North Uist 20
Longbridge Deverill, Wiltshire 12–14, 22, 45–7,
   52–6, 66, 70, 119–20, 195–6, 229–31
Lookout Plantation, Northumberland 60,
   210–12
Lower Slackbuie, Inverness 72–3

MacKie, Euan 18–19, 92–4, 96–7
magnetometry 12, 45–6
   see also geophysical survey
Maiden Castle, Dorset 8–9, 52
Malleville-sur-le-Bec (Eure) 188–92
Manching, Bavaria 9–10, 29
Marcigny, C. 187
Mason, David 219–20
Mattingly, D. 219–20
McCord, Norman 134
Meadowend Farm, Kennet, Clackmannan 207–8
Meare, Somerset 8
Meillionydd, Llŷn, Caernarvonshire 167–8
Mellor, Greater Manchester 65
Melsonby, Yorkshire 59, 61, 64
Melton, Humberside 59, 229
Melville Nurseries, Dalkeith, Midlothian 210–12
Meole Brace, Shrewsbury 59
Meon Hill, Hampshire 9
Micklefield, Yorkshire 132–3
middens 38
Middle Burrow Farm, *see* East Worlington, Devon
Middle Farm, Dorchester, Dorset 52, 54, 63–4
Midhowe, Rousay, Orkney 102
Milton Loch, Kirkcudbrightshire 3–5
Mingies Ditch, Hardwick-with-Yelford,
   Oxfordshire 52, 54, 63–4
Moel Goedog, Harlech, Merionethshire 166–7
Moel y Gaer, Rhosesmor, Flintshire 15–16, 56
Moel y Gerddi, Merionethshire 166–7
Moneylawn Lower, Co. Wexford 166, 184–6
Moore, T. 158–9
Moss Carr, Methley, Yorkshire 84–7, 153
Mousa, Shetland 96–7
Mucking, Essex, South Ring 188
Munro, Robert 2–6
Musson, Chris 214
Must Farm, Cambridgeshire 45, 66–9,
   229–30, 246

Navan, Co. Armagh 84–7, 150, 175–9, 186–7
Neal, C. 224
Ness, Caithness 97
New Kinord, Aberdeenshire 106
Nijnsel, Noord-Brabant 187
Nowakowski, J. 171

O'Brien, W. 175–7
O'Driscoll, J. 175–7
Oldbury, Wiltshire 141
Old Kinord, Aberdeenshire 106
Oldmeldrum, Aberdeenshire 210–11
Old Scatness, Shetland 21, 88, 93–4, 97, 107–11
Oswald, A. 21–2
ovens, corn drying/malting 218–19

palaeopathology 27, 38
pallozas 200–1
Park Brow, Sussex 9
Parker Pearson, M. 21–2
pastoralism 87, 121, 124–7, 132, 135, 186–7,
    201, 234–5, 237–8
Patteson's Cross, Devon 173–5
Pegswood Moor, Northumberland 135–9
Pequeno de Neixón, Galicia 199
Phoenixtown, Co. Meath 183–4
Pierowall Quarry, Orkney 100–2
Piggott, Mrs C. M. 1–17
Pilsden Pen, Dorset 141–2
Pimperne, Dorset 12–15, 17, 22, 45–7, 56,
    65–71, 74, 143–4, 228–31, 235–6, 244–5
pit-alignments 135–7
'pit-dwellings' 2, 8–10
    see also Grubenhäuser
pits, storage 10, 14–15, 141, 188–90, 243–4
Pitt-Rivers, Lt-Gen A. H. L-F. 8–10
Plédéliac (Côtes d'Armor) 188
Pluciennik, M. 33–4
Plumpton Plain, Sussex 212
Pocklington, Yorkshire 29
Poole, C. 32
Pope, Rachel 22–3, 76, 210–12
Portgordon, Moray 151–3
Porth y Rhaw, Pembrokeshire 170–1
Poses-sur-la-Mare (Haute-Normandie) 193–5
Potterne, Wiltshire 38
Poulton, Cheshire 65
promontory forts 170–1
publication 32–4

Quanterness, Orkney 100–2
quarrying 90–2
Quinnell, H. 171

radiocarbon dating 18, 20–1, 26, 88, 98
Raffin, Co. Meath 177
Rathcoran 179–80
Rathcroghan, Co. Roscommon 27, 84–7,
    175–9, 186–7
Rathgall, Co. Wicklow 180
Reading Business Park, Berkshire 52–3,
    193, 234–5

rectangular houses 1–2, 6–8, 23–4, 72, 144–5,
    155–6, 158–61, 165–6, 168–70, 192–6,
    198, 201, 216–18, 223, 232–4
Redlands Farm, Northamptonshire 217–19
Regan, R. 104
Reynolds, Peter 14–16, 43–4, 47–9, 52, 63–4,
    70–1, 93–4, 143–4, 146, 156–7, 200–1,
    229, 235–6, 243–4
Richards, C. 203
Riley, Derrick 153
ring-barrows 186
ring-works 82, 188
Ritchie, Anna 147
Roberts, Brian 34
Robinson, Mark 234–5
Romankiewicz, Tania 89–92, 107
Roskams, S. 224
Ross Bay, Kirkcudbrightshire 59–60, 210–12
roundhouse cosmology 21–4
'rounds', Cornish 146, 171–3
Roxby Moor, Yorkshire 61, 64, 66
Ruano, L. 35–6
Rubh' an Dunain, Skye 19

Sacaojos, León 199
Salmondsbury, Gloucestershire 52, 54, 153
Sangmeister, E. 18–19
Sanfins, citânia de, Porto 199–200, 233–4
Santa Luzia, citânia de, Viano do
    Castello 199–200
Sastre, I. 40–1, 198
Scotstarvit, Fife 76, 145–6
Scott, Sir Lindsay 19
Scottish Crannog Centre, Loch Tay,
    Perthshire 2–3, 5
Seafield West, Inverness 84, 151–3
Sharples, N. 36–7, 202–3
Shearplace Hill, Sydling St Nicholas,
    Dorset 212–13
Sheffield University SEARCH programme 20
Shotton, Northumberland 135–7
Smith, Reginald 9
Snailwell, Cambridgeshire 38–9
social structure 11–12
    see also hierarchy
souterrains 22–3, 106, 196–8, 238–9, 243–4
South Shields, Tyne and Wear 61, 64
Standlake, Oxfordshire 153–4
Stanton Harcourt, Oxfordshire, *see* Gravelly Guy
Stanwick, Northamptonshire 67, 216–18
Stanwick, Yorkshire 219–23
Staple Howe, Yorkshire 18
Steer, Kenneth 16
Stevens, C. E. 17
Stevenson, R. B. K. 16–17

276 INDEX

St David's Head, Pembrokeshire 170–1
Strabo 237, 243–4
Street House, Loftus, Yorkshire 56–8
'structured deposits' 21–2
'structuring principles' 22, 32–3
survey, laser 27, 92–3
   LiDAR 179–80
Swallowcliffe Down, Wiltshire 9
symbol stone, Pictish 110–11

Tap o' Noth, Aberdeenshire 139–41
Tara, Co. Meath 175–7, 186–7
   Ráith na Rígh 177–9
   Rath of the Synods 177–9
Tarlogie dun, Inverness-shire 105
Teigncombe, Devon 173
Terroso, cividade de, Porto 199–200, 233–4
Thainstone, Inverurie, Aberdeenshire, Business
   Park 52, 55
   East 80–1, 196–8
theory, archaeological 34–6
Threemilestone, Cornwall 171–3
Thrumster, Caithness 97
Thwing, Paddock Hill, Yorkshire 80–3, 188
timber supplies 92
   see also woodland management
Toft's Ness, Sanday, Orkney 100–3
Topping, Patrick 20
trackways, landscape 82, 113, 135,
   137–9, 186–7
Tre' Ceiri, Llŷn, Caernarvonshire 2, 140–1
Trethurgy, Cornwall 146, 171–3
Trevelgue Head, Newquay, Cornwall 171
Trinovantes 238

typology 18–21, 26, 79–80, 99, 163–6,
   232–3, 238–40

unenclosed platform settlement 17, 139–41,
   173, 206
'unit villas' 219–20

Wakerley, Northamptonshire 49, 56, 59
'washing line settlements' 130
Wattle Syke, Yorkshire 130–3, 224–6
Wedigs Project 107
Welwyn, Hertfordshire, *see* burials
West Brandon, Co. Durham 17, 59, 62, 74–6, 245
West Brunton, Northumberland 134–6
Wester Rarichie, Easter Ross 105–6
West Harling, Norfolk 74, 144–5
West Plean, Stirlingshire 54
West Stamford, Lincolnshire 62–3, 72
Wetwang Slack, Yorkshire 61
Wheeler, Sir Mortimer 9–10, 219–20
Whitegait, Caithness 93–4
White Meldon, Peeblesshire 139–41
Whitton, Glamorgan 168–70, 223
Wideopen, Northumberland 139
Winterborne Kingston, Dorset 237–8
Winterton, Lincolnshire 156–7
Wolsty Hall, Cumbria 65–7, 157–8
Woodcuts, Dorset, Down Farm 159–60
woodland management 19–20, 92, 227, 235–6
Wood-Martin, W. 2
Woodside, Dyfed 168–70

Yarnton, Oxfordshire 114–16, 122, 215–16, 234–5
Yarrows, Caithness 97, 234